T0281286

Audio Anecdotes III

Audio Anecdotes III

Tools, Tips, and Techniques for Digital Audio

Edited by

Ken Greenebaum

Ronen Barzel

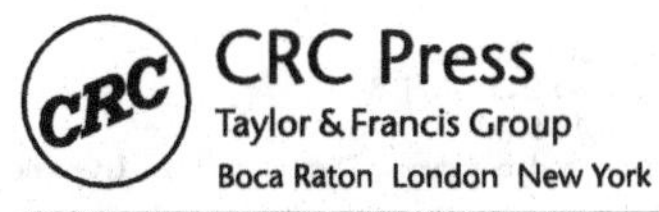

CRC Press is an imprint of the
Taylor & Francis Group, an **informa** business
AN A K PETERS BOOK

First published 2007 by A K Peters, Ltd.

Published 2019 by CRC Press
Taylor & Francis Group
6000 Broken Sound Parkway NW, Suite 300
Boca Raton, FL 33487-2742

First issued in paperback 2019

ISBN 13: 978-0-367-45285-8 (pbk)
ISBN 13: 978-1-56881-215-1 (hbk)

Visit the Taylor & Francis Web site at
http://www.taylorandfrancis.com

and the CRC Press Web site at
http://www.crcpress.com

Library of Congress Cataloging-in-Publication Data

Audio anecdotes : tools, tips, and techniques for digital audio / edited by Ken Greenebaum, Ronen Barzel.
p. cm.
Includes bibliographical references.
ISBN 13: 978-1-56881-215-1 (vol. 3)
ISBN 10: 1-56881-215-9 (vol. 3)
1. Sound--Recording and reproducing--Digital techniques. I. Greenebaum, Ken, 1966- II. Barzel, Ronen.

TK7881.4.A93 2003
621.389'3--dc22

2003057398

Cover art: Pablo Picasso (1881–1973), *Guitar on a Pedestal.*

Cover design by Darren Wotherspoon.

Contents

Preface

This third volume completes the collection of *Audio Anecdotes* that was begun in 2004 and that has involved many contributors and advisors. The extensive and positive feedback from the digital audio community has convinced me that our combined efforts have been well worthwhile and that we have achieved our goal of helping researchers and practitioners to be more effective in developing and integrating digital audio solutions. I hope that, in a small way, we have been able to raise the bar for digital media quality and capabilities.

Amazing strides have been taken since the time this series was conceived (with much progress even in the relatively short period of time since the second volume was published). It was during this period that digital media technologies have come into their own and become mainstream instead of being limited to deep-pocketed professionals, dedicated early-adopting enthusiasts, or the curious wealthy.

The following are only some examples of the technologies that have spawned exciting new products and sometimes entire industries.

Voice over IP (VoIP) has been a technology buzzword for a long while, but with the growing popularity of Skype, it has become not only mainstream but also a valuable enterprise, as Skype's recent multibillion-dollar acquisition impressively underscores. While not yet mainstream, IP-based PBXs, such as the open-source Asterisk, have already begun outselling conventional PBXs and may just become mainstream in the near future.

Personal digital media players have become a common accessory, lead by the phenomenal success of the iPod, and they continue to evolve, offering video capabilities and integrating with other equipment, such as car stereos.

Legal, convenient, digital audio content download and streaming services are rapidly gaining in popularity and are already outselling all but the largest brick-and-mortar outlets for music. Purchase and subscription models are being experimented with in the laboratory of the marketplace.

Digital video downloads of television and movie content are now available from services such as CinemaNow, MovieFlix, and iTunes. Services such as these will forever change how media is distributed and may just eliminate physical distribution entirely.

The verb *to TiVo* has entered our lexicon with PVR *time-shifting* capabilities rapidly becoming a ubiquitous offering for hard-disk video recorders, cable television boxes, and media PCs.

Perhaps the most exciting phenomena has been the democratization of media creation and distribution.

The word *podcast* has been added to the venerable *OED*, and the *New Oxford American Dictionary* declared it to be "the 2005 word of the year." Perhaps, this record-time for a neologism to be added to the self-proclaimed "definitive record of the English language" underscores individuals' desire to share their thoughts whether written (blog), spoken (podcast), or performed (video blog, video podcast).

Video production and distribution are no longer limited to those governments, individuals, or corporations who can afford studio time and television broadcast rates. Do-it-yourself video is not only possible but has never been easier or more affordable with now inexpensive digital video cameras, the ubiquitous high-speed digital video interfaces such as USB2.0 and 1394 on computers, and even non-linear digital video editing applications available inexpensively or even bundled free with many new computers. Even the bandwidth costs associated with distributing video over the internet have been defrayed by technologies such as *bit torrent*, which uses networks of interested parties to redistribute already downloaded content, in effect scaling content servers with the popularity of the media being (re)distributed.

I continue to be amazed by the wonderful group of people who have helped take *Audio Anecdotes* the concept and make it a successful reality. Most of the people who made these books possible are explicitly recognized as contributors, without whose dedication and patience *Audio Anecdotes* would not have been possible. I want to take a moment to thank others who have made major contributions.

Thanks to Alice, Klaus, and the rest of the wonderful A K Peters publishing family.

Special thanks to those who volunteered for the project: Howard Good (our build and CD meister), Eric Lee (for his help and enthusiasm), Robert Quattlebaum (for his desire of excellence and Mac OS X expertise), John Nordlinger (for his strategic vision), and Michelle Steinberger (for her constant support even through the late nights and lost weekends).

Finally, thanks to all my dear friends, colleagues, and family, who have contributed ideas, read early drafts, leveled with me when I failed to communicate, and otherwise helped and encouraged me through this long project.

Ken Greenebaum, Cupertino, June 2007

Introduction

Welcome to *Audio Anecdotes III*! Those of you already familiar with the series will find a variety of exciting new content in a familiar format. Those of you new to *Audio Anecdotes* should be able to dive right in and quickly find yourself at home; however, for the best experience please have the earlier volumes available since articles often build on and reference articles from earlier volumes.

Continuing the series, the articles in this volume also explore creating, recording, processing, and analyzing many forms of sound and music. While the book discusses all manner of audio phenomena, it emphasizes techniques for digitally representing, manipulating, and processing media. These digital-media techniques present profound opportunities over former analog methods and are increasingly enabled by the seemingly endless progression toward ever more powerful, less expensive, and universally available digital computation.

To ensure the broadest impact of the material presented, the accompanying CD-ROM provides audio and video files, interactive demos, and cross-platform open-sourced computer source code. We go to this effort to help the reader not only understand the material but also hopefully incorporate it into existing projects, and ultimately to help stimulate the creation of new products and services.

As the near ubiquity of audio-centric consumer electronic devices like the cell phone and, more recently, the portable digital audio player remind us, it is still far too easy to forget in our visually focused society just how fundamental our sense of hearing is. Perhaps we in this society forget or undervalue sound both because hearing is such a subtle sense that we often don't recognize its effect on us and because most of us no longer rely on it to hunt or save us from becoming prey.

Yet, sound's influence is profound, and it influences us in a powerfully primordial way. Consider that the sound of our mother's beating heart may be the first sound of which we are aware, and no matter what our age, resting our head on a loved one's chest and listening to their heartbeat may be the safest and most comforting place we know. Or, consider how music can seemingly affect our emotions directly, whether we try to resist or not. Music can quickly stir our hearts and senses. Finally, it is both fascinating and enlightening to consider that most of the world's religions teach that creation began with a sound; whether that sound be an utterance or the universal Om.

In *Audio Anecdotes* we explore both sound and our sense of hearing; the one sense which never sleeps and works omni-directionally across vast distances. *Audio Anecdotes* attempts to present opportunities to improve the audio experience where sound already exists or to encourage the integration of sound into presently mute applications, leading to richer, more expressive, more engaging, and ultimately more valuable applications.

Structure

Each *Audio Anecdotes* volume is composed of articles that cover a wide range of audio-related topics. Written by experts, the articles' topics span the breadth of sound- and music-related fields and take a number of forms. The types of articles include topic introductions, essays, in-depth technical exploration of algorithms, and practical presentation of tools and techniques.

Audio Anecdotes is different than other books. We encourage our authors to write using their individual voices and many articles contain the authors' personal anecdotes and hard-earned experience from having worked in the trenches. We therefore encourage readers to consult the biography section at the end of the book to learn a little about an author's background before diving into their article.

Our articles explore deep topics that individually could fill entire books. Consequently, the articles are designed to act as *jumping-off points* for readers to discover new topics, receive motivation as to why a technique or algorithm might be appropriate, facilitate experimentation via interactive demos, provide explanation with a bit of background, and finally, point to other references to further explore the topic. Each article contains an annotated list of references that serve not so much to document the sources of the article, but to direct readers to significant texts and further sources of information on the topic area. Where possible, articles reference other articles in this or other *Audio Anecdotes* volumes. We introduce a topic in an early *Audio Anecdotes* volume and then return in a future volume to cover the same topic in a deeper or more abstract way.

Articles in each *Audio Anecdotes* volume are grouped into chapters by topics organized along an arc spanning the following topic areas:

- Fundamentals: the physics, measurement, and human perception of sound
- Recording and playback of sound: whether of music, voice, or nature
- Synthesis: rendering sounds including the synthesis of musical instruments, voice, or sound-effect (Foley Sound)
- Signal processing: the mathematical analysis and manipulation of sound
- Signal processing applications: from compression techniques to signal detection and recognition
- Computer techniques: efficiently implementing robust, low-latency, precisely synchronized audio systems
- Music theory: the mathematics of both western and non-western music
- Creative topics: music composition and sound design
- Nature, mind, and body: how sound exists in nature and affects the mind and body

The motivation for this topic arc is rooted in the belief that to understand any topic, or to be able to make informed engineering trade-offs in design or optimization, a solid understanding of the physics and human perception of the phenomena is required. Great engineering accomplishments, such as the design of the telephone system, color television, and digitally compressed media such as the DVD, all demonstrate a mastery of the interplay between physics and human perception. From the fundamentals, the arc extends to the abstract through the applied and creative, to again revisit human perception from a different perspective.

While each *Audio Anecdotes* volume can't include articles covering every topic area, the articles are organized according to this arc. *Audio Anecdotes III* contains the chapters described below.

Chapter 1. Recording Music

This chapter greatly expands the basic audio recording articles found in the first two *Audio Anecdotes* volumes.

We begin with a pair of articles that provide music recording industry insiders' perspectives on recording techniques. The first article explores the analog multi-track era, providing many examples from classic contemporary recordings, many of which the author participated in. The second article describes the current situation where most recording is performed digitally and is edited using easy-to-use, nondestructive, nonlinear editors. Not surprisingly, it takes time to refine new tools and to create appropriate methodologies. This article discusses some of the strengths and perils of using these new digital tools.

The next article provides an incredibly intuitive introduction to the artistry of sound mixing. The author explains mixing from an almost painterly perspective instead of the classic clinical perspective of level setting and equalization. The article describes a large number of techniques and provides audio versions of these on the accompanying CD-ROM.

Audio Anecdotes last explored audio scene analysis in the first volume. The final article in this chapter applies the principles of audio scene analysis to audio mixing, providing a theoretical framework to understand how audio recording and mixing techniques are perceived by the listener. This article may also provide insight into anecdotal techniques and rules of thumb.

Chapter 2. Sound Synthesis

In this chapter we return once again to explore sound synthesis, a topic featured in every *Audio Anecdotes* volume.

This chapter begins with a detailed introduction to granular synthesis, a technique that uses many simultaneous instances of sound, called seeds, to create results that are very difficult to emulate using other synthesis techniques. This technique is particularly effective at creating the sounds of nature such as the roar of waterfalls or the crash of waves. However, other sounds directly lend themselves to this technique such as synthesizing the sound of the maraca, a traditional instrument usually consisting of a hollow guard filled with seed and shaken. Code and examples of these and more exotic sounds are included on the CD-ROM.

The final two articles build on the second volume's introduction to physical modeling. The first article adds a model of string excitation due to *stiction* to the physically modeled traveling wave equation presented in the previous volume. This is needed to emulate the effect of rosin applied to the bow sticking, melting, and solidifying in rapid succession in the bow-string interface that allows a violinist to so beautifully excite their instrument's strings. Code and examples of a bowed string violin synthesizer are provided on the CD-ROM.

The second article of the pair presents modal synthesis, a highly efficient alternative to physical modeling complex resonant models. The technique employs a bank of resonators tuned to emulate the measured resonances of actual objects. The result is a realistic, high fidelity model of the actual object that can be excited to simulate the effect of striking or scraping the modeled object. Code and examples are provided on the CD-ROM.

Chapter 3. Voice Synthesis

This chapter introduces the topic of voice synthesis to *Audio Anecdotes.* Voice synthesis has been possible for a long time; however, it has become more mainstream as the trend toward designing computers and other devices to interact directly with people on human terms accelerates. Increasingly specialized, computer-centric interfaces, such as computer keyboards and video displays, are being displaced by other, more natural devices and modes of interaction whenever possible. An example, with which most of us have interacted, is a telephone-based banking, reservation, or other system that employs speech synthesis and, more recently, voice recognition.

While devices have employed the playback of voice since before the invention of digital computers, these devices have traditionally been limited to repeating the same pre-recorded phrases or sentences and consequently could only provide content variation by recording every anticipated permutation of the message. We begin this chapter with a practical article describing how to record and process segments of speech so that they may later be dynamically stitched back together in real-time to form full sentences with variable detail. Without a methodology such as the one introduced in this article, it can be very difficult to form natural sounding sentences.

The next article provides an unusual perspective on voice synthesis. While developers have traditionally focused on improving the clarity and intelligibility of their voice synthesis systems, this author's research involves creating realistic voice especially as an artificial replacement voice for people who are loosing their own ability to speak. Since our unique voice is a large part of our individual identities, the ultimate goal of such synthesis is to recreate the unique qualities of an individual's natural voice. This article provides an introduction to the subject by surveying the history of speech synthesis techniques.

Phonemes are the distinct units of sound that make up the spoken word. Surprisingly, every language uses an overlapping but distinct subset of the sounds a human vocal tract can produce. While modern speech synthesis algorithms don't string together recordings of phoneme sounds to form words (this produces crude and mechanical sounding speech), it is very helpful to be familiar with phonemes. This chapter's final contribution is a table of the phonemes found in the English language.

Chapter 4. Speech Processing

This chapter continues Chapter 3's theme by considering the processing of speech. The human vocal tract is a very specialized instrument that creates a very unique signal. Consequently, conventional sound processing can fail horribly when applied to speech, or at least not perform as well as those designed specifically for speech. Speech processing requires a solid understanding of both the physics and perception of voice.

The first article begins by providing an introduction to the physics, physiology, and acoustics of speech. This article describes the vocal tract and identifies the distinct features unique to voice based on the physics of the human vocal tract. It is specifically these features that the next two articles exploit.

The remaining pair of articles explores the manipulation of the speech signal. The first articles describes a method to speed up or slow down the rate of speech without significantly affecting it's intelligibility or its perceived pitch. Such a system is useful whenever we might want to slow speech down (when transcribing), or speed voice up (when reviewing recorded notes, or catching up on a missed television episode in a fraction of the originally aired time).

The second article of the pair describes, conversely, how to use related techniques to change the apparent pitch of the speech without affecting the playing time. This technique could be useful for correcting the pitch of voice or song to make it *on key* or to simply alter the quality of the speaker's voice.

Chapter 5. Applied Signal Processing

In this chapter we return to the subject of signal processing, this time exploring applications.

The first article introduces audio dynamic range compression. Not to be confused with data compression (reduces the encoded size of data), dynamic range compression (and its opposite, expansion) changes the relative amplitude of the loudest and quietest portions of a signal. Dynamic range compression is heavily used in the music recording and broadcast industries for both creative and practical purposes and has many applications in other fields. This article deeply explores compression theory, application, and challenges. MATLAB models are provided.

An important component of speech communication systems is the speech, or energy, detector. For instance, a speech detector enables a system to be able to discriminate between valuable speech and unwanted noise. Such an equipped system could disable its transmitter when speech is not present thus increasing battery life. Bi-directional speech detectors are used to eliminate feedback in speakerphone systems when only one party is speaking. The next article presents a simple and computationally inexpensive speech activity detector translated from its original 8-bit assembly language implementation.

The last article expands on the signal detection theory articles from the first volume by providing an introduction to sound classification. The implementation for an actual sound classifier that can distinguish between the sounds of different propeller aircraft is presented to help illustrate these concepts. The working classifier with example sounds is provided on the accompanying CD-ROM.

Chapter 6. HRTF Spatialization

Audio Anecdotes II included a chapter on multiple-speaker spatialization techniques as well as articles on binaural sound. In this chapter we return to the topic of sound spatialization by introducing the head-related transfer function (HRTF). The HRTF models the spectral filtering caused by the human torso and pinna (outer ear). The characteristics of this filter are highly dependent on the sound's incident angle to the head, which allows us to sense the sound source's position in space. While most sounds heard in the environment are processed in this way, it has also become possible to synthetically process sound to control spatial characteristics.

We begin the chapter with an article describing the nature of true three-dimensional sound, why it is best listened to on headphones, and how the spatial cues break down when listened to on stereo loudspeakers. Be sure to listen (with headphones!) to the collection of binaural recordings the author recorded himself, using a special in-ear microphone apparatus, on the accompanying CD-ROM.

The next article describes a novel application for spatialized sound; a dance club. This article demonstrates that spatialized sound is not limited to computer graphic applications or headphone wearers.

The final article provides a mathematical model for deriving and understanding the HRTF from first principles. The author provides a mathematical derivation of the HRTF angle-dependent spectral filtering based on a simplistic model of the head (resembling a bowling ball). This analysis is unusual since the HRTF is usually not synthesized but rather is constructed based on measuring in-ear microphones' spectral response to a movable sound source.

Chapter 7. Synchronization

A major goal of *Audio Anecdotes* is to share algorithms, techniques, and actual code to help individuals build robust applications that combine sound and other media. This chapter extends the audio-sample *plumbing* articles presented in previous *Audio Anecdotes* volumes to address the challenging subject of synchronizing digital media.

The first article attempts to provide a solid introduction to the often-confusing subject of synchronization. To do this it defines the major terms, provides motivation for solving the problem, and describes some of the challenges and strategies for solution, including a variety of approaches.

The next article adds a historical context for synchronization by describing the twenty year-long technical struggle to marry a synchronized soundtrack to the then silent motion picture. This effort finally yielded the *talkie* that we today recognize as the modern movie. This is a colorful story from which we can still learn today as we attempt to perfect multimedia synchronization on modern computers.

The final two articles describe in detail the two major components of synchronization first presented in the introductory article: *start synchronization* (the process of ensuring that media streams are begun at individually appropriate times to ensure that they are synchronously presented at a designated time in the future) and *dynamic synchronization* (the process of constantly comparing the relative positions of multiple streams in a presentation, measuring their drift from ideal, then dynamically adjusting their rates to keep the streams approximately synchronized). Pre-roll, resampling, and control theory are among the subjects introduced. Code examples are provided on the CDROM to use and experiment with.

Chapter 8. Music Composition

Audio Anecdotes II included a chapter introducing music theory. This chapter builds on that base to provide two rather different articles on composition.

Music has generally fit into two categories: the composed repertoire (consider classical music) and improvisational (consider jazz). While many live performances may blur these distinctions, it is certainly true that all recorded music is presented virtually identically every time it is played. The recent application of computer technology to the performance of music has begun to change the static, linear, repeatable nature of recorded music. Unlike in a movie where scenes are a set length and order, in an interactive video game the user may take a different length of time to complete a goal, and increasingly video-games are being designed to allow more free-form exploration that allows the user to direct the order of encounters or scenes. The first article describes special considerations for composing music to accompany such non-linear experiences as video games strive to become more and more cinematic in both quality and presentation.

The second article expands on the description of musical meter from the second volume by introducing and exploring polyrhythm, a topic that can be alien to the western mind and ear. The article is designed to be interactive, suggesting exercises that the reader can perform to experience polyrhythm themselves. Further, this article provides a perspective from ethnomusicology on rhythm and polyrhythm, suggesting how different cultures came to develop very distinct rhythmic structures.

Chapter 9. Human Experience

Every *Audio Anecdotes* volume closes with a chapter that returns to the human experience of sound.

As scientists, we attempt to understand the physics of phenomena (like the creation, propagation, and perception of sound described in *Audio*

Anecdotes I). As engineers, we attempt to make calculated tradeoffs to create reliable, efficient devices that produce output perceived to be as high quality as possible, using technologies that are currently available (topics *Audio Anecdotes* returns to again and again). However, as artists, we have a different set of goals that are more difficult to describe, and we constantly change the rules. The first article suggests how video-game sound engines may be modified to produce a less technically accurate but much more engaging sonic experience for the user. This manipulation mimics the inaccurate and often completely unrealistic sound commonly employed in film and theatre.

Audio Anecdotes I extensively explored the human perception of sound and the mathematics used to measure sound based on human perception. Our second article continues this theme by introducing the fundamentals of psychophysics: detection, discrimination, scaling, and identification. The article then uses these principles to explore the psychoacoustic implications for quantization in the digital audio playback. For instance, does the 16-bit quantization of sound (as used in the CD Red-book standard) exceed human perception? If 16 bits are insufficient, then what would be the optimal number of bits of quantization before the human ear could no longer recognize an improvement?

Finally, we close the chapter and this book with an essay examining the history of technology and the human condition that ponders the future of man-machine interaction. The author suggests that traditional computing environments have reached "a crisis of complexity" that requires novel approaches to solve. Future machines will need to fully engage all human senses including hearing (under appreciated in our culture for historical reasons). Hence, the inevitability of the "audiocomputer."

Glossary, Contributor Biographies, and Index

Following the main chapters are an extensive glossary (defining many of the audio terms used throughout the book), contributor biographies, and an index.

CD-ROM

Audio Anecdotes III is accompanied by a CD-ROM containing materials intended to supplement the articles: audio files, video files, and executable demo programs including C-language source code. Demos support the Microsoft Windows, Apple OS X, and Linux platforms. Wherever possible, articles reference these materials so that readers can immediately listen to examples and experiment with the concepts introduced in the articles. Please be sure to explore the CD-ROM's contents, via the HTML-based tour, since materials are constantly being added to the CD-ROM and may not be explicitly mentioned in the text. In addition to the executable formats mentioned above, programs are also distributed as C-language source code with a makefile-based build system to facilitate experimentation and to allow code to be easily incorporated into the reader's own projects.

This material is distributed on the CD-ROM as tar balls (*tar*'ed compressed archives). A wizard-based installer is provided for automatic installation on our supported platforms. README files provide installation information if the installation wizard doesn't automatically start upon CD-ROM insertion. Once installed on your computer, the demo material is organized by chapter and author.

Unless otherwise specified, the contents of the CD-ROM are protected by the BSD license, and the reader may use the source code provided on the CD-ROM for any purpose as long as the following statement is prominently displayed: This product includes code from *Audio Anecdotes III*, edited by Ken Greenebaum and Ronen Barzel, published by A K Peters, 2006. The code is to be used at your own risk: Ken Greenebaum, Ronen Barzel, and A K Peters make no claim regarding the suitability of this material for any use.

A Note on Patents and Trade Secrets

Our authors have certified that their articles do not contain trade secrets. In some articles, authors have explicitly stated that the algorithms that they describe are patented. However, even algorithms that lack such statements may be under some form of patent protection. For many reasons, including the long gestation of patent applications (so-called submarine patents), we cannot vouch for the suitability of using these algorithms for any use other than educational purposes.

Please Participate

Visit us at the *Audio Anecdotes* website (http://www.audioanecdotes.com) to find errata, download code updates, or find out what's new.

Audio Anecdotes was created as a forum to share tools and techniques with the greater audio community. The subjects covered in this volume only scratch the surface of topics that we would like to cover. If you have been inspired by *Audio Anecdotes*, we encourage you to share your own tools, techniques, or experiences. If you find an error in the text or code, or have a code improvement, please send it to errata@audioanecdotes.com.

A Final Thought

We wanted to create books that would be fun to leaf through or read cover-to-cover, books that would be useful both as a reference and a source of creative inspiration. We hope that we have succeeded!

Recording Music

How Recordings Are Made I: Analog and Digital Tape-Based Recording

Daniel J. Levitin

Most modern movie-goers and television watchers are aware of the various forms of "trickery" involved in bringing scenes to cinematic life. We take for granted that there were probably multiple takes; that the dialog might have been dubbed in later to fix poor location recording; or that the sound of a blender mixing up a smoothie or a pistol being fired were added later in a sound effects suite. What most people don't realize is that this same level of sophisticated production is found in most modern audio recordings. The techniques used in music recording are fascinating in their own right, and they can enhance one's appreciation of the final product. See also Rogers' article "The Art and Craft of Song Mixing" (page 29) later in this chapter for a discussion of how such techniques are used to artistic effect.

I'll start this article by providing some background about the "traditional" hardware that is available in the recording studio. (Until recently, I would have called this the "modern" hardware, but the development of digital hard-disk-based recording is changing studio hardware, as discussed in the next article. Still, the traditional principles and techniques described in this chapter carry forward into that world.)

1 Multitrack Recording

Most popular music (rock, country, alternative) CDs use *multitrack* recording, in which different instruments (or different parts of an instrument) are recorded on distinct, separate regions of recording tape or a computer's hard disk. The most common systems use 24-tracks. In tape-based recording, several of these machines can be linked together to create 48-track and 72-tracks. In virtual or disk-based recording, additional tracks are subject to the number of *buses* available, the disk access speed, and the memory limitations of the computer.

If this concept of multiple tracks is new to you, consider your stereo cassette player or CD player. These have two tracks known as left and right, that is, two independent channels of audio information. The information on one track is processed using completely separate electronics from the other track, and this is why you are able to hear separate information coming from your two stereo speakers. (If you have more than two speakers, in a surround arrangement, the information coming from the third through nth speakers used to be extracted artificially from the two stereo tracks, and was not created in the original recording session. True multichannel audio recordings are just beginning to be commercially released on DVD-audio and SACD). Now, by convention, what we hear coming from the two speakers are parts of the same song and they are time-locked (synchronized) so we can listen to both tracks together and they make sense. But this does not have to be so; I have a CD of Leonard Bernstein discussing Beethoven's "5th Symphony," in English on the left channel (one of the stereo tracks) and in German on the right channel (the other stereo track). Using the balance knob on my amplifier, I can choose to listen to only one of the tracks or both. Theoretically, record companies could manufacture CDs with two mono tracks in parallel, of different performances, and you would get twice as much music on one CD. So for example, on older recordings of Duke Ellington's Orchestra (made before there was stereo), you could have two Ellington albums on one CD–you'd just have to set the balance knob so that you wouldn't hear the cacophony that would be created by playing back both at the same time.

Now, extend the concept of two tracks to a multitrack tape recording system which has 24, 32, or 48 independent tracks. The output of each of these tracks feeds a separate preamplifier built into a mixing console in the studio, or a virtual console on your computer monitor. Instead of having a balance control with 48 positions (awkward, to say the least), a recording engineer can decide which of the tracks to play by adjusting a separate volume control for each, or turning each track on and off with a switch (called the *mute* button). It is important to understand that these 24 (or however many) tracks are both time-locked and distinct. They can be recorded or played back one at a time or in any combination, without interfering with each other. This simple fact enables a number of interesting recording techniques.

First, the musicians don't all have to perform their parts at the same time. If a band decides to add a saxophone solo after they've finished recording a song, the sax player just adds her part to an empty track. It doesn't disturb parts that were already recorded. Conversely, if the group decides that they don't want to use a guitar solo they had recorded earlier, they just don't turn that track on (they can even erase it) and the rest of the parts remain undisturbed. Many groups exploit this feature of multitrack recording and add all kinds of parts just to see what they sound like–background vocals, horns, strings, and so on–and let the producer or mixing engineer decide later what to keep and what to throw out. The mixing engineer is the engineer who combines all the tracks into a two-channel "mix," and decides how to allocate the various instruments to the left-right stereo soundfield.

Second, a given musician can play more than one instrument, and listen back to the previously recorded instruments while he is doing so to provide a reference. The guitarist and inventor Les Paul was the first to employ this technique, and Stevie Wonder, Prince, and The Beatles have all used it to great effect.

A third advantage of separate, multiple tracks is that each track can be modified or processed *individually* without affecting other tracks. Signal processing devices, such as compressors, expanders, tonal equalizers, noise gates, digital reverberation simulators, and digital delays can be applied to any one or multiple tracks, and they can be applied after the sound was recorded. Most high-end recording consoles and digital audio workstations have built-in parametric equalizers (EQ) on every track, allowing the engineer a wide range of tonal control over every track. For example, suppose that an electric guitar, electric bass, and acoustic guitar are recorded on three separate tracks. Maybe the electric guitar sounds too shrill, the bass sounds too muddy, and the acoustic guitar sounds too dark. Any time during the recording process, the engineer can modify these sounds by applying EQ to them individually. Multiple signal processing devices can be chained, so in this case, the engineer might EQ the bass to make it less muddy, run it through a noise gate to get rid of hum that was present in the background of the studio that day, then run it through a compressor (to even out the overall volume of the performances), and finally, another stage of EQ. This specific scenario is actually not all that uncommon.

2 The Basic Tracks

The typical way that rock and country music are produced is to record the rhythm section first–usually the drums, bass guitar, and maybe a rhythm guitar. At this time, the vocalist records a *scratch* vocal—a temporary vocal track just to help the rhythm players keep track of where they are in the song. The vocalist typically doesn't give it his all at this stage and the engineer doesn't always bother to set up a particularly good microphone, because the plan is to replace this vocal (overdub it) later with a better performance. You can often find a lot of joking around on these scratch vocal tracks.

John Lennon was working on a new album in 1980 which eventually became *Milk and Honey.* He had recorded scratch vocals to accompany the musicians' basic tracks, but he was killed before any final vocals were recorded. The vocals you hear on the version of the album that has been released were what Lennon had intended only as temporary vocals, and so they contain a certain degree of casualness—and an absence of full voice singing—that would not normally be found on a final vocal.

The various instruments used in the rest of the piece are usually added one at a time. Musicians adding a new part can listen to any combination of the instruments already recorded, in any volume mix that they choose. A rhythm guitarist might want to hear lots of bass and drums so he can keep time; a lead guitarist might want to hear lots of keyboards so he can hear the chord changes better.

This is the norm in popular and country recording. Traditional jazz, classical, bluegrass, and folk have followed a different tradition. In these genres, the musical communication between players is considered an essential part of the performance, and they would never consider playing separately from one another. Neil Young is an example of a rock artist who tends to favor *live* recordings with minimal overdubs, but he is an exception in the rock world. One of the issues here is purely technical: To create a clean rock recording with loud electric guitars is difficult to do when the guitar amps, the drums, and the vocalist are all playing in the same room at the same time, because the sound of the instruments leaks into the microphones of the other instruments, creating a muddy sound. If you care to, listen to *Led Zeppelin III* and *Houses of the Holy* to hear the radical difference in recording quality as the group moved from live recording to an overdub approach, the latter of which allowed for sonic isolation between the instruments and the attendant improvements in sound quality.

There is also a movement, at the vanguard of audio engineering, to use as little audio processing as possible. These engineers often boast on album covers that they have used no EQ, no digital reverberation, etc. The results can sound stunningly lifelike, but pulling this off requires a great sounding musician to begin with, and a great deal of skill on the part of the engineer. One famous example of an album with no equalization is Steely Dan's *Countdown to Ecstasy*, recorded by Grammy-award winning Roger Nichols. To record an entire album without any outboard effects is a challenge, but it does not guarantee a superior product. Some of the best engineers in the world—Roger Nichols, Bruce Swedien, and George Massenburg, for example—use outboard signal processing devices judiciously to create beautiful recordings, and in many cases, to create interesting *hyperrealities*.

3 Soundscape

3.1 Illusions of Perspective: Realism versus Hyperrealism

One of the most interesting aspects of cinematography is that we are able to see on the movie screen things that we could never see in real life. A classic example of this is the movie chase scene. In the theater, we can see the pavement speeding by from a camera mounted on the door of the car, or we can see the road ahead from a camera mounted on the front bumper. In a sense, these are very *unrealistic* vantage points—we rarely are able to put our eyeballs in these positions. An even more startling example of an impossibility is when the director cuts from one of these cameras to another, allowing you to see two very different perspectives in rapid succession. What the director and cinematographer are conveying is an intentionally unrealistic view of the world; they are providing a set of impossible perspectives in order to provide excitement and a sort of *hyper*realism. Please see Bailey's article "Spatial Emphasis of Game Audio" (page 399), where such techniques are applied to video games to create hyperrealistic cinematic experiences.

Of course, chase scenes aren't the only use of techniques that create unreal perspectives. Even simple *head shots* of someone talking give the illusion that your eye is only three inches from the person's face, revealing pores and details most of us never see. Modern recording also uses technology to create hyperrealities.

3.2 Microphone Placement

One common technique is based on a simple concept—microphone placement. For example, when recording an acoustic guitar, the engineer might use two microphones, one at each end of the guitar, and record these onto two separate tracks. During mixing, one of these tracks is assigned to the left stereo field, and the other to the right stereo field. If you listen back at home and your speakers are eight feet apart, it sounds like the guitar is eight feet wide! (It also sounds like your head is right in the middle of the guitar, which of course it couldn't be in real life, or the guitarist would be strumming your face.) In headphones, the illusion of your head being right inside the guitar is even more compelling because there is virtually no air between the transducers and your ear. The guitarist Alex deGrassi records his acoustic guitars using this technique, which is particularly evident on his albums *The World's Getting Loud* and *Slow Circle.*

Any instrument can be recorded in this way, known as *stereo mics split panned. Split panning* refers to the two mics being split in the stereo image, so that one is assigned completely to the left channel and the other is assigned completely to the right channel (the *pan pot* used for *panning* is an abbreviation for the control knob which is officially called a *panoramic potentiometer*). With only one mic, the instrument can be assigned to one speaker or the other, or to any arbitrary point between them. Only by rendering the signal with two mics, however, can the sound break free of *point source localization* and begin to take up more space in the stereo image, the ultimate being the illusion that the instrument is surrounding the listener. Grand pianos are often recorded this way, too, in popular, jazz, and classical music, because it gives the listener a sense of being enveloped in sound.

Other instruments lend themselves to different spatial effects. Drums are typically recorded with one microphone on each individual drum, and these are panned in a semicircular arc, emulating the sound that a drummer would hear sitting at the drums: the high-hat just to the left, the ride cymbal on the right, the snare and kick drums in the middle, and the tom-toms sweeping around the arc of a semicircle, from left to right. The sound we hear through our speakers and headphones, however, is typically much better than the drummer actually hears; because the mics are placed adjacent to each sound source, each percussive component conveys the sound it would if your ear were right up next to it. Stevie Wonder was one of the first to do this, working with engineers Malcolm Cecil and Bob Margouleff, on his album *Music of My Mind.*

The same is true with vocals—the engineer typically places a very sensitive microphone an inch or two in front of the singer. This makes it sound as though your ear is just in front of the singer's mouth. In ballads, this adds intimacy to the performance, especially when listening back in headphones; in heavy metal, it adds a great deal of power, and gives the vocals a presence that keeps them from being swallowed up by the other instruments in the mix. Again, in real life, our ears are never just two inches from the singer's mouth, but through recording we experience this illusion. For years, my favorite example of this was Paul McCartney's vocal on "Honey Pie" from the Beatle's *White Album.* The mic—probably a Telefunken M49—is so close to his mouth, you can actually hear his lips part just before he pronounces the "p" in the word "pie"; when he sings the word "crazy," you can hear the air moving as he sets his mouth to pronounce the "c." Recently, I found a recording that conveys this effect even better—Aimee Mann's vocals on "Jacob Marley's Chain," from her album *Whatever* (recorded with Neumann's version of the M49, a U49). She uses vocal dynamics artfully to create the illusion she is practically whispering the song in your ear. Mixing engineer Bob Clearmountain added a great deal of compression to the vocal to even out the dynamics, so that loud and soft passages appear to be at the same volume, even as Aimee goes from very soft to very loud. Now imagine listening to a group and all of the instruments have been recorded with the microphones right on top of them—this is called *close miking* and it is how most rock records are made. The listener experiences the ultimate in hyperrealistic perspective—hearing each instrument as though her ear was right up against it, all at the same time! This is equivalent to the rapid edits in a movie, except with albums, you, the listener, get to decide when to switch your attention from one instrument to another, or whether to take in the whole scene.

It is interesting to consider the cognitive differences between seeing and hearing. Because visual information is spread out across *space* and auditory information is spread out across *time*, the two sensory experiences are fundamentally different. When we shift attention from one visual stimulus to another, we have to move our eyes. To shift attention from one auditory stimulus to another, we don't move our ears; we simply focus our attention on a different aspect of the sound that is impinging on our eardrums. In a musical performance, we can concentrate on an individual instrument or on the whole (the *Gestalt*). In a visual performance, such as a movie, we can only have the equivalent degree of control if we are provided with multiple views—for example, if the director splits the image up into several parts. Note also that in a movie, the director and cinematographer often use an assortment of lighting and image-composition tricks to get you to look at exactly the part of the screen they want you to, whether that's focusing on the face of a character who's making some significant expression or looking off to the side in anticipation of a monster about to jump in. Audio engineers can accomplish some of these same framing effects by the proper use of signal processing: equalization that carves out a notch in frequency space for a particular instrument, for instance, or reverberation that places certain instruments at a specific depth in the overall auditory space of the recording.

3.3 Reverberation

In the old days, engineers would take the signal of Elvis Presley's vocal, play it through a speaker in the corner of a small, tiled room, and pick up the sound of the room reverberating with a microphone suspended from the ceiling. In recent years, the acoustic echo chamber has all but been replaced by digital reverberation simulators. Whereas the live echo chamber provided only one sound (adjusting parameters like reverb time required moving the mic around in the tiled room), the modern devices simulate dozens of spaces, such as a small tiled room or a large woodpaneled church. Because each instrument can be run through special effects separately, you can hear something else on albums you never hear in the real world, a band in which the snare drum sounds like it is inside a 50-gallon oil drum, a guitar that sounds like it's underwater, and a lead vocal that seems to be coming from the far end of the concert hall.

The various microphone and mixing techniques described earlier define the location of a sound in the left-right plane; reverberation defines a sound's location in depth. The three-dimensionality of recordings comes from the listener's impression that the various instruments occupy different places in depth as well as in the left-right stereo field. By applying different reverb programs to different instruments, the depth of a recording is greatly increased, giving the sense that each instrument occupies its own place in the sonic landscape.

Additional tricks can be applied to alter location in the sideways or $x - y$ plane. With clever manipulation of phasing, engineers can make it seem as though sound is coming from *beyond* (outside of) the stereo speakers (not just between them). Engineer Bruce Swedien experimented with these placements on Michael Jackson's *Bad* and *Dangerous* albums. Of course, if used indiscriminately, all these techniques can create a cheap, gimmicky sound, but if used properly, they can create excitement.

Pink Floyd, The Beatles, and Laurie Anderson pioneered the use of the studio as another musical instrument to enrich their artistic product, and this has now become commonplace.

4 Editing Parts

Multitrack recording brings with it another possibility—the ability to edit individual parts. Remember that in the typical case, a rock band might record the *basic tracks* of their song first—the drums, bass guitar, and rhythm guitar. Because each instrument can be recorded on its own track, it is a simple matter to repair any mistakes on a given track without altering the other tracks. If the producer and the band decide that a particular take has the right *feel*, they might decide to use it even if it contains some mistakes. If the bass player played some wrong notes, or her timing was off by a bit, it is simple to go back and fix *just those* notes. The engineer plays the tape back to the bass player and she plays along with the tape. When the tape gets to the part where the mistake occurred, the engineer hits the *record* button for the bass player's track only. Now the bass player's new performance is put on tape, erasing the old one, and the engineer can hit the *stop* button any time to stop recording and return to the part that was formerly recorded.

This technique is called *punching in*. It is simple to punch in and out of very tight spots—it is not unusual, for example, for a musician to try to repair a passage with only a 16th note space on either side of it. As long as an instrument was recorded on a separate track, and was isolated from the sound of other instruments during recording, it is difficult to tell a repair from the original. After spending three and a half minutes recording one take for a basic track, a group might spend hours making repairs to those basics.

Soloists and vocalists also routinely punch into a track to repair or improve performances. If a vocalist misses a high note, there is no need to redo the whole performance, obviously—he can just punch in and fix the troublesome phrase. If you listen carefully, you can actually hear where the punches are on Michael Jackson's vocals on some of the songs off *Thriller*, and on Crosby, Stills and Nash's song "Helplessly Hoping." You can hear the punches because they occurred while the singers were taking a breath and the punch interrupts the sound of them breathing in. Interestingly, a musician with only marginal technique can use punching in to make himself sound better than he really is, creating flawless performances that he would never be able to otherwise execute in real time.

(I am a marginal guitarist in real life, but on tape I sound pretty good, only because I, like many of my friends, used to spend six hours recording one eight-bar solo.)

Conceptually, punching in is equivalent to the old-time method of editing analog tape with a razor blade and splicing tape. The difference is that punching in only affects one or a few tracks at a time and editing usually involves cutting the entire piece of tape and splicing it to a new one. Symphony orchestras typically record an entire performance, and then go back and replay any sections that had mistakes. Later, an editing engineer splices in the fix. In traditional jazz, the combo might play several versions of the same song, but it would be an artistic scandal if two different takes were edited together; because jazz is primarily an improvisational form, each take is considered a completed and inviolable work.

Since jazz and classical sessions are generally recorded without overdubs, you might think they don't need all these tracks, but they are still commonly recorded multi track so that mixing engineers can make balance decisions about the relative levels of instruments after the performance. In the case of classical, many people believe this is the conductor's job, and that engineers should not presume to change the balance from that which the conductor and orchestra have so carefully achieved. Engineers may work closely with conductors to achieve the conductor's ideal of how the instruments ought to sound. This idea of punching in fixes is extended in the technique of *compositing* performances.

5 Composite Performances—Creating a Master Take

The ability of an artist to punch in and out of a track to make fixes eventually spawned the idea of creating composite tracks. Originally, an artist might have recorded two or three takes of their vocal, and then, along with the producer, picked the best take and systematically fixed any problems by punching in. Some time ago, a clever engineer figured out that he could mix and match the various parts of these three vocal takes, taking the best parts from each one and dubbing them into an empty track on the tape.

The way this is often implemented now is that the vocalist will sing the song across several different days, compiling maybe 20 different vocal takes of the song. Then, the vocalist, engineer, and producer will sit down with a lyric sheet and listen carefully to every take, indicating which take contains the best version of a particular musical line. Then the engineer creates a composite vocal track that combines all these distinct performances.

Vocalists who are really compulsive (they shall remain nameless) sometimes even edit down to the syllable level. I've observed several of these *compositing* sessions in which the poor engineer had to extract a "th" from one track and an "e" from another to create the perfect "the." In this ultimate application of punching in, what you end up with is a performance that is better than the artist had actually done—a truly *master* performance. Once a composite master has been compiled, the artist, whether she is a singer or a guitarist or whatever, studies and practices this master so that they can duplicate it in concert. An example of a composite guitar solo is Jimmy Page's solo on Led Zeppelin's "Stairway to Heaven." This solo was pieced together from several different solos, to create the unified piece we now hear.

6 Impressionism and Realism

For several hundred years, beginning in the Renaissance, painters strived to bring increasing realism into their works. The discovery of the use of perspective, which had eluded earlier artists, laid the groundwork for fantastic advances in rendering scenes in oil with lifelike qualities. Around the middle of the nineteenth century, a popular movement overshadowed the realists; the impressionists strove to create scenes that didn't rely on realistic depiction to convey their emotional message. What caused this sudden change in style?

One explanation of art historians is that the invention of the camera around 1840 meant that everyone, without any special training, could suddenly capture scenes realistically. Impressionism and, subsequently, cubism were the styles adopted by artists to create engaging artistic works as a reaction to the ease with which realism could now be created.

For many years in audio, recording engineers strove to create ever more realistic recordings; to recreate the sound of a musical group on stage inside everyone's living room. In classical, folk, and traditional jazz, this is still the norm. Naturalistic microphone techniques and a minimum of processing are used to accomplish this. One notable exception is the cycle of Beethoven symphonies recorded by Herbert von Karajan and the Berlin Philharmonic in the early 1980s. Karajan insisted that the instruments be close-miked. The result was a complete loss of the normal depth in the soundscape of the orchestra. Instead of the French horns sounding as though they were off in the distance, they and all the other instruments sounded as though they were right in your face. Many critics and the public found the recordings so disorienting as to be unlistenable. The Maestro was unabashedly pleased with the result, commenting that for the first time in his life, he could now hear the orchestra as he had always heard it in his head.

In the 1970s, recording technology reached the point where it succeeded in recreating the sound of a live band with great fidelity. The cutting edge of audio production since then has been to create something more than reality—to sculpt sound pictures that evoke feelings and thoughts unconstrained by reality: soundscapes that push the envelope of the technology available to create a sort of auditory impressionism. Artists, producers, and engineers are now able to create all the sounds that they hear in their heads, not just the ones that would occur in real life.

These days in rap, hip-hop, house, techno, and electronica, it is common for the engineer to entirely compose and perform music by grabbing samples from previous works, looping them, combining them with drum machines, editing, etc. The distinction between engineering and performing has become increasingly blurred, and the sounds created for a track can be more important than chords and notes. In acousmatic music, a branch of electroacoustic music, compositions are created out of *found sounds*, environmental sounds—such as jack hammers, breathing, turbine engines, and waves crashing—that have been recorded and reprocessed, then sculpted together to create a composition. Samplers and editing stations are considered to be musical instruments by many musicians these days, and have allowed a greater number of people to participate in the making of music. The increased sophistication and affordability of advanced technology has been a great equalizer, making music creation accessible to a larger number of people, and not just a select few with conservatory educations.

We continue this discussion in "How Recordings Are Made II" (page 15) by exploring how recent advances in computers and digital recording have affected the recording industry.

How Recordings Are Made II: Digital Hard-Disk-Based Recording

Jay Kadis and Daniel J. Levitin

1 The Brave New (Digital) World

The last five years or so have seen what may be the biggest change in recording technology since the introduction of multi-track recording in the 1960s—the move to hard disk-based digital recording. This may represent an even more profound change than the introduction of digital recording in the 1980s because hard-disk-based recording allows for editing and manipulation of the signal in ways that are fundamentally different from that which came before, even with digital tape. Because developments in this domain have been so rapid, there is a danger that anything we write today (summer of 2005) may become quickly outdated; nevertheless, we will attempt to discuss principles, techniques, and technologies as they exist today. While some details may change, we believe that the fundamental principles will apply for some time (as the principles and techniques of tape-based recording, discussed in the previous article, still apply). We will examine the many advantages that computer-based recording systems provide along with the related implications and difficulties.

Recording engineers and composers have long eyed the computer's potential for making and manipulating sound recordings, but early computers were too slow and expensive to be practical. As personal computers became faster and cheaper, desktop computers acquired the ability to perform functions that previously necessitated a building full of expensive electronic devices. This fueled a race among software developers to find new ways of making and processing music. The now-widespread availability of tools previously available only to professionals has facilitated an explosion of music created by musicians previously unable to realize their ideas. The democratization of the recording process also brings the predictable result whenever powerful tools are placed in the hands of less-skilled operators: overuse of gimmicky production tricks and poorly composed and performed music in abundance. Simply using professional tools does not guarantee the production of professional-quality recordings, and providing access to a professional recording environment does nothing to improve musical composition. Whether boon or bane, we will see how the personal computer has altered the relationship between music creators, their tools, and the listener.

The fundamental difference between the older and newer systems for recording and manipulating sound is the manner in which the signals are encoded and stored. Prior to the development of digital audio recording, sound recordings were made by processing continuously varying voltages generated by microphones or electronic instruments. These voltages were converted into proportional magnetic fields in analog tape recorders and stored on magnetic tape. The term analog indicates that the signal voltage is directly proportional to the original sound pressure level and is continuous in nature (the term "analog" comes from the same root as the word "analogy"). Any manipulation of the analog sound representation had to be made in what is called *real-time*, meaning simultaneously as the musicians or tape recorder played.

In contrast, digital audio devices first convert the continuously varying voltage signals into a series of numbers that represent the signal amplitude. This process, called *sampling*, requires that the measurements be made very frequently so that the digital representation closely reflects the analog signal. To understand sampling, imagine that you wanted to obtain an estimate of how much traffic passes by your living room window, the room in which you plan to set up your new recording system. If the cars are going by slowly enough, you can see a car, look down to your notebook, and write it down. If they're going by quickly, in the time it takes you to look down in your notebook and write it down, another car or two may have passed and you will have missed counting them. You can see intuitively that the amount of time you spend looking out the window (sampling) the traffic has to be related to how long it takes a car to pass by and how long it takes to write down each entry. In the case of an audio signal, the rate of voltage change is somewhat analogous to the speed of the cars: the higher the signal frequency, the faster the voltage is changing.

In audio sampling, we store only the values that we measure at the sample times and do not save information about what happens between samples; thus, sampling a signal results in a discrete representation, one that is not continuous. When we choose the sampling rate properly (according to the Nyquist theorem of 1928), we don't have to worry about missing important information. Another analogy comes from the world of film-making. A film camera does not record continuous images; it samples them, putting each image into a portion of a continuously moving piece of film, called a *frame*. The standard frame rate for professional film cameras is 24 frames per second (fps), standard NTSC video in North America is 30 fps, and faster frame rates exist also. This sampling rate is sufficient to give the flicker-free illusion of smooth motion when the projected image is viewed (the projector double shutters to display 48 images per second, which is beyond the human eye's fusion rate). This system works well as long as no element of the picture moves too quickly with respect to the frame rate. For example a quickly spinning wagon wheel, whose rotation takes less than two frame times to complete, will not appear to spin at the correct rate when projected and might even appear to rotate slowly backwards. This phenomenon is known as aliasing and can be prevented by limiting the frequency of the signal being sampled to less than half of the sampling rate (that's the Nyquist theorem again).

The very high speed of modern computers allows the digital samples representing the recording to undergo significant signal processing in the short time between when new samples are acquired or played. Effects may also be applied to existing digital recordings. This is especially useful for effects that require too many resources to run in real-time on today's processors. Many effects that we could not easily accomplish using analog techniques are possible, from editing performances in very small pieces to shifting individual notes in time by tiny fractions of a second or correcting the pitch of a singer's performance. We can create sounds directly by computer synthesis and use sampled sounds and loops of music to create new compositions. We can make mathematical models of instruments that allow computer programs to simulate the physical behavior of real and imaginary instruments, and the sounds of those instruments can be played by the computer. We can cut and paste musical sounds as easily as we do text in a word processing program, moving them freely in time or pitch space to create special effects or to improve a flawed performance.

The advances mentioned thus far apply to digital recordings: music stored as a series of digital samples of acoustic pressure over time as acquired by microphones fed into analog-to-digital converters. In addition, computers enable the capture and manipulation of the gestural information pertaining to how a musician actually manipulated an instrument to create the performance. Specially outfitted instruments must be used, which encode the musician's performance as a stream of instructions pertaining to which note was struck, when it was struck, how hard it was struck, and when it was released. This stream of information may then be edited and played back through a synthesizer or even an actual instrument such as a modern player piano. This entire approach is reminiscent of the player piano rolls of old, but it retains more gestural information than piano rolls did.

This is the result of a technology known as MIDI (Musical Instrument Digital Interface), providing a digital instruction language and hardware connection standard that links electronic instruments to each other and to computers. MIDI sends data that contain instructions on when to play notes (note-on), how dynamically the notes sound (velocity), how loud it should play (volume), and when the note should stop (note-off or velocity 0) as well as many special controller values and device-specific commands (sys-ex). MIDI allows synthesizers to play back digital scores stored in computer memory as sequences of events. MIDI permits selecting and altering the sounds to use for playback and any effects like reverberation that may be produced by the devices. MIDI networks connect racks of different synthesizers so that they operate as one instrument, allowing composers and arrangers to hear a symphony played by sampled instruments, for example. Popular music may be produced entirely in this manner without the creator being able to play any instruments at all! MIDI may also be used to connect the devices in a studio so that their operation is controlled from a central location, often the mixing console, using MIDI machine control instructions. MIDI time code can be used to synchronize playback from different sources such as tape recorders and synthesizer sequencers. While MIDI allows the fledgling arranger to try out ideas and textures before bringing them to live musicians, it will not prevent the arranger from writing notes that cannot be played within the range of a real instrument or requiring playing in other impossible ways.

Not everything in the production of music has changed fundamentally as a result of moving to digital audio. Many techniques of mixing and creating effects are still accomplished in a fashion similar to that of the analog studio. For instance, a mixing console is as central to a digital studio as it was to an analog studio, although it may now exist completely in software with virtual knobs and sliders on the computer display which may be moved with a mouse instead of a hand. The engineer still needs to have the ability to change several parameters quickly and perhaps more than one at a time. The mouse is a poor substitute for a mixer full of controls; consequently, digital studios often interface devices with physical knobs and sliders reminiscent of the analog mixing panel to their software mixers. The digital audio workstation, or DAW, is modeled on the recording studio of old because the methods developed in the traditional recording studio are still sensible and adequate ways to record and assemble multitrack recordings, albeit the DAW does have some advantages over studios of yore.

One of the major advantages of digital audio is the nondestructive nature of editing and recording. Now we can have as many tracks as the speed and memory of the computer will allow rather than the fixed number of tracks provided by a dedicated tape recorder. If we wish to add material, we can *punch in* without overwriting the previously recorded tracks. We may select parts of tracks to be combined in a *playlist*, a listing of pieces of sound that are to be played back in the order we specify regardless of when the pieces were originally recorded. This process is automated and recallable, so we can make small changes and listen to multiple versions easily. The ability to independently manipulate pieces of data is known as *nonlinear editing*. Using analog systems, tracks recorded synchronously to tape cannot easily be moved in time relative to each other whereas digitally recorded tracks can be accessed freely and independently.

Another advantage of the computer-based studio is the cost savings of using software for simulating the hardware devices found in the traditional studio. Signal processors like compressors, limiters, delays, reverberators, and other special-effects devices were plentiful but expensive in the traditional studio. These hardware devices are now being modeled in software (often called *plug-ins* because they are add-ons to the basic software package), creating programs that process the digital information much like the analog gear of old. The advantage is that rather than buying a new compressor when we exhaust our supply, we need only click a button to install another copy of the software emulation and we're ready to go on with the mix. The number of copies that we may use is limited only by the power and speed of our computer. Add-on signal-processing cards are available to increase the amount of processing power a computer may provide, including both complete recording and mixing systems like Digidesign's ProTools TDM and add-on digital signal processing (DSP) systems like the Universal Audio UAD-1, designed to augment host-based recording systems like Apple's Logic.

2 Trouble in (Digital) Paradise

Digital audio continues to evolve rapidly, taking advantage of the constant stream of faster computers and new interface formats that allow more data to be transferred and stored. The speed of this evolution is both an advantage and one of the potential problems plaguing users of the new technologies. Issues of incompatibility are exacerbated when the elements of the system are all changing quickly, and often independently. While analog technologies were also constantly improving, an analog tape recorder (like Studer or Ampex) or analog consoles (like Neve or SSL) were usable for decades. Digital hardware and software change quite rapidly and completely, requiring frequent upgrades to remain compatible. This state of constant change makes it harder to train new engineers and the need to continually learn new software and hardware takes time away from the job of recording music for experienced engineers. The software is complicated and may contain *bugs* that cause system failures in special circumstances not discovered by the programmers, leading to computer crashes, lost information, and angry customers. Selecting add-on audio and MIDI interfaces for the computer is complicated by differing requirements of the various computer systems and recording software packages. Recording engineers now also need to be computer technicians to be assured of the ability to keep their studios operational.

For all its advantages, digital audio introduces some problems that did not exist with the analog approach. A friend of ours, a famous producer/engineer who has a studio in his home, spent several months getting the various components of his system running: the computer hardware, operating system, recording software, sequencing software, various input/output devices, plug-ins, etc. During this time, a minor upgrade to the computer's operating system was released, but since it wasn't compatible with the plug-ins, our friend decided (of course) not to do the upgrade.

He began to record an album, and after four months, his computer's motherboard failed. The manufacturer offered to send our friend a brand new computer, with a faster processor and more hard disk space, and the whole package was sent by next day air. Unfortunately, the new computer came with a newer version of the operating system (one that was incompatible with the plug-ins) and the new computer's logic board was incapable of operating under the previous system. This meant that the album production had to stop completely. With the plug-ins and various other I/O devices not working, the producer could not maintain continuity between what he had done before and after the hardware change. This demonstrates that the complex interdependency of hardware, peripherals, operating systems, drivers, and applications demands a thorough understanding on the part of those depending on such systems for production.

Software and hardware incompatibilities aren't the only source of potential trouble. Time synchrony is required when sampling, since we must guarantee that the timing of the sample measurements is correct for every track we record. While most digital systems are able to automatically synchronize with themselves and with each other, the accuracy of the clock that determines the sample time must be consistent throughout the entire system.

For instance, if devices clock each sampled word at different times, clicks may be generated in the audio data stream. Or, if the reference clock is not perfectly regular, digital data may be output with slightly different intervals between words, altering the audio data produced and potentially affecting the perceived stereo image. There is also an issue of delays created in the digital system as data are moved around inside the devices. In order for many tracks of recorded music to be played simultaneously, each must have undergone exactly the same internal delays, or *latency*.

If simultaneously-recorded, live tracks are played back with different delays, they combine to produce peaks and dips in the frequency response as certain frequencies reinforce and others cancel to produce an unwanted comb filter effect. This is a particular problem with stereo tracks where the sound is simultaneously recorded but played back slightly apart, causing the stereo image to shift. (When tracks are overdubbed, this is not so much of an issue since the sounds were not time-locked to start except by the musician's timing accuracy, which is nothing like the microscopic resolution of the sample clock.) Each process, analog-to-digital conversion, data storage, data manipulation, and digital-to-analog conversion must delay all tracks the exact same amount in order for them to be played back synchronously.

Loss of synchronization is not just an abstract problem but one that occurs frequently in practice. In the analog world, tape machines typically have two *heads* over which the tape passes and which read or write material onto the tape. One head is used for high quality playback, and the other is used to record. This is because the physical processes of recording and reproducing magnetic signals are different and optimization requires different head designs for each process. If one wants to *overdub* (add an instrument to one that has already been recorded), a potential problem exists.

Suppose that you've recorded drums and now you want to add bass. If the record head and the playback head are not in the same physical

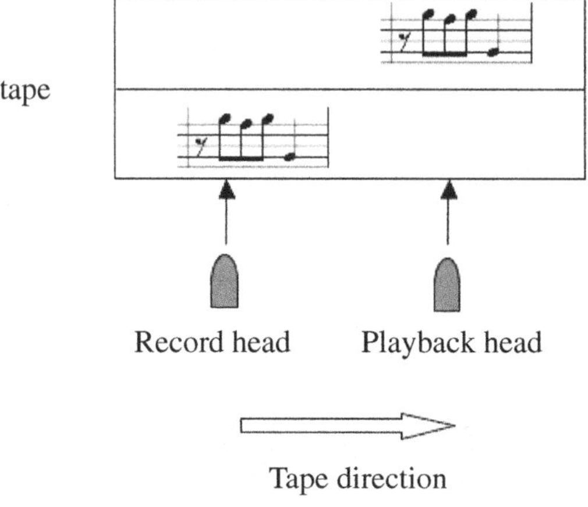

Figure 1.

location along the tape's path, there will exist an asynchrony. You'll hear the drums playing the moment the tape passes the playback head, of course. As you play bass along with those drums, the record head will put the signal on tape, but if the record head is an inch or so away from the playback head, your bass part will be out of synchronization with the drum part by the distance between the two heads. At 15 inches per second (IPS) with an inch between the heads, this one inch would cause the bass part to be recorded 66 ms later, or the equivalent of 1/16th note at 64 beats per minute (bpm).

This problem was solved in analog recording by combining lower fidelity playback electronics on the same physical component as the recording head, in what is often called a *sync head.* This permitted the musician to hear back the previously recorded track (at somewhat lower fidelity) and add something to it virtually instantaneously, and in (virtually) perfect synchrony.

In the analog world, no matter what happens to the master tape, the performances on it will remain synchronized with one another so long as they started out synchronized; not necessarily so in the computer-based digital world. The two of us had to mix a song once for which the session file had become corrupted. We still had access to the individual sound files of the performance—the basic tracks and all the overdubs—but the ProTools session file that contained instructions for how the tracks were to line up in time had been destroyed. We had to import each individual sound file—for the kick drum, snare drum, bass guitar, vocals, etc.—into a newly created session file. Because some of the drum files were edited after recording to get rid of noise at the beginning, and because some of the files were from overdubs not recorded with the basic tracks, lining up all the sound files in the mix/edit window did not succeed in synchronizing them. In fact, there was no information available at all to tell us where to place the files with respect to one another. Lining up the snare drum and kick drum was time-consuming but not complicated because it was obvious how those parts were intended to fit together (and bleed-through in the mics gave clues). Lining up the vocals and the guitar solo, however, was extremely difficult. In some cases we knew roughly (within half a second or so) when they were supposed to occur, but the vocals and solo had been performed with a particular feel, a very specific relationship to the beat that we were unable to recapture. We spent hours nudging the parts around by 10 and 20 milliseconds to get what sounded good to us, with no objective information about how the singer had intended to place his vocals with respect to the beat. To make matters worse, there were pieces of vocal and guitar performances—a few notes here and there—that had been recorded on separate tracks as repairs or fixes, and we had no idea where *they* were supposed to go or what they were intending to repair or fix.

The ease with which files are created by computer recording often leads to sessions with huge numbers of individual sound files. This demands careful attention to file naming and recordkeeping. Every time you create a new track, give it a name that indicates what it is. Good names: Lead Vocal I, Snare Drum, or Replacement Rhythm Guitar. Bad names: Audio 6 (the default name the computer software might assign), RE20 (the name of the microphone you used—but what instrument did you record?), or July 7. Take as many notes as possible about the track and write them directly to the computer or in a project journal: the microphone used, mic pre-amp, time of day, compression settings, and what the part was intended to do (that is, how it was intended to fit into the final mix). The microphone and signal processing notes will help you if you want to go back and recreate that sound. Be sure to distinguish tracks that were intended as retakes or replacements as opposed to primary parts, so that you or some poor mixing engineer doesn't waste days trying to figure out if two parts are redundant or not.

In the digital domain, it takes a small but often noticeable amount of time for a digitally-recorded signal to be converted to analog. Suppose that it takes 20 milliseconds for a signal to wind its way through an A-to-D or D-to-A converter, and you want to play bass along with a previously recorded drum part. The drums take 20 ms to get through the converters, so your speakers get them 20 ms after the computer "plays" them. Now, if you're sitting 8 feet from your speakers, assume that it takes another 7 ms for the sound to reach your ears. (While we usually think of overdubs employing headphone monitoring, some performers, reportedly including Frank Sinatra, dislike performing with headphones and favor loudspeaker monitoring for overdubs, allowing a more natural performance.) You play along as best you can, but it takes the computer another 20 ms for the sound from your bass to get through the A-to-D converter on the way back in. Your sound is now recorded 47 ms *after* the drum track (not unlike the case with analog overdubs that we just spoke about). For more information see Derek DiFilippo's "Perceivable Audio Latencies" in *Audio Anecdotes I.*

The software designers, in theory, know how long the hardware converters take to process sound, and part of their job is to build in a synchronization function that should synchronize your overdub with the previously recorded track automatically. The only thing that they can't take into account is the small delay from the speakers to your ear because that will vary from room to room. The hypothetical 7 ms in our example is truly insignificant when it is the only delay, but it can make a noticeable difference when it adds up with other sources of delay. Most semiprofessional and professional software recorders have a way to minimize, though not eliminate, converter delay. Known by names such as *low latency* or *overdub mode*, this options shrinks the buffer size during playback to give you the fastest playback possible. This is usually at the expense of being able to use large amounts of built-in processing, such as compressors, equalizers, reverbs, etc., which take time to employ but which can be added back in during mixdown. Alternatively, you can monitor inputs directly and not listen through the digital device, eliminating the digital monitoring delays entirely.

3 Summation for the Defense?

As we are beginning to realize, every technological revision comes with a cost. When fuel injection replaced carburetors in automobiles (new cars haven't had carburetors since the early 1990s), it provided a more reliable system for delivering fuel. Gone are the cold mornings when the car wouldn't turn over at all, the sudden sputtering during high altitude climbs, and much of the pollution caused by imprecise air/fuel mixtures. Fuel injection works well without requiring maintenance for many times the miles between carborator tune-ups, but when the fuel injection computer fails, it fails all at once and no amount of tinkering will get you back on the road. A carburetor failed gradually, gracefully—you had warning coughs and sputters as gaskets decayed or springs lost their tension, and if you knew what you were doing you could enrich or lean out the mixture to accommodate changing climate, elevation, or wear.

When analog tape, or for that matter tube electronics (amps, compressors), fail, they often do so gradually; the tubes begin to leak and performance is compromised, but the hardware is still useable. Old analog tapes eventually wear out as a function of age, poor storage conditions, or too many playbacks, but on their way to wearing out they are still useable. The loss of high-frequency information or occasional drop-outs are often the first clue that a tape is deteriorating. But, with digital recording as found on digital tape, hard-disk recording, or even CDs and DVDs, the deterioration is masked by error-correction schemes. Error correction ensures that even imperfect media (ever hold a CD up to a light source and notice the pinholes?) can play back bit-for-bit accurate sound—that is, until the deterioration exceeds a threshold where the error correction can no longer cope, potentially rendering the recording utterly and instantly unusable. While some professional gear will report digital media's bit error rate to allow an engineer to monitor potential deterioration of media, this feature is far from universal. In a pinch, we could always use a partly compromised analog tape (as was done for many CD reissues—that's why some of your favorite albums don't sound all that great on CD), but a digital recording that has been corrupted cannot be used at all.

What advantages does digital recording technology offer to the musician? With MIDI-based sampling systems like Tascam's GigaStudio, a composer can hear a close approximation of a symphony playing her composition using only the computer. A musician can record music in a bedroom studio and experiment with different arrangements, perfecting songs without requiring the participation of other musicians. Recordings may be edited to produce near-perfect performances, and slight timing and pitch problems may be eliminated. Bands can record their own albums, taking as much time as they desire without spending a fortune for studio time. Musicians in far-flung areas of the world can collaborate in recording by sending music over the Internet or through the mail for others to contribute to and return. Musicians can now record, master, duplicate, and offer for sale at performances their own CDs. Digital music is easily distributed over the Internet, so unknown bands can find an audience that they could never meet physically. This represents a true democratization of the recording and distribution process.

Recent developments in Internet technology may result in an even more active method of collaboration: real-time interactive performance over the network. It is now possible to reduce the time lag associated with digital audio systems connected to the Internet to a delay short enough to allow musicians around the world to play together. Our research groups at Stanford and McGill have worked on particular algorithms for reducing broadband latency as much as possible, and members of the Stanford and McGill jazz community have conducted several live, "low latency" internet jam sessions to demonstrate the technology. We are still at the beginning of such possibilities, and there are some inherent limitations to the process, but digital audio promises to provide new capabilities to musicians and music lovers in the future that are difficult to imagine.

The Internet and digital music also present a problem for the creators of music due to the ease with which sound files can be exchanged. Current digital delivery media like the compact disc contain no method of copy prevention, so anyone can extract, or *rip* the digital audio files from a commercial CD to their computer and send them over the Internet to anyone else with a computer. Preventing unauthorized copying is one reason for developing new digital media. It has also helped promote the development of new digital techniques of representing music that both provide improved sound quality and easier protection from copying. Super audio compact discs (SACD) use different encoding of the audio data that simplify playback circuitry while preventing computers from reading or playing the discs. Future media for music distribution will likely be secure from unauthorized copying. While this protects the commercial producers of music, it also makes it more difficult for independent musicians to use the technology.

While many of the signal-processing devices, synthesizers, and sequencers now available provide preset, instant sounds, it is important to fight the tendency to overuse them! In most cases, the designers of these presets intended them as a starting point for exploration, not an end point. The danger of using presets is that music will become increasingly homogenized as everyone starts to use the same effects, reverbs, or synth sounds. It also introduces the danger of music sounding dated: as soon as new sounds come out, everyone rushes to be the first to use them, and then after several years those sounds become associated with a particular era. As always, the best way to make fresh, creative, and high-quality recordings is to let your ears guide you. Whether it is a digital reverberation device, a new string synthesis program, or a guitar amplifier simulator, we recommend that you play around with and modify the parameters to your liking. Even small modifications will give you a more individual, customized sound.

The popularity and accessibility of computer-based recording systems has increased the number of people making music recordings, greatly expanding the market for recording equipment. The demand for inexpensive microphones, preamplifiers, mixers and monitor speakers has been met with a new generation of manufacturers who produce equipment in places where labor is cheap and who sell devices that look much like the expensive equipment of the traditional recording studio. Many of these look-alikes actually perform their tasks well, however some simply resemble the original device and fail to sound anything like the gear after which they are modeled. The availability of decent inexpensive recording equipment has significantly increased, but one must know how to evaluate and select from the plethora of new devices (and presets) introduced. The increased access to sophisticated recording equipment enabled by the personal computer has led to a shift in the way musicians think about recording: where once a commercial studio was the only place to make recordings, many people now favor doing it themselves at home. Several large and well-known studios have ceased operation in part due to the dwindling business caused by the shift to personal and project studios. Since many of the do-it-yourself practitioners have limited knowledge and experience, the average quality of the music recordings may have declined. However, as more and more hobbyist recording engineers gain knowledge and experience, we may expect a positive effect on the quality of music recordings.

While a considerable community still regards music recording as a job for analog tape, the computer-based recording system is here to stay. The flexibility, power, and economy that it provides are too compelling, and young recordists adopt the computer naturally. Although early digital systems were open to criticism for inferior sound quality when compared to analog recorders, significant improvements have resulted in comparable sound from computer-based systems. The convenience of the editing and mixing capabilities of these systems are a final impetus to join the move to adopt this recording technology for many. As we become comfortable with the new technical requirements of digital computer-based studios, they will seem as familiar as the old analog studio.

Although technology will continue to change rapidly, fundamental principles do not: the purpose of music recording has *always* been to convey the music as expressively as possible. Except for those rare cases when the purpose is to demonstrate gear in a hi-fi store, a high quality recording of a song no one likes will never take the place of a low quality recording of a great song. When excellence in both comes together, the results are long-lasting. Learning to make good recordings, even with high-quality and easy-to-use computerized equipment, takes time like anything else. Care, attention to detail, and a good ear are as important as they ever were, and those are things that are not likely to change in the next five or even fifty years.

The Art and Craft of Song Mixing

Susan E. Rogers

Music in stereo is almost like a magic trick. Listen to a modern recording in front of a pair of speakers and you will hear the singer directly in front of you—where no speaker exists. While the bass may be in the middle, the guitars could be off-center, and the drums could occupy the width of your room. Some instruments will probably sound distant and others up close. This is an illusion created by spectral and timing cues in the audio signal. Audio engineers add these cues during the mixing process. This article will discuss how mixers create a two-dimensional (left/right, front/back) stereo space from a multitrack recording. It would be nice if I could tell you that a mix will make you believe Simon is taller than Garfunkle, but as of today the third dimension (high/low) is yet to be commercialized. Beyond any sleight of hand is the final impression of the act, so this chapter will also discuss mixing as an art form.

Mixing a popular song is the art of combining many individual recordings into one panoramic auditory scene. Recorded tracks—the parts of a composition—can number as few as one (even a solo voice can be embellished with signal processors to create a mix) or more than one hundred separate sounds. To use a better analogy, the mixer's job is almost like that of a visual artist's—she blends individual elements to communicate an idea or evoke a feeling.

Early on, the visual artist will struggle to learn technique, refining her eye and controlling her muscles to draw the perfect barn, tree, cloud, and bridge to suit her purpose. Although she may master each of these individually, arranging them in the same scene may say no more to her audience than "here is a picture of a barn, a tree, a cloud, and a bridge." If she wants to capture the essence of a pastoral scene, she needs to understand how these objects collectively can represent an idea not necessarily present in the parts.

This is the case in song mixing where (typically) no single instrument carries the entire message. Melody, harmony, rhythm, and lyrics are expressed in individual tracks, but it is their *relation* to one another that forms an overall impression in the listener—the song's essence. The performer's message may be lost or changed by altering the blend between the instruments in a balanced mix.

This is not to suggest that there is only one perfect mix for each song. Depending on the song and the arrangement, it is possible to create a different emotional impression by remixing a multitrack recording. A finished mix can sound natural, as if the musicians are playing together in one room, each occupying a location within a single space, or the same song can sound artificial with some instruments echoing off distant walls while others appear to come from cracks in the floor. A listener may find the song equally pleasing regardless of which mix he hears, although one may suggest that the singer is contemplative and the other that he is disgruntled (see tracks 1 and 2 on the CD-ROM). Part of the mixer's job is to understand what the artist intends to say and to create a sonic image that either supports the text or counterbalances it with subtext.

If you doubt that a blend of level, equalization, and reverb can carry such associations, consider another comparison with vision. Flip through channels on a television set, and you will notice a distinct difference between the look of a videotaped sitcom on one channel and an old Technicolor film showing on another. Along with each visual impression, you may have an implicit knowledge of cultural trends associated with each technology. Since audio technology has changed as rapidly as visual technology, a modern song can be mixed in a decades-old style, thus adding subtext to the performer's message.

For example, a recording engineer might create a monophonic 1960s sound using an 8-track analog tape recorder, tube microphones, and signal processors made from discrete, rather than integrated circuit, components. Assuming that he finds this rare equipment (and blank tape), he and the musicians are limited to filling only 8 tracks. The final product is a relatively bare recording with audible tape hiss and certain analog distortions. Despite these infidelities, some would say the analog sound is "fatter" and "warmer" than modern digital recordings. For an auditory example, listen to any Sly and the Family Stone record from the early '60s (also see track 3 on the CD-ROM).

A mixing engineer can approximate this analog sound from digital recordings. First, he may elect to use only the basic parts of the composition, say 8 to 12 tracks, in the final mix. Then, he can route the digital tracks through tube signal processors, or even re-record them onto analog tape, adding the sound of tape saturation and hiss. Most digital recording software includes plug-ins designed to sound like analog equipment. The final mix can sound close enough to the original style that listeners draw comparisons between the new artist and his inspiration. Lenny Kravitz is a good example of a modern artist who appropriated his forerunner Jimi Hendrix's recording sound.

Mixers today can pursue high fidelity or low fidelity; most listeners readily accept both, judging by current popular music. Just as musicians use cheap drum machines and early-model synthesizers, mixers sometimes reach for low quality gear when the song calls for it. Mixing studios offer both old and new equipment to let the engineer add distortion or keep it clean. While distorting the electric guitar created a new sound in the '50s, overdriving a mic pre-amplifier with vocal tracks creates something equally valid today. The aim is not to achieve the highest fidelity but to make an auditory statement. Likewise, a portrait painter can represent a barn in a realistic manner or in a gesture drawing. Sometimes just a few lines—the *idea* of a barn—are enough to convey what a barn represents. If a mix can evoke an emotion, a memory, or an idea in a listener, it is working as the writer and performers intended. It is communicating.

The following mixing techniques are tips for shaping and blending individual tracks. Learning techniques will make the beginning mixer a better artisan; learning to convey a message will make him an artist. This short chapter can help with the former. I think only practice (and maybe a few visits to an art museum) can help with the latter.

1 Techniques

1.1 Finding the Resonant Frequency

Due to their physical properties, materials and cavities resonate at certain frequencies when struck with a moderate force (see Perry Cook's article "Introduction to Physical Modeling," in *Audio Anecdotes I*). This resonance is indirectly related to the fundamental frequency of played notes; it refers to where a vibrating body generates the most power. A hollow wooden instrument such as a violin is built to resonate at a frequency complementing the timbre it produces. Its size, shape, type of wood, and surface finish all contribute to its resonance. Likewise, pipes open at one end (flutes, oboes, etc.) resonate at a frequency the wavelength of which is one fourth the pipe length. Singers instinctively recognize this and work on exercising their vocal chords to expand their range from their own resonant frequency—the easiest note to sing. For musical instruments and singing voices, the *resonant frequency* is often where the most pleasant timbre is found. During recording, a microphone or its placement can inadvertently diminish this part of the spectrum, but a multiband equalizer can help bring it back (see track 4 on the CD-ROM).

When two or more instruments are playing similar parts but need to be acoustically separated, find the resonant frequency of each before deciding what to boost or cut. Boost each frequency band one at a time and listen for the timbre changes. There may be more than one "sweet spot," particularly with quality instruments. A ten-band graphic equalizer is perfect for the job, but a parametric equalizer may be used if you dial the Q (sharpness of the filter) to its narrowest setting before sweeping through the bands.

The resonant frequency can be unpleasant if the instrument is damaged or if it overpowers all other tones coming from the source. Cutting the unpleasant frequencies of one instrument creates a dip in the overall sonic spectrum that another instrument can fill, preferably with its own "sweet spot." Instruments with non-overlapping resonant frequencies may be panned to the same location in stereo space and both will sound clear. This is especially useful for instruments that are typically placed in the middle and share a frequency range, such as kick drum and bass or lead vocal and snare drum.

If you find that two instruments share the same resonant frequency, play in synchrony, and must be panned to the same spot—pull the resonant frequency out of just one of them and let the other instrument represent that frequency band for both. Each will sound distinct and full (see tracks 5 and 6 on the CD-ROM).

1.2 Depth of Field

One obvious method for creating depth of field is to apply a lot of reverb to the instrument you want in the background and a smaller amount to the foreground instrument (see tracks 7 and 8 on the CD-ROM). Two alternate techniques may be combined to create even greater depth, however. The first capitalizes on the proximity effect inherent in directional microphones.

As a sound source moves from four feet to two feet away from a mic, the mic capsule experiences a four-fold increase in air pressure as the distance is halved. If the sound source continues moving inward, this large increase in the pressure gradient causes the bass frequencies to seem louder in relation to the rest of the spectrum. Within two feet of the receiver, the high frequencies begin to deflect around the mic (or listener) and, due to phase cancellation, lose some of their power at the capsule (or eardrum). Once a sound source gets *very* close to a listener's ear, space does not permit most of this deflection, so both the lowest and highest frequencies of the sound's range are once again present.

To create the impression that a voice is very close, add more detail to its frequency spectrum by boosting its most natural sounding upper highs and lowest lows. Do the *opposite* for any sound you want to place in the back of the room. Consider that the walls will absorb some of the highest frequencies (> 4 kHz) before a distant source can reach the listener's ear, so decrease this band by a decibel or two. Keep the mid-frequency band (150 to 1 kHz) flat while decreasing the bands below 100 Hz or so (see tracks 9, 10, and 11 on the CD-ROM).

If you are looking to create a realistic sonic image, be aware that the loudest sounds (snare drums, powerful vocals, electric guitars) are never likely to be really close to the listener. By using equalization to position them farther back, you can make them seem truly powerful. Remember that an approaching freight train sounds increasingly brighter (more high frequencies, or treble) as it nears (this is the Doppler effect, and it is responsible for the apparent pitch shift of the train whistle as it passes you). Hearing only the lowest frequencies (< 150 Hz) from an object can make us think that something sonically enormous is in the distance. Slightly boosting this range in a broadband instrument (electric guitar, for example), while reducing the highest frequencies, can help give the impression that it is a distant object with great power.

Once two objects have been equalized to appear near and far, apply a second technique to increase the perception of depth. Use *signal delays* (also called *echo*) of different lengths on your near and far sources to create the distancing effect of reverb but with greater clarity and definition.

Reverberation results from sound waves contacting reflective surfaces at different angles. Any angle of reflection is dependent on the path length from the source to a surface. Since musical instruments and voices radiate sound pressure waves in all directions, these waves strike the walls and floor at slightly different points. Unless immediately absorbed by soft materials, sound waves bounce from one surface to the next until their energy dissipates. This bouncing around takes some time—a typical reverberant room will permit a high-energy signal to reflect for several seconds before dying out. Thus, the reverb portion of a signal consists of a very large number of phase-shifted delays, with each frequency band losing energy at different rates.

The sound of this phenomenon can be compared to a visual image from an unfocused camera lens. Blurring the boundaries between an object and its background has a softening effect, but, by adding so many random events to the clean, direct signal, it also adds noise. You can achieve dimension without the noise by imposing a shadow rather than a blur on the auditory object. Route the near and far voices to two separate stereo delay lines. For the near object, try adding 124 milliseconds of delay to the left channel and 126 milliseconds to the right. Double this amount for the far voice by putting 248 milliseconds of delay on the left and 252 milliseconds on the right. The small time difference between channels will have a phase-shift effect, helping to give the perception of three-dimensional space. If your delay lines have a feedback function, add a small amount of this feature for a more realistic picture. When more instruments are brought into the mix, the direct voices with their delays will occupy two distinct spaces in the picture. A little reverb can be added to them, of course, but you may find that you don't need it. Change the delay times, keeping a few milliseconds difference between left and right channels, to move a voice closer or farther away (see track 12 on the CD-ROM).

Another way to add clarity and depth to your sonic picture is by using the *pre-delay* feature on your digital reverb (or patching a delay device to the input of your echo device). As mentioned, adding reverb to the direct signal blurs the boundaries of sonic space. Putting 40 to 80 milliseconds pre-delay between the direct and reverberant signal separates the clear from the blurred image. To visualize it, imagine a physical object and its shadow. Mentally pick up the shadow and move it back some distance from the object. This distance is like adding space between the direct signal and the reverberant one (hence the name pre-delay). This gives a nice balance between a well-defined auditory object and its softer "shadow," thus creating depth in the picture (see track 13 on the CD-ROM).

1.3 Changing Dynamics

Compressors reduce intense peaks in an audio signal by scaling back a proportion of the peak reaching the output (see Kolber and Lee's article "Audio Dynamic Range Compression" on page 199). For example, when a compressor's gain reduction is set to 4:1, an eight-decibel spike at the input becomes a two-decibel spike at the output of the unit. This has a smoothing effect on the auditory signal and, if set optimally, evens out performance dynamics. Because changing dynamics is a musical component that the brain follows, reducing the amount of change draws attention away from that property of the signal. This can result in increased attention paid to the changes happening in other areas, such as melody or lyrics.

When a rhythm player changes the dynamics of his performance, usually while coming out of one song section and going into the next, he can easily (but unintentionally) shift his timing. Using compression on rhythm tracks (e.g., bass, drums, rhythm guitar) is a trick that the mixer uses to give listeners the impression that the tempo is steadier than in reality. For example, a mixer can set the compressor to have a fast attack and slow release time. When the sharp peaks of the loudest signals hit the compressor, the spike is quickly reduced, matching the softer peaks of the average signal, and then held for a moment before resuming normal operation. Smoothing out dynamic changes like this keeps the listener's attention focused on the big picture, rather than on the details of the rhythm track (see tracks 14 and 15 on the CD-ROM). Compressing melodic instruments, too, can draw focus away from loudness changes and make the overall melody more noticeable. Applying this effect to the lead vocal makes lyrics stand out over the mechanics of the vocal performance.

Nature has outfitted the human ear with a built-in compressor to protect it from very intense, nonimpulsive, sounds. When exposed to signals above 78 dB, the muscles of the middle ear contract. This action, called the *middle ear* (or *acoustic*) *reflex*, is slow (roughly 100 milliseconds onset time) and mostly attenuates low frequencies. A compressor can be set to mimic the middle ear reflex and fool the listener into believing the sound source is very loud, even when played at moderate levels. This is probably why many producers ask mixers to compress the entire mix; the result can make the whole performance sound more exciting. (It is worth noting here that, unfortunately, the middle ear reflex offers little protection against sharp, impulsive sounds like gunshots, cymbal crashes, and snare drum hits).

According to the inverse square law of acoustics, when a sound source doubles its distance from a listener, intensity is reduced by six decibels (see the various articles from *Audio Anecdotes I* regarding sound pressure levels, the decibel, and sound propagation). The law can only be applied outdoors or in an anechoic chamber. In enclosed environments, the inverse square law only holds for the direct, nonreflected sound. The intensity of signals reaching the listener from the back of a room change very little with distance because reflected signals contribute to the overall power spectrum. From this you can see that adding compression to a signal—leveling it out—has the effect of placing distance between the performer and the audience. This effect is especially natural if it is combined with reverberation. Taking this into consideration, a mixer can choose to compress some instruments and not others, giving precedence to certain parts of the composition. If compression is combined with equalization, delay, and reverb, mixers can achieve a great deal of control over instrument placement in the soundscape.

1.4 Blending

What the mixer and the artist want the song to convey affects decisions about which instruments to favor in a composition. The song's lyrics and, to some extent, nuances of the vocal performance provide the obvious text; supporting lead and harmonic instruments either underscore the text or add counterpoint to the message. Imagine a lead vocalist singing of frustration against the backdrop of a cheerful chord progression, and you see the point. Although the artist and producer will have made these choices before the mix, altering the blend between instruments changes the arrangement by shifting the listener's focus.

When mixing, it is important to listen to all the elements of the composition and play with the blend to decide the best way of complementing the arrangement. Some songs benefit from featuring the most evocative melodic part, so other instruments must serve supporting roles. Other songs derive power from synchronization. In these, melodic instruments can be "nested" in a bed of rhythm tracks where repetition is the star. Typically, many musicians will have contributed to the song, so each part brings a unique interpretation or feel to the piece. Just as the painter can move the barn, tree, cloud, and bridge around her sketchpad before deciding where they will end up, the mixer can move elements of a song around to look for changes in the emotional effect or impression. The changes may be very subtle but awareness of this aspect of mixing can make the difference between a mix that does not serve the song and one that just sounds right.

1.5 Layering

Statisticians tell us that if you poll 100 college undergraduates on what they think of tattoos, asking number 101 for his opinion is unlikely to add anything meaningful. Each new opinion adds something until all of the likely responses are collected. After this point, anything more is a waste of time; you have already gotten the message. Technically speaking, adding more variables than you need lowers the signal-to-noise ratio.

It is the same with audio signals. Layering voices or instruments to create a thick, rich sound works up to a point. Once you have saturated the part to where you no longer hear tonal differences between instruments, adding one more will result in diminishing returns. As the noise level climbs, the dramatic impact of the fat signal is reduced—the listener has gotten the message. This is something to be aware of whether the layering is natural from overdubbing many instruments or artificially created with signal processors. The trick is to know when fewer are more. Should you decide to recreate Phil Spector's "Wall of Sound," remember that his early recordings were three-channel monophonic on analog tape. Layering to digital tape will not give the same saturation effect that made his early sound so distinctive.

The reason for this is in the difference between analog and digital tape recording. Recording tape has permanent magnets embedded in the tape oxide. On blank tape, the magnets are polarized randomly so that the net force on any piece of tape is zero. If you play it back, you will hear nothing. The recording process aligns the magnets to correspond to changes in the original, electrical, signal. On playback, the aligned magnets reproduce the audio signal (see Kadis and Levitin's article "How Recordings Are Made II," page 15).

As the input level to analog tape is increased, it reaches a point where the tape is fully magnetized and additional input will not result in greater signal gain. This point is called *tape saturation*. If you keep adding level past the saturation point, the tape machine will distort in a not unpleasant way. Many engineers deliberately disregard the peak meters and drive their analog tape to saturation.

In a digital recording system, a signal exceeding the maximum allowable level will "clip." The top of the waveform will be cut off because information above the threshold is unavailable to the processors. This has a very unpleasant sound, nothing like analog distortion. All digital signal processors, not just recorders, respond this way to being overdriven. A mixer with an analog tape machine can always re-record his digital tracks onto it, saturating the tape for an analog sound.

2 Conclusion

The points discussed in this article were learned on the job, taught to me by other engineers, or deduced from reading books on acoustics and signal processing. Like most people, I usually discover what works by accident and later go looking for a technical explanation to help me do it again.

I do know that a great mix is invisible, or perhaps inaudible is a better word, since the listener becomes completely engaged in the performance and is oblivious to the artistry that helped create his experience.

Annotated Bibliography

[1] D. M. Huber and R. E. Runstein. *Modern Recording Techniques,* Sixth edition. London: Elsevier, 2005.

This book is a classic text on recording technique.

[2] B. Owsinski. *The Mixing Engineer's Handbook.* Auburn Hills: Intertec, 1999.

Owsinski's handbook provides more information on mixing, including interviews with famous mixers.

Creating Mixtures: The Application of Auditory Scene Analysis (ASA) to Audio Recording

Wieslaw Woszczyk and Albert S. Bregman

1 The Art of Recording: The Creation of Mixtures

The focus of this article will be on the application of principles of auditory scene analysis (ASA) to the art of recording. In order to follow the present discussion, please also refer to "Controlling the Perceptual Organization of Sound: Guidelines from Principles of Auditory Scene Analysis" (see *Audio Anecdotes I*). To summarize, ASA describes how the auditory system sorts out the complex sense data received from a mixture of sounds into separate perceived sound sources, such as distinct voices or instruments. When many sounds are heard at the same time, the brain receives a whole array of sensory features of the signal. To hear the distinct sounds in the mixture, the brain has to create bundles of features that it treats as belonging to the same sound (the process of integration), and to treat them as distinct from other bundles that are attributed to different sounds (the process of segregation). There are two types of organization involved: (a) sequential organization—those processes that integrate or segregate the sounds in a sequence, deciding whether they come from a single sound source; and (b) simultaneous organization—those processes that integrate or segregate frequency components or other sensory features that are present at the same time.

Many of the decisions made by the recording engineer are closely related to ASA because they are about the segregation or blending of parts, where the parts are the different tracks that have been recorded of acoustic instruments and voices, synthetic and sampled natural sounds, effects (transformed sounds), room sounds, ambiances, etc. (see the articles by Dan Levitin, "Instrument (and Vocal) Recording Tips and Tricks" (see *Audio Anecdotes I*) and "How Music Recordings are Made" (page 3).

2 General Guideline

The general guideline from which all the detailed ones follow comes from the definitions of *integration* and *segregation*: to cause sounds to be distinct, strengthen the ASA cues that favor segregation, and to blend them, weaken those cues. We are not implying that ASA principles can tell recording engineers how to pursue their craft. Perhaps, however, by becoming aware of the general principles of perceptual grouping, as they have been uncovered in the laboratory, recording engineers can understand why their methods are successful. It is also possible that ASA principles might supply a framework upon which their craft could be systematized.

3 The Use of Space (Loudspeaker Separation)

An important technique that the audio engineer uses is the spatial placement of the numerous recorded tracks into two, three, five, or more spaced apart loudspeakers. One aspect of the art of mixing is to decide which of the original recorded tracks to mix into the same loudspeaker, which to separate into different speakers, and which to distribute across speakers.

As a crude first step, one could say that if you mix two sounds, A and B, into the same speaker, or into all speakers, they will blend, and if you mix them into separate speakers, they will be perceived as more distinct. However, research has shown that unless A and B differ in other ways, as well as in their spatial locations, their separation in space will do little to segregate them. In other words, if A and B are synchronous in onset, have the same amplitude envelopes, and the same kinds of attacks, spatial separation won't segregate them very well even though they have different pitches and timbres. Therefore, separating two steady-state sounds in space doesn't make them easier to segregate [1]. Spatial separation seems to work by accentuating the segregation that is based on other dissimilarities between the sounds. Happily, in any two sequences of sounds outside the psychophysicist's laboratory, there are many differences between them from moment to moment: Their amplitude envelopes are rarely exactly correlated. Their attacks don't exactly overlap in time. Their pitches usually don't change in parallel. This is why spatial differences can be used effectively by the audio engineer to segregate signals, especially when they differ in their temporal characteristics, and when their difference in distance or angular separation is large. Similarly, mixing different instruments into the same loudspeaker, or spreading all of them out over a few speakers will contribute to the blending of their sounds.

4 Filtering and Equalizing

We know that the sequential grouping of sounds is affected by their timbres; this means that the ear will be more easily able to follow the same instrument or voice over time, if it has a unique timbre. There are two ways in which timbre might affect perception: (a) by providing features that the listener can track voluntarily over time; and (b) by influencing the automatic, bottom-up grouping of the sounds in a sequence. It is by no means certain that every feature that permits voluntary tracking is also a basis for automatic sequential grouping.

For both these forms of grouping, two of the most important features of timbre are the formant structure of a sound (layout of major peaks in its spectral envelope), and its onset and decay transients. Each musical instrument has a distinctive formant structure, which provides it with an "auditory signature" that can be tracked over time. However, transient structure (onset and offset) as well as dynamic envelope and fluctuations are also very important for the identification and tracking of a sound source. Playing any recorded sound backward preserves its spectral shape, but makes the source difficult to recognize particularly in the case of percussion, bells, piano, and plucked instruments. Audio Example 5 which appears on the accompanying CD-ROM presents four ten-second recordings of different solo instruments played backwards. Can you recognize the instruments? You can find the answers at the end of this article.

It has been demonstrated that when onsets of instrumental sounds are edited out, leaving only the sustained sounds, perception and classification of musical instruments is confused. A cornet, for example, can be mistaken for a violin, a cello for a bassoon, a French horn for a flute. Possibly, because onsets precede the sustained portions and are free of their own reverberation, transients can provide reliable cues in source identification. The nonstationary and resonant nature of musical sounds makes them very robust carriers of redundant auditory cues—cues that allow them to be blended together or separated by the actions of the musicians.

Other identifying features are "brightness," "sharpness," and "roughness." Brightness and sharpness are qualities of experience that occur when the high partials of a sound are of greater intensity than its low partials (an intensity relation that raises the spectral "center of gravity"). Roughness is an experience that results from the beating of the partials of concurrent sounds at unrelated rates, either because the fundamentals of the two sounds are not in good harmonic relations with one another or because the sounds, in themselves, are inharmonic. Differences in any of these qualities will allow our voluntary attention to separate individual sounds, and their similarities over time will allow the sounds from a single source to be tracked. While not all these properties have been studied in the context of automatic sequential integration, it is known that "brightness" (spectral center of gravity) influences the d (combined difference in properties) that affects sequential grouping. Filters and equalizers can play a role in accentuating differences in brightness and can modify the spectral balance of formants and transients. A gradual high-pass filter will make the sound brighter whereas a gradual low-pass filter will make it duller. Segregating sounds by artificially induced differences in brightness may be undesirable from an esthetic point of view, but filtering a short phrase or two in the music in this way could clean up a muddy stretch of sound. Conversely, bandpass filtering of two sounds with the same filter settings will increase their tendency to blend.

Since each microphone is a filter, and each microphone placement captures a different spectrum of the source, engineers responsible for recording and balance use microphone selection and placement to shape the character and aural identity of the source that will make it distinct from others. Further equalization and filtering will be used to fit, isolate, match, and blend sounds with each other depending on the musical requirements of the mix. The entire process of composing, performing, recording, and mixing involves a careful consideration of which sounds should be fused together and which should be segregated so that the music can communicate its intended purpose clearly and fully.

Filtering can also be employed to bring out the pitch of a particular instrument, A. Since only a few harmonics, particularly the low ones, are needed to define a pitch, if there is a region in the spectrum where the lower harmonics of A are not mixed with those of other instruments, boosting the intensity of this spectral region will strengthen the pitch of A. Finding such a region is easier if A is a bass instrument, whose lower harmonics are substantially lower than those of the other instruments in the ensemble.

5 Temporal Synchrony

By employing a rubato style, instrumentalists and vocalists take themselves out of exact synchrony with the accompanying instruments (assuming that the latter stay in synchrony with one another). This causes their sound to stand out from the rest of the ensemble. In the recording or post-production process, the recording engineer can achieve the same result by time-shifting the tracks that need to be emphasized relative to the other tracks. A delay of as little as 20 to 30 msec can be effective for an instrument whose tones have abrupt onsets that are well defined. Longer delays will be needed for slower onsets. This technique has to have musical and expressive justification and be used sparingly, perhaps causing the isolated instrument to be sometimes ahead of and sometimes behind the others. Otherwise, the time-shifted instruments will sound "out of time" and outside the context of the music.

Delaying or advancing a track with respect to others during post-production can also be used to synchronize tracks that were recorded out of synchronization with others; this can increase the perceptual integration of the group of instruments when this is desired.

A group of similar instruments (say electric guitars) can be blended into an ensemble when their individual envelopes are trimmed into synchrony using gates or keyed (synchronous) expanders. One of the envelopes is used as a master and is imposed dynamically on the other instruments to align their onsets with that of the master.

6 Spatial and Pitch Motion

The recording engineer can impose common motion in order to achieve a greater sense of ensemble, and create unity out of independent sources. Modern digital and analog processors allow group modulation of gain, frequency/pitch, time delay, and spatial position. For example, all reverberation sources in the mix can be modulated (or gated) by a single source signal, producing gated reverberation. Several sources or the entire mix can be compressed in amplitude by a compressor that imposes common dynamic changes. The result is always increased blend and interdependence of sounds subjected to the commonality of motion. Common spatial panning of several instruments segregates them out of the mixture and groups them in the unity of motion. Pitch modulation or Doppler modulation, achieved when sources are reproduced via a rotating Leslie loudspeaker or its digital emulation, does the same to impose distinct aural characteristics blending the sounds together. The common spectral side-bands created by modulation are derived from the individual spectra and thus bind the individual sound together.

7 Reverberation

Even adding reverberation to an entire signal, or just a part of it, can affect perceptual organization. It can do so in two ways:

(1) An individual sound with reverberation added to it will stand out from a mixture (from other potentially masking sounds) because of the lengthening effect of reverberation. Reverberant decay sustains the spectral content of the source by delaying and recirculating this signal for as long as the reverberation time is set (on a digital room simulator, for example, the reverberation time indicates the time needed to achieve a 60 dB drop in reverberation level at mid-frequencies). The spectral content of the source is represented in the reverberant sound and is thus available for auditory evaluation because reverberation acts as a temporary (leaky) storage of that sound. This "running reverberation" (following the source closely in time) may help the perceived continuity of a stream of sound, by strengthening sequential integration. The lengthening can especially help the auditory system to more clearly register the pitch of short notes (since the pitch computation takes time) because these notes can still be heard in the reverberation even after a quick decay of the primary source. Each distinct reverberation pattern accompanying each different sound source will help to segregate these sources from one another by providing lengthening and differentiating characteristics (spatial or timbral) to these sounds.

(2) A mixture of sounds combined with a single reverberation derived from this mixture (by sending a number of tracks to the same reverberator) will act to blend and integrate these sounds. This is because the temporal, spectral, and spatial structure of the reverberator—either from the natural one (a room) or an artificial one (a digital room simulator)—will become the common attribute of all these sources. This common lengthening and spatializing of sounds

will enhance their similarity and thus promote their blending and integration. For example, background vocals should use the same reverberation if the intent is to provide a well-blended ensemble sound.

Adding the same type of reverberation to all tracks, or to the final mix, can reinforce the listener's sense that they are all in the same spatial context, lending a kind of esthetic unity to the mix. However, this effect is probably due to higher-level cognitive processes based on learning, and not on the low level, "bottom-up" processes that have been studied in ASA research, and which are believed to be innate.

It is also possible that by adding reverberation to one track (A) and not to another (B), this can help B to stand out against A, since B's attacks will be clearly heard against the smoother sound of A. This effect can be obtained in a weaker form by passing A and B through different reverberators that smooth A more than B.

For example, one reverberation (A_r) may give the impression of a small room while the other (B_r) of a large ballroom. The ASA will act to separate the two sounds, based on their reverberation difference including reverberation decay time and delay time of early reflections.

Here, we should perhaps point out that whenever the source produces sound in a large reverberant room, the auditory system subdivides the inputs into two streams. All direct sounds from the source plus the immediately following reflections that cannot be perceptually separated from them (e.g., floor reflection and that from the nearest wall or an object) are grouped to create the impression of the source. All indirect sounds created by the later arriving acoustic response from the room are grouped to produce an image of the room. Therefore, a listener is aware of the source and the surrounding enclosure as separate sounds, the source as a sequence of distinct sounds, and the enclosure as a continuous reverberation. In addition, a listener may identify and track other perceptually distinct sources such as that annoying flutter echo or a slap back from the rear or rumble of the ventilation system. All available sounds compete for membership in these perceptual structures on the basis of similarity and plausibility.

It is assumed that qualitatively similar sounds heard within the auditory system's integration limit will fuse together. The limit is generally considered to be between 5 ms and 40 ms, depending on the transient nature of the sounds, beyond which auditory fusion breaks down and the sounds are segregated [4]. Of course, strongly dissimilar sounds are able to maintain their perceptual independence and are not subject to the integration. Imprecise attacks in a group of instruments such as strings will be largely unnoticed, due to integration. Late attacks by instruments of different tonal characteristics (woodwinds, for example) will be more noticeable. It is considered that the permissible range of delayed starts of instruments in the orchestra is 50 ms.

Because the acoustic room response has similar tonal characteristics to those of the sound that caused it, perceptual integration of the source and early response of the room operates over a longer time span, perhaps as much as 80 ms, depending on the nature of the transients of the source. Beyond that delay, the "room sound" becomes separated from the source and is perceived independently from it. This is why we do not have a strong awareness of the acoustics in small rooms where room response decays quickly. Large rooms and concert halls provide a strong sense of a "separate" acoustic space having its distinct onset and decay pattern as if it were an independent musical instrument.

The classical recording engineer tries to capture and frame these two distinct images of source and enclosure using microphones. The pop recording engineer more often creates synthetic environments to enrich sources that have been captured in a dry studio. Both of them are fully aware that the right acoustic environment must be used to establish a unique mood and atmosphere able to enhance the intended musical illusion of time and place.

8 Transposing the Pitch

It is technically possible to transpose the pitch of a tone while keeping all its frequency components in the correct harmonic ratios. This processing can be used for improving the blend of tracks with one another. When a voice or instrument is out of tune with others, it has three distinct effects:

(1) It causes some beating that can be heard as roughness.

(2) It gives the impression of more voices (the "chorus" effect).

(3) Since consonant harmonic relations increase perceptual fusion, and being out of tune destroys these harmonic relations, it increases the segregation of concurrent sounds that would have been in good harmonic relations had they been in tune.

A more complex effect produced by a "chorus effects processor" (usually present in DSP multi-effect devices) can blend a number of distinct sounds (say, a group of instruments) into a softer "mass" of sound by imposing common pitch and phase modulation.

The simple chorus effect, which is created by adding the track to itself several times, each time with a small delay, tends to "fill out" the music so that the slightly asynchronous onsets of individual instruments in, say, the violin section are lost and the instruments blend together.

In other cases, the tendency to segregate may be undesirable. For example, in polyphonic classical music, segregation of the parts is usually desired in the middle of a phrase or section of the music. However, at the *ends* of phrases or sections, the parts usually come together into strongly fused chords. This fusion maintains the unity of the music despite its polyphony. Good harmonic relations at these points of fusion are important; if one instrument is slightly out of tune, it is important to use pitch transposition to correct this, in order to maintain the unity of the whole. At other places, the mistuning, as long as it is not sustained for long, can be tolerated, or even appreciated. For example, mistuning may lend a desirable human voice-like quality to electronic keyboard synthesizers. An interesting example of mistuning that is perceptually desirable is that applied by piano tuners who often tune (acoustic) pianos with the low end pushed just a little too low, and the high end just a little too high, in order to achieve proper perceived interval (melodic or harmonic distance) between extreme notes of the piano. Because very high and low pitches of the piano have many inharmonic components (due to the physically imperfect nature of metal strings), equally tempered melodic tuning would cause the pitch intervals to sound too close together in the absence of additional outward stretching of pitch.

A device called a harmonizer can be used to generate chords or additional notes transposed to a chosen pitch interval relative to the original track, all playing along with that track. The harmonic chorus effect created this way has a thicker, more immediate texture, but is usually used only sparingly to support the source itself or is fed to a reverberator to support the source through gentler ambient sound.

9 Interactions Between Modalities

Auditory and visual perception are not two independent processes functioning in isolation. Both modalities cooperate towards improving human efficiency and ability to track "objects" and "events" in a surrounding environment. When auditory information is supported by matching visual information, or when visual information is reinforced by a matching auditory cue, the cooperative interaction between the modalities reinforces human awareness of the stimulus. The matching of auditory and visual data triggers perceptual synergy between modalities and promotes intermodal fusion. A powerful form of audio-visual interaction can be seen in a phenomenon called the "McGurk effect." When a video picture shows a person saying one consonant, and the audio has the person saying a different one—with the two signals appropriately synchronized—the observer hears (does not merely *decide upon*, but actually *hears*) a consonant that is maximally compatible with both sources of information, rather than hearing the sound that has been presented in the audio signal [3]. Later research has shown that the effect is very powerful. It occurs even when the auditory and visual stimuli are presented by different genders, or when the face is blurred. Even when the auditory stimuli lags behind the visual stimuli by as much as 180 ms, the McGurk effect is apparent.

This effect is taken by advocates of the "motor theory of speech perception" as showing that the speech recognition system does not use sound to recognize speech directly, but to infer the talker's vocal tract activity; then it hears the sound that this activity would have created. This is why the visual evidence can so strongly influence what is heard. From the point of view of ASA, the effect illustrates the potency of synchronizing picture and sound to achieve cross-modal integration. Movies with effective sound tracks also show the power of the same integrative force.

Another important intermodal phenomenon is the "ventriloquism" effect. When sounds are synchronized with a picture that comes from a different location, listeners hear the sound as coming from the location of the picture, or close to it [2]. This, too, appears to be automatic on the part of the listener. The pulling effect can be observed in delays of up to 200 ms, and spatial displacements of up to 30 degrees. In all cases of audiovisual integration, sound reduces the ambiguity of picture and helps to define it, while picture reduces the ambiguity of sound or its position and helps to define its purpose.

The scientific evidence of the interdependence of hearing and vision shows that this synergetic perceptual interaction depends on the matching between auditory and visual data displayed to the viewer [6].

The important matching factors are

(1) Temporal coincidence (synchrony),

(2) Spatial coincidence,

(3) Congruence of auditory and visual movement,

(4) Balance between picture size and the loudness of sound,

(5) Balance between picture quality and sound quality.

10 Conclusion

We hope that this exploration of the applications of ASA to music and recording will provide new insights into these rich arts and perhaps provide the craft of the recording engineer with a scientific foundation.

11 The Answers to Audio Example 5: Musical Instruments Heard Backwards

(1) Trumpet

(2) Guitar

(3) Cello

(4) Xylophone

These are anechoic sounds that are played backwards; so no room reverberation precedes the decay of the instrument.

The sounds were provided by Bang & Olufsen A/S and were prepared by Geoff Martin at Multichannel Audio Research Laboratory, at the Centre for Interdisciplinary Research in Music Media and Technology, and at McGill University, Faculty of Music.

Annotated Bibliography

[1] P. L. Divenyi and S. K. Oliver. "Resolution of Steady-State Sounds in Simulated Auditory Space." *Journal of the Acoustical Society of America* 85 (1989), 2042–2052.

This study created a simulated auditory space by using separate "transfer functions" for the two ears, simulating, over headphones, what the listener would have heard in real free-field listening. Listeners were asked for separate localizations of two sounds presented concurrently. Relatively untrained listeners required quite large separations (perhaps as large as 60 degrees). Complex sounds were easier to separate than pure tones.

[2] C. E. Jack and W. R. Thurlow. "Effects of Degree of Visual Association and Angle of Displacement on the Ventriloquism Effect." *Perceptual and Motor Skills* 37 (1973), 967–979.

Sounds that co-vary with visual stimulation originating at a different spatial location are localized at or closer to the visual display (the "ventriloquism" effect). This research used a display consisting of a videotape of a human speaker with the voice separated from the picture, and showed that the ventriloquism effect was greatly reduced when a lag of 200 ms was introduced between the visual and auditory stimulation. With co-variant auditory-visual stimulation, the effect operated over a separation as large as 30 degrees of visual angle.

[3] H. McGurk and J. MacDonald. "Hearing Lips and Seeing Voices." *Nature* 264 (1976), 746–748.

This brief paper reports the McGurk effect. It depends on the joint presentation of a video picture of a person saying one syllable and a sound track in which a different syllable is said. The resulting experience incorporates information from both sources to make a completely new percept. For example, when the picture of the face saying /ga/ is presented with the auditory syllable /ba/, the subject will perceive /da/. Like /ga/, /da/ doesn't involve a lip closure (which is absent in the picture), but it sounds more like /ba/ than /ga/.

[4] H. Wallach, E. B. Newman, and M. R. Rosenzweig. "The Precedence Effect in Sound Localization." *American Journal of Psychology* 62 (1949), 315–336.

Showed that the upper limit of the time interval over which fusion of separate sound stimuli (presented sequentially) takes place is about 40 ms for complex stimuli such as speech or music.

[5] F. Winckel. "Music, Sound and Sensation." New York: Dover Publications, 1967.

This small, yet excellent, book translated from German, combines physical acoustics in music with the evaluation of the art of music, the subjective character of musical hearing, and the analysis of musical structures and speech. The author who himself has a thorough understanding of music provides composers, musicians, and recording engineers/producers with a better understanding of physical acoustics and psychoacoustics by reviewing, in the context of music, the astonishing sensitivity of the ear to temporal, spectral, and dynamic properties of sound.

[6] W. Woszczyk, S. Bech, and V. Hansen. "Interactions Between Audio-Visual Factors in a Home Theater System: Definition of Subjective Attributes." *Proceedings of the 99th Convention of Audio Engineering Society*, Preprint No. 4133, October 1995, New York.

This paper reviews broad evidence of interactions between seeing and hearing, and explains an experimental design developed for measuring interactions in a home-theater viewing experience. The authors propose to test four dimensions of audio-visual experience, where cooperative interactions between vision and hearing can deliver convincing illusions: action, motion, mood, and space. The approach has been used successfully to assess the subjective quality of home-theater systems using Dolby Surround programs. The companion paper (Bech, Hansen, Woszczyk, "Interaction Between Audio-Visual Factors in a Home Theater System: Experimental Results," Proceedings of the 99th Convention of Audio Engineering Society, Preprint No. 4096, October 1995, New York) presents the results of these experiments.

Sound Synthesis

Implementing Real-Time Granular Synthesis

Ross Bencina

1 Background

Granular Synthesis, or *Granulation*, is a flexible method for creating animated sonic textures. Granular Synthesis may be employed to generate or process sound in musical and sound design applications. Sounds produced by Granular Synthesis have an organic quality sometimes reminiscent of sounds heard in nature: the sound of a babbling brook, or leaves rustling in a tree. Forms of granular processing involving sampled sound may be used to create time stretching, time freezing, time smearing, pitch shifting, and pitch smearing effects. Perceptual continua for granular sounds include gritty/smooth and dense/sparse. The metaphor of *sonic clouds* has been used to describe sounds generated using Granular Synthesis [10]. By varying synthesis parameters over time, gestures evocative of accumulation/dispersal and condensation/evaporation may be created.

The output of a Granular Synthesizer or *Granulator* is a mixture of many individual *grains* of sound. The sonic quality of a granular texture is a result of the distribution of grains in time and of the parameters selected for the synthesis of each grain. Typically, grains are quite short in duration and are often distributed densely in time so that the resultant sound is perceived as a fused texture. Algorithmic means are usually employed to determine when grains occur in time and to select their synthesis parameters, which often include duration, amplitude, panning, pitch, and envelope shape. A *Stochastic* Granular Synthesizer uses random number generators to determine grain onset times and synthesis parameters. Usually, the probability functions of these random number generators constitute the parameters of the Granulator as a whole and are often varied over time.

A Granulator synthesizes individual grains by applying an *amplitude envelope* to a *source* such as a synthetic or sampled waveform. One criterion that has been used to classify different types of Granular Synthesis is the method used to generate the source sound for each grain [15]. According to this classification scheme, types of Granular Synthesis include:

- *Tapped Delay Line Granular Synthesis.* Uses a delay line to store samples from a real-time input stream. Each grain reads sound from the delay line with a potentially different delay time and playback rate. This form of granular synthesis is appropriate for "effects" processing of real-time input.

- *Stored Sample Granular Synthesis.* Generates each grain by reading sample values from a wavetable. It can be used to process pregenerated or sampled sounds.

- *Synthetic Grain Granular Synthesis.* Describes a broad class of Granular Synthesizers that employ standard synthesis techniques such as oscillator or FM synthesis to synthesize each grain, thus creating purely synthetic sound textures. (See the other articles in this chapter for additional techniques which could be used to create synthetic grains).

Granular Synthesizers can also be classified in terms of the method used to distribute grains in time:

- *Asynchronous Granular Synthesis.* Distributes grains in time according to a stochastic function that is traditionally specified in terms of *grain density:* the number of grains per unit time.

- *Pitch Synchronous Granular Synthesis.* Sequences grains at regular intervals in time to create periodic or pitched sounds.

Granular Synthesis differs from many other audio synthesis techniques in that it straddles the boundary between algorithmic event scheduling and polyphonic event synthesis. Conventional synthesis techniques are typically employed in the creation of individual musical "notes," whereas Granular Synthesis may employ thousands or millions of relatively simple grains to articulate a single sonic gesture. One implementation of Granular Synthesis using MIDI synthesizers was described as "Rapid Event

Deployment" highlighting the central role of event scheduling in Granular Synthesis [17].

Interested readers are advised to consult the literature for further information on the theory and applications of Granular Synthesis. The annotated reference section of this article provides some starting points [4], [11], [14]. Hesham Fouad's article "Ambient Synthesis with Random Sound Fields" (see *Audio Anecdotes II*) discusses a related technique in which ambient sound fields are synthesized using randomized event scheduling.

1.1 Overview

The remainder of this article describes a flexible architecture for implementing Real-Time Granular Synthesis and documents implementation strategies for various components of the architecture. Section 2 describes forces that influenced the architecture's design. Among these forces are the points of variation across existing implementations and the presence of multiple implementation strategies for some aspects of the system. Section 3 introduces the abstractions that participate in a Granular Synthesizer and identifies their roles within the system. The ways in which these abstractions interact to synthesize sound samples is described in Section 4. Section 5 examines the strengths and weaknesses of the architecture and identifies some details that have been left to implementation. The remaining sections discuss the implementation of various aspects of a Granulator. Section 6 describes how the architecture accommodates three common types of Granular Synthesis: Tapped-Delay Line, Stored Sample, and Synthetic Grain Granular Synthesis. Section 7 describes three efficient algorithms for generating grain envelopes. Section 8 discusses techniques for determining grain onset times. Section 9 presents a technique for passing initialization parameters to individual grains. Section 10 describes the use of generic programming to compose implementations of the various abstractions into a Granular Synthesizer; and finally, Section 11 discusses some common implementation strategies for improving the efficiency of implementations. A C++ implementation of the framework described in this article, along with working example programs, is provided on the CD-ROM accompanying this book.

1.2 A Note on Design Patterns

Some readers may recognise that this anecdote follows the design pattern form. A design pattern is a reusable pattern of (software) design that is common to, and may be applied across, multiple implementations.

The design pattern form was chosen for this article because it provides a useful framework for documenting the design forces and describing the abstractions employed within the architecture. Readers interested in further investigating this fascinating topic are encouraged to read Erich Gamma et al.'s *Design Patterns* book [6].

1.3 About the Diagrams

The software design diagrams in this article employ the Unified Modelling Language (UML) notation. Although familiarity with this notation is not essential (as an explanation of each diagram is provided), readers who are unfamiliar with UML may wish to consult a reference on the topic for additional insight into the meaning of the symbols [5].

2 Motivation

As described in Section 1, known points of variation between different types of granular synthesizers include the method used to synthesize each grain and the method used to distribute grains in time. Another point of variation is the method used to synthesize grain envelopes. This section considers the implementation requirements of each variation in order to provide motivation for a generalized architecture that accommodates them all.

The method used to synthesize the source for each grain is one criterion that has been used to classify Granular Synthesizers. This classification scheme encompases Tapped Delay Line, Stored Sample, and Synthetic Grain Granular Synthesis. Both Tapped Delay Line and Stored Sample Granular Synthesizers require information such as a wavetable or delay line to be shared between all grains. Internally, they both use interpolated sample look-up whose complexity is dependent on the desired interpolation quality. Maintenance of the delay line and implementation of variable rate delay taps for each grain results in Delay Line Granulation having greater implementation complexity than the other types of Granular Synthesis described here. Synthetic Grain Granular Synthesis has the potential to be simpler than Delay Line and Stored Sample Granular Synthesis as no state is shared between grains. However, its implementation complexity is primarily dependent on the synthesis method used as the source of each grain.

Various algorithms for grain amplitude envelope generation and grain onset sequencing may be employed interchangeably in the implementation of the aforementioned types of Granular Synthesis. The following envelope algorithms can each be implemented with similar efficiency: Parabolic, Trapezoidal, and Raised Cosine Bell. Another common, but possibly less efficient, method of generating grain amplitude envelopes is the use of a look-up table containing the envelope function. Selection of a particular envelope algorithm is often based on the level of flexibility desired in specifying the envelope's attack, sustain, and decay characteristics. In some applications, such as analysis/resynthesis, the spectral characteristics of the grain envelope may determine which algorithm is chosen.

Asynchronous and Pitch Synchronous forms of Granular Synthesis differ in the method used to distribute grains in time. Asynchronous Granular Synthesis typically specifies a *grain density*—the number of grains per unit time, whereas Pitch Synchronous Granular Synthesis specifies a grain rate. For real-time operation, where it is necessary to schedule grains in time-sequential order, a useful concept is *interonset time*: the time between the onset of successive grains. When implementing Asynchronous Granular synthesis, it is possible to generate interonset times as a function of grain density. In Pitch Synchronous Granular synthesis, the interonset time is directly related to the grain rate, and hence the period of the resultant sound.

A Granulator may be required to synthesize thousands of grains per second, with common grain durations falling in the range from 10 to 70 milliseconds. This typically corresponds to between 10 and 100 concurrently active grains. Although individual grains are often simpler to synthesize than traditional synthetic "notes," the large number of grains involved in a typical granular texture often leads to significant processing overhead in scheduling, generating, and passing parameters for each grain. Implementations of Granular Synthesis which utilise the standard event sequencing and scheduling facilities of general-purpose synthesis systems can exhibit poor or non-real-time performance due to the overhead involved in initialising and passing parameters to each grain. This overhead is often the result of a generalized or text-based interface between the "instrument" (grain) and the "score" (grain sequencer). Such overhead is typically not significant for event rates associated with note-based music; however, the higher event rates of Granular Synthesis place significant demands on the process of note activation and deactivation. Unifying grain scheduling, parameter generation, and synthesis within a Granular Synthesizer can significantly reduce this overhead, resulting in significant efficiency improvements over implementations where these functions are performed at different structural levels of a program, or by separate hardware systems.

An efficient implementation of Granular Synthesis requires grain scheduling, synthesis, and mixing to be executed with a minimum of overhead. It is desirable to employ an architecture that accommodates the various grain source synthesis types, envelope algorithms, and grain scheduling policies without forfeiting efficiency.

3 Structure

Section 2 identified a number of properties that differentiate various types of Granular Synthesis. These included the algorithm used for grain source synthesis, the grain envelope generation algorithm, and the algorithm used to determine grain onset times. The object-oriented structure illustrated in Figure 1 allows all of these algorithms to be varied independently by encapsulating the sources of variation in the three abstract classes: Source, Envelope, and SequenceStrategy.

The class diagram in Figure 1 shows the main participants and associations in a Granulator and indicates that SequenceStrategy, SourceData, Source, and Envelope are *abstract,* meaning that they may have multiple concrete implementations.

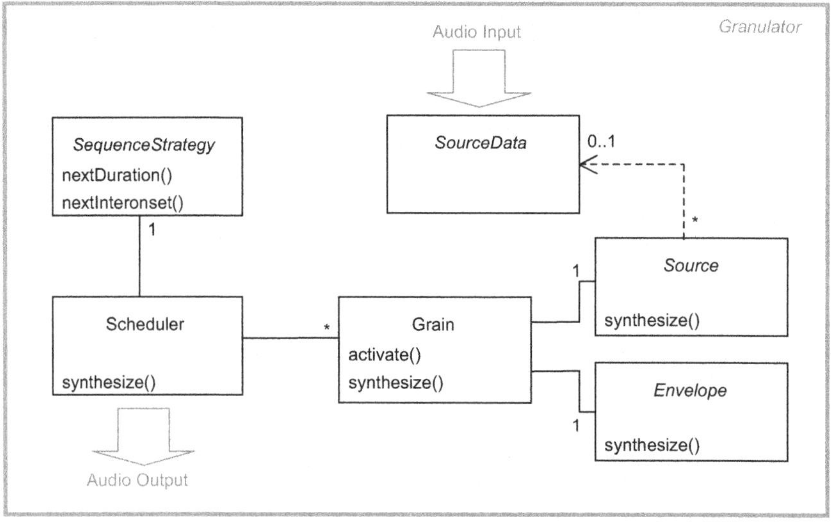

Figure 1. Object-oriented Granulator structure.

3.1 Participants

- **Granulator (DelayLineGranulator, StoredSampleGranulator, SyntheticGrainGranulator)**
  - Top-level container responsible for the lifetime of its component parts.
  - Mediates between external audio streaming services, the Scheduler and possibly the SourceData, for example a Delay Line in the case of a Delay Line Granulator.
  - Manages dynamic parameter modulation or acts as a Façade [7] to allow clients to modulate synthesis parameters.
- **SequenceStrategy**
  - Provides an interface allowing the Scheduler to determine when the next grain should occur and what its duration should be.
- **Scheduler**
  - Maintains state necessary for activating grains according to Grain onset times and durations supplied by a SequenceStrategy.
  - Exposes a method for synthesizing samples of sound by mixing together the output from its active Grains.
  - Manages grain allocation; for efficiency, it may maintain a pool of reusable Grains.
- **Grain**
  - Provides an interface for activation, synthesizing samples, and querying whether the grain has completed.
  - Contains an Envelope and Source, which are used by the Grain's synthesis method.

- **Envelope (TrapezoidalEnvelope, ParabolicEnvelope, Raised-CosineBellEnvelope)**
  - Synthesizes an amplitude envelope.
- **Source (DelayLineSource, SampleSource, SyntheticSource)**
  - Generates the source waveform for a grain.
  - Maintains a reference to the Granulator's SourceData in Granulator variants where SourceData is required.
- **SourceData (DelayLine, StoredSample)**
  - Maintains shared state used by all instances of Source within the Granulator: a delay line in the case of a Delay Line Granulator, a wavetable in the case of a Stored Sample Granulator.

4 Collaborations

- In response to a request from an audio streaming service, Granulator requests that Scheduler synthesizes samples of sound.
- Scheduler synthesizes sound by requesting each of its active Grains to synthesize sound. The result of each Grain's output is mixed and returned to the client.
- Grain synthesizes samples in response to requests from the Scheduler. This is achieved by requesting that Envelope generate an amplitude value, which is then used by Source to synthesize a sample at the appropriate amplitude.
- Scheduler requests a grain interonset time and grain duration from SequenceStrategy and uses these to determine when the next grain should be activated (the next grain onset time) and its duration.
- At the next grain onset time, Scheduler activates a new Grain.

The sequence diagram in Figure 2 shows the interaction that occurs when samples are requested from a Granulator. It illustrates how Grain obtains the current envelope value from Envelope and passes it to Source, while avoiding any implementation dependence between Source and Envelope.

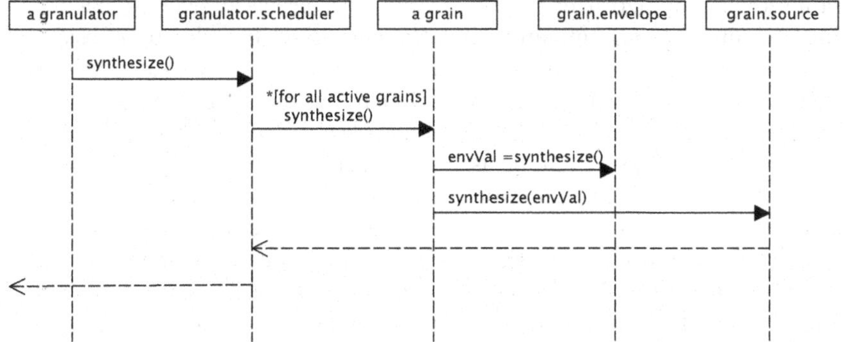

Figure 2. Event sequence when samples are requested from a Granulator.

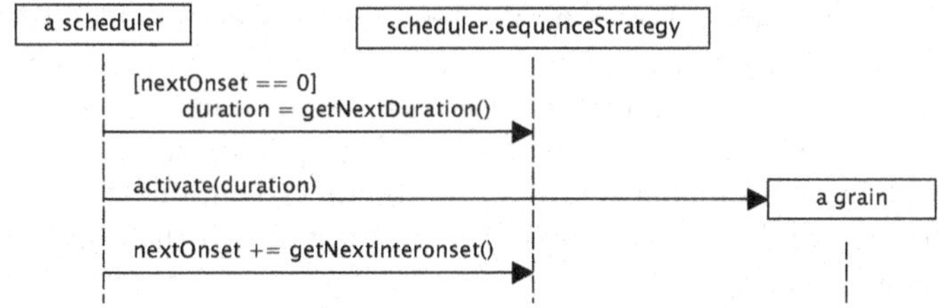

Figure 3. Event sequence when it is time to activate a new Grain.

The sequence diagram in Figure 3 shows the interaction that occurs between Scheduler, SequenceStrategy, and Grain, when the Scheduler determines that it is time to activate a new Grain. Notice that SequenceStrategy is responsible for determining the duration of the activated Grain, and for determining when the next grain will occur.

5 Consequences

As stated in Section 3, this design allows various algorithms for Source, Envelope, and SequenceStrategy to be used interchangeably. More subtle benefits of this design arise from the allocation of responsibilities between participants; Grain passes the current envelope value to Source to control Source's output amplitude, also allowing Source to utilize the envelope value for additional purposes. For example, the value can be used as an FM modulation index in Synthetic Grain Granular Synthesis [16]. SequenceStrategy controls both Grain duration and onset time, enabling grain sequencing algorithms where grains must precisely overlap, such as time domain pitch shifters and Pitch Synchronous Granular Synthesis.

This design leaves open the problem of selecting individual synthesis parameters for each activated grain. Depending on the degree and flexibility of parameterization required, Source and Envelope, the Scheduler, or an additional object could be assigned this responsibility. A subsequent section describes a flexible approach that allows the grain parameter generation strategy to be varied independently of Envelope and Source.

The primary strength of this design is also its greatest weakness: It uses interchangeable, largely autonomous building blocks with little centralized control. This decomposition is well suited to common forms of Granular Synthesis such as Stochastic Granular Synthesis, where the random generation of each grain parameter is independent of all other grain parameters. However, it may be less appropriate when correlated grain parameters are required. For example, SequenceStrategy determines grain onset times and durations, but has no control over grain pitch or transposition, thus making it difficult to use this design to implement a Granulator that can play rhythmic melodies. If required, such control can be achieved by introducing a (possibly abstract) coupling between SequenceStrategy and Source in order to pass pitch or other information from SequenceStrategy to Source.

6 Granulator Variants

The following subsections describe three different types of Granular Synthesis using the architecture presented above. Note that these Granulators vary only in terms of Source, SourceData, and external signal routing topology. They can be implemented using any of the Envelope and SequenceStrategy algorithms described later. Additional notes germane to the implementation of each type of Granulator are provided where relevant.

6.1 Delay Line Granulator

Each Grain Source in a Delay Line Granulator implements an independent delay tap on a Delay Line shared by all Grain Sources. Each delay tap may read the delay line from a different position to create delay and/or time smearing effects, and at a different rate to create pitch shifting and/or pitch smearing effects. Writing to the delay line may be temporarily halted to facilitate "time freezing." If a delay tap has a playback rate greater than unity, care must be taken to avoid the noncausal case of

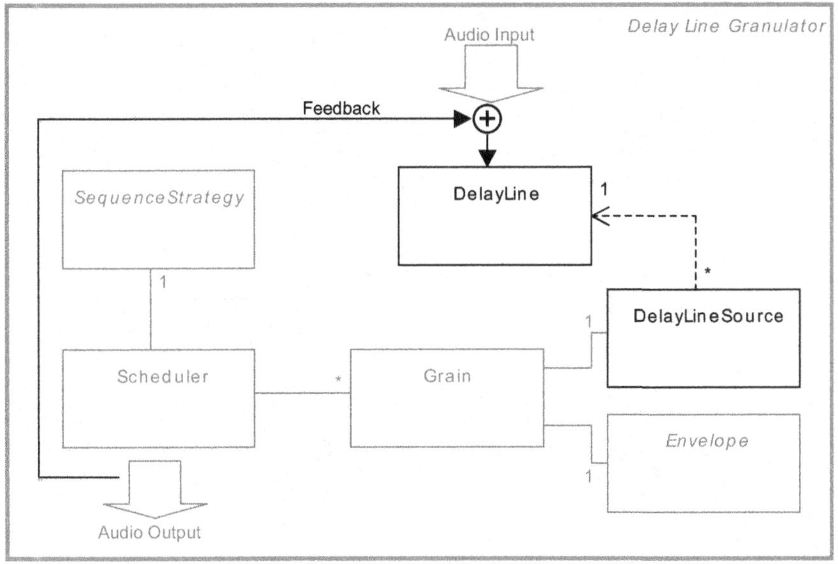

Figure 4. Delay Line Granulator.

trying to read "future samples" from the delay line. One solution to this problem is to increase the initial delay time according to the requested grain duration and playback rate.

The output of the Delay Line Granulator may be mixed back into the delay line input to create feedback effects, which vary in sonic quality according to the granulation parameters. For example, feedback combined with pitch-shifted grains creates stacked transpositions (chords) spaced according to the transposition factor. Due to the unpredictable phase and amplitude response of the sum of active grains, it may be necessary to insert a compression or limiting element in the feedback loop to avoid instability.

6.2 Stored Sample Granulator

Grain Sources in a Stored Sample Granulator read sound from the stored sample at independent positions and rates. Ramping the initial read position across the stored sample for successive grains creates time stretching or time dilation effects. Each Source's initial read position can be modulated by a small random factor to decorrelate source phases and create a more animated timbre.

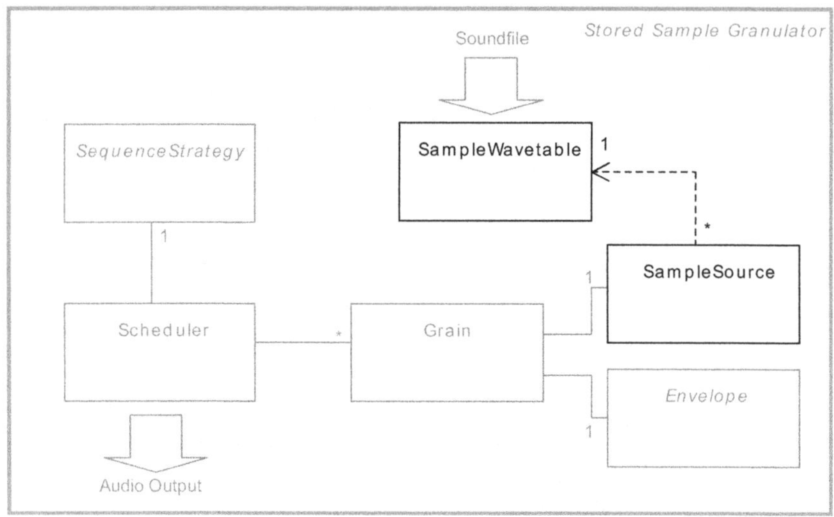

Figure 5. Stored Sample Granulator.

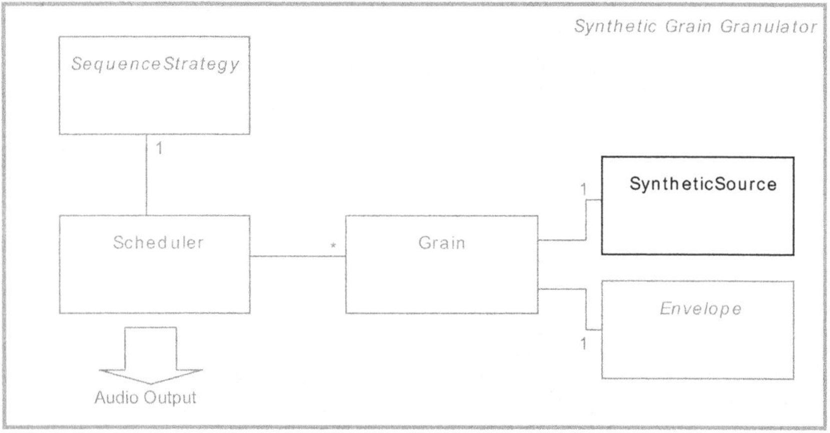

Figure 6. Synthetic Grain Granulator.

6.3 Synthetic Grain Granulator

Grain Sources in a Synthetic Grain Granulator are responsible for synthesizing their waveform without any reference to a SourceData object. The available choices for SyntheticSource synthesis method are as limitless as the range of known sound synthesis methods. Traditionally, performance concerns have lead to the use of simple techniques such as single modulator FM or two oscillator additive synthesis.

6.4 Enhancements

Enhancements to the above types of Granular Synthesis include independent filtering (such as bandpass filtering) of each grain, independent panning of each grain to create spatially diffused textures, and ramping the source playback rate of each grain to create glissandi grains or "chirps" [10].

7 Grain Envelopes

A number of factors can influence the choice of grain envelope algorithm including spectral response, flexibility of available envelope shapes, and efficiency of generation.

Due to the short duration of individual grains, amplitude envelopes may introduce noticeable spectral artifacts, especially when grain durations are less than 10 to 15 milliseconds. Of the envelope algorithms presented below, trapezoidal envelopes introduce the greatest spectral distortion due to the second order discontinuities at each envelope state transition—raised cosine bell envelopes provide decreased spectral distortion at the cost of increased processing time. A formal analysis of the spectral artifacts introduced by various grain envelopes will not be presented here; however, it is interesting to note that a related synthesis technique, *FOF synthesis*, uses the spectral effects of a specific grain envelope shape to simulate vocal tract formants [12].

Although classical Granular Synthesis utilizes symmetrical grain envelopes, there are advantages to providing flexible grain envelopes with parameters to control envelope shape. For example, these parameters can be randomized to decorrelate artifacts introduced by the envelope. When the grain density is low and grain durations are relatively long, variations in envelope shape are easily perceived. As a result, a flexible grain envelope may be musically useful; for example, a granular texture consisting of grains with slow attacks and fast decays can be made to sound like reversed tape playback.

The three envelope generation algorithms presented below may be implemented using iterative algorithms that employ a small number of state variables. This enables efficient implementation on modern processor architectures where memory access overhead may discourage the use of stored tables for grain envelopes.

7.1 Parabolic Envelope

Parabolae provide smooth grain envelopes; however, they only allow parametric control over grain amplitude and duration. Successive samples of a Parabolic Envelope may be computed efficiently using the following pseudocode [8, page 6]:

```
amplitude = amplitude + slope
slope = slope + curve
```

Initial values for amplitude, slope, and curve may be computed as follows:

```
amplitude = 0
rdur = 1.0 / durationSamples
rdur2 = rdur * rdur
slope = 4.0 * grainAmplitude * (rdur - rdur2)
curve = -8.0 * grainAmplitude * rdur2
```

7.2 Trapezoidal Envelope

The Trapezoidal Envelope is considered a degenerate envelope due to the spectral artifacts introduced by its discontinuities. However, it may be

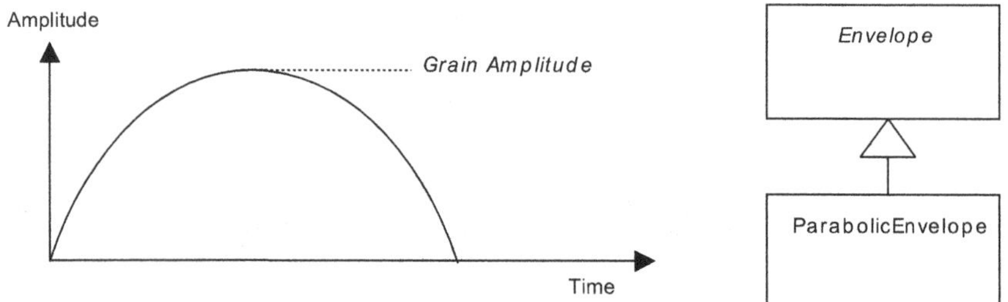

Figure 7. Parabolic Envelope.

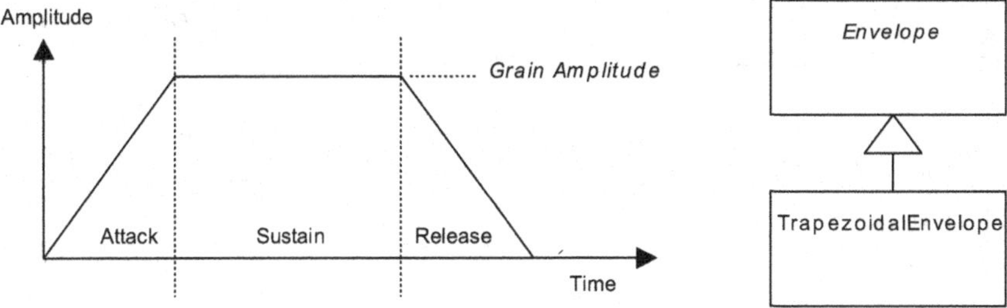

Figure 8. Trapezoidal Envelope.

implemented efficiently, making it a candidate for real-time implementations. It provides the flexibility of independently variable attack, sustain, and release times.

Successive samples of a trapezoidal envelope may be computed using an accumulator:

```
nextAmplitude = previousAmplitude + amplitudeIncrement
```

Where `amplitudeIncrement` varies according to the current envelope segment:

```
attack:
    amplitudeIncrement = grainAmplitude / attackSamples
sustain:
    amplitudeIncrement = 0
release:
    amplitudeIncrement = -(grainAmplitude / releaseSamples)
```

`AmplitudeIncrement` need only be updated at envelope segment boundaries. A separate counter may be employed to determine when the next envelope segment boundary has been reached.

7.3 Raised Cosine Bell Envelope

The Raised Cosine Bell Envelope is a second-order continuous envelope which allows independent specification of attack, sustain, and release times. The attack and release portions of the envelope are transposed cosinusoidal segments:

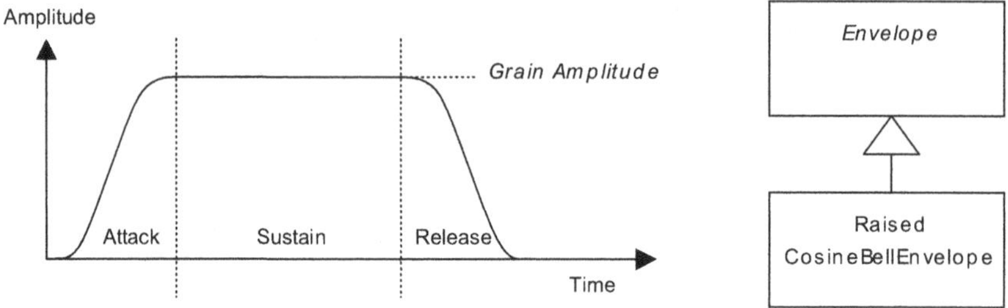

Figure 9. Raised Cosine Bell Envelope.

```
attack:
    amplitude = (1.0 + cos(PI + (PI * (i / attackSamples) *
                (grainAmplitude / 2.0)
sustain:
    amplitude = grainAmplitude
release:
    amplitude = (1.0 + cos(PI * (i / releaseSamples)) *
                (grainAmplitude / 2.0)
```

where `i` is the number of elapsed samples for the current envelope segment.

The following pseudo-code generates sinusoidal waveforms using only a single multiply-accumulate per sample; `y0` is the current value [8, page 5]:

```
y0 = b1 * y1 - y2;
y2 = y1;
y1 = y0;
```

The state variables may be initialized as follows, where `w` is the phase increment and `ip` is the initial phase, both expressed in radians:

```
b1 = 2.0 * cos(w)
y1 = sin(ip - w)
y2 = sin(ip - 2.0 * w)
```

This algorithm can be used to compute the cosinusoidal function in the attack and release portions of the Raised Cosine Bell Envelope. As with the Trapezoidal Envelope, state variables only need to be re-initialized at envelope segment boundaries.

8 Grain Scheduling

Traditionally, grain onset times have been derived from a density parameter expressed as *grains per unit time*. Such temporally uniform grain distributions have a "natural" quality like rain on a tin roof. Non-real-time implementations can directly implement this type of distribution by allocating a buffer containing all output samples and randomly distributing grains across the buffer according to the required density.

For real-time operation new grains must be activated in time-sequential order. The basic variable controlling grain density in a real-time granulator is the *interonset time*—the time between temporally adjacent grain onsets. Using interonset times, a simple grain activation mechanism may be used whereby a counter is set to the next interonset time at each grain activation. For each subsequently generated sample the counter is decremented until it reaches zero, at which point the next grain is activated and the process repeats:

```
float Scheduler::synthesize(){ // returns the output sample
    if( --nextOnset == 0 ){
        activateGrain( sequenceStrategy.nextDuration() );
        nextOnset = sequenceStrategy.nextInteronset();
    }

    return synthesizeActiveGrains();
}
```

In many situations, the parameter(s) controlling the generation of interonset times may be modulated by an external controller such as a human performer, or a higher level control algorithm. In such cases, it may be desirable for significant reductions in interonset time (for example, from 1 second to 10 milliseconds) to take effect immediately, rather than to wait for the next onset counter to reach zero. Implementing such a scheme requires additional communication between Scheduler and SequenceStrategy so that, for example, the Scheduler can periodically ask the SequenceStrategy whether the previously issued interonset time should be reduced.

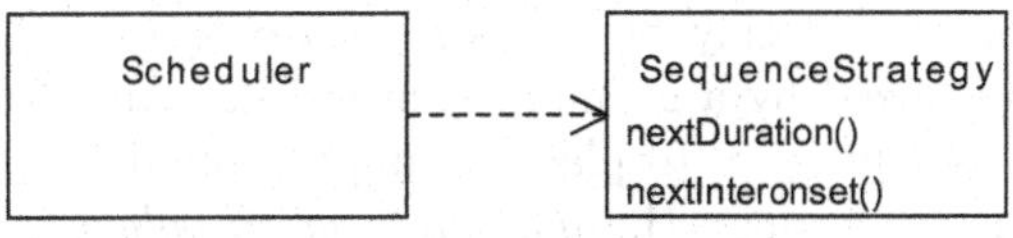

Figure 10. Grain Scheduling.

8.1 Direct Interonset Specification

The simplest method of calculating grain interonset times in a real-time Stochastic Granulator is to express the interonset time as a random range:

```
interonset = minInteronset +
             (frandom() * (maxInteronset - minInteronset))
```

where `frandom()` is a function returning real numbers from 0 to 1. As this method constrains interonset times to a specified range, it is capable of creating subjectively "smoother" fused textures than the density-per-unit time method described next. When the minimum and maximum interonset times are equal, grains are scheduled periodically, creating interesting amplitude-modulation style spectral effects.

8.2 Interonset Time as a Function of Density

To create classical granular textures with a specified grain density per unit time, it is necessary to use a SequenceStrategy that generates interonset times as a function of density. The following pseudocode generates interonset times based on an average grain density of `D` grains per second [9]:

```
interonsetTime = -log( frandom() ) / D
```

where `log()` is the natural logarithm and `frandom()` is a function returning real numbers from 0 to 1.

8.3 Onset Quantization

An interesting extension to stochastic methods of grain onset scheduling is to quantize grain onsets to(wards) fixed quantization boundaries, thus creating rhythmic or "pulsed" textures. The quantization boundaries may be determined from a global time base, or by maintaining a countdown to the next boundary. This technique has been implemented in the various granulators available in the author's AudioMulch software synthesizer [2].

8.4 Limiting Grain Polyphony

In real-time contexts, it may be necessary to constrain the number of processor cycles utilized by a granular synthesizer. An effective method of limiting processor usage is to place an upper bound on the number of simultaneously active grains—the *maximum grain polyphony*. The maximum grain polyphony can be hard-coded into the Scheduler, specified by the user, or dynamically varied according to processor usage information provided by the operating system.

Implementing a grain polyphony limit involves the Scheduler discarding any potential new grains, or deferring activation of new grains until existing grains have completed while the grain polyphony limit is exceeded. Traditional note-based synthesizers sometimes limit polyphony using "voice stealing," whereby an active note (or grain in our case) is prematurely terminated to make way for a new note. However, voice stealing is inappropriate for granular synthesis since a prematurely terminated grain is likely to create undesirable audible artifacts, whereas the perceptual effect of omitting a grain from a grain stream will often be negligible.

9 Initialising Grain State

The Granular Synthesizer architecture described earlier did not specify which object or objects are responsible for generating synthesis parameters for newly activated Grains. This section presents a solution motivated by the following two design considerations:

- *Modularity.* A variety of Source and Envelope algorithms are available; each of these algorithms requires a different set of initialization parameters. In the interest of allowing different algorithms to be used interchangeably, it is best to insulate other elements of the system such as the Scheduler and SequenceStrategy from the varying initialization requirements of each Source and Envelope algorithm.

- *Accessible parameter control.* Initialization parameters for individual Grains are usually derived from parameters specified for the Granulator as a whole. For example, in Stochastic Granular Synthesis, the parameters of individual grains are chosen randomly according to probability distribution parameters defined for the Granulator as a whole. These parameters are usually modulated by an external entity such as a separate sequencing object or a graphical user interface. Thus it is desirable for all of the Granulator's parameters to be accessible from a single location.

The method of initializing Grain state shown in Figure 11 requires that each implementation of Source and Envelope define their own specialized initialization parameter type. For the remainder of this article, these initialization parameter types are referred to as "Essences,"

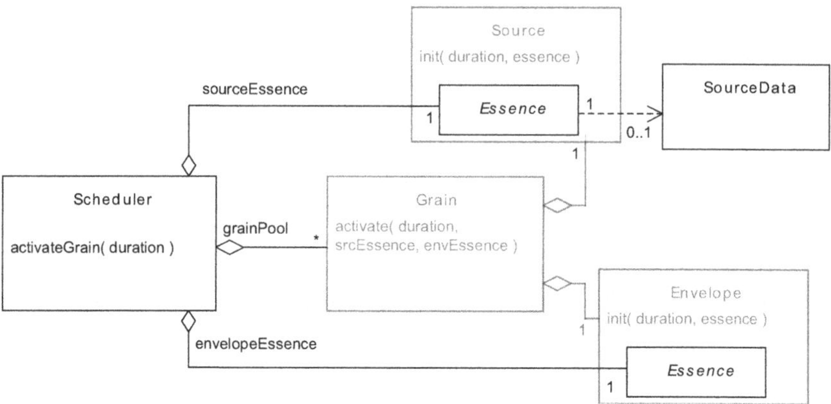

Figure 11. The relationship between Scheduler, Grain, Source, Envelope, and their respective Essences.

after the design pattern of the same name. The Essence design pattern uses a separate object (the Essence object) to store initialization parameters for the object being created, in our case, a Grain Source and Envelope [3].

Figure 11 illustrates the relationship between Scheduler, Grain, Source, Envelope, and their respective Essences. Each concrete Source and Envelope class specifies a nested Essence type that fulfills their specific initialization requirements. If Source and Envelope Essence are defined as abstract types, multiple parameter generation strategies can be used with each concrete Source and Essence. If a separate abstract Essence hierarchy is constructed, it may also be possible to use the same concrete Essence class with multiple Sources or Envelopes.

The Scheduler contains a single instance of Envelope::Essence and Source::Essence. Depending on the implementation, the Granulator or an external client may access these Essences in order to modulate synthesis parameters. In the case of Delay Line and Stored Sample Granulators, the Granulator may need to register the delay line or stored sample with `scheduler.sourceEssence` before synthesis begins. Alternately, the Source Essence could be designed to directly contain the Delay Line or Stored Sample.

When the Scheduler needs to activate a new Grain it calls `Grain::activate()`, passing the grain duration along with references to EnvelopeEssence and SourceEssence. In turn, Grain passes the duration and respective essences to the `init()` methods of Source and Envelope

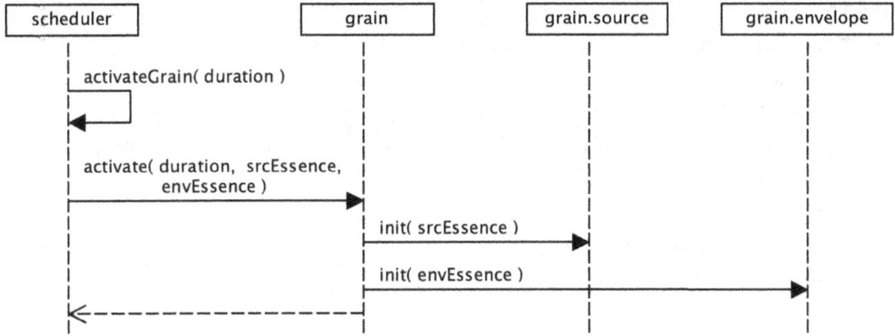

Figure 12. An implementation which uses methods to activate grains taken from a fixed pool.

enabling them to initialize themselves from parameters stored in their Essence. The sequence diagram in Figure 12 illustrates this process.

From a high-level perspective, grain activation is best viewed as object construction. However, the high rate of grain allocation in a typical Granulator makes it desirable to use some form of object pooling to optimize grain activation and deactivation. The implementation described in Figure 12 uses the `Grain::activate()`, `Source::init()`, and `Envelope::init()` methods to activate grains taken from a fixed pool. In C++, grain activation could be implemented as object construction by replacing `Grain::activate()`, `Source::init()`, and `Envelope::init()` with constructor calls, and grain pooling could be implemented using the placement new operator.

10 Compile-Time Composition

Although the preceding discussion defined SequenceStrategy, Source, Envelope and their respective Essences as abstract or polymorphic types, they could also be considered as generic programming "concepts" [1]. In the present context, the distinction is primarily one of implementation methodology—by viewing them as concepts rather than abstract types a granulator may be efficiently implemented in C++ by using templates to create specialized versions of Grain and Scheduler at compile time:

```
template< class SourceT, class SourceEssenceT,
          class GrainEnvelopeT, class GrainEnvelopeEssenceT >
class Grain{
```

```
public:
    typedef SourceT source_type;
    typedef SourceEssenceT source_essence_type;
    typedef GrainEnvelopeT envelope_type;
    typedef GrainEnvelopeEssenceT envelope_essence_type;
    ...
private:
    source_type source_;
    envelope_type envelope_;
};

template< class SequenceStrategyT, class GrainT >
class Scheduler{
public:
    SequenceStrategyT sequenceStrategy;

    GrainT::source_essence_type sourceEssence;
    GrainT::envelope_essence_type envelopeEssence;
    ...
private:
    grain_type *grainPool;
};
```

An implementation of a Stochastic Delay Line Granulator using a stochastic density SequenceStrategy and a parabolic Envelope would look like this:

```
class StochasticDelayLineGranulator{
    typedef Grain<
        DelayLineSource< StochasticDelayLineSourceEssence >,
        StochasticDelayLineSourceEssence,
        ParabolicEnvelope< StochasticAmplitudeEssence >,
        StochasticAmplitudeEssence
    > grain_type;

    typedef Scheduler<
        StochasticDensitySequenceStrategy, grain_type
    > scheduler_type;

    scheduler_type scheduler;
    DelayLine delayLine;
public:
```

```
    DelayLineGranulator(int maxGrains, int maxDelayTime)
        : scheduler( maxGrains )
        , delayLine( maxDelayTime )
    { scheduler.sourceEssence.setDelayLine( delayLine ); }

    float synthesize( float input ){
        float result = scheduler.synthesize();
        delayLine.write(input + result * .2);// 20% feedback
        return result;
    }

    // additional facade methods for accessing synthesis
    // parameters in scheduler.sequenceStrategy,
    // scheduler.envelopeEssence and scheduler.sourceEssence
    // go here
};
```

Note that `DelayLineSource<>` and `ParabolicEnvelope<>` are parameterized by Essence types. This reflects the abstract nature of `Envelope::Essence` and `Source::Essences` as described in the previous section, and allows other (perhaps nonstochastic) Essences to be used in combination with the existing implementations of DelayLineSource and ParabolicEnvelope.

Without the benefits of compile-time specialization as provided by language facilities such as C++ templates, this type of abstraction would not be practical for constructing an efficient real-time Granulator.

11 Optimizations

A common approach to improving the performance of software synthesis algorithms is to synthesize a vector (array) of samples at a time. This allows synthesis state variables to reside in registers or level 1 cache for the duration of the vector computation, reduces the number of function calls per generated sample, and provides optimizing compilers with opportunities to unroll loops.

11.1 Vectorizing Grain Scheduling

As grain scheduling must, in general, be sample-accurate, the scheduling method must accommodate activation of grains at any time, thus precluding scheduling only on fixed vector boundaries. A simple way of accomplishing sample-accurate scheduling is to use variable length vectors expressed as a pointer to their first element and an integer representing the vector's length. The implementation of `Scheduler::synthesize()` below extends the previously described per-sample synthesis function to accommodate both vectorized synthesis and sample-accurate grain scheduling:

```
void Scheduler::synthesize( float *out, int length ){
    synthesizeActiveGrains( out, length );

    while( nextOnset < length ){

        Grain& grain = activateGrain(
                       sequenceStrategy.nextDuration() );
        grain.synthesize(out + nextOnset,
                        length - nextOnset );
        nextOnset += sequenceStrategy.nextInteronset();
    }
    nextOnset -= length;
}
```

Handling the case where `activateGrain()` fails to locate an available grain has been omitted for clarity. Note that all active grains are synthesized prior to activating new grains, this allows grains that complete during the current vector to be reactivated immediately if necessary. A more efficient implementation might interleave synthesis and activation as it iterates through the grain pool.

11.2 Hoisting Grain Synthesis Boundary Conditions

Many software synthesis primitives may be split into two parts: First, compute a resultant sample (with possible state variable updates) and second, check for deterministic boundary conditions such as circular buffer wrap-around or envelope segment transition. These boundary conditions will be true for only a small fraction of generated samples, however, when computing audio one sample at a time, they must be checked for each sample generated. In a vectorized implementation, it may be more efficient to hoist boundary checks outside inner loops, provided that the inner loops can be guaranteed to halt before the boundary conditions occur:

```
void Grain::synthesize( float *output, int length ) {
    int remaining = length;
    do{
```

```
        int nextBoundary =
         envelope_.nextBoundary(
          source_.nextBoundary( remaining ) );

        float *end = output + nextBoundary;
        do{
            *output++ += source_.synthesize(
                           envelope_.synthesize() );
        }while( output < end );

        envelope_.checkBoundary( nextBoundary );
        source_.checkBoundary ( nextBoundary );
        remaining -= nextBoundary;

    }while( remaining > 0 && !envelope_.atEnd() );
}
```

This requires Source and Envelope to implement their synthesis algorithms as three separate functions:

- `nextBoundary( maximum )`. Returns the lesser of `maximum` and the number of samples until the next boundary condition. Algorithms with no boundary condition such as the Parabolic Envelope algorithm presented earlier can simply return `maximum`.
- `synthesize()`. Calculates the next sample and updates any internal state, but does not check for boundary conditions.
- `checkBoundary( samplesPassed )`. Notes the number of samples which have passed and performs boundary checks and state transitions (such as envelope segment state transitions) as necessary.

This technique is only applicable when the overhead of computing `nextBoundary()` is low. Often, `nextBoundary()` can be implemented by simply returning the value of an internal counter.

12 Final Remarks

This article has been primarily concerned with defining an architecture that facilitates simple and efficient implementation of many of the known variants of Granular Synthesis. It has made only passing reference to some significant forms of Granular Synthesis such as Pitch Synchronous

Granular Synthesis and related techniques such as FOF synthesis, which can also be implemented using this architecture. Discussion of generating grain parameters has been limited to stochastic techniques, although many other possibilities exist. The treatment of Synthetic Grain Granular synthesis has been minimal. The fact that these topics fall outside the scope of this exposition reflects the breadth and depth of the granular concept.

The separation of concerns between SequenceStrategy, Scheduler, and Grain can be considered a computer music design pattern with applications beyond Granular Synthesis. It is hoped that this article has presented a new angle on an old idea and may inspire others to explore some of its latent possibilities hitherto unheard.

Readers are invited to explore a C++ implementation of the Granular Synthesis Framework described here which is provided on the CD-ROM accompanying this book. Working examples of Granulators using FM synthesized grains, sampled grains, and delay line granulation are provided, along with an implementation of FOF synthesis built using the Granular Synthesis framework.

13 Acknowledgments

I owe a debt of gratitude to Curtis Roads for his pioneering work in the field of Granular Synthesis and for introducing me to a number of its variants. Many thanks to Barry Truax for his 1988 *Computer Music Journal* article which started me on my journey of implementing Real-Time Granular Synthesis. Thanks to Gordon Monroe for providing me with the density to interonset time function presented in this article. Thanks are also due to Dean Walliss, Ken Greenebaum, and Ronen Barzel for their kind assistance and comments during the preparation of this manuscript.

Annotated Bibliography

[1] Matthew H. Austern. *Generic Programming and the STL.* Reading, MA: Addison-Wesley, 1998.

This book is a guide to applying generic programming techniques to C++; within this context, it presents a complete reference to the C++ Standard Template Library.

[2] Ross Bencina. *AudioMulch Interactive Music Studio.* Melbourne, 2004. Software available from (http://www.audiomulch.com/).

AudioMulch is a real-time modular synthesizer; it includes modules that implement a number of Granular Synthesis variants including Delay Line, Sampled Sound, and Filtered Grain Delay Line Granular Synthesis. All of the Granular Synthesizers implement Grain Quantization as mentioned here.

[3] Andy Carlson. "Essence." In *Pattern Languages of Program Design 4*, edited by N. Harrison, B. Foote, and H. Rohnert, pp. 33–40. Reading, MA: Addison Wesley, 2000.

This article describes the Essence design pattern, which involves using a separate class to encapsulate the initialization parameters for one or more other classes.

[4] Sergio Cavaliere and Aldo Piccialli. "Granular Synthesis of Musical Signals." In *Musical Signal Processing*, edited by Curtis Roads et al., pp. 155–186. Lisse: Swets & Zeitlinger, 1997.

This article describes an analysis/resynthesis architecture based on Granular Synthesis. An extensive analysis of the spectral properties of granular signals is presented.

[5] Martin Fowler with Kendall Scott. *UML Distilled: Applying the Standard Object Modeling Language.* Reading, MA: Addison Wesley, 1997.

This book provides a concise reference for using the Unified Modeling Language to develop and document object-oriented designs.

[6] Erich Gamma et al. *Design Patterns: Elements of Reusable Object-Oriented Software.* Reading, MA: Addison Wesley, 1995.

This book jump-started the design patterns movement—it is an excellent source of reusable object-oriented design patterns.

[7] Erich Gamma et al. "Façade." In *Design Patterns: Elements of Reusable Object-Oriented Software*, pp. 185–193. Reading, MA: Addison Wesley, 1995.

The "Façade" design pattern referred to here is concerned with providing an external interface to a set of collaborating objects in order to simplify or hide their internal details.

[8] James McCartney. "Synthesis without Lookup Tables," *Computer Music Journal* 21(3) (1997): 5–6.

This article describes a number of computationally efficient techniques for synthesizing envelope functions and periodic signals.

[9] Gordon Monroe. "A Note on Interonset Times." Private correspondence, 1998.

In this note, Gordon Monroe provided the mathematical function approximating density to interonset time conversion used here. An exact, but more complex, function was also described.

[10] Curtis Roads. "Automated Granular Synthesis of Sound," *Computer Music Journal* 2:2(1978), 61–62. Reprinted in *Foundations of Computer Music,* edited by C. Roads and J. Strawn, pp. 145–149. Cambridge, MA: The MIT Press, 1985.

The 1985 version revises and expands Curtis Roads' seminal article on Granular Synthesis. The theory of Granular Synthesis is introduced in the context of Gabor's theory of acoustic quanta, and Xenakis' compositional theory of sound grains. Two implementations of Granular Synthesis and their compositional applications are discussed.

[11] Curtis Roads. *Microsound.* Cambridge, MA: MIT Press, 2001.

This book offers a wide-ranging treatment of microsound—sound particles lasting less than a tenth of a second. It presents an extensive survey of Granular Synthesis techniques and an analysis of their application to various musical tasks.

[12] Xavier Rodet, Yves Potard, and Jean-Baptiste Barrière. "The CHANT Project: From the Synthesis of the Singing Voice to Synthesis in General. *Computer Music Journal* 8:3 (1984), 15–31.

This article describes the CHANT singing synthesis project and its FOF (format wave function). FOF synthesis is based on quasiperiodic sequences of enveloped sinusoidal grains.

[13] Curtis Roads. *Computer Music Workshop at the Next Wave Festival.* Unpublished Lecture, Melbourne, 1998.

At this lecture, Curtis Roads presented an extensive exposition of Granular Synthesis concepts. Included were discussions of grains with internal glissandi and the application of independent bandpass filtering to individual grains.

[14] Barry Truax. "Discovering Inner Complexity: Time-shifting and Transposition with a Real-Time Granulation Technique," *Computer Music Journal* 18:2 (1994), 38–48.

This article discusses the application of Granular Synthesis to pitch- and time-based transformations.

[15] Barry Truax. "Real-Time Granular Synthesis with a Digital Signal Processor." *Computer Music Journal* 12:2 (1988), 14–26.

This article describes an implementation of real time granular synthesis for the DMX-1000 signal processor. The article makes the useful distinction between delay line, sampled sound, and synthetic grain granular synthesis that is used here. A system for varying synthesis parameters over time is also presented.

[16] Barry Truax. "Real-Time Granular Synthesis with a Digital Signal Processor." *Computer Music Journal* 12:2 (1988), 14.

[17] Rodney Waschka, II and Toze Ferreira. "Rapid Event Deployment in a MIDI Environment," *Interface, a journal of new music research* 17:4 (1988), 211–222.

This article describes an implementation of the granular concept using an Atari 1040stf connected to a MIDI synthesizer.

Physical Synthesis of Bowed String Instruments

Stefania Serafin

1 Introduction

In this article, we describe how bowed string instruments such as the violin, viola, cello, and bass can be modeled using equations that describe their most significant physical attributes.

We describe a model of a bowed string that is accurate enough to simulate the behavior of a real instrument, yet efficient enough to be played in real time given the performance of modern computer platforms. This model is an extension of the waveguide model described in Cook's article "Introduction to Physical Modeling" (see *Audio Anecdotes I*). We suggest reading that article first in order to understand the basics of waveguides and physical synthesis, which is a recommended background for this article.

Furthermore, this model can be extended beyond the possibilites of real instruments to create interesting sonorities for composers and performers.

Section 2 describes the structure of a bowed string instrument; Section 3 presents a description of the development of the research on vibrating strings; Section 4 proposes a waveguide model of a bowed string; and Section 5 proposes some improvements. Section 6 shows how to control this model, and Section 7 presents the conclusions.

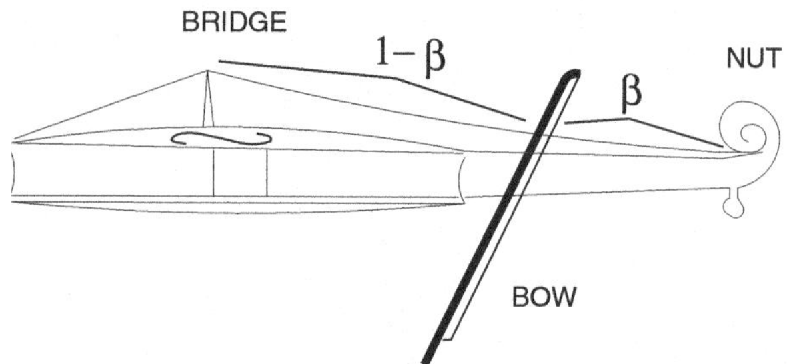

Figure 1. A bowed string instrument.

2 Description of a Bowed String Instrument

Figure 1 shows a schematic representation of a contemporary bowed string instrument.

The sound produced by a bowed string instrument is obtained by drawing a bow across one of the four tensioned strings. As Figure 1 shows, from now on we will call β the normalized distance between the bow and the nut (0 represents the nut; 1 represents the bridge; 0.5 represents the middle of the string).

To produce sound, energy from the vibrating string is transferred to the body of the instrument. The strings are supported by the "bridge," which acts as a mechanical transformer, since it converts the transverse forces of the strings into the vibrational modes of the sound box. The combination of bridge and body resonances play a key role in the overall tone of the instrument. In this article, however, we focus on modeling the interaction between a bow and a string.

3 Research on Bowed Strings

Scientific understanding of vibrating strings started in the seventeenth century with Galileo Galilei (1564–1642) and Marin Mersenne (1588–1648).

The violin itself was deeply studied by Felix Savart (1791–1841), who examined the vibrations of top and back plates in Stradivarius and Guarnerius violins, deducing the function of the soundpost.

Herman Von Helmholtz (1821–1894) [16] contributed to the understanding of bowed string instruments via physical and psychoacoustical experiments. In 1877, using a stroboscope, he observed that the displacement of the string when driven by a bow follows a triangular pattern at

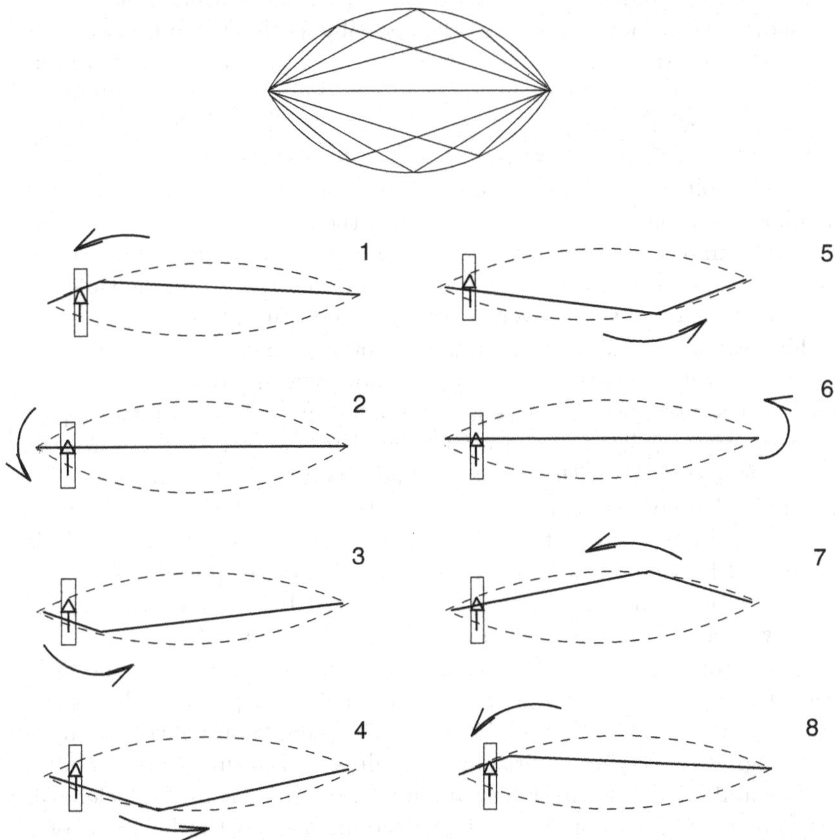

Figure 2. Representation of the motion of a bowed string as observed by Helmholtz [16].

whatever point considered. In this motion, shown in Figure 2, a sharp corner shuttles back and forth around the envelope of the string vibration. As the corner passes the bow, it triggers transition between sticking and sliding friction and vice versa. The result is a velocity waveform at the bow like the one shown in Figure 2.

In this motion, now known as Helmholtz motion, the string sticks to the bow for most of the time, slipping rapidly backwards just once per vibrational period. The role of the bow is to supply enough energy in order to maintain this motion.

In 1909, the Indian physicist Raman [9] extended Helmholtz's work and showed that there are many other possible periodic solutions for the bowed string. In fact, Raman showed that all periodic motion of the string involved traveling corners and that with only one corner, Helmholtz motion was the simplest case.

In real instruments, however, it is rare to observe any other motion than Helmholtz's one, and psychoacoustical studies [1] have shown that Helmholtz motion is the only motion that the ear finds acceptable. The only other kinds that have been observed are known as double-slip motion, which corresponds to two traveling corners on the string, and multiple fly-back, where three, five or seven traveling corners are present.

The player produces the Helmholtz motion, controlling mainly three parameters with his bow, which are the bow pressure, the bow velocity, and the bow position. The intensity, quality, and subtlety of sound produced by great violinists is strongly related to the way they control the Helmholtz waveform with the bow. The quality of sound produced by any violin therefore depends as much on the bowing skills of the violinist as on the physical properties of the instrument. An important role is also played by the left hand of the player, which is responsible for pitch changes, vibrato, and glissando. As mentioned before, however, in this article we focus our attention on modeling the right hand.

Computer simulations of bowed string instruments started in the early 1980s, mainly thanks to the mathematical models proposed by McIntyre, Schumacher, and Woodhouse ([4, 5]), which were soon converted to efficient signal processing algorithms by Julius O. Smith [14, 15]. Today, the availability of powerful hardware and the development of efficient algorithms allows us to simulate the subtle nuances of the behavior of a bowed string, resulting in accurate models that capture most aspects of a real instrument and can be played in real time [12].

4 Description of the Model

Musical instruments such as the clarinet, the flute, and the bowed string can be defined as *self-sustained*, which means that sound is produced as long as a source of energy is provided to the instrument.

The structure of these instruments can thereby be simplified as having an exciter—which is the source of energy—and a resonator, as shown in Figure 3. In the case of the clarinet, the excitation is given by the player blowing into the instrument, and the resonator is the bore of the instrument. For bowed string instruments, the excitation is the bow–

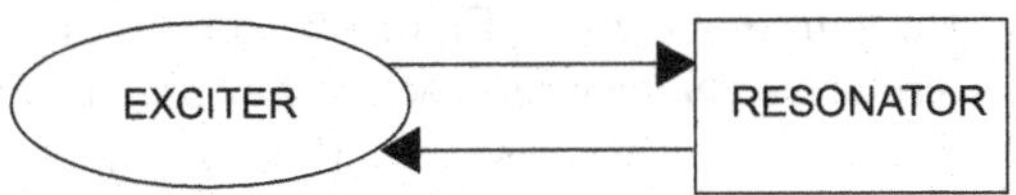

Figure 3. Simplified structure of a self-sustained oscillator.

string interaction, while the resonator is the vibrating string connected to the body of the instrument. In building a bowed string physical model, a simple model of a one-dimensional digital waveguide which represents the string's vibration has been described in Cook's aforementioned article. The same approach used to simulate a plucked string can be used to model a violin string. In order to model the position of the bow along the string, two delay lines are needed, which model waves propagating along the string in the two sides of the bow (one delay line for the waves going from the bow to the bridge, and another delay line for the waves propagating toward the nut).

Let's assume, for example, that we are modeling a violin A string (440 Hz) at a sampling rate of 44100 Hz. In this case, the string has $44100/440 \approx 100$ samples. If the bow is exciting the string at a normalized bow position $\beta = 0.1$ where 0 represents the bridge and 1 represents the nut, then the delay line containing waves propagating toward the bridge is made of $100 \cdot 0.1 = 10$ samples, while the delay line containing waves propagating toward the nut is made of $0.9 \cdot 100 = 90$ samples. This situation is shown in Figure 4.

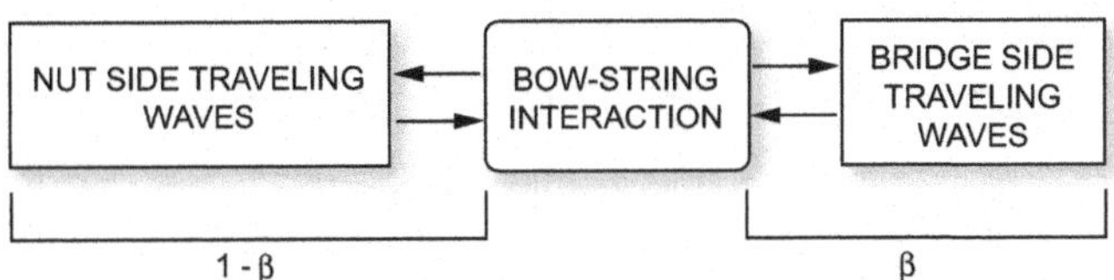

Figure 4. Schematic representation of a waveguide bowed string physical model; β represents the normalized bow position.

4.1 Modeling the Excitation

The excitation mechanism in a bowed string instrument is given by friction, the tangential force between objects in contact. The player, in order to increase friction between the string and the surface of the bow, coats the bow with sticky rosin. Early experiments on violins have shown that the resulting relationship between the frictional force and the relative velocity between the string and the bow is highly nonlinear and can be approximated by the curve shown in Figure 5. The straight line in the vertical axis at zero relative velocity represents the case in which the string is sticking to the bow. In the other cases, friction exponentially decreases when the relative bow-string velocity increases.

It is possible to mathematically represent the curve of Figure 5 using Equation 1,

$$\mu = \mu_d + \frac{(\mu_s - \mu_d)v_0}{v_0 + v - v_b}, \tag{1}$$

where v, v_b, and v_0 are the string velocity, bow velocity, and initial bow velocity, respectively, and $\mu_d = 0.3$ and $\mu_s = 0.8$ are the dynamic and static coefficients of friction, respectively. This model has been used for many years as a convenient mathematical approximation which yields closed-form results for the bow-string interaction [5, 4, 7]. Using this curve, it is possible, in fact, to find analytically the value of the velocity of the string when excited by a bow, as described in the following section.

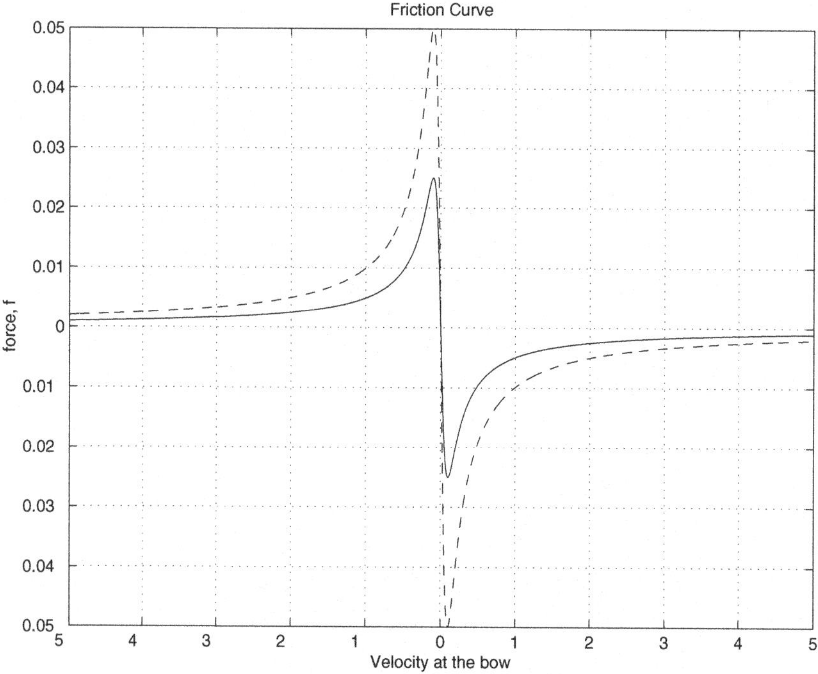

Figure 5. Friction curve. Horizontal axis: relative bow–string velocity. Vertical axis: friction force.

4.2 Connecting the Excitation and the Resonator

In this section, we describe how the linear and nonlinear part of the model are connected together. In a first approximation, we assume that the bow is exciting the string in a single point. The single-point bow-string model is classic and was first introduced in [4]. This model approximates bow-string contact at a point which is at a normalized distance β from the bridge, where $\beta = 0.5$, as before, represents the middle of the string. Again, bow velocity and the bow force at the contact point are denoted v_b and f_b, respectively. At the contact point, two physical variables are considered: the friction force f, where $f = \mu f_b$, where μ is given by Equation 1, and the transverse velocity of the string v. Friction and velocity are nonlinearly related via the bow-string contact parameters [13].

When the velocity v_b of the bow is equal to that of the string v, they are "stuck together," otherwise they are sliding.

The algorithm works as follows: at a given time t, it is possible to calculate the incoming velocity at the bow point v_h (where h traditionally stands for history), which is given by the contribution of the reflected waves v_{i_n} and v_{i_b} coming from the nut and the bridge, respectively, where v_{i_n} and v_{i_b} are the traveling waves propagating along the two sides of the string, in the portion that is not in contact with the bow:

$$v_h = v_{i_n} + v_{i_b}.$$

At this point, it is necessary to find the value of the friction force f and of the velocity v at the contact point. This is done by solving Equations 2(a) and 2(b):

$$f = 2\,Z(v - v_h), \tag{2a}$$

$$f = \mu f_b, \tag{2b}$$

where $f = 2Z(v - v_h)$ represents the linear vibration behavior of the string (Z is the string impedance), and μ is the hyperbolic friction curve of Equation 2(a). Formulating the friction curve using a hyperbola allows one to analytically solve Equations 2(a) and 2(b). The C++ code provided on the accompanying CD-ROM shows how to find the values of f and v giving this friction curve.

Once the new values for f and v have been calculated, the new outgoing waves v_{o_n} and v_{o_b} are calculated using Equations 3(a) and 3(b):

$$v_{o_n} = v_{i_b} + \frac{f}{2Z}, \tag{3a}$$

$$v_{o_b} = v_{i_n} + \frac{f}{2Z}. \tag{3b}$$

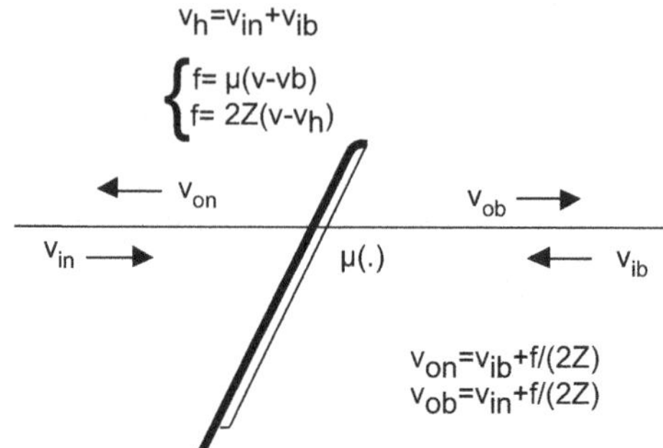

Figure 6. Description of a simplified model of a bowed string instrument.

Equations 3(a) and 3(b) are obtained considering that $v = v_{i_n} + v_{o_n} = v_{i_b} + v_{o_b}$, and accounting for Equation 2(a). The overall equations of the model are summarized in Figure 6.

Despite its simplicity, the model shown in Figure 6 is able to reproduce many phenomena that occur in a real instrument. For example, it is able to reproduce the Helmholtz motion and the higher types of motions described by Raman. However, to obtain a high quality violin synthesizer, other phenomena need to be taken into account, as discussed in Section 5.

5 Improving the Model

The model presented in the previous section can be improved in order to obtain more realistic sonorities.

A first improvement consists of accounting for torsional waves. It has been proved [17] that torsional waves allow the Helmholtz motion to be established faster, since they are more lossy then transversal waves. When accounting for torsional waves, the model, starting from rest, achieves the Helmholtz motion in a shorter number of periods. Torsional waves can be modeled by adding an additional pair of delay lines, traveling 5.2 faster than transversal waves.

Another improvement consists of accounting for string stiffness. String stiffness is particularly important for cello and double bass strings, in which the diameter of the string is not negligible compared to the length of the string. In the case of stiff strings, high-frequency components, traveling faster, reach the Helmholtz corner sooner than low-frequency components. The consequence of this is the fact that the corner becomes rounded, which is audible in the resulting sound.

Stiffness can be efficiently taken into account inserting into the model a cascade of all-pass filters whose order and coefficients are estimated from the frequency-dependent delay of the strings. We noticed [11] that modeling stiffness improves the quality of the synthesis.

Further improvements consist of examining more refined friction models, which account also for the bow width [7, 8], or for the thermodynamical properties of rosin [13].

As proved in [13], the friction force during sliding is not determined only by the instantaneous sliding speed, as stated by the model described in this article. A more complex behavior at the contact point appears in which friction depends on the thermodynamical properties of rosin. Rosin, in fact, melts and solidifies according to the temperature of the contact point. Finally, it is important to model the body of the instrument, whose complex resonances contribute to its characteristic sound [3].

A simplified approach consists of accounting only for the low-frequency resonances of the body, which can be modeled using resonant filters. In this way, the computational efficiency is maintained but the precision is

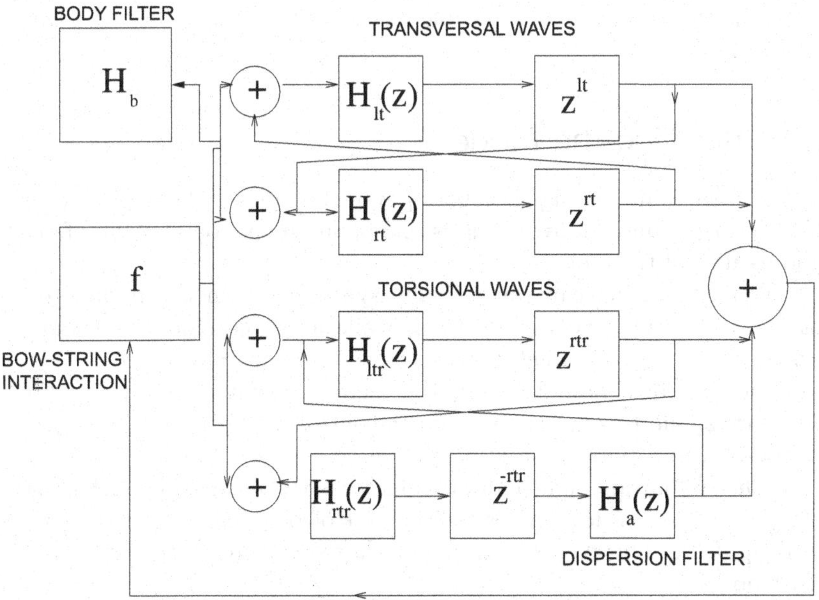

Figure 7. Structure of a refined bowed string model, which accounts for torsional waves, stiffness of strings, and the body of the instrument.

lost, since the complex high-frequency resonances of the body of a musical instrument are an important component of its rich sonorities.

To cope with this problem, it has been suggested [2] to use a waveguide mesh which can be designed to have a modal distribution which is psychoacoustically equivalent to the resonances of the violin body at high frequencies.

Figure 7 represents the structure of a refined model of a bowed string. As before, f represents the frictional force, while $H_{\mathrm{lt}}(z)$ and $H_{\mathrm{rt}}(z)$ are the filters that model the losses of the left-going and right-going transversal waves propagating toward the bridge and the nut, respectively.

The left-going and right-going delay lines are represented by z^{-lt} and z^{-rt}, respectively. The filters $H_{\mathrm{ltr}}(z)$ and $H_{\mathrm{rtr}}(z)$ model the losses of the left-going and right-going torsional waves propagating toward the bridge and the nut, respectively.

Moreover, z^{-ltr} and z^{-rtr} represent the left-going and right-going delay lines for the transversal waves, and $H_{\mathrm{a}}(z)$ represent the cascade of all-pass filters used to model dispersion.

Finally, H_b is the filter that accounts for the body resonances.

This complex structure, if driven by an appropriate controller such as the one described in Section 6, is able to reproduce realistic bowed string sonorities.

6 Controlling the Model

One of the most interesting aspects of physical models is the fact that the evolution of parameters over time is one of the main components of the sound quality of the model itself.

A complete model can sound really synthetic when the parameters that drive it do not evolve over time, while a simple model can sound realistic if driven by parameters that evolve in a natural way.

In the case of a bowed string, the main parameters that drive the model correspond to what the player can control with his right hand, i.e., bow velocity, bow position, and bow force.

Another important right-hand parameter is the inclination of the bow on the string, which determines the amount of bow hair in contact with the string itself. This control parameter allows us to recreate the characteristic bow noise.

Concerning the left hand, the player can control the length of the string to change pitch and obtain vibrato, glissando, or flautato. In terms of the model, bow force and velocity influence the bow-string interaction

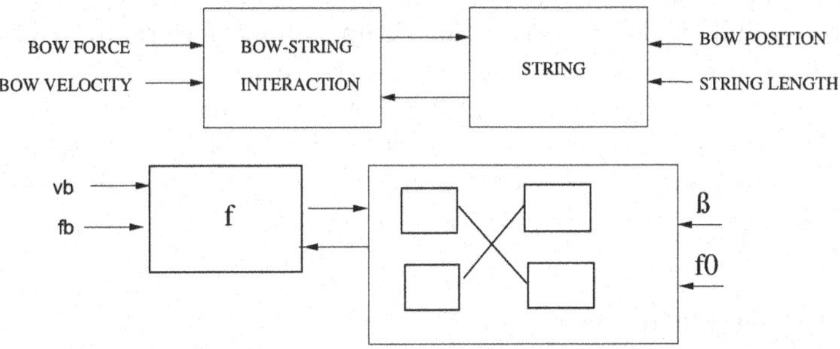

Figure 8. Input parameters for the bowed string model.

part, while the left-hand parameters and the bow position are input to the string, as shown in Figure 8.

The combination of all these parameters create a vast timbral space that can be explored in real time. In order to take advantage of all the possibilities offered by the model while playing it in real time, suitable controllers are necessary.

For example, a Wacom graphical tablet [10] is a controller which has the advantage of being commercially available with a number of degrees of freedom high enough to allow us to control most of the parameters of the virtual instrument. The graphical tablet is provided with a pressure sensitive pen. We mapped the pressure of the pen of the tablet to the bow pressure. Moreover, the tablet is able to detect the absolute horizontal and vertical position of the pen. We mapped this data to the velocity of the bow and the position of the bow in the string, respectively.

An advantage of the tablet is the intuitive mapping between its input parameters and the parameters driving the bowed string. One problem of the tablet is the fact that it lacks force feedback, which is a natural characteristic of real instruments, where the strings react to the action of the player complementing the auditory loop between the instrument and the player with the haptic loop. In her dissertation, Sile O'Modhrain [6] proved that force-feedback controllers improve the playability of virtual bowed string instruments.

7 Future Directions on the Research on Physical Models of Bowed Strings

This article describes an efficient implementation of a physical model of a bowed string instrument based on digital waveguides.

Today, the behavior of bowed string instruments is reasonably well understood, and efficient synthesis algorithms allow us to reproduce most of the phenomena that appear in real instruments. In the source code provided on the accompanying CD-ROM, the implementation of the hyperbolic friction curve is provided. This friction model, when connected to the waveguide implementation described in Cook's article, as described in Section 4, allow us to simulate basic bow strokes.

Annotated Bibliography

[1] L. Cremer. *The Physics of the Violin.* MIT Press, Cambridge, MA, 1984.

Book explaining all the components of a violin from an acoustician's point of view.

[2] Patty Huang, Stefania Serafin, and Julius O. Smith. "A waveguide mesh model of high-frequency violin mode resonances." In *International Computer Music Conference, Berlin.* Computer Music Association, 2000.

Description of the use of a waveguide mesh to model complex resonators such as the body of the violin.

[3] Matti Karjalainen and Julius O. Smith. "Body modeling techniques for string instrument synthesis." In *Proceedings of the 1996 International Computer Music Conference, Hong Kong*, pages 232–239. Computer Music Association, Aug. 1996.

Different techniques to model the body of musical instruments are presented.

[4] Michael E. McIntyre, Robert T. Schumacher, and James Woodhouse. "On the oscillations of musical instruments." *Journal of the Acoustical Society of America*, 74(5):1325–1345, Nov. 1983.

[5] Michael E. McIntyre and James Woodhouse. "On the fundamentals of bowed string dynamics." *Acustica*, 43(2):93–108, Sept. 1979.

[6] Sile O'Modhrain. *Playing by Feel: Incorporating Haptic Feedback into Computer-Based Musical Instruments.* Ph.D. thesis, Music Department, Stanford University (CCRMA), 2000.

Proof that haptic feedback improves the playability of virtual instruments.

[7] R. Pitteroff. "Modelling of the bowed string taking into account the width of the bow." In *Proceedings of the Stockholm Musical Acoustics Conference (SMAC-93)*, pages 407–410, Stockholm, July 1993. Royal Swedish Academy of Music.

Physical model of a bowed string with finite bow width simulation.

[8] R. Pitteroff. "Mechanics of the contact area between a violin bow and a string. Part i: reflection and transmission behaviour. Part ii: Simulating the bowed string. Part iii: Parameter dependance." In *Acustica-Acta Acustica*, pages 543–562, 1998.

Physical model of a bowed string with finite bow width simulation.

[9] C. V. Raman. "On the mechanical theory of vibrations of bowed strings, etc." *Indian Assoc. Cult. Sci. Bull.*, 15:1–158, 1918.

First article explaining motions of bowed strings different from the Helmholtz motion.

[10] Stefania Serafin, Richard Dudas, Marcelo Wanderley, and Xavier Rodet. "Gestural control of a real-time physical model of a bowed string." International Computer Music Conference, Beijing, Oct. 1999. Computer Music Association.

This paper describes how a physical model of a bowed string can be controlled using a Wacom tablet.

[11] Stefania Serafin and Julius O. Smith, III. "Modelling stiffness in virtual bowed string instruments." In *Proceedings ASA*, Atlanta meeting, june 2000. Acoustical Society of America.

Waveguide model of a bowed string that accounts also for string stiffness.

[12] Stefania Serafin, Christophe Vergez, and Xavier Rodet. "Friction and application to real-time physical modeling of a violin." International Computer Music Conference, Beijing, Oct. 1999. Computer Music Association.

This paper describes a bowed string model in which different friction models are tested to represent the bow-string interaction.

[13] Jonathan H. Smith and James Woodhouse. "The tribology of rosin. Part I: Dynamic friction measurements. Part II: Thermal modelling.

Part III: Stick-slip simulation." *Journal of the Mechanics and Physics of Solids* 48(8):1633–1681, August 2000.

Article describing thermal models for bow-string interaction.

[14] Julius O. Smith. "Synthesis of bowed strings." In *Proceedings of the 1982 International Computer Music Conference, Venice.* Computer Music Association, 1982.

Essentially fully contained in [15].

[15] Julius O. Smith. *Techniques for Digital Filter Design and System Identification with Application to the Violin.* Ph.D. thesis, Electrical Engineering Deptartment, Stanford University (CCRMA), June 2000.

Lots of techniques for filter design that are still used.

[16] H. L. F. von Helmholtz. *On the Sensations of Tone as a Physiological Basis for the Theory of Music.* Dover, New York, 1954.

Pioneer work on acoustics and psychoacoustics where among other things the motion of a bowed string is explained. English translation of 1863 (German) edition by A. J. Ellis.

[17] James Woodhouse and A. R. Loach. "The torsional behavior of cello strings." *Acustica/Acta Acustica* 85(5):735–740, Sept./Oct. 1999.

Paper describing physical parameters of a cello D string.

Modal Synthesis for Vibrating Objects

Kees van den Doel and Dinesh K. Pai

1 Introduction

When a solid object is struck or scraped, or engages in other external interactions, the forces at the contact point causes deformations to propagate through the body, causing its outer surfaces to vibrate and emit sound waves. Examples of musical instruments utilizing solid objects like this are the marimba, the xylophone, and bells.

The sounds made by objects like this are important for interacting with our environment because they provide useful information about the physical attributes of the object, its environment, and the contact events, including the force (or energy) of the impact, the material composition of the object, the shape and size, the place of impact on the object, and finally the location and environment of the object.

In order to create the sounds of objects like this in an interactive digital environment, such as a video game or a simulation, we need real-time synthesis, as we do not know the stimulus of the (virtual) objects before they occur, and sustained intimate user interaction like touching and scraping an object needs a continuously parametrizable sound.

A good physically motivated synthesis model for objects like this is modal synthesis [37, 15, 25, 6, 10, 9, 26, 13], where a vibrating object is modeled by a bank of damped harmonic oscillators which are excited by an external stimulus. The frequencies and dampings of the oscillators are determined by the geometry and material properties (such as elasticity)

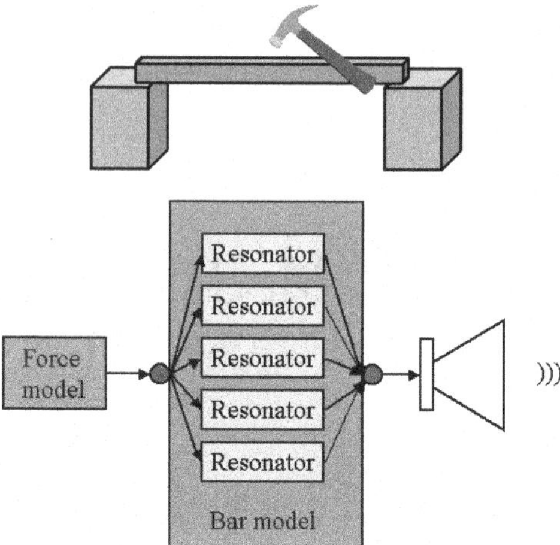

Figure 1. Modal synthesis of the sound made by hitting a bar with a hammer. The hammer force is modeled by a contact force model and sent to a bank of resonators, which is the modal model of the bar. Each resonator has a characteristic frequency, damping, and gain and the outputs of the resonators are summed and rendered.

of the object and the coupling gains are determined by the location of the force applied to the object.

The modal synthesis model is physically well motivated, as the linear partial differential equation for a vibrating system, with appropriate boundary conditions, has as solutions a superposition of vibration modes. See Figure 1 for an illustration.

Modal synthesis can also be used to model other types of physical systems which can be modeled by excitations acting on resonances, such as car engines, rumbling sounds, or virtual musical instruments. For musical instruments with a harmonic spectrum, modal synthesis can be used, but it is computationally quite demanding because of the large number of modes needed. Waveguide models [30, 5] are in most cases much more efficient for these types of sounds. The sound made by a modal model can be computed very efficiently with an $O(N)$ algorithm [15, 11, 7] for a model of N modes, as described below.

The remainder of this article is organized as follows. Section 2 defines modal synthesis and explains the physical motivation behind it. An efficient synthesis algorithm is derived formally, and we show how to implement it. In Section 3, we discuss the construction of excitation signals to the modal models for a number of applications. Concluding remarks are presented in Section 4. A set of Java classes implementing these ideas is provided on the accompanying CD-ROM, and discussed in detail in this text. An implementation in C is also provided.

2 Modal Resonance Models

2.1 General Properties

We can formally describe a modal model $\mathcal{M}$ utilizing N modes at K different locations (contact points) on an object as $\mathcal{M} = \{\boldsymbol{f}, \boldsymbol{d}, \boldsymbol{A}\}$, where $\boldsymbol{f}$ is a vector of length N whose components are the modal frequencies in Hertz, $\boldsymbol{d}$ is a vector of length N whose components are the (angular) decay rates in Hertz, and $\boldsymbol{A}$ is an $N \times K$ matrix, whose elements a_{nk} are the gain coefficients for each mode.

The Java class **ModalModel** encapsulates a modal model. It contains the public member variables,

```
public double[] f;
public double[] d;
public double[][] a;
```

which define $\mathcal{M}$. This class also contains the member variables,

```
public double fscale;
public double dscale;
public double ascale;
```

which provide a convenient means to uniformly scale the frequencies, dampings, and gains of an entire model. The class constructor `ModalModel(String fn)` reads the modal parameters from a text file in a self-explanatory format. By convention, a modes file has the extension `.sy`. Several examples of modal models are provided with code examples on the accompanying CD-ROM.

The impulse response $y(t)$ of $\mathcal{M}$ at location k is given by

$$y(t) = \sum_{n=1}^{N} a_{nk} \exp(-d_n t) \sin(2\pi f_n t), \tag{1}$$

for $t \geq 0$ and is zero for $t < 0$, where $y(t)$ denotes the audio signal as a function of time. The impulse response represents the sound that the virtual object makes when struck with a unit impulse at time $t = 0$ at location k. The decay rate d_n of each mode is an object property which is strongly influenced by the material, which determines the internal dissipation of energy during vibration. According to a simple material model explained in [38, 22], the dampings d_n are just proportional to the modal frequencies f_n, i.e., $d_n = \rho f_n$, with the proportionality constant ρ determined by the internal friction parameter. Small values of ρ produce models which are relatively undamped, characteristic of metal objects, whereas larger values produce highly damped models characteristic of materials such as plastic and wood. In real objects, this relation between damping and frequency is only approximately valid [7], but this simple model is capable of evoking the illusion of materials reasonably well as was shown in perception studies [21]. The impulse response y as given in Equation 1 is characteristic of physical systems that obey the linear wave equation for solid bodies, which is of the form

$$(A - \frac{1}{c^2}\frac{\partial^2}{\partial t^2})\mu(\boldsymbol{x}, t) = 0 \tag{2}$$

on some domain, where μ is the deviation of the surface as a function of time, and A is a (usually very complicated) spatial differential operator. The solution of Equation 2, together with a radiation model which we do not discuss here, in principle allows the calculation of the modal parameters in Equation 1; however, this is very complicated. In [11], the calculation was performed for some simple shapes. Finite element methods were used in [27, 26].

The provided modes file `s100.sy` contains the computed modal data for an ideal string, with 100 modes and 20 contact locations. Taking the string to lie on the interval [0 1], the computed contact locations are at the K discrete points $p = (k+1)/2K$, where $k = 0, \ldots, K-1$. The demo **DemoBowedString** uses this modes file to synthesize an ideal string bowed by white noise. You can set the bow point with the bottom slider whereas the upper slider sets the pitch (or string tension). A linear model with a noise excitation oversimplifies the physics of a bowed string, which is nonlinear and quite complicated [29]. Nevertheless, the resulting sound is quite convincing.

The sound model parameters for a given object can also be obtained experimentally by recording the impulse response of the object and fitting the model parameters to the recorded sound. We can think of this as designing a digital filter of a specific type with a given impulse response (the recording). Various off-the-shelf tools are available to display spectrograms and sonograms of sounds, and these can be used to measure the modal parameters. For example, in Figure 2 we depict the spectrogram of a recording of a church bell (`bell4.wav`). An algorithm to automatically

Figure 2. The spectrogram of a church bell. The x-axis is time; frequency corresponds to the y-axis. The decibel level is mapped to darkness.

extract a modal model from a recorded impulse response at one location was given in Van den Doel's thesis [7]. A modified version of the algorithm was used to extract the modes of the bell which can be found in the file `bell4.sy`. This algorithm is also capable of integrating data from multiple contact points into a single modal model and is described in [28]. The corresponding demo is **DemoBellStrike**. The lower slider in the UI dialog sets the number of modes used in the synthesis, from 1–50, and the upper slider sets the hardness (see Section 3.1) of the virtual mallet used to strike the bell.

The Active Measurement Facility (ACME) at the University of British Columbia [28] has the capability to automatically acquire sound measurements by moving a sound effector around the surface of a test object with a robot arm. At selected points on the surface, the sound effector hits the object with an impulsive force and records the sound produced by the impact. The modes file `calona0.sy` contains the modes extracted from measurements at ACME on a glass bottle. The corresponding demo is **DemoBottleHit**. The lower slider in the control panel sets the location of the impact point on the bottle, mapped to the interval [0 1], and the upper slider sets the hardness (see Section 3.1) of the virtual mallet used to strike the bell.

Sometimes it is desirable to construct a modal model by hand (and ear), for example using a modal model editor [4]. An example of a resonance model for engine sounds is given in `car1.sy`, which is used in the **DemoEngine** demo which takes command line arguments pointing to the modal model and the excitation model. We will discuss this demo further in Section 3.3.

2.2 Derivation of a Modal Synthesis Algorithm

We shall now derive the modal synthesis algorithm, show how it can be implemented most efficiently, and then show that it is in fact a bank of reson filters (resonant band-pass filters) operating on the interaction force. If we assume a linear model, the response to any kind of input force is determined completely by the impulse response. It follows from Equation 1 that the sound produced by an impulsive force of magnitude F at time s can be described by the imaginary part of the complex wave form

$$y(t) = \sum_n a_n e^{i\Omega_n(t-s)} H(t-s)F, \tag{3}$$

where the sum is over the complex eigenfrequencies Ω_n (the imaginary part determines the damping of a mode). Here, $H(t) = 0$ for $t < 0$ and $H(t) = 1$ for $t \geq 0$. If we substitute $F = 1$, $s = 0$, and $\Omega = 2\pi f_n - id_n$ and assume $t > s$ so that $H(t-s) = 1$, we recover Equation 1 from this.

A continuous stimulus force $F(t)$ can be represented formally as an infinite sum of infinitesimal impulses

$$F(t) = \int_0^\infty \delta(t-s)F(s)ds,$$

where $\delta(t)$ is the Dirac delta distribution, assuming the force is zero for negative times. Using the principle of linearity, the output of the model driven by this force can be written as a sum of infinitesimal contributions from each of these impulses:

$$y(t) = \int_0^\infty ds \sum_n a_n e^{i\Omega_n(t-s)} H(t-s)F(s).$$

Discretizing this equation in time, with sampling rate S_R, gives

$$y(m) = \sum_{l=0}^{m} \sum_n a_n e^{i\frac{\Omega_n}{S_R}(m-l)} F(l),$$

with $y(m) = S_R y(t_m)$ and $t_m = m/S_R$. This convolution equation can be rewritten as a recursion relation by defining the functions $y_n(m)$, one for each partial. The complex signal is written as a sum of modal contributions y_n:

$$y(m) = \sum_n y_n(m).$$

For the partials $y_n(m)$, we have

$$y_n(0) = a_n F(0),$$

and the recursion relation

$$y_n(m) = e^{i\frac{\Omega_n}{S_R}} y_n(m-1) + a_n F(m) \tag{4}$$

determines the audio signal $\mathrm{Im}(y)$. As $|e^{i\frac{\Omega_n}{S_R}}| < 1$, the recursion relation is always stable. Equation 4 requires five multiplications per sample point, which can be reduced to three as we will now derive.

To simplify the notation, let us drop the n subscripts which label the modes, and write $y(m) = u(m) + iv(m)$, with u and v real. The recursion can now be written as

$$\begin{aligned} u(m) &= c_r u(m-1) - c_i v(m-1) + aF(m), \\ v(m) &= c_i u(m-1) + c_r v(m-1), \end{aligned} \tag{5}$$

with

$$c_r = e^{-d/S_R} \cos(\omega/S_R),$$

$$c_i = e^{-d/S_R} \sin(\omega/S_R),$$

$$d = Im(\Omega),$$

and

$$\omega = Re(\Omega).$$

We can eliminate u from Equation 5 as

$$u(m) = v(m+1)/c_i - c_r v(m)/c_i$$

and arrive at the second order recursion for the quantity of interest, v, in the form

$$v(m) = 2R\cos(\theta)v(m-1) - R^2 v(m-2) + aR\sin(\theta)F(m-1), \tag{6}$$

with

$$R = e^{-d/S_R},$$

and

$$\theta = \omega / S_R.$$

Equation 6 is precisely the equation for a reson filter [31] with transfer function $\mathcal{H}(z) = 1/(1-2R\cos\theta z^{-1}+R^2z^{-2})$, operating on the input signal $aR\sin(\theta)z^{-1}F$. Note that because of the Nyquist theorem, all modal frequencies must be less than half the sampling rate, so both $\sin > 0$ and $\cos > 0$.

To synthesize the sound in real-time, we repeatedly compute an audio buffer of length T. The synthesis algorithm fetches the values of the coefficient arrays as well as the external force F for the time interval T. Equation 6 is then used to sequentially add contributions of the modes v_n until all modes have been added or until a certain deadline has been passed. Note that this can't be done in-place and requires accumulating intermediate results in separate buffers. If the modes are sorted in a decreasing order of importance, this allows for a graceful degradation in the quality of the synthesized sound, when the time available for audio synthesis is not constant.

2.3 Implementation of Real-Time Algorithm

A number of Java classes are provided which implement audio synthesis based on the algorithm presented mathematically in Section 2.2.

The **AudioForce** interface provides a single method which fills a given buffer with samples of the output produced by the object implementing it:

```
public interface AudioForce {
    public void getForce(double [] output, int nsamples);
}
```

Stimulus forces will be represented by objects implementing **AudioForce**, but vibrating objects also implement this interface, in which case they can send their output (obtained through `getForce()`) directly to the audio hardware; they apply their "audio force" to the air. Objects can also excite each other, the output of one becoming the input of the other. This "patch-based" design has been used for a long time in computer music [24].

An object which produces sound is represented by the abstract base class **SonicObject**:

```
public abstract class SonicObject
           extends Thread implements AudioForce
```

A **SonicObject** is capable of rendering itself to the audio hardware in real-time by creating a thread using the `start()` method which it inherits from its superclass **Thread**, which will call the `run()` method. Its `run()` method

```
public void run() {
    float [] y = new float[bufferSize];
    RTPlay pb = new RTPlay(bufferSizeJavaSound,srate,16,1,
                           true);

    while(true) {
        this.getForce(y,bufferSize);
        // Unimportant code omitted ...
        pb.write(y);
    }

}
```

obtains the output of the **SonicObject** using its own **AudioForce** interface which classes derived from it must implement. It renders the result using the utility class **RTPlay** which we wrote to provide a convenient interface to the standard Java audio API (JavaSound, which is part of Java 2) through its `write()` method, which places a buffer on the playback queue and blocks if the queue is full. This design is illustrated in Figure 3.

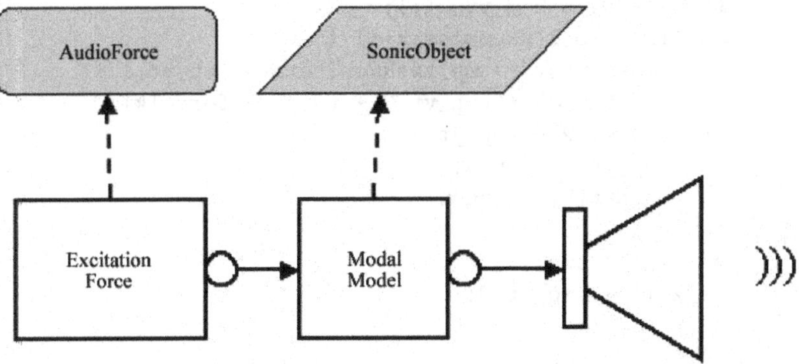

Figure 3. The model for the excitation implements the **AudioForce** interface. It sends audio buffers to the modal model, which derives from the abstract class **SonicObject**, which also implements **AudioForce**.

The Java class **ModalSonicObject** derives from **SonicObject** and implements the modal synthesis algorithm from the previous section. It contains a reference to a **ModalModel** and a reference to an object `audioForce` which implements the **AudioForce** interface method and which encapsulates the input to the modal resonators. We call it "AudioForce" to stress its interpretation as a rapidly fluctuating physical contact force on a material object.

ModalSonicObject implements its own **AudioForce** interface with the following:

```
public void getForce(float [] output, int nsamples) {
    audioForce.getForce(scratchBuf, nsamples);
    computeSoundBuffer(output, scratchBuf, nsamples);
}
```

Its core method is `computeSoundBuffer()`:

```
private void computeSoundBuffer(float[] output,
                  float[] force, int nsamples) {
    for(int k=0;k<nsamples;k++) {
        output[k] = 0;
    }
    int nf = modalModel.nfUsed;
    for(int i=0;i<nf;i++) {
        float tmp_twoRCosTheta = twoRCosTheta[i];
        float tmp_R2 = R2[i];
        float tmp_a = ampR[i];
        float tmp_yt_1 = yt_1[i];
        float tmp_yt_2 = yt_2[i];
        for(int k=0;k<nsamples;k++) {
            float ynew = tmp_twoRCosTheta * tmp_yt_1 -
                tmp_R2 * tmp_yt_2 + tmp_a * force[k];
            tmp_yt_2 = tmp_yt_1;
            tmp_yt_1 = ynew;
            output[k] += ynew;
        }
        yt_1[i] = tmp_yt_1;
        yt_2[i] = tmp_yt_2;
    }
}
```

The bank of `nf` reson filters has filter coefficients `twoRCosTheta` and `R2`, which correspond to the variables occurring in Equation 6, and gains `ampR`. In the outer `for` loop the filter coefficients are stored in temporary variables to avoid array access in the inner loop. The inner `for` loop adds the contribution of reson `i` to the `output`, using the input buffer `force`. The member variables `yt_1` and `yt_2` remember the last two outputs from one buffer to the next. (Note that we have ignored the one sample delay in the force occurring in Equation 6, as it has no audible effect as long as we don't create any feedback loops using this filter.) Note that the factor $R\sin(\theta)$, which multiplies the input force in Equation 1, has been absorbed in the rescaled gains `ampR`.

There are two types of buffer sizes that concern us here. The first is the buffer size `bufferSize` used in calls to `computeSoundBuffer()`, which has an effect on the latency. It should be set to a low value. However, a low value will introduce more overhead in calls to `computeSoundBuffer()`. The demo class **DemoModalBenchmark** can be used to monitor the performance of the algorithm by varying various parameters like `bufferSize`. It times `computeSoundBuffer()` and then computes how many modes could be synthesized maximally in real-time on the machine. On a 450 Mhz Pentium III, one can synthesize 800 modes at a sampling rate of 22050 Hz, for a buffer size of 128. If we set `bufferSize` to 1 (which will give the lowest latency but the highest overhead), we can do only 200 modes.

In the C sample code directory we also provide a similar benchmark implemented in C. For a buffer size of 128, it was found that we could synthesize 1000 modes, making the C code about 25% more efficient.

The second buffer size is `bufferSizeJavaSound` which should be set to the smallest possible value to obtain the lowest possible latency. The current JavaSound implementations require this buffer size to be rather enormous on most platforms, with very large latencies, but this may improve in the future.

Real-time interaction with a running **SonicObject** is achieved by changing the modal model parameters and/or the contact location. The modal parameters can be accessed directly. Once the **SonicObject** is running, changing the modal parameters has no effect until `computeFilter()` is called, which then computes the filter coefficients occurring in the synthesis loop. There is a potential race condition here, as `computeSoundBuffer()` may be accessing these variables in the synthesis thread whereas a control thread is changing them by calling `computeFilter()`. We have not encountered any such problems in practice and, therefore, have not bothered writing the appropriate `synchronized` accessors.

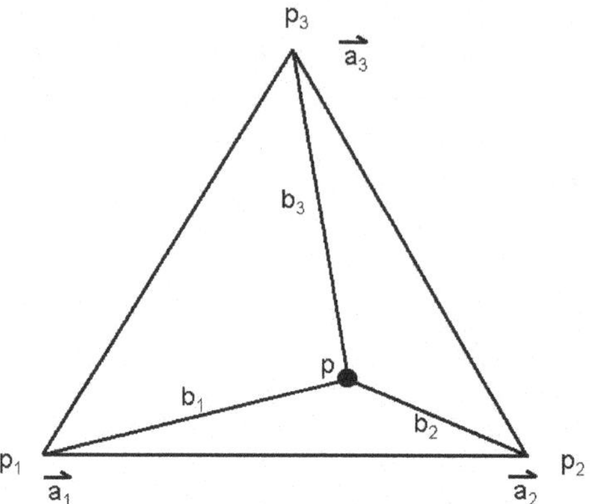

Figure 4. Interpolation of gain vectors which are defined at the corners of the triangle. The gain vector associated with point $\mathbf{p}$ inside the triangle is the linear combination with the three barycentric coordinates b_i as weights.

The manner in which the location on the object is set is somewhat involved. The modal model $\mathcal{M}$ contains gains on a discrete set of location points. These location points will usually correspond to geometric locations on some two-dimensional contact surface. In order to allow for interpolation in between the data points, we specify the location by providing three discrete location points `p1 p2 p3`, which index the gain arrays. We then draw an imaginary triangle (see Figure 4) between the physical geometrical points on our actual object (of which the audio objects have no knowledge) and provide three barycentric coordinates `b1 b2 b3` to specify the position within this triangle. The gain coefficients are then appropriately averaged over the three discrete data points. For one-dimensional objects, such as bars or strings, we can simply use two significant discrete points `p1 p2` and as long as $b3 = 0$, the third point is irrelevant.

3 Audio Force Models

In order to create sounds with a modal model we need good interaction force models to provide an input to the real-time algorithm described in Section 2.3. The **SonicObject** contains a single **AudioForce** object for the input excitation force, though it could easily be extended to contain many which operate on different locations. In this section, we consider four types of interaction models:

- impact forces, used for collision sounds;
- continuous contact forces for sliding and rolling;
- combustion engine forces;
- live data streams.

3.1 Impact Forces

When two solid bodies collide, large forces are applied for a short period of time. The precise details of the contact force will depend on the shape of the contact areas as well as on the elastic properties of the involved materials. For example, a rubber ball colliding with a concrete floor will experience a contact force which will increase faster than linearly with the compression of the ball, because the contact area also increases during the collision. A generic model of contact forces based on the Hertz model and the radii of curvatures of the surfaces in contact was considered in [19]. A Hertzian model was also used to create a detailed model of the interaction forces between the mallet and the bars of a xylophone [3].

To create a simple model of a collision force to drive the audio synthesis, we assume that the two most important distinguishing characteristics of an impact on an object are the energy transfer in the strike and the "hardness" of the contact. A psychophysical study of perceived mallet hardness [14] of xylophones showed that this is indeed a very perceptible parameter of an acoustic event. The hardness translates directly in the duration of the force, and the energy transfer translates directly in the magnitude of the force profile.

We have experimented with a number of force profiles and found that the exact details of the shape are relatively unimportant. A very simple phenomenological model of a finite duration impact force can be constructed from a single period of a cosine function. The model which we implemented in a class **BangForce** approximates the contact force by a function of the form

$$F(t) = F_{max}(1 - \cos(\frac{2\pi t}{T})) \tag{7}$$

for $0 \leq t \leq T$, with T the total duration of the contact. This function has the qualitative correct form for a contact force. The force increases slowly in the beginning, representing a gradual increase in contact area, and then rises rapidly, representing the elastic compression of the materials. The sounds of soft contacts (with large T) are recognizable as such, which shows that this model can produce this perception.

In order to hit a running **SonicObject** with a **BangForce** you call `hit()` on the **BangForce**, and the next time the **SonicObject** calls `getForce()`, a strike profile is returned. Typically, a duration of about 50 ms will be perceived as a very soft "thud," and anything with a longer duration is too smeared out in time to be audible.

More complex interactions during contact may have an important effect in some cases. For example, the hammers in a piano are covered with felt, so during the contact between the hammer and the string, they damp the higher modes of vibration. How this actually occurs is quite complicated [16, 17, 18, 33] and potentially important, especially for high-quality musical instrument modeling. As another example, experimental data [32] shows that there are sequences of very fast contact separations and collisions during hard impacts. These micro-collisions are caused by modal vibrations of the objects involved, and can be simulated by a short burst of impulse trains at the dominant modal frequencies [9].

The **DemoBellStrike** class contains a demonstration of the impact forces. It tolls a bell with a **BangForce** whose duration can be set with a slider. Of course, if you don't like bells, any modal object can be substituted for the bell. A second slider allows you to set the number of modes used, to get a feeling for the degradation in quality when using fewer modes. Its `main()` method contains the lines

```
sob1 = new SonicObject(new ModalModel(args[0]),
                  srate,bufferSize,bufferSizeJavaSound);
af1 = new BangForce(srate);
sob1.setAudioForce(af1);
sob1.start();
new HelperThread().start();
new DemoBellStrike (new java.awt.Frame (), true).show ();
```

which creates a **SonicObject** loaded from a modes file, assigns a **BangForce** to it, and launches a control thread which hits the bell:

```
while(true) {
    sleep(t_control);
    af1.hit();
}
```

When you move the upper slider, the mallet hardness is set by the user interface thread by

```
af1.setDuration(x);
```

where `x` is set by a slider.

The same bell model is also implemented in C, without a user interface, using the PABLIO audio library for rendering.

3.2 Continuous Contact Forces

An important ingredient in synthesizing realistic scraping and rolling sounds is a surface interaction model. A lot of research has been conducted on models of contact interactions between solids [34, 35, 23, 20, 1, 2], but they usually focus on predicting forces at a coarser time scale than needed for our purposes, though not all [36]. Nevertheless a rigid body simulator is able to provide information about the contact force magnitudes and the friction forces at the contact areas which may be used as inputs to a contact force model.

This model should be able to generate contact forces at the audio sampling rate for a specific type of contact given the contact force at the simulation rate (usually orders of magnitude slower than the audio rate) and the sliding speed. The roughness profile of both surfaces will determine the effective force stimulus to the object and therefore have an important effect on the sound.

A solution we found to be satisfactory is to use a looping digital sample with pitch shifting and volume control to adjust the speed and force of the contact. The physical picture behind this contact model is that the sample encodes the shape of the surface and the object scraping it is following this surface profile exactly, like the needle in a phonograph. Note that aliasing will occur for large values of the looping speed which we find to make a positive contribution to the effect in many cases, creating a richer variation with speed. With a small set of short samples representing a variety of textures, a great variety of contact surface profiles can be imposed upon the vibration models. Surface profiles were created by simply scraping a real object with a contact microphone.

Another solution is to directly synthesize the contact force from a stochastic noise model, which is quite involved and will not be described here; see [9].

The Java class **LoopForce** represents a looping audio sample with controllable looping speed and volume. Its constructor reads an audio file and calls to `getForce()` return buffers obtained by looping through the sample buffer at the current speed. The method `getNextSample()` implements pitch shifting by linear sample interpolation. Experiments with a more accurate quadratic sample interpolation algorithm did not result in an audible improvement.

The demo class **DemoMouseScrape** allows you to scrape a modal model with the mouse. It samples the mouse position at a fixed sampling rate (say 50 Hz) and uses a low-pass differentiating filter to obtain the mouse velocity, which is used to set the looping speed of the excitation.

3.3 Engine Forces

Engine sounds are very difficult to achieve in computer games, as they are essentially continuous sounds which need real-time control. Racing games are very popular and a properly modeled car sound that responds in a realistic way to input parameters would greatly enhance the audio in such games.

It is not obvious that combustion engines can be modeled with our techniques, as the sources of sound are explosions and very complicated gaseous phenomena. Rather surprisingly, we found that reasonably convincing sounding interactive models can be made by driving some resonance object (a lumped model of everything that is vibrating) with a rather simple-minded model of a combustion engine.

The first model which we created is a four-stroke engine. The driving force is obtained by constructing a looping audio sample divided into four regions which represent the four stages of the engine. The sample driving the resonances as depicted in Figure 5 (`car1.wav`) contains an intake stroke, a compression stroke (silence), a combustion stroke, and an exhaust stroke. The intake stroke was modeled as white noise enveloped with a bell curve. The exhaust stroke is modeled as white noise, rapidly decaying in time, inspired by a high pressure gas mixture being released when the valve opens. The combustion stroke consists of an enveloped burst of $1/f$ noise. It was found, after trying various $1/f^{\alpha}$ noises, that this gives the most realistic sound. The reason is perhaps that the combustion takes place inside the cylinder, so the shock wave is transmitted to the mass of metal of the engine block, which acts as a low-pass filter.

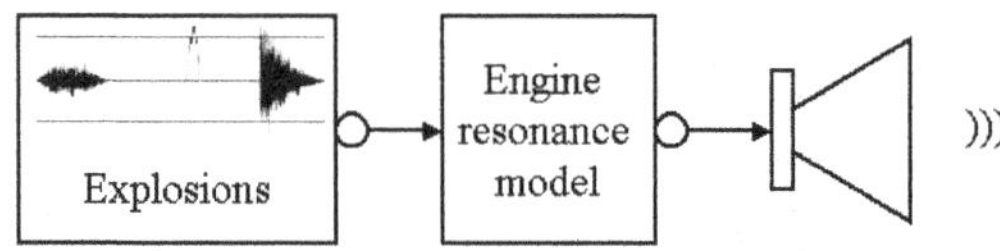

Figure 5. A hand-constructed looping .wav file represents the four strokes of a simple engine model. The rest of the car, including muffler, is modeled as a lumped resonance model.

The sample is looped at an adjustable rate, corresponding to the running speed of the engine. For added realism, the engine is allowed to "misfire" once in a while, which we implement by skipping a section in the looped sample. The Java class **CombustionEngineForce** is a subclass of **LoopForce** and has the additional method `setBeatupness(double prob)` which sets the probability per call to `getForce()` that the engine misfires.

This simple driving force model can generate a variety of engine sounds by coupling it to various vibration models. Models with relatively high frequency resonances with high damping give a "lawn mower" effect, whereas a low frequency object gives a motorcycle sound.

A slightly different sound is produced by adding a background pitched sound to the sample at all four stages. This simulates the sound of the fan, and perhaps other rotating parts. For the pitched sound, a short noisy note played on a Persian ney (a type of flute) was used, which is very satisfactory. The audio file is `car2.wav`.

Yet another engine sound was obtained by creating a four-cylinder version. We assume that the four cylinders fire $90°$ out of phase and simply add the samples from the one cylinder engine four times, with a relative phase shift of $90°$. If we just use this driving force as-is, the result is not very good. The reason is probably that in a real engine, the four cylinders are attached to the intake manifold at different locations and therefore sound different. To incorporate this, we adjust the volumes of the four one-cylinder samples individually, and when they are set all differently, the resulting sound is much better. The audio file is `car3.wav`.

The demo class **DemoEngine** creates a **SonicObject** off a modes file, `car1.sy` for example, and applies a **CombustionEngineForce** to it which is loaded from an audio file. The top slider sets the speed and the bottom slider sets the "beatupness." We noticed that the result is strongly dependent on the type of audio speakers used for playback, so you may want to tune the model parameters to your audio set-up.

In a real game application, one would certainly spend a lot more time on the actual modeling of the car engine than we have done here. But our simple models show that a reasonable result can already be obtained using extremely simple models. To create richer engine sounds, different cylinders may be coupled to different exhaust manifolds or muffler pipes.

3.4 Live Data Streams

An interesting interface to this type of synthesis is a sensor that measures real interaction forces. This can be demonstrated with a contact microphone. When touching and scraping real objects, the audio signal can be sent to a synthesis process, where this audio signal is then interpreted as a force to whatever vibration model is currently loaded. We can then scrape some interface object and transfer the measured signal to the audio synthesis to create the impression of touching a virtual object. Another type of application is to use the output of an electrical guitar as the driving force for some virtual guitar body.

The Java class **MikeAudioForce** obtains its output "force" buffer from the audio input of the soundcard:

```
protected RTAudioIn pai;
    public void getForce(double [] output, int nsamples) {
        pai.read(output,nsamples);
    }
}
```

It makes use of the utility class **RTAudioIn**, which provides a convenient access to the audio input through JavaSound. The class **DemoMikeIn** loads a **ModalSonicObject** from a given modes file and attaches a **MikeAudioForce** to it. It works well when using a contact mike for scraping various surfaces. You can also plug the output of your electrical guitar in and have a modal guitar effects box.

4 Conclusions

We have given a theoretical and practical introduction to modal synthesis, which we believe to be very useful for the real-time synthesis of a variety of sounds. After discussing the physics leading to the model, we derived an efficient algorithm, which turns out to be a familiar bank of reson filters. A Java class **ModalSonicObject** implements a modal model which can render itself. It contains an object which implements the **AudioForce** interface, which provides it with its input.

A **SonicObject** must implement its own **AudioForce** interface which allows one **SonicObject** to act as the input to another, in effect creating a filter graph.

Force models to excite the modal models were discussed, and examples were given of impact forces, scraping forces, combustion engine forces, and live data streams.

The efficiency of the synthesis algorithm was measured with the provided class **DemoModalBenchmark**, and we found that on a 450 Mhz

Pentium III, one can synthesize about 800 modes at a sampling rate of 22050 Hz using Java, whereas C is about 25% more efficient.

The Java code examples presented here for tutorial purposes are, with slight modifications for presentational purposes, part of JASS, which is a unit-generator-based audio synthesis programming environment written mainly in Java [12], but which also includes platform-specific code for low latency audio on Windows, LINUX, and Macintosh OS X (CoreAudio). The JASS development environment is available for noncommercial use from the JASS web site, www.cs.ubc.ca/~kvdoel/jass [8], where you can also try out several interactive audio synthesis applets which run in all modern web browsers.

Annotated Bibliography

[1] D. Baraff. "Dynamic Simulation of Non-Penetrating Rigid Bodies." Unpublished Ph.D. dissertation, Cornell University, 1992.

[2] D. Baraff. "Dynamic Simulation of Non-Penetrating Flexible Bodies." *Computer Graphics* 26:2 (1992), 303–308.

[3] A. Chaigne and V. Doutaut. "Numerical Simulations of Xylophones. I. Time Domain Modeling of the Vibrating Bars." *J. Acoust. Soc. Am.* 101:1 (1997), 539–557.

[4] A. Chaudhary, A. Freed, S. Khoury, and D. Wessel. "A 3-D Graphical User Interface for Resonance Modeling." In *Proceedings of the International Computer Music Conference.* 1998.

[5] P. Cook. "Introduction to Physical Modeling." In *Audio Anecdotes*, edited by K. Greenebaum and Ronen Barzel, pp. 179–198. Natick, MA: A K Peters, Ltd., 2003.

[6] P. R. Cook. "Physically Informed Sonic Modeling (PhISM): Percussive Synthesis." In *Proceedings of the International Computer Music Conference*, pp. 228–231. 1996.

[7] K. v. d. Doel. "Sound synthesis for virtual reality and computer games." Unpublished Ph.D. dissertation, University of British Columbia, 1998. Available from World Wide Web (http://www.cs.ubc.ca/~kvdoel/publications/thesis.pdf)

[8] K. v. d. Doel. *JASS web site.* Available from World Wide Web (http://www.cs.ubc.ca/~kvdoel/jass), 2003.

[9] K. v. d. Doel, P. G. Kry, and D. K. Pai. "FoleyAutomatic: Physically-Based Sound Effects for Interactive Simulation and Animation." In *Proceedings of SIGGRAPH 2001, Computer Graphics Proceedings, Annual Conference Series*, edited by E. Fiume, pp. 537–544. Reading, MA: Addison-Wesley. 2001.

[10] K. v. d. Doel and D. K. Pai. "Synthesis of Shape Dependent Sounds with Physical Modeling." In *Proceedings of the International Conference on Auditory Display 1996*. 1996.

[11] K. v. d. Doel and D. K. Pai. "The Sounds of Physical Shapes." *Presence* 7:4 (1998), 382–395.

[12] K. v. d. Doel and D. K. Pai. "JASS: A Java Audio Synthesis System for Programmers." In *Proceedings of the International Conference on Auditory Display 2001*. 2001.

[13] K. v. d. Doel, D. K. Pai, T. Adam, L. Kortchmar, and K. Pichora-Fuller. "Measurements of Perceptual Quality of Contact Sound Models." In *Proceedings of the International Conference on Auditory Display 2002*. 2002.

[14] D. J. Fried. "Auditory Correlates of Perceived Mallet Hardness for a Set of Recorded Percussive Sound Events." *J. Acoust. Soc. Am.* 87:1 (1990), 311–321.

[15] W. W. Gaver. "Synthesizing Auditory Icons." In *Proceedings of the ACM Interchi*. 1993, pp. 228–235. New York: ACM Press, 1993.

[16] D. E. Hall. "Piano String Excitation in the Case of Small Hammer Mass." *J. Acoust. Soc. Am.* 9:1 (1986), 141–147.

[17] D. E. Hall. "Piano String Excitation II: General Solution for a Hard Narrow Hammer." *J. Acoust. Soc. Am.* 81:2 (1987), 535–545.

[18] D. E. Hall. "Piano String ExcitationIII: General Solution for a Soft Narrow Hammer." *J. Acoust. Soc. Am.* 81:2 (1987), 547–555.

[19] K. L. Johnson. *Contact Mechanics.* Cambridge: Cambridge University Press, 1985.

[20] J. B. Keller. "Impact with Friction." *Journal of Applied Mechanics*, 53:1 (1986), 1–4.

[21] R. L. Klatzky, D. K. Pai, and E. P. Krotkov. "Perception of Material from Contact Sounds." *Presence* 9:4 (2000), 399–410.

[22] E. Krotkov and R. Klatzky. "Robotic Perception of Material: Experiments with Shape-Invariant Acoustic Measures of Material Type." In *Preprints of the Fourth International Symposium on Experimental Robotics, ISER '95.* 1995.

[23] P. Løtstedt. "Numerical simulation of time-dependent contact and friction problems in rigid body mechanics." *SIAM J. Sci. Stat. Comput.* 5:2 (1984), 370–393.

[24] M. V. Mathews. *The Technology of Computer Music.* Cambridge, MA: MIT Press, 1969.

[25] J. D. Morrison and J.-M. Adrien. "Mosaic: A Framework for Modal Synthesis." *Computer Music Journal* 17:1 (1993).

[26] J. F. O'Brien, C. Chen, and C. M. Gatchalian. "Synthesizing Sounds from Rigid-Body Simulations." In *Proceedings of the 2002 ACM SIGGRAPH/Eurographics Symposium on Computer Animation*, pp. 175–181. New York: ACM Press, 2002.

[27] J. F. O'Brien, P. R. Cook, and G. Essl. "Synthesizing Sounds from Physically Based Motion." In *Proceedings of SIGGRAPH 2001, Computer Graphics Proceedings, Annual Conference Series*, edited by E. Fiume, pp. 529–536. Reading, MA: Addison-Wesley, 2001.

[28] D. K. Pai, K. v. d. Doel, D. L. James, J. Lang, J. E. Lloyd, J. L. Richmond, and S. H. Yau. "Scanning Physical Interaction Behavior of 3D Objects." In *Proceedings of SIGGRAPH 2001, Computer Graphics Proceedings, Annual Conference Series*, edited by E. Fiume, pp. 87–96. Reading, MA: Addison-Wesley, 2001.

[29] S. Serafin. "Physical Synthesis of Bowed String Instruments." In *Audio Anecdotes III*, edited by K. Greenebaum and Ronen Barzel, pp. 85–72. Natick, MA: A K Peters, Ltd., 2003.

[30] J. O. Smith. "Physical Modeling Using Digital Waveguides." *Computer Music Journal* 16:4 (1992), 75–87.

[31] K. Steiglitz. *A Digital Signal Processing Primer with Applications to Digital Audio and Computer Music.* New York: Addison-Wesley, 1996.

[32] D. Stoianovici and Y. Hurmuzlu. "A Critical Study of the Applicability of Rigid-Body Collision Theory." *ASME Journal of Applied Mechanics* 63 (1996), 307–316.

[33] A. Stulov. "Hysteretic Model of the Grand Piano Hammer Felt." *J. Acoust. Soc. Am.* 97:4 (1995), 2577–2585.

[34] Suresh Goyal, F. W. S., and Elliot N. Pinson. "Simulation of Dynamics of Interacting Rigid Bodies Including Friction I: General Problem and Contact Model." *Engineering with Computers* 10 (1994), 162–174.

[35] Suresh Goyal, F. W. S., and Elliot N. Pinson. "Simulation of Dynamics of Interacting Rigid Bodies Including Friction II: Software System Design and Implementation." *Engineering with Computers* 10 (1994), 175–195.

[36] C. Ullrich and D. K. Pai. "Contact Response Maps for Real Time Dynamic Simulation. In *Proceedings of the IEEE International Conference on Robotics and Automation*, pp. 1019–1025. 1998.

[37] J. Wawrzynek. "VLSI Models for Real-Time Music Synthesis." In *Current Directions in Computer Music Research*, edited by M. Mathews and J. Pierce. Cambridge, MA: MIT Press, 1989.

[38] R. P. Wildes and W. A. Richards. "Recovering Material Properties from Sound." In *Natural Computation*, edited by W. Richards. Cambridge, MA: MIT Press, 1988.

Voice Synthesis

Voice Concatenation: "A Stitch in Time Saves Nine"

Craig Utterback

1 Introduction

In this article, we present and discuss a number of issues involved in the design, planning, and development of concatenating voice features for interactive products, specifically for games with a limited vocabulary and highly scripted grammar. For a more general and technical analysis, please consult Bunnell's articles "Introduction to Speech Acoustics" (page 159), "Timescale Modification of Speech" (page 173), and "Pitch Modification of Speech Writing Using PSOLA" (page 187) describing the structure of voice. Debbie Yarrington's article "Synthesizing Speech for Communication Devices" (page 143) deals with the challenges of voice synthesis and puts speech concatenation into a larger context.

Let's start out by saying that voice concatenation is the process of dynamically stitching together words and phrases to make sentences and/or a continuous stream of words, phrases, and sentences using specially designed and prepared speech segments. In an interactive game, the results might be used to provide an ongoing commentary for **color**, a description of **play-by-play**, and/or react to **input response** events as they occur.

In the seven years that I've been working with this process, I've always called it voice "stitching"; consequently, I will be using the terms "concatenation" and "stitching" synonymously throughout this article.

2 What Is It Good For?

Concatenation provides a solution to the problem of automatically dispensing verbal information, specific to a given set of circumstances (button push on a touch tone phone or player actions in a computer game). Many of the principles discussed here apply equally well to nongaming technologies such as an automated customer support phone service as long as the dialogues required are well enough understood and constrained.

For computer games, data size matters. *A lot.* Concatenation helps address the need for manageable data sizes by reusing as much of the content as possible to achieve a balance between data size versus number of features versus depth and variety of features versus audio quality.

There are several sizes to consider:

Delivery media size. What is the size of the delivery media and how much space will be allowed for audio content? For an older cartridge style game with 4 Mb TOTAL storage, 512 Kb for audio would be generous. For a CD-ROM game with 650 Mb total storage, 200+ Mb for audio might be appropriate depending on the importance and desirability of the audio content. For newer DVD-ROM console and computer games with 6+ gigabytes total storage, there is lots of room for audio (until the graphics folk figure out how to fill that space up with textures or whatever).

Installation size. On older computer systems, hard drive space was at a premium such that the size limits and options for installing content might be determined by performance issues—hard drives could access data much faster than a CD-ROM—if playback latency was problematic, content needed to be installed on the hard drive. Even with the larger disk drives available today, moderate size limits are observed to reduce lengthy installation times and alleviate the "snowball" effect of installing numerous games on a hard drive—if you install 10 games with a 100 Mb of audio content each, it would consume a gigabyte of drive space. More recently, CD-ROM and DVD technologies have improved their performance sufficiently to provide speedy access to content without installing large amounts of data on a hard drive. Also, hard drive sizes have increased dramatically, so the size considerations for installing content on disk drives are becoming less of an issue.

RAM size. Another size to be considered is for content that needs to be loaded into system RAM. Low-latency sound effects that sync to game action need to be loaded into RAM. Streaming audio from DVD or CD-ROM is often sufficient for voice content that is not concatenated; however, there are a number of integration schemes that provide sufficient bandwidth to meet low-latency requirements without using prohibitive RAM sizes (preloading files into RAM just before they are needed and clearing RAM once the content is heard; or using RAM buffers to load, play, and dump content as it is needed).

Online bandwidth—speed versus size. More recently, concatenation has become useful for delivering content over the Internet, where bandwidth is at a premium and larger data sizes require longer download times.

A naive alternative to voice stitching would be to record and produce complete cues for every combination of every feature for an entire product. Obviously, if there were very many variables and each variable had many possible values, the number of unique sentences that would have to be recorded separately would be huge and the storage requirements astronomical.

A game designer might want an announcer to utter a sentence of the following form:

> This is [name]'s [number] [action] this game!
> Ex: "This is Craig's tenth foul this game!"

A vocabulary of 20 names, 10 numbers, and 5 actions would require the sentence to be recorded 1000 different ways! Changing the name of one player would require 50 sentences to be re-recorded! Adding a new action adds 200 sentences ...

Other alternatives might include limiting oneself to printed text, using limited voice content and text together, or using a text to speech synthesis technology. Speech synthesis (text to speech technology), while a promising technology, is still a long way from being mature. Synthesis offers an unlimited vocabulary, but doesn't convey the sense of real speech patterns because of the unfortunate sacrifices, not only the richness of recorded voice but much intelligibility too—the results often sounding like a drunken Swede.

(Please see Yarrington's aforementioned article for a much more thorough examination of voice synthesis techniques, promise, and limitations).

3 The Challenge

The real challenge related to concatenation is getting voice features that sound convincing. In this day of desktop digital audio recording (see

Manley's article "How to Make Great Voice Recordings" in *Audio Anecdotes I*), it's fairly easy to use concatenation of recorded voice to say almost anything; however, making it sound natural and convincing when stitched together—this is a far more difficult matter and is the subject of this anecdote.

The voice content heard in most strategy, action, fantasy-role playing, and first person shooter game genres is indeed developed and produced in its final delivered state. The designers of these applications don't need to consider the complexities of stitching because they can achieve the desired features using this method.

Sports games, however, need and use voice concatenation to integrate their announcer features, which can be heard in numerous football, baseball, basketball, golf, soccer, hockey, and other products released by Sierra On-line/Sierra Sports, Electronic Arts/EA Sports, and Microsoft, among other publishers.

For the sake of this article, I'm going to examine some of the issues that had to be considered in the conception, design, planning, and development of the play-by-play announcer for the *Sierra Sports Professional Bull Rider* and *Sierra Sports PGA Championship Golf* computer games.

4 Script Planning

Thorough planning and careful scripting are essential to the success of any concatenating voice integration. When possible, a real-life model is the best reference. For sports, attend an event, or watch and listen to a broadcast. Having the cooperation, enthusiasm, and licensing of the PGA of America, Inc. and Professional Bull Riders, Inc. organizations provided a wonderful depth of resource, by allowing us access to knowledgeable people and official information, all-area access at certain events, and permission to make reference recordings from the main mixer during actual events. Detailed examination of those recordings helped provide a reference for the features we needed and a preliminary "framework" for the script.

There are, of course, pitfalls to be avoided when planning a script for concatenation: single word stitches, soft phoneme stitches, and trying to stitch together more than three chunks (two stitches) to produce phrases. All of these approaches have difficulty sounding convincing (more on these topics coming up).

When designing the script for *PBR (Professional Bull Rider)*, a number of decisions needed to be made regarding game/voice features. Discussions with the designers, programmers, and artists helped to determine desirable features for our game announcer. The programmers and I went over every proposed feature to verify that it could be successfully hooked to events in the game. Input from the artists and animators helped determine the context and specific language for many of the features in our script (such as bull and bullfighter movements and injuries). To provide depth and variety, multiple cues were scripted and produced for many of the features. Here are some examples of just a few of the features that we needed for our announcer:

- welcome the player to the game (start of game)
- welcome the player to the arena (start of arena)
- make remarks before a ride
  - match-ups for bulls and riders
  - bull thrashing in the chute
  - player gives the nod (start ride)
- make remarks during a bull ride
  - general excitement cues (lots and lots and lots)
  - bull belly rolls left
  - bull changes direction
- make remarks after a ride
  - rider gets injured
  - thumbs-up (successful ride)
  - no score (unsuccessful ride)
  - rider appreciation
- make remarks between rounds
  - standings
  - check leader board
- congratulate championship winners
- game wrap-up and kiss–off

4.1 Gender Considerations

When planning a script for a product that has both male and female players and characters, be sure to watch features that include gender-specific content. All cues containing the words "he, him, his, he's" must have duplicate cues containing the words "she, her, hers, she's."

4.2 Features that Grow and Size Considerations

As I said earlier, for computer games, data size matters. *A lot.* For *PBR*, we tried to achieve a balance between data size versus number of features versus depth and variety of features versus audio quality, by reusing as much of the content as possible. Some of the features we wanted required large numbers of files (cues). For the NAMES feature, we created cue templates for Rider NAMES, Bullfighter NAMES, and Bull NAMES. These templates show (to some degree) how the cues will integrate when they are stitched together (more detailed information on stitching integration related to templates and file naming coming up in the Concatenation Schemes section).

> Scripting Template for Rider NAMES and stitching cues (8 iterations):
> [1st *and last name]* takes 1st.
> *[Here's* 1st *and last name]* to start us off.
> *[This is* 1st *and last name]* to get us started.
> [1st *name]* gets bucked off.
> *[And,* 1st *name]* gets a thumbs-up.
> Next up,[1st *and last name]*.
> 78 *[for* 1st *and last name]*.
> Great ride *[by* 1st *name]*.
>
> Scripting Template for Bullfighter NAMES and stitching cues (8 iterations):
> *[bullfighter name]* takes 1st.
> *[Here's, bullfighter name]* to start us off.
> *[This is bullfighter name]* to get us started.
> *[bullfighter 1st name]* gets hurt on that one.
> *[And, bullfighter name]* gets punished.
> Next up, *[bullfighter name]*.
> That's 78 *[for bullfighter name]*.
> Great fight *[by bullfighter name]*.

Scripting Template for Bull NAMES and stitching cues (6 iterations):
[bull name] bucks him off.
[Now, bull name] turns left mostly.
Next up *[bull name]*
Here's Cody Hart, *[on bull name]*
That's 78 *[for bull name]*
He got hurt *[by bull name]*

46 Rider NAMES times 8 iterations	368 cues
5 Bullfighter NAMES times 8 iterations	40 cues
40 Bull Names times 6 iterations	240 cues
Total	648 cues

Now, 648 NAMES cues for the *Professional Bull Rider* game aren't really a very large number; however, consider the larger number of cues needed for similar features if you wanted to develop a football game:

400+ Player NAMES times 8 iterations	3,200+ cues
20+ Team NAMES times 8 iterations	160+ cues
20+ City NAMES times 8 iterations	160+ cues
Total	3,520+ cues

Over 3,520 cues just for NAMES!!! Staying with football for a moment, consider the number of cues needed for STATS, SCORES, and YARDAGE features. Here's a few YARDAGE related cues:

"He's taken down after a 36 yard run."
"First and 10, from their own 14 yard line."
"Pass completed for a 72 yard gain."
"He gets sacked for an 8 yard loss."

And there are plenty more cues with 50 to 100 instances for each "yardage" feature—tens of thousands of variations are possible. So be watchful for features that grow in size, and try to achieve a balance between data size versus number of features versus depth and variety of features versus audio quality.

4.3 Stitching Numbers

Features that involve numbers also tend to grow in size. I have tried several approaches to scripting and integrating NUMBERS, and getting multiple stitched numbers to sound convincing is extremely difficult. In my opinion, if you want the numbers to sound like someone actually said them in context, then get the voice talent to perform every iteration for every number for every cue. This is not usually feasible due to vast number of cues required and limitations of size, time and endurance of the voice talent.

For *PBR*, we designed NUMBER cues that would allow score stitching up to the number 1,000 (which would be desirable for announcing scores at the end of an event or tournament). As I recall, this feature required the voice talent to read about 500+ cues from which I would manually build all 1,000 cues (so they would not require CPU overhead or suffer from stitching latency at runtime) and stitch them with other content to achieve our scoring features.

After producing this content, I used my sound editor to stitch together some cues as a test and was displeased with the results, which (to me) did not sound adequately convincing. Since the announcing scores at the end of an event or tournament feature would not be heard very often in the game, we decided to omit this feature and instead we scripted cues that directed the player's attention to a scoreboard where the scores were displayed.

We also designed a separate score stitching feature for individual bull rides where we needed cues for scores between 70 and 100 (in .5 point increments) only. Since this feature would be heard much more often (at the end of most bull rides or about every 25–30 seconds in the arcade), we wanted the best possible sounding content. We decided to record our scores in context to the content using stitching schemes that worked with the Rider, and Bullfighter, and Bull NAMES (yes, you could play as the bull!), thereby attaining the desired results—no stitching required. Here are some example bull ride score cues:

"The judges give him a 92 point 5."
"They give him a 93."
"That'll give him a 93 point 5."
"That ride earns him a 94."
"They're gonna give him a 94 point 5."
"He earns himself a 95."
"That's gonna be worth a 95 point 5."
"That's gonna earn him a 96."

5 Performance Issues

The really ticklish part of concatenation involves stitching segments together within a phrase. In order to get successful phrase stitching, the script must be written in such a way that the voice talent can perform "normal" sounding cues, from which desirable segments can be excerpted for concatenation. Some script material is prepared for no other reason than to serve as a "vehicle" to get the desired segments (and the unused pieces are later discarded).

Keeping the voice talent on his "mark" is imperative to meet the following vocal performance criteria: the pitch (high-low) of each segment has to match, the tempo (speed) of each segment has to match, and the tenor (attitude/excitement) of each segment has to match (more on this subject coming up).

5.1 Voice Talent

For the *Professional Bull Rider* game, we used a real arena announcer, which proved valuable to our product in terms of providing convincing sounding content. His expert knowledge provided additional script input in terms of contributing numerous cues to features, thereby improving the depth and quality of those features.

5.2 Phonemes, Formants, and Other Articulation Issues: What Works and what Doesn't

When scripting for stitching within a phrase, I've come up with some guidelines for what works and what doesn't. In general, phrase segments that begin or end with hard-sounding phonemes and formants offer decent opportunities for successful stitching; phrases that begin or end with soft sounding phonemes and formants are less likely candidates. Here are some examples of phrases containing hard sounds at the stitch point. In each example, the cue is designed to be stitched together with a rider's name at the end of the phrase with the word "by" in front of the name.

A great effort... *by Ty Murray*
A terrific job... *by Chris Shivers*
Sensational bull ride... *by Troy Dunn*

The word "effort" ends with a hard "T" sound. When forming the "T," the tongue touches the back of the teeth momentarily stopping airflow at the plosive "T" sound. The word "job" ends with a hard "B" sound. When forming the "B," the lips come together, momentarily stopping airflow at the plosive "B" sound. The word "ride" ends with a hard "D" sound. When forming the "D," the tongue touches roof of the mouth momentarily stopping airflow at the plosive "D". When viewed with a software sound editor, you can observe that the amplitude goes to (or near) zero at the location of many of the hard plosives in the content. Because of the hard plosive cutoff of these words, it was possible to edit clean segments that stitch successfully with all of the rider names—we have reusable content!

Unfortunately, depending on semantic context of the cue and the vocal performance (pitch, tempo, and tenor), it can be difficult to make a clean usable phrase segment even when working with hard phonemes. Whenever possible, I attempt to script cues that have a natural pause at the stitch point. In some cases, I direct the voice talent to hesitate slightly at the stitch point when performing a cue.

As mentioned above, soft phonemes offer less opportunity for successful stitching. When listening to normal speech, many soft phonemes transition (cross fade) between other phonemes. An example of this is the word "man"—say it a couple of times and try to separate the sounds of the "M" from the "A," and the "A" from the "N." Soft phonemes do indeed provide the connecting flow between words and phrases, making it extremely difficult to excerpt content to produce convincing stitches.

I've had some success using soft sounds like *"fffff"* and *"sssss"* to stitch at the beginning and end of phrases; and, it is possible to "force" a stitch by scripting material prepared for no other reason than to get the desired segments. For example, I needed the cues "FOR bullfighter name" and "ON bull name," beginning with soft phonemes, that were designed to be stitched at the end of a phrase for all the bull and bullfighter names. So, I scripted the following material:

"That's 78 *for Roach Hedeman.*"
"Here's Cody Hart, *on Snakeskin.*"

I scripted a phrase that contained a hard "T" sound just before the "FOR" and "ON" to allow me to excerpt the desired segment from each phrase.

5.3 Scripting Pitfalls

As with any project design and development, one "occasionally" encounters soft phoneme scripting pitfalls that usually serve to inhibit successful concatenation features. In the Workaround Strategies and Extraordinary

Rescue Measures section of this article, I've cited an example of unsuccessful soft phoneme scripting I encountered and rescued (with the help of some audio mojo) while working on a feature for *Sierra Sports PGA Championship Golf 2000.*

6 Recording Session

Integrated voice features may need to be heard in different ambient scenes, which makes it desirable to make the recording in an isolation booth that is anechoic (no echo—acoustically dead). This allows post-production or software ambiance effects to be applied more convincingly than if the recording contained any room sound at all.

Effort spent to obtain a signal path with as much signal and as little noise as possible is essential to the success of feature integration. A typical signal path would include: a microphone, running into a mic preamp (or mixer channel), with a compressor (or limiter) inserted prefader, feeding into an A/D converter—at which time the signal is turned into digital format and routed to a DAT, or a computer, or any digital recording device. Dynamic processing during the recording should be sufficient to get a fairly hot signal, gently compressed (take the tops of the peaks off), without raising the noise floor significantly, or removing the life from the voice talent's performance.

During post-production, more dynamic and normalization processing are used in the digital domain, and steps must be taken to avoid the artifacts that can appear when using multiple processes and reduced resolution data formats. Aliasing, interpolation distortion, and noise reduction artifacts all contribute to audible peculiarities and the apparent noise floor; so, hot (but not too hot) and clean (but never clean enough) is the engineering formula for success.

An effort to get the voice talent to understand concatenation and how you plan to use the content being recorded will greatly improve chances for a smooth running and successful session. Getting the voice talent to closely match phrasing, pitch, and tenor through a reading of several hundred NAME and NUMBER cues can be boring and exhausting for everyone involved, which makes it very important to record these features when the voice talent is warmed up and settled into their stride. Try not to leave long reads until the end of the session. Previewing the script and discussing these features can help the talent successfully get through the long parts. Session tip: Plan to record some "fun" and less repetitive cues before long reads, and take a break afterwards.

For a more in-depth examination of voice recording, see Manley's aforementioned article.

7 Integration Considerations

7.1 Sweeping Generalities

It is important to keep the number of stitches per phrase to as few as possible. The more cues that are stitched together to make a phrase, the less likely the phrase will stitch successfully. Multiple stitched phrases/cues (especially using single words) can sound pretty bad—for example: automated phone information for airline flight arrivals and departures.

It is advantageous to script a number of unstitched/generic cues to be mixed in with stitched cues, thereby increasing the overall variety of features. Sometimes unstitched/generic cues are needed to provide certain contexts to existing features.

One of the features that we desired for *Professional Bull Rider* was the ability for the player to create their own rider character (with a new name) which required a set of generic cues to function in the place of the Rider NAMES feature for that player's Rider character.

7.2 Considerations for Subsequent Revisions and Additions

Successful computer games are often followed by a sequel, so it may be desirable to add features to existing content. It is possible to (re)produce content that closely matches the original audio by carefully documenting all recording and post-production processes.

About a year after the initial recording sessions for *Professional Bull Rider*, we brought the same announcer back to our studio to perform a new script and make new recordings. Several existing features were to be revised and supplemented (including Rider and Bull NAMES) and numerous new features were to be added for *Professional Bull Rider II*. I was able to reproduce (as much as possible) the exact recording and post-production process, because I had documented the make, model, and settings for every piece of equipment used and the signal path and all level indications. I documented where the talent sat in the room and the position of the microphone relative to the voice talent's mouth. During post-production, I had created presets and documented all processes used and was sure to include the order in which all processes were performed. Many of the *PBRII* features had phrases that were stitched together, using cues that were recorded a year apart, and they sounded great.

7.3 Concatenation Schemes

While the focus of this article is on the audio side of development, it is necessary to have some understanding of the concatenation "structures" that are used to integrate content into a product. For *PBR*, I needed a way to easily communicate my concatenation schemes to the programmers on the project. Here's a concatenation scheme that we used to integrate the Bull NAMES feature (described earlier in this article). This example defines structures for file names, function, and stitching position for all Bull NAME cues, and includes several models using both variable file names and instances of actual content for specific file names.

File naming scheme for Bull NAMES: BNAME?nn.WAV where:

BNAME = "prefix" for all classes of bull names

? = letter representing class of bull name—there are 6 classes of bull names ... they are:

A = [*bull name*] STITCHES IN FRONT (beginning of cue)
B = ["NOW" + *bull name*] STITCHES IN FRONT (beginning of cue)
C = [*bull name*] STITCHES IN BACK (end of cue)
D = ["ON" + *bull name*] STITCHES IN BACK (end of cue)
E = ["FOR" + *bull name*] STITCHES IN BACK (end of cue)
F = ["BY" + *bull name*] STITCHES IN BACK (end of cue)

nn = 2-digit integer number that specifies individual bull names ... they are:

01 - Moody Blues	11 - Tuff E Nuff
02 - Promised Land	12 - Tropical Depression
03 - Palace Station	13 - Clayton's Pet
04 - Baby Face	14 - Scat Cat
05 - Hollywood	15 - Outlaw Willie
06 - Panhandle Slim	16 - High Rise
07 - Red Wolf	17 - Jim Jam
08 - Sports Machine	18 - Nitro
09 - Locomotive Breath	19 - Rampage
10 - Sky King	20 - Hard Copy

Here are some examples:

File name	Contents	
BnameE14	"for Scat Cat"	["FOR" + *bull name*] STITCHES IN BACK (end of cue)
BnameA06	"Panhandle Slim"	[*bull name*] STITCHES IN FRONT (beginning of cue)
BnameF18	"by Nitro"	["BY" + *bull name*] STITCHES IN BACK (end of cue)

BULL STITCHING CUES and STITCHING SCHEMES:

Here the files named BST??_?? contain Bull Stitching cues identified by function and iteration.

File name	Function of contents
	(multiple cues for each stitch feature)
BST01_03	BULL BUCKS RIDER OFF: STITCHES in BACK of *BnameA??* cues MODEL: *BnameA?? + BST01_?? =* *[bull name] "bucks him off"* *BnameA03 + BST01_02 =* *"Palace Station bucks him off"*
BST02_01	RIDER GETS BUCKED OFF: STITCHES in FRONT of *BnameF??* cues MODEL: *BST02_01 + BnameF?? =* *"He gets bucked off" [by bull name]* *BST02_01 + BnameF07 =* *"He gets bucked off by Red Wolf"*
BST03_02	RIDER GETS HURT: STITCHES in FRONT of *BnameF??* cues MODEL: *BST03_?? + BnameF?? =* *"He gets beat up" [by bull name]* *BST03_02 + BnameF14 =* *"He gets beat up by Scat Cat"*

This approach worked well for my programmer colleague, who was pleased that we didn't resort to earlier (and inferior) documentation methods for feature and integration schemes.

8 Authoring and Busting

8.1 Processing Issues and Considerations

When authoring digital audio, always use the best resolution possible, especially when applying any kind of process to your source material. Using better/higher resolution file formats helps to reduce unwanted side effects of processing, such as interpolation distortion, the built-in sizzle of 8-bit audio, and/or aliasing. It is especially important to observe this practice when delivering content at lower resolutions (lower resolution material suffers more from processing degradation than higher resolution material that is processed then down-sampled).

Although there are various computers, operating systems, sound cards, audio editors, and related tools that could successfully accomplish the desired authoring and processing tasks discussed in this article, the system configuration and tools I used to develop *Professional Bull Rider* included: Intel-based PC running Microsoft Windows, Digidesign Audiomedia III soundcard, Syntrillium Software Cool Edit Pro audio editor, Sonic Foundry Sound Forge audio editor, Waves Native Bundle plug-ins.

When we recorded the content for *PBR*, some analog compression was used to keep the signal level up and to keep peak levels down a little. When attempting to concatenate content that may have been recorded months apart, it is necessary to "normalize" the content so that the apparent loudness and dynamics are fairly equal from segment to segment. After "evaluating" the raw audio files, and trying a few test processes, I used the compressor/limiter plug-in of my audio editor to reduce the dynamic range and raise the level of the quiet parts while setting a "brick-wall" limit on the overall signal to -1 db below maximum amplitude. The raw files were authored and processed at 44.1 kHz, with the knowledge that the content would be downsampled to 22 kHz. So, I used the EQ plug-in to produce a slight increase in frequencies over 7 kHz to compensate for the reduced frequency response provided by the lower sample rate.

8.2 Documenting Settings

During post-production, create presets and document all processes used and be sure to include the order in which all processes were performed, as mentioned earlier in Section 7.2. This will greatly improve your ability to create new audio that matches the sometimes subtle qualities of existing content at a later date.

9 Editing and Proofing

9.1 Out of Product Concatenation Testing and Tuning

By using the macro and scripting features in my audio editor, I could test concatenated announcer features and audition them quickly, thereby providing the means to determine what features worked (or didn't work), and what kind of "tweakage" would be possible to improve acceptable features. When editing audio to be stitched, sometimes it's desirable to add a few milliseconds of silence (breath pause) to the stitch end(s) of your files to fine tune the timing of certain cues. Since the stitching integration for *PBR* produced almost no latency, I had to add these breath pauses to several cues because the chunks being stitched together sounded rushed.

9.2 Workaround Strategies and Extraordinary Rescue Measures: "A Fish Story about Golf"

When planning and scripting features, sometimes a feature gets overlooked, or just doesn't sound right once it's integrated into the product, and recalling the voice talent for a pick-up recording is not an option. It then becomes necessary to come up with a strategy to work around the problem. Some possible scenarios might include:

- Plan, script, record, and produce extra features for your product—some features work and sound better than others; use the features that sound best! Accountants and schedulers don't like this approach, but I like to consider it insurance—time and money well spent, especially when a sequel is possible.

- Find another (existing) cue to use as a substitute. More repetitive, but if you really, really need the feature, this is an easy way to add a feature by reusing existing content.

- Search the script and content for pieces of phrases that could be used to build a substitute feature—the "fishing expedition."

The "fishing expedition" can be a very time intensive (and moderately unrewarding) approach to rescuing features; however, both the time and reward factors can be greatly improved if the person(s) on the rescue mission are intimately familiar with fishing expeditions and the material in hand—i.e., they wrote the script, directed the talent in the recording sessions, and authored and post-produced all of the content.

During the development of *Sierra Sports PGA Championship Golf 2000,* I was asked to assess the degree of difficulty required to "fix" a feature desired for the play-by-play announcer—*say the number of yards from the location of the player's ball to the flag (within 5 yards).* It started to look like I was going on a "fishing expedition"; and, except for a two-page stitching "guide" that I had emailed to the developer two years earlier, it was my first "contact" with this voice content. Also, I was not going to get any filename or script documentation. It turns out I'd be going on a "*blind* fishing expedition." Yikes!

I played the game to listen to the existing integration and it sounded great to me. The play-by-play and color announcer voices that the developer selected were real pro golf broadcast announcers, which contributed plenty to the convincing sound of this product. Since I had no file name or script documentation, and to get some sense for the range and depth of features, I fired up my audio editor and listened to the total voice audio content as individual .WAV files.

The developer sent me the materials that they had produced for the desired *yardage to the flag* feature integration for evaluation. They had scripted and recorded a set of cues intended to be integrated using two stitches to concatenate three audio chunks (BEGINNING + YARDAGE + ENDING)—a BEGINNING chunk, stitched to a YARDAGE chunk, stitched to an ENDING chunk, which would in combination form a desired yardage cue. The BEGINNING and ENDING chunks were designed to provide variety to the cues, while giving the YARDAGE information (which remains constant for any given yardage).

Here are some examples of the materials the developer had produced that show the intended concatenation scheme:

BEGINNING	+	YARDAGE	+	ENDING
It looks like it's		*about* 315 yards		to the pin.
It's going to be		*about* 250 yards		to the hole.
He's got		*about* 175 yards		to the flag.

The big problem was that the content had been scripted (and produced) using a soft phoneme stitch scheme between the BEGINNING and YARDAGE chunks. They had planned to stitch in front of the letter "A" in the word "ABOUT," which would severely limit the potential for convincing sounding stitches – all of the YARDAGE chunks began with the word "ABOUT," (more on the word "ABOUT" just ahead).

Another problem was that the "pitch," "tenor," and "volume" of the BEGINNING chunks didn't match audio and performance quality very well with the YARDAGE chunks ... strikes 2, 3, and 4!

At this point, I wasn't very optimistic about the successful rescue of this feature based on "fixing" the content the developer sent. However, I decided to go through and listen to all of the content again (a few thousand cues) in an attempt to find BEGINNING chunk candidates that might be successfully stitched with the YARDAGE chunks.

There were scattered possibilities throughout the content; however, the rescue solution showed up in a group of files all related to PUTTING. The developer had existing play-by-play announcer cues for a "*footage to the flag*" feature. All of the "*footage to the flag*" cues were scripted and produced as complete phrases—NO STITCHING was used for this feature.

Several of these cues began their phrase such that the word "ABOUT" occurred right before the "*footage to the flag*" number. Eureka! I had found a possible rescue. Because the "*footage to the flag*" cues were performed the same way I would have scripted them for making stitching cues (the word "ABOUT" ends with a hard "T" plosive), I was able to excerpt 13 BEGINNING chunks from the PUTTING cues, of which there were 6 different phrases, some with multiple variations of "pitch," "tenor," and "volume" for each phrase.

Here are the BEGINNING chunks I used to build the revised YARDAGE cues.

He's got about	(+ YARDAGE)
It's about	(+ YARDAGE)
It's gotta go about	(+ YARDAGE)
Looks close to about	(+ YARDAGE)
Looks like about	(+ YARDAGE)
This one's about	(+ YARDAGE)

So, I went through the 100+ YARDAGE cues and manually removed the "ABOUT" from the front of each chunk. Using the scripting feature of my audio editor, I then stitched together some test cues from the BEGINNING chunks (excerpted from the PUTTING feature), and the revised YARDAGE chunks. The results of this test gave me a great deal of optimism for the rescue of this feature, but revealed limited success for producing convincing cues by stitching the BEGINNING chunks to the YARDAGE chunks *from software during game play.*

I decided to "manually" stitch a BEGINNING chunk to each YARDAGE chunk, thereby allowing this feature to be integrated with only one stitch per cue—YARDAGE + ENDING. By this time, I had established that the ENDING chunks prepared for this feature would work convincingly; so, when the revised YARDAGE chunks stitched together with the ENDING chunks, they sounded acceptable and would work fine for our purposes.

Finally, I set up another script in my audio editor to manually stitch every BEGINNING chunk with each individual YARDAGE chunk. I listened to the resulting cues, picked the best sounding cue (of 13 versions), and when necessary, I "tweaked" pitches and volumes by hand for all 100+ YARDAGE cues.

I was able to produce a complete set of convincing sounding "*yardage to flag*" cues for the desired announcer feature, albeit, with less randomization than if the cues were stitched in software. However, there's a built-in variety factor, since the "manually" stitched BEGINNING and YARDAGE chunks were chosen based on the best-sounding of 13 candidates for each cue. Also, the probability was quite low that the player would be consistently hitting from the same distance, thereby reducing the likelihood of hearing the same cue repeated very often.

A successful rescue mission accomplished!

9.3 Kiss-Off

Executing a successful voice concatenation project is a complex undertaking that requires a great deal of careful planning and preparation. Deciding what features are desirable and feasible, obtaining useful reference material, designing a voice script, following appropriate recording engineering practices, establishing standard authoring and post-production processes, and documenting your work in progress are all issues that must be observed to keep a project "on track." Most importantly, never quit listening—trust your ears; they are your most valuable asset.

Annotated Bibliography

The information given here is derived from empirical observations and discoveries that I have made during the development of numerous products (that use voice concatenation) and from dialogs and discussions I had in 1996 with Rob Bailey at *Electronic Arts* (thanks, Rob). No other references or resources were used in the development of this article.

Synthesizing Speech for Communication Devices

Debra Yarrington

1 Introduction

While originally envisioned as having limitless uses, today, synthetic speech has two primary applications: Synthetic speech is used in telephony, and synthetic speech is used in devices for people with disabilities. While many issues overlap for both uses of synthetic speech, synthesis for the telephone industry centers on developing rules for name pronunciation and creating a system that allows for synthesis of all phonemes in all languages. The use of synthetic speech for people with disabilities tends to serve two purposes: to serve as a "read-aloud" and alerting mechanism for people who have difficulty reading (e.g., people with visual impairments), and to serve as a "voice" for people who have difficulty communicating vocally. Those who use synthetic speech as a read-aloud mechanism are concerned with being able to control the speed of voice output, being able to stop and start instantly, and related controls such as scanning text and systematically representing acoustically systems such as web pages, user interfaces, etc. Those who use synthetic speech as a voice, on the other hand, are concerned primarily with intelligibility, but also with naturalness, the ability to emote, and voice characteristics that are age, gender, and regionally appropriate and, if possible, unique to the individual. This article will focus on synthetic speech used in communication devices by individuals who have difficulty communicating vocally.

2 Communication Devices

To use synthetic speech as a substitute for vocal communication, users must first enter what they want to say into a communication device. Most commonly, this is done using a typical keyboard, an enlarged keyboard, a joystick, or a track ball. However, input can also be entered using a touch screen with graphical images, a scanning system in which images, words, or letters are scanned, or an eye-gaze system that can also be used with graphical images, words, or letters. A simple on-off switch can be used with scanning systems to select items as they are scanned. A two-switch system can also be used to input Morse code (one for dashes and one for dots). Once the desired text has been entered, it must be converted to speech output. The simplest conversion system is one in which the entered text or keystrokes directly specifies a set of prerecorded words and phrases that have been stored in the communication device. The input triggers playback of one of these prerecorded phrases, whose quality and naturalness are limited only by the recording and playback mechanism in the communication device. For communication devices used by people who need only a limited vocabulary, this is an adequate speech output solution. However, for devices in which storage space is limited and in which unlimited speech or new and unique phrases should be an option, direct playback is not feasible. Even if a person had the tenacity to record and a device had space to store all possible words, appending individually recorded words to create phrases and sentences does not result in acceptable speech. (See Utterback's article, "Voice Concatenation: A Stitch in Time Saves Nine" (page 123), describing the challenges of using speech concatenation in computer games.) In natural speech, talkers will emphasize words that are important for the listener to attend to, and deemphasize words that are less important, either syntactically or semantically. Talkers will also indicate the ends of phrases and sentences using cues such as phoneme and syllable duration changes, and pitch changes. Such cues are lost when words are recorded in isolation. Words that should be emphasized may not be, or, more likely, words that should be de-emphasized will be emphasized. Prosodic contours (e.g., pitch contours, amplitude changes, and phoneme and syllable duration variations) will be choppy and disjointed. The resulting speech will be very unnatural. Also new words, either a new proper name or a newly invented word in a language, will not be available. For devices that may be required to output new and unique utterances, speech must be synthesized.

3 Methods of Synthesizing Speech

There are three basic approaches to synthesizing unlimited speech: articulatory synthesis, formant synthesis, and concatenative synthesis. All three approaches can be used in conjunction with one another, so the categories are not mutually exclusive. However, for descriptive purposes, it is simplest to separate the three approaches (for a very thorough overview of all aspects of speech synthesis, see [4]).

4 Articulatory Synthesis

The first approach is known as articulatory synthesis. Speech that is synthesized using rules that model the vocal tract falls under this category (see Bunnell's article, "Introduction to Speech Acoustics" (page 159), for a more in-depth explanation of the vocal tract). Using this method, there is a source function that models the sound source (created in humans from vocal fold vibration plus air from lungs and friction created by air passing through constrictions within the vocal tract) and an algorithm that models the acoustics of the vocal tract, treating it as a tube that can be altered in shape by the action of articulators such as the lips, jaw, and tongue. For every vocal gesture, a sequence of vocal tract shapes is identified. These can be determined using imaging techniques such as x-rays, ultrasound, magnetic sensing devices, or, more recently, MRI. Each vocal tract shape is then modeled in a piecewise manner as a series of short cylinders of different diameter that approximate the cross sectional area function of the vocal tract from glottis to lips. The acoustics of the vocal tract are then estimated numerically from the tube approximation of the vocal tract.

Currently, methods for estimating the area functions have taken two different directions. In one case, the motion of the articulators is modeled, and the area functions of the vocal tract are estimated from the model. This is how area functions are estimated for the articulatory synthesizer being developed by Haskins Laboratory (a nonprofit speech research laboratory located in Connecticut). In the other, the area functions are modeled directly with no reliance upon articulator position. This is the approach used in the articulatory synthesizer being developed by Bell Labs (a research and development laboratory focusing on telecommunications).

Articulatory synthesizers have the ability to include a noise source anywhere that constriction might occur along the vocal tract (e.g., for obstruents such as "s," "f," "k," "b," etc.), and may also have a side branch to model the nasal cavity. In theory, this system should be able to model the transitions between phonemes more naturally than other types of rule-based synthesizers because it focuses on articulator movements rather than simply smoothing the transitions between target values identified at particular locations within a phoneme. However, at this point, the rules for controlling the articulators are not understood well enough to be practical for real-time synthesis and, unless the parameters are identified correctly and in great detail, the resulting speech is very unnatural sounding if not unintelligible. In the future, acoustic synthesis may be used in communication devices, but at present, it is only used as a research tool.

5 Formant Synthesis

The approach most commonly used in communication devices today is rule-based, or formant synthesis. When we speak, our vocal folds vibrate. We also contract and relax the tongue, lips, jaw, and velum, etc. to shape the vocal tract. The vocal fold vibrations are resonated and dampened along the vocal tract depending on its shape. Formants are spectral prominences due to vocal tract resonations at the frequency locations of the prominences. Formant bandwidths can be narrow, meaning that the spectral prominence occurred over a narrow frequency range, or the bandwidths can be wide because the spectral prominence occurred over a wide range of frequencies. In speech, most formant bandwidths tend to be around 100 Hz. Higher frequency formants tend to have wider bandwidths, and the formant bandwidths in women's speech tend to be wider. Both the frequency and the bandwidth of formants are the results of the position of articulators. In speech, there can be many formants, but the ones most important to the perception of speech tend to be the three formants with the lowest frequencies, known as F1, F2, and F3, whereas F4 and F5 play more of a role in naturalness and less of a role in intelligibility.

For formant synthesis, text is converted to phonemes. Each phoneme, a set of target values, is defined in a look-up table. Target values include formant frequencies, formant bandwidths, amplitudes, characteristics of the source function, and other parameters needed for synthesis. A few target locations over the duration of each phoneme are normally defined, and parameter values for speech between the target locations are determined by an interpolation algorithm that estimates smooth trajectories for each synthesis parameter in a succession of discrete time frames (typically one frame every 10 ms). These target values are used to control a source function and a set of resonators. The source function is the sound source, which is specified by certain target values (e.g., voicing/noise ratio), and its output activates the resonators.

The formant resonators in rule-based synthesis can either be used in parallel (parallel formant synthesis) or serially (cascade formant synthesis). With parallel formant synthesis, the source function excites the resonators simultaneously and the output of the resonators is summed. Parallel formant synthesis usually has four formant resonators. For each formant, frequency and amplitude are calculated. The bandwidths of each formant are often fixed, although some systems do allow the bandwidths to vary. Parallel formant synthesizers are easier to control than cascade formant synthesizers—it is easier to adjust the output of the synthesizer to match that of natural speech. Parallel synthesizers can even mimic singing. Parallel formant synthesizers have an extra resonator that allows them to model frequencies below the fundamental frequency (F0) to aid in modeling nasals or nasalized phonemes fairly accurately. The nasal cavity adds a side channel to the vocal tract. The nasal cavity also has the effect of damping the acoustic spectrum. This damping effect is achieved by adding one or more zeros (antiresonators) to the system. Because parallel synthesizers allow individual control of the amplitudes of each resonator, nasals are more easily synthesized with a parallel synthesizer. The most notable and extensive parallel formant synthesizer was developed by John Holmes. By carefully adjusting formant frequencies, amplitudes, source parameters, and other parameters, Holmes's synthesizer is able to match recordings of natural speech very closely [3]. However, pure rule-based synthesis is less well developed for parallel synthesizers than it is for cascade formant synthesizers.

Cascade formant synthesis also consists of a source function and a series of resonators. Beginning with the formant with the highest frequency (typically the fifth highest, or F5), the output of successive formant filters is used to excite the next formant filter. As with parallel formant synthesizers, cascade formant synthesizers may use five or more formants, but the frequencies of formants above the third are generally fixed at talker-specific values. Formant amplitudes are not explicitly controlled in cascade synthesizers. Instead, formant amplitudes vary as a function of formant bandwidth, formant frequency, and the proximity of formants to one another. Because of the complex interactions between formant frequencies and bandwidths in determining formant amplitudes, it is more difficult to mimic specific natural utterances with cascade synthesizers than with parallel synthesizers. However, for rule-based synthesis, cascade synthesizers are more easily controlled because amplitude relationships among formants tend to automatically simulate those of natural speech. The most well-known version of a cascade synthesizer is DECTalk, which is a descendent of MITalk and its predecessor Klattalk, developed by Dennis Klatt. (For more information on MITalk's rule system, see [1].) DECTalk is a rule-based system in which target values are automatically computed via a complex set of rules that predict formant frequencies, bandwidths, source amplitudes, phoneme durations, pitch values, etc. These target values are then converted to synthetic speech using the DECTalk cascade formant synthesizer. DECTalk uses a parallel synthesizer in conjunction with the cascade synthesizer to model fricatives because more information is in the higher frequencies for fricatives, and control of the amplitudes of higher frequencies is more easily achieved with a parallel branch in the synthesizer.

For both types of formant synthesizers, the sound source can be a periodic pulse for voiced speech, a noise source for unvoiced speech, or a combination of both for voiced fricatives. Currently, source models have been adopted that allow the voice source to be modified in terms of the proportion of time the vocal cords are open within each pitch period, the abruptness with which the vocal cords close, the breathiness of the signal, and so forth. Older source models provided less control over the sound source, but control over the properties of the source function is very important in producing natural sounding synthetic speech.

The rules for governing the formant synthesizer are complex and fairly talker-specific. In order to create new and unique voices, a new set of rules must be developed manually—there is currently no way to generate these rules automatically. The creation of female voices also raises new issues. Female voices are not simply higher-pitched male voices. Formant values, harmonic spectrum differences, breathiness differences, and even different speaking strategies distinguish female voices from male voices. The intelligibility of rule-based synthesizers can be very high, however. Studies have found that the intelligibility of synthetic speech generated using the best rule-based systems approaches that of natural speech in meaningful sentences [5]. Thus, formant synthesizers are well suited for devices in which intelligibility is the most important factor. For instance, for reading devices for people with visual impairments, rule-based systems are ideal because intelligibility is the most crucial factor, as well as the ability to speed up the system to rates much greater than those of natural speech. Because of its high intelligibility, a formant synthesizer (i.e., DECTalk) is used most frequently with communication devices as well.

6 Concatenative Synthesis

A third type of synthesis is known as concatenative synthesis. Rather than use rules to create synthetic speech that mimics natural speech, concatenative speech appends units of recorded speech to synthesize new words and phrases. The smallest logical unit of speech that could be recorded, stored, and concatenated to create unlimited synthetic speech are phonemes. There are about 40 phonemes in American English (see the chart of American English phonemes in the appendix to this article). However, when we speak, we tend to move our articulators in preparation for upcoming sounds, and we don't always move our articulators out of position immediately when we finish a sound. The effect this has on the acoustic properties of a particular phoneme within speech is known as coarticulation. We also consistently produce phonemes differently in different contexts. For instance, the "t" in "torch" is pronounced differently than the "t" in "cat." These different pronunciations of the same phoneme are known as allophones—a set of sounds that are similar, but occur in different contexts and, when substituted for one another, don't change the meaning of a word. Taking coarticulation effects on phonemes and including allophones, there are about 50 phoneme/allophones in American English, still quite a manageable size to record and store for synthesis. However, when stored phonemes/allophones are simply pasted together, the discontinuity in their acoustic properties (e.g., formant values, bandwidths of the formants, etc.) at the boundary between the two sounds is very jarring and unnatural, and may make the speech unintelligible.

A solution to the problem of jarring concatenation points is to record and store the transitions between phonemes, rather than the phonemes themselves. Theoretically, every example of a phoneme will have a location (typically its center) where its acoustic properties will be most similar to those of other examples of that phoneme. Thus, appending speech segments that run from the center of one phoneme to the center of an adjacent phoneme should result in better acoustic boundary matches and less jarring speech. This idea was first proposed by Wang and Peterson [9]. Based on the technology available to them, they spliced together pieces of analog magnetic tape and played the results back. Segments were cut from a portion of speech beginning at the middle of one phoneme and ending at the middle of the subsequent phoneme. These units are known as diphones. With only about 40 phonemes, and with not every possible phoneme combination existing in the English language, it is possible to synthesize most English words with only about 1,200 diphones. The resulting speech has the voice qualities of the person recorded, without requiring complex rules to model the individual's voice. Unfortunately, continuous speech is more than just a set of transitions. Coarticulation effects extend farther than just to adjacent phonemes. The acoustic properties of individual phonemes are also affected by prosodic factors such as whether the phoneme occurs in a stressed or unstressed syllable, its location in a phrase, whether it is in a position of focus, etc. As a result, the acoustic properties of phoneme centers are not necessarily consistent. When speech units are concatenated, these inconsistencies lead to acoustic discontinuities that can result in unnatural glitches in the speech, possibly even rendering the synthetic speech unintelligible.

There are a few different approaches to eliminating boundary discontinuities in concatenative synthesis. One approach involves storing speech in a parameterized form rather than as a waveform. A commonly used method of parameterization is Linear Predictive Coding (LPC). LPC analysis is based on the assumption that, to a certain extent, speech is redundant and predictable. It estimates the parameters of a filter to model the predictable information in the speech signal. The unpredictable information emerges as a residual signal by inverse filtering the speech with the LPC filter. The speech signal can be reconstructed by using the residual signal to excite the filter, resulting in speech that is virtually identical to the original signal. Because one aspect of speech that is unpredictable is its pitch, pitch information is largely contained within the residual signal. Thus, if we wanted to alter the pitch of an utterance, we could discard the residual signal and replace it with an approximation consisting of one or more pulses that represent the pitch contour of the utterance and some aspects of the residual signal. When the LPC filter is excited with this pulse residual signal, the resulting synthetic speech is less natural sounding. Whether residual or pulse excitation is used for LPC in concatenative synthesis, the boundary discontinuities can be reduced by smoothing the boundary coefficients before the waveform is reconstructed. Differences in pitch can be accommodated by altering the residual signal. However, with these alterations, the resulting speech looses some of its naturalness and possibly intelligibility as well.

Another approach to smoothing the boundaries in concatenative synthesis (although it applies only to pitch discontinuities) is to use the Pitch-

Synchronous Overlap-Add (PSOLA) technique. PSOLA also makes it possible to manipulate the pitch of speech throughout a synthesized sentence, not just at boundaries. (See Bunnell's article, "Pitch Modification of Speech Using PSOLA" (page 187), for more details on this technique).

A simpler (at least in theory) approach to reducing the effects of acoustical and prosodic mismatches at appended boundary locations is to reduce the number of boundaries. Regardless of how this is accomplished, if unlimited synthetic speech is the goal, the amount of stored speech will be larger than that of diphone speech. This leads to the question of what speech units should be used that do not result in huge amounts of stored speech. One type of unit proposed is the demisyllable. Based on the assumption that coarticulation effects are less likely to extend across syllable boundaries, the demisyllables extend either from the beginning of a syllable to the center of the syllable nucleus (usually a vowel), or from the center of the syllable nucleus to the end of the syllable. One result of this is that consonant clusters (e.g., "spl," "tr," etc.) are kept together within demisyllable units [2]. The resulting speech has fewer boundaries, and the boundaries don't occur within consonant clusters, thus reducing the acoustic mismatches caused by coarticulation. More recently, an approach that has become popular is to record, label, and store large databases of speech. Then, when speech is synthesized, the database is searched for acoustic units that most closely resemble the desired speech with the fewest boundary mismatches. This approach was first proposed by ATR in Japan [8]. Large corpora of speech are recorded, and then labeled for phoneme boundaries, and in some cases, prosodic features such as stress, pitch, and pitch accents. During synthesis, a search algorithm is used to find units of speech that match the desired speech most closely. The unit choice is weighted by a cost function that increases as the acoustical mismatches at boundaries increases. Thus, the search is more likely, but not guaranteed, to find the longest unit of speech in the database. If the speech to be incorporated into the database is chosen wisely, words and phrases that are used most frequently will be incorporated into the database and the resulting synthesis will be comparable to that of recorded speech. The quality of the synthesized speech resulting from the database is dependent on what speech is stored in the database, on how well the speech is labeled for storage, and on the algorithm that chooses the speech units for concatenation. While this approach results in very natural sounding synthetic speech, recording large databases (usually hours) of speech may prove prohibitive for people with limited attention spans (e.g., children) or weak voices (e.g., people with Amyotropic Lateral Sclerosis, a.k.a. Lou Gehrig's Disease or

ALS). In order to transfer the benefits of this technology to people with communication difficulties, recording limitations must be taken into consideration. One way of limiting recording requirements while retaining the quality of large recorded databases is to combine database synthesis with diphone synthesis [10]. By recording the most common words and phrases and storing them in a database with a complete set of diphones recorded by the same person, most common words and phrases will have the quality of recorded speech. Less common and novel utterances will have the quality of diphone synthesis, but will be in the same "voice" as the more common words. Recording requirements are greater than those for diphone synthesis, but significantly less than that of database speech. Issues to be considered with this combined approach are the content of the database, the amount of recording versus the quality of the resulting synthesized speech, and the acceptability by users of the quality of completely novel utterances (e.g., utterances created almost completely with diphones as the speech units).

Currently, concatenative speech synthesis is not used in augmentative and alternative communication devices. However, it holds potential for being a very desirable method for communication devices. Concatenative synthesis reproduces the voice recorded and stored in the database used for synthesis. The production of new voices is not hindered by complex rules used to recreate vocal features that make each voice unique. Accents and dialects are automatically captured in the stored speech. The ability to create unique age, gender, and regionally appropriate synthetic voices makes this method very appropriate for users of communication devices.

7 Conclusion

For people who use synthetic speech as their personal voice, synthetic speech is invaluable. However, there are still issues that need to be addressed more thoroughly. For instance, the prosody in synthetic speech still needs work to be considered natural. Individual variability is not sufficiently captured. Rules governing prosody are largely based on formal reading and tend to sound formal and monotonous rather than conversational. Also, there is really very little work being done to capture emotions in speech. What little work has been done has focused on basic emotions like anger, sadness, happiness, fear, etc. [6] Methods of conveying more complex information like sarcasm, disbelief, surprise, etc. have barely been considered. For people using communication devices, these emotive abilities are highly desirable.

Appendix A: Phoneme Chart

Table 1 lists 40 of the English phonemes for the *General American* (GenAm) English dialect. Here, we have only reproduced the phonemes for a single dialect of English; other possibilities exist, including *Received Pronounciation* (RP, also known as the prestige British accent) and *Australian English* (AuE). Fully representing the entire English phoneme alphabet would be considerably more complex, and unfortunately beyond the scope of this article. Among speakers of General American English, the pronunciation of vowels varies considerably; thus the "same" word will be represented by different phonemes in different varieties of GenAm English. For example, in East Coast GenAm English, the words "cot" and "caught" will be /kɒt/ and /kɔt/, but in West Coast GenAm English, they will both be /kɑt/.

A more complete table can be found in [1,2], and an in-depth discussion of phonemes and dialects can be found in [3].

Acknowledgments Kim Silverman and Caroline Henton assisted with assembling and correcting this table.

Phoneme	Description	Example
	Vowels	
ɑ	low back vowel	ma, father
æ	low front vowel	cat, lad, ran
ʌ	central vowel	but, run, enough
ɔ	mid back vowel	law, caught
ɒ	rounded back vowel	cot[1]
ɛ	mix front vowel	bet, bed
ɪ	front high vowel	it, city
i	front high vowel	eat, see
o	mix back vowel	so, no
ʊ	back high vowel	soot, put
u	back high vowel	suit, soon, through
ə	schwa	about
	Diphthongs	
eɪ	diphthong	bay, day
aɪ	diphthong	pie
aʊ	diphthong	cow
ɔɪ	diphthong	boy

Table 1. Phonemes for General American English and their IPA symbols, with some examples taken from [2].

Phoneme	Description	Example
Consonants		
b	voiced bilabial plosive	boo
p	voiceless bilabial plosive	pie
d	voiced alveolar plosive	do
t	voiceless avelolar plosive	tie
g	voiced velar plosive	goo
k	voiceless velar plosive	key
h	voiceless glottal fricative	he
v	voiced labiodental fricative	very
f	voiceless labiodental fricative	foo
ð	voiced dental fricative	this
θ	voiceless dental fricative	think
ʒ	voiced postalveolar fricative	mirage
ʃ	voiceless postalveolar fricative	shoe
z	voiced alveolar fricative	zoo
s	voiceless alveolar fricative	sue
ʤ	voiced alveopalatal affricate	joe
ʧ	voiceless alveopalatal affricate	chew
j	voiced palatal approximant	yo
w	voiced labiodental approximant	wary
l	alveolar lateral	leaf
ɹ	alveolar approximant	reef
m	voiced bilabial nasal	moo
n	voiced alveolar nasal	new
ŋ	voiced velar nasal	sing

Table 1. *cont.*

Annotated Bibliography

[1] J. M. Allen, S. Hunnicutt, and D. Klatt. *From Text to Speech: The MITalk System.* Cambridge, England: Cambridge University Press, 1987.

[2] H. Dettweiler and W. Hess. "Concatenation Rules for Demisyllable Speech Synthesis." *Acustica* 57 (1985), 268–283.

[3] J. N. Holmes. *Speech Synthesis and Recognition.* Berkshire, England: Van Nostrand Reinhold (UK) Co. Ltd., 1988.

[4] The International Phonetic Alphabet, 2005. http://www.arts.gla.ac.uk/IPA/ipa.html

The official guide for phonetic symbols and their meaning. The IPA is not specific to English, and there are many phonemes in the IPA that are not used in English.

[5] IPA chart for English, Last visited: October 17, 2006. http://en.wikipedia.org/wiki/English_phonemes

Wikipedia includes a more complete English phoneme chart, and they also list variations for British English and Australian English as well as General American English.

[6] D. Klatt. "Review of Text-to-Speech Conversion for English." *Journal of the Acoustical Society of America* 82:3 (1987), 737–793.

[7] P. Mirenda and D. Beukelman. "A Comparison of Speech Synthesis Intelligibility with Listeners from 3 Age Groups." *Augmentative and Alternative Communication* 3 (1987), 120–128.

[8] I. R. Murray, J. L. Arnott, and A. F. Newell. "HAMLET – Simulating Emotion in Synthetic Speech." *Proceedings of Speech '88, The 7th FASE Symposium*, pp. 1217–1223, 1988.

[9] I. R. Murray and J. L. Arnott. "Toward the Simulation of Emotion in Synthetic Speech: A Review of the Literature on Human Vocal Emotion." *J. Acoust. Soc. Am.* 93:2 (1993), 1097-1108.

[10] K. Takeda, K. Abe, and Y. Sagisaka. "On the Basic Scheme and Algorithms in Nonuniform Unit Speech Synthesis." In *Talking Machines: Theories, Models, and Designs*, edited by G. Bailly, C. Benoit, and T. R. Sawallis, pp. 93–105. Amsterdam: Elsevier Science, 1992.

[11] W. S-Y. Wang and G. E. Peterson. "Segment Inventory for Speech Synthesis." *Journal of the Acoustical Society of America* 30:8 (1958), 743–746.

[12] John C. Wells. *Accents of English.* Cambridge, UK: Cambridge University Press, 1982.

A classic text describing in great detail the various dialects of English from all over the world and their effect on phonetic representations of words.

[13] D. Yarrington, S. R. Hoskins, J. B. Polikoff, and H. T. Bunnell. "Personalized Synthetic Voices for AAC." In *Proceedings of ISAAC 2000—The Ninth Biennial Conference of the International Society for Augmentative and Alternative Communication*, pp. 700–702.

Speech Processing

Introduction to Speech Acoustics

Tim Bunnell

1 Introduction

An understanding of the physics of speech can provide much insight into how to synthesize, process, and recognize or decode the human voice. This anecdote attempts to provide a basic introduction to speech acoustics. It was written to complement and provide the background to get the most from my speech pitch and timescale articles, "Pitch Modification of Speech Using PSOLA" (page 187) and "Timescale Modification of Speech" (page 173), as well as Debra Yarrington's article "Synthesizing Speech for Communication Devices" (page 143). A list of references is provided at the end of this article for the reader to further explore our evolving understanding of the mechanisms of speech.

1.1 General

Speech, like the sound produced by many musical instruments, results from the interaction of a sound source with a resonator (see [9] for one of the most thorough early treatments; [20] provides the most in-depth recent treatment; [16] covers much of this area as well, in a way that is more accessible to nonengineers). For speech, there are fundamentally two sound sources: *frication*, the broadband turbulent noise source we use in sounds like /s/ and /f/[1], and *phonation* or *voicing*, the periodic sound

[1]It is common to write symbols associated with speech sounds (phonemes) between forward slashes using a set of symbols called the International Phonetic Alphabet (IPA) where each symbol corresponds to only one speech sound. Many IPA symbols are also standard letters, but they do not necessarily sound like one would expect. For instance, while the first phoneme in the word *sat* is /s/, the symbol /a/ does not correspond

source that is characteristic of all vowels and many consonants. Frication is produced by forcing air through a constriction in the vocal tract, forming a narrow stream of air which strikes a baffle such as the teeth [19]. This, in turn, creates turbulence that we hear as the frication sound. The aperiodic sound produced by rushing air past partially adducted vocal cords is sometimes treated as a third type of sound source called *aspiration*, however, we will consider that to be a special case of frication.

The voicing source is produced by inducing rapid periodic vibration of the vocal cords located in the larynx [15]. If you've ever made a screeching sound with a balloon by blowing it up and then stretching the neck while letting the air back out, you've experienced the basic principles of phonation at work. The periodic opening and abrupt closure of the air passage produces a periodic sequence of negative pressure spikes which give rise to a buzzing sound. This sound has a fundamental frequency (F0) equal to the inverse of the pressure spike rate. Its spectrum is characterized by harmonics at integer multiples of the fundamental frequency. What we hear as voice pitch is the speech F0. We vary voice pitch over the course of an utterance to produce an intonation contour.

The spectral envelope of both frication and voicing is fairly diffuse and unstructured. For frication, the spectral envelop is quite broad and rolls off gradually above about 1600 Hz [20]. A typical voicing source has its highest amplitude at the fundamental frequency and rolls off at about 12 dB per octave for higher frequency harmonics [9].

Cavities in the vocal tract above or in front of (i.e., closer to the lips) the location of a sound source serve as resonating chambers that impose structure on the source spectrum. For voiced nonnasalized[2] sounds, where the source is located in the larynx, the entire vocal tract from the larynx to lips comprises the resonator. If the vocal tract were uniform in a cross sectional area—imagine a cardboard tube like the core of a toilet paper roll, but narrower—it would have evenly spaced resonances at frequencies determined by its length. For the average adult male, the vocal tract is about 17 cm long, leading to an expectation of resonances at 500 Hz, 1500 Hz, 2500 Hz, and so forth. For the neutral vowel /ə/ (the *a* sound in *about*), these are, in fact, approximately the resonances of an adult male vocal tract. For most other speech sounds, the vocal tract is not even

to the vowel sound in *sat*. The /a/ phoneme is the vowel sound in the word *Bob*. Benjamin Franklin tried to introduce a new spelling system for English in which, like the IPA, letters corresponded to sounds.

[2]A nasal or nasalized speech sound is one for which the velum at the back of the oral cavity is open, allowing the nasal passages to couple acoustically to the oral vocal tract. This complicates the resonant properties of the vocal tract.

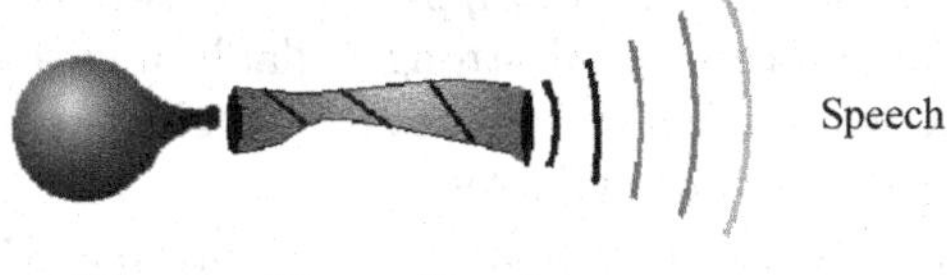

Figure 1. The source-filter model of speech production (simplified).

approximately uniform in a cross sectional area—imagine some kinks in that cardboard tube—and as a result, formant frequencies vary from those of a uniform tube. This accounts for the acoustic differences among the various speech sounds. This model of speech production is illustrated in Figure 1.

In continuous speech, talkers vary the characteristics of the sound source and the shape of the tube (their vocal tract) more or less continuously. The way that vocal tract shape, source location, and source type vary to produce fluent speech is a topic that is beyond the scope of this discussion. For the remainder of this section, we will concentrate specifically on the temporal and intonational structure of speech. First, we will examine these factors at the broad (e.g., phrase or sentence) level, and then look more closely at the fine structure of the speech signal for insight into how speech timing and intonation can be altered without adding unnecessary distortion to the speech.

1.2 Rhythm and Timing in Speech

Speech has rhythm; you can tap to it. Take any sentence and start repeating it over and over. With each repetition, start tapping a finger to the "beats" you perceive. You will find that there are certain syllables in the sentence that attract the down beats. These are called *strong* or *stressed* syllables. In English[3], strong syllables are thought of as being the first beat in rhythmic groups called feet that correspond roughly to musical measures, but each foot contains only one stressed syllable which is followed by all the unstressed syllables up to the next stressed sylla-

[3]It is important in discussing all aspects of speech, including prosody, to be clear about the language under discussion. For example, English is said to be "stress timed" indicating that the perception of rhythmic structure is related to the timing of its stressed syllables. Even though related to English, French is said to be "syllable timed" with each syllable being given more nearly equal weight. The rhythmic structure of Japanese is based on a unit called the mora and not the syllable. When Japanese talkers are asked to count "beats" in speech, they count mora, not syllables.

ble[4]. For instance, the word *Mississippi* contains two feet and each foot contains two syllables, the initial strong syllable and a following weak syllable, while the word *candidate* contains a single foot with one strong syllable followed by two weak syllables.

Even if one distorts the stress pattern of a word like *Mississippi* (e.g., produce it as four separate and equally strong syllables such as MISS-IS-SIPP-I), we are likely to understand the word because all the phonetic segments are the same no matter how we stress them. Since stress and rhythmic patterns are largely independent of phonetic segments and are defined over larger units than phonetic segments (i.e., syllables, words, and phrases), they are, along with intonation as we will discuss later, termed *suprasegmental* properties.

Suprasegmental properties, while distinct from segmental or phonetic properties, are nonetheless an integral part of spoken language. For instance, English contains some word pairs that are distinct *only* in their stress pattern. Consider the difference between the noun **con**vict (someone in jail) and the verb con**vict** (the act of assigning someone to a jail term). The first syllable of the noun is strong and its second syllable weak, but the stress pattern is reversed for the verb. A similar stress difference is found in English between compound nouns such as hotdog and greenhouse that are built from the combination of an adjective and noun, but refer to a specific class of objects. In compound nouns, the first syllable (corresponding to the adjective) receives stronger stress than the second syllable, but in true adjective-noun pairs (a hot dog or a green house), the noun receives stronger stress than the adjective, all other factors being neutral.

In phrases and longer length utterances, the rhythmic patterns of individual words are incorporated into an overall rhythm in which additional levels of syllable strength or emphasis appear. The additional levels of syllable strength generally serve the pragmatic function of emphasizing or focusing attention on specific words. Additionally, syllable duration is used to mark the locations of phrase boundaries. Syllables immediately before a phrase boundary are lengthened to mark the boundary (this is called *phrase-final lengthening*). Thus, suprasegmental properties provide

[4]One note of caution regarding the rhythmic structure of speech: Although rhythm entails regular timing in music, and although the timing of stressed syllables in speech often seems to be regular like musical beats, virtually every careful study of normal speech timing over the last 50 years has concluded that stressed syllables do not, in fact, fall at equal temporal intervals like musical beats. We seem to hear regularity that is not present. The basis for this disparity between our perception of speech and its physical structure remains unknown.

lexical information (regarding word meaning), syntactic information (regarding phrasal units), and semantic information (the point a talker is trying to make).

In acoustic terms, suprasegmental properties are conveyed by three factors primarily:

(1) Duration. Strong syllables are generally longer than weak syllables.

(2) Amplitude. Strong syllables are often louder than weak syllables.

(3) Pitch. Strong syllables can receive a form of intonational marking called a pitch accent ([10], [11], [3], [4]). We turn now to consideration of pitch, or fundamental frequency, and intonation in speech.

1.3 Fundamental Frequency and Voice Pitch[5]

Everyone is familiar with the general use of intonation in speech to signal, for example, the difference between a statement (falling pitch at the end of a sentence) and a question (rising pitch at the end of a sentence).[6] There are other familiar intonation contours as well, such as the *calling contour*, the high followed by low pitch your mother may have used to call you in for lunch when you were a child, or the *contradiction contour*, the sort of exaggerated questioning intonation one uses to express disbelief at a preposterous claim:

Pam: "I just saw Elvis buying tickets for the next Redskins game."
Joe: "There were tickets available for a ***Redskins*** game!?"

We tend to think of the intonation contour as being continuous over an utterance, but of course, it is really only defined over the voiced segments within the utterance. Perceptually, we seem to interpolate pitch over voiceless segments, giving us the illusion of a continuous contour. Additionally, it is not certain what information in the time-varying pitch

[5]Technically, fundamental frequency or F0, is a physically measurable property of sound, but pitch is a perceptual property that is correlated with F0. Not all measurable differences in F0 are perceptible as differences in pitch, and in some extreme cases, the normal relationship between F0 and pitch can break down completely. Nonetheless, we will tend to use the terms F0 and pitch more or less interchangeably in discussing intonation.

[6]As with the previous discussion of timing and rhythm, the use of pitch is language-specific. Some languages (Mandarin, for example) use tone to signal phonemic contrasts as well as prosodic contrasts. Even when languages use intonation only for prosodic effects, they evidence significant differences that nonnative listeners tend to hear as part of the "accent" associated with the language.

contour is most crucial for our perception of intonation. Some people have argued that changes in pitch are more important than the specific pitch values (e.g., [14]), while others argue that specific pitch targets are most important and that the pitch changes between targets are merely necessary transitions from one target to another (e.g., [17], [2], [1]). Thus, for example, one prominent account of intonation suggests that there are only two *tones* in English, a high tone and a low tone which can occur singly or in combinations throughout an utterance and which determine the overall intonation contour.

The high and low tones of English are not absolute pitch values. Obviously pitch targets of children, women, and men tend to be quite different. Further, each talker has a characteristic pitch range that they use and each talker's high and low tones seem to be relative in some way to that pitch range. Finally, the pitch associated with high and low tones varies depending on the location of the tone in the utterance: There is a general trend for pitch to decline over the course of an utterance (this is termed *pitch declination*) and for the range of pitch values to compress over the course of the utterance as well. As a result, high and low tones tend to be both higher in pitch and further apart at the beginning of an utterance compared to values seen at the end of an utterance [18].

While it is clear that tones are not associated with absolute F0 values, and while it is not certain that tones are even associated with specific *relative* F0 values, it is clear that maxima and minima in the F0 contour lend prominence to the syllables with which they are associated. Simply put, one way to make a word sound very important in the context of an utterance is to place an F0 peak on the primary stressed syllable of the word. High tones in particular commonly occur as pitch accents within utterances to add emphasis and mark specific words. Because tones or tone combinations are aligned relative to stressed syllables, there is a correlation between stress and pitch, with stressed syllables having on average higher pitch than unstressed syllables.

From this brief description, it may be clear that the suprasegmental features of speech—F0, amplitude, and syllable duration/timing—are important in helping listeners to parse the grammatical structure of speech and to interpret the speaker's meaning.

Suprasegmental features are also extremely important in conveying the impression of naturalness in speech. For these reasons, considerable effort has been exerted toward an understanding of how to manipulate suprasegmental structure in both natural and synthetic speech (e.g., [12], [6], [5], [7]). This effort has resulted in a number of very effective and computationally efficient methods of altering the timing and pitch of natural speech in ways that introduce minimal distortion. These methods exploit aspects of the temporal fine structure of speech. Consequently, to understand these methods, it is first important to understand the temporal fine-structure of the speech signal, a topic to which we now turn.

1.4 The Temporal Fine-Structure of Speech

As we mentioned previously, there are two primary modes of speech: voiced (corresponding to periods of phonation) and voiceless (corresponding to periods of silence and frication). Because there is no pitch associated with silence or frication, and because the temporal fine-structure of voiceless speech is either nonexistent (silence) or nearly random (frication), there is little to discuss regarding the temporal fine-structure of voiceless speech. Consequently, we will restrict discussion here to the structure of voiced speech. To do this, let us begin by considering the aerodynamic/acoustic events within the larynx that produce the voicing source signal.

Figure 2 plots both air flow (top curve) and air pressure (bottom curve) as might be measured in the larynx, just above the vocal cords. The signals shown in Figure 2 are synthetic illustrations of these functions, not signals actually measured from a speaker. Two cycles of glottal opening and closing, corresponding to periods when the vocal cords move apart and back together again are shown in the figure. The region labeled

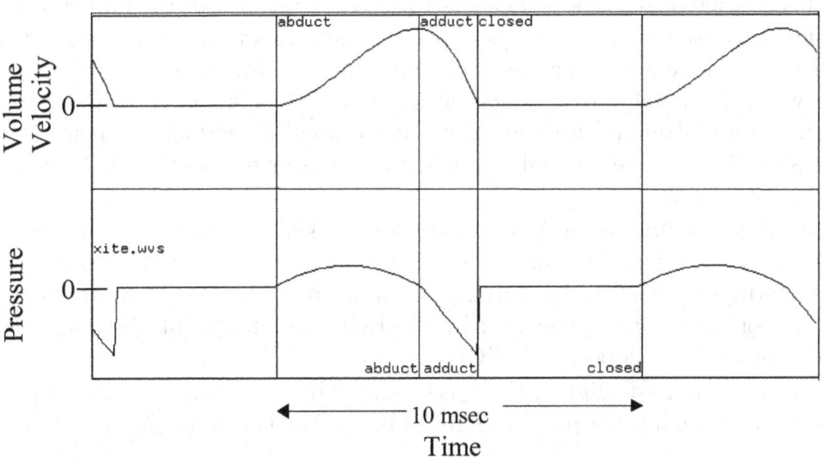

Figure 2.

"abduct" in the top curve corresponds to a period during which the vocal cords are spreading increasingly further apart. As they open, air flow rises from zero to some maximum flow (the scale here is arbitrary and irrelevant) at the moment when the vocal cords are furthest apart. In the region labeled "adduct," the vocal cords are in the process of closing and air flow is reducing. During the closed phase of a glottal cycle, no air flows because the vocal cords are closed completely, preventing air from escaping from the lungs. Notice that air flow rises more gradually during the abduction phase of the glottal cycle and drops more abruptly during the adduction phase. This is typical of most speakers and results from the fact that while air pressure differences between the lungs and supralaryngeal vocal tract account for the opening phase, both muscle tension and a Bournelli effect are responsible for the rate of closure.

The pressure waveform shown in the bottom of Figure 2 corresponds to the first derivative of the air flow. It is actually the pressure waveform which is the excitation function for the vocal tract. Note that there are fairly sharp negative pressure spikes associated with each closure. Each of these spikes excites the vocal tract, producing a single *pitch period.*[7] Of course, the rate at which pitch periods are produced corresponds to the fundamental frequency.

This is further illustrated in Figure 3, which shows a few pitch periods recorded from natural speech in the top curve and a corresponding EGG signal that was simultaneously recorded. The EGG is a device that measures the variation in impedance across the *glottis*, which is the opening between the vocal cords. When the vocal cords are closed, the impedance is low because there is complete tissue contact. When the vocal cords are open, the impedance increases substantially because there is an air gap between the vocal cords. Thus, peaks in the EGG signal correspond to periods of glottal closure and valleys correspond to periods of openness. This makes the EGG signal approximately the inverse of the air flow as shown in Figure 2.

The top signal displayed in Figure 3 is the speech waveform measured by a microphone near the lips. Comparing the EGG signal with the speech waveform, one can see that pitch periods begin at the time of most rapid vocal cord closure as estimated by the EGG signal (i.e., at the point of greatest positive slope in the EGG signal).

Unlike the EGG signal, the speech signal displays considerable structure within each pitch period. This additional structure is introduced by

[7]The pitch period is literally the period of the source function, that is, the duration of each cycle in the source function.

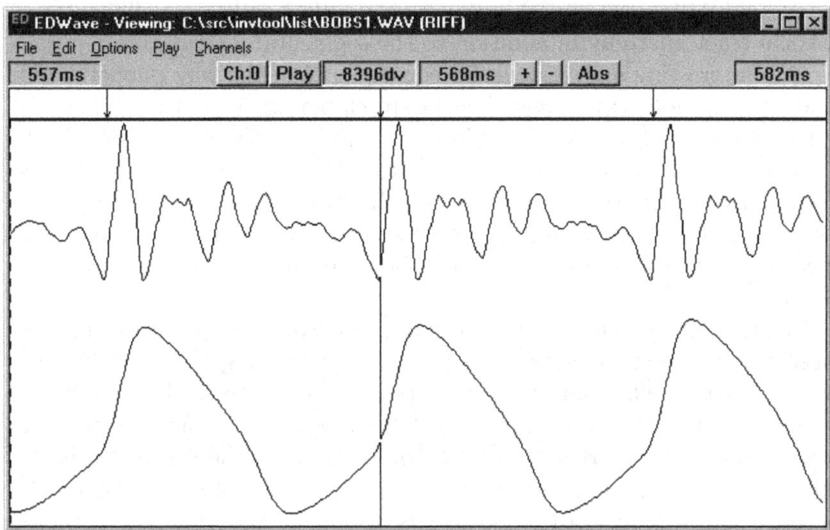

Figure 3. A display of the speech waveform (upper signal) and Electroglottograph (EGG) signal (lower signal). The x-axis is time (shown in msec) and the y-axis is a linear amplitude scale with the two signals offset for display purposes. Since the displayed signals cover a range of about 25 msec, the fundamental period of each cycle is about 8 msec and corresponds to an F0 of about 120 Hz.

the resonances of the vocal tract. Following the point of excitation for each pitch period, the vocal tract responds by "ringing" at its resonant frequencies, and this introduces the additional waveform cycles within each pitch period. By analyzing the fine structure of each pitch period, it is possible to estimate the frequencies of the first one or two vocal tract resonances (termed F1 and F2, respectively). Notice in Figure 3 that one cyclic pattern repeats five or six times within the pitch period suggesting an F1 frequency of between 600 and 720 Hz. The second F1 cycle in the pitch periods in Figure 3 is flat on top, and in the flat area of that cycle, one can just make out very small cycles of a waveform that is three or more times the frequency of F1. This difficult-to-see pattern is due to sound energy at the frequency of F2.

Since the waveform structure within pitch periods represents the contribution of the vocal tract to the speech signal, it is highly specific to the phonetic segment being produced by the talker; different vowels or voiced consonants will have different waveform structure with each pitch period. Additionally, the within-pitch-period variations reflect many features of the individual talker's speech because they reflect talker-specific features of vocal tract anatomy in addition to the segmental information.

One interesting and very useful consequence of the way phonetic and other information is "packaged" within pitch periods is that pitch periods can be thought of as being fundamental units of the speech signal. If one is careful to avoid waveform discontinuities, individual pitch periods can usually be removed or duplicated with virtually no audible distortion. This is not true if one ignores pitch period boundaries in removing or duplicating waveform sections no matter how carefully one avoids waveform discontinuities.

To summarize, this very brief introduction to speech acoustics has focused primarily on the suprasegmental properties of speech, its rhythm, and intonation. The main reason for this focus is to provide some background for the other articles which delve into methods for altering the suprasegmental properties of speech while retaining the segmental intelligibility of the signal. Before turning to a discussion of speech timescale modification, a final word of caution is in order. Although the methods described in those articles are relatively low in distortion, they are not distortion-free and, if pushed beyond their normal limits, can introduce substantial distortion to the signal. A good rule of thumb when mucking about with speech is that just about anything you do will distort the signal in some way; we seek methods that minimize distortion, but it is clear that we are some way off from having methods of manipulating speech without introducing any distortion at all.

After reading the speech modification articles and experimenting with the code examples found on the CD accompanying this book, the reader will hopefully find these techniques both useful in their existing form and useful as a starting point toward creating more sophisticated processes.

Annotated Bibliography

[1] M. E. Beckman and G. M. Ayers. *Guidelines for ToBI labeling*, vers2.0. Manuscript and accompanying speech materials. Ohio State University, 1994. [Obtain by writing to tobi@ling.ohio-state.edu].

This manuscript contains a tutorial on labeling the prosody of English utterances using the Tone and Break Index method developed as a collaboration of several research groups. This represents an attempt to standardize the way researchers store, describe, and communicate information about speech prosody. The tutorial contains example waveforms with prosodic labels and is mainly intended for use with the

Entropic Waves+ speech processing software that is commonly used on UNIX systems in research laboratories.

[2] M. E. Beckman and J. B. Pierrehumbert. "Intonational Structure in Japanese and English." *Phonology Yearbook* 3 (1996), 255–309.

This manuscript illustrates how one can describe varied intonational structure in two very different languages using a simple system of tones used singly or in combination.

[3] H. T. Bunnell, S. R. Hoskins, and D. Yarrington. "Interactions Among F0, Amplitude, and Duration in the Perception of Focus." *J. Acoust. Soc. Am.*, 102:5 (1997), 3203. See Bunnell, Hoskins, and Yarrington, in review.

[4] H. T. Bunnell, S. R. Hoskins, and D. Yarrington. "Acoustic and Perceptual Features of Focus." In review (draft available at http://www.asel.udel.edu/speech/).

This paper describes a series of experiments and acoustic analyses intended to assess the contributions of three acoustic features (loudness, pitch, and duration) to the perceived emphasis placed on particular words in spoken sentences. The manuscript illustrates the use of timescale and pitch modification to alter natural speech in ways that allow us to find answers to questions about acoustic phonetics and human speech perception.

[5] T. H. Bunnell, D. Yarrington, and K. E. Barner. "Pitch Control in Diphone Synthesis." *Proceedings of the 2nd ESCA/IEEE Workshop on Speech Synthesis* (1994), 127–30.

This describes an alternative approach to PSOLA for altering pitch in the time domain. It involves running speech through filters designed to prolong pitch periods when speech is shifted down in pitch and truncate pitch periods when speech is shifted up in pitch. The algorithm is computationally more demanding than PSOLA and represents a perceptual improvement only under very specific conditions. (We tried, but it's hard to improve on PSOLA).

[6] E. Moulines and F. Charpentier. "Pitch-Synchronous Waveform Processing Techniques for Text-to-Speech Synthesis Using Diphones." *Speech Comm.* 9:5/6 (1990), 453–67.

This is a more accessible description of PSOLA and related techniques than the actual patent document (Hamon, 1988). It is also a well-written and extensive discussion of the overall topic of altering speech prosodic properties.

[7] M. Covell, M. Withgott, and M. Slaney. "MACH1: Nonuniform Time-Scale Modification of Speech." *Proceedings of ICASSP* (1998), 349–352.

This paper from a recent meeting of the International Conference on Acoustics, Speech and Signal Processing reported the use of PSOLA to achieve substantial time compression of the speech signal by paying careful attention to the way talkers locally adjust speaking rate when speaking rapidly. It illustrates the advantages of respecting articulatory and perceptual constraints in optimally maintaining speech intelligibility.

[8] T. H. Crystal and A. S. House. "Articulation Rate and the Duration of Syllables and Stress Groups in Connected Speech." *J. Acoust. Soc. Am.* 88 (1990), 101–112.

This and several earlier papers by the same authors involved extensive analyses of a multitalker speech database. Such studies have only been feasible in recent years because of the development of reliable computational tools for handling massive amounts of speech. One of the important lessons learned from studies of large collections of continuous speech is the extent to which predictions based on the results of carefully controlled laboratory speech studies fail to reflect more natural speech settings.

[9] G. Fant. *The Acoustic Theory of Speech Production.* The Hague: Mouton and Co., 1960.

This is now a dated publication in some ways, but it was truly seminal in the development of modern conceptions of how speech should be characterized in source/filter terms. Since much of Fant's work was presented from a physical and engineering perspective, it has aged wonderfully.

[10] D. B. Fry. (1955). "Duration and Intensity as Physical Correlates of Linguistic Stress." *Journal of the Acoustical Society of America* 27:4 (1955), 765–768.

[11] D. B. Fry. (1958). "Experiments in the Perception of Stress." *Language and Speech* 1 (1958), 126–152.

These two papers by Fry report his pioneering research on the acoustic correlates of stress. They are noteworthy because he approached the study of prosody using instrumental experimental procedures coupled with speech synthesis to test hypotheses generated from the instrumental studies. Additionally, the results reported by Fry are fundamentally valid today except for a distinction that was not recognized in his time between stress and pitch accents.

[12] D. W. Griffin and J. S. Lim. "Signal Estimation from Modified Short-Time Fourier Transform." *IEEE Transactions on Acoustics, Speech, and Signal Processing* 32 (1984), 236–243.

This describes a method for speech compression or expansion that is based on very different principles than the time domain approaches presented here.

[13] C. Hamon. "Procédé en dispositif de synthése del parole par addition-recouvrement de formes d'ondes." Patent no. 8811517.

The PSOLA patent document.

[14] J.'t Hart, R. Collier, and A. Cohen. *A Perceptual Study of Intonation: An Experimental Phonetic Approach to Speech Melody.* Cambridge, UK: Cambridge University Press, 1990.

This book provides an excellent and in-depth account of the best alternative to the tone levels approach. Many Dutch investigators have held the view that the perceptually most salient aspect of intonation is related to changes in pitch rather than to a simple sequence of tone levels. From psychological studies of perception, this appears to be a well-motivated view.

[15] H. Hirose. "Investigating the physiology of laryngeal structures." In *The Handbook of Phonetic Sciences*, edited by W. J. Hardcastle, and J. Laver, pp. 116–136. Oxford, UK: Blackwell Publishers Ltd., 1997.

This is an excellent chapter on laryngeal aspects of speech production. The book that it is in contains many other excellent chapters on speech and phonetic sciences. This is an extremely good source book for those interested in having a good place to start in doing thorough literature reviews in any of the aspects of the scientific study of speech and phonetics.

[16] J. M. Pickett. *The Acoustics of Speech Communication: Fundamentals, Speech Perception Theory, and Technology.* Needham Heights, MA: Allyn & Bacon, 1999.

Pickett's book is an excellent textbook on Acoustic Phonetics with additional forays into speech perception and speech technology by several highly knowledgeable contributing authors. The book provides a thorough coverage of the field that is accessible to those of us who do not have a graduate degree from MIT.

[17] J. B. Pierrehumbert. "The phonology and phonetics of English intonation." Ph.D. diss. MIT, 1980.

For serious students of intonational linguistics, Pierrehumbert's dissertation is a "must read."

[18] J. B. Pierrehumbert. "The Perception of Fundamental Frequency Declination." *J. Acoust. Soc. Am.* 66 (1979), 363–368.

This article focuses specifically on the phenomenon of pitch declination and its implications for theories of intonation.

[19] C. H. Shadle. "Articulatory-Acoustic Relationships in Fricative Consonants." In *Speech production and speech modeling*, edited by W. J. Hardcastle and A. Marchal, pp. 187–209. Dortrecht: Kluwer Academic Publishers, 1990.

Shadle's work on fricative production is well-founded in physics and engineering, as well as in anatomy and physiology. This and other of her publications are good reading for people who are interested in modeling the production of speech sounds from a physical acoustic perspective.

[20] K. N. Stevens. *Acoustic Phonetics.* Cambridge, MA: MIT Press, 1998.

This book is the single best technical reference available on the study of speech acoustics by a renowned scholar in the field. It is not, however, good reading for a novice, nor would it be a good textbook for any class except an upper-level graduate seminar.

[21] G. H. Yeni-Komshian and H. T. Bunnell. "Perceptual Evaluations of Spectral and Temporal Modifications of Deaf Speech." *J. Acoust. Soc. Am.*, 104:2:1 (1998), 637–647.

This is a recent article describing studies of how prosodic factors influence the perceived normalcy of speech. It contains a fairly complete overview of literature related to the question of how prosodic and segmental properties interact in determining both intelligibility and the perceived naturalness of speech.

Timescale Modification of Speech

Tim Bunnell

1 Introduction

Timescale modification is the general term applied to various methods for altering the temporal structure of speech without altering other aspects of the signal such as its pitch or the voice quality of the speaker. Timescale modification can be applied globally to change the perceived speaking rate of an utterance by uniformly increasing or decreasing the durations of all the syllables in the utterance. It is also possible to apply timescale modification locally within an utterance to alter the duration of just a particular region of the utterance, say, to lengthen a single syllable. The two approaches can be combined to mimic the nonuniform duration/rate changes that talkers actually produce when speeding up or slowing down their speech (e.g., [1]). Several methods have been developed for timescale modification with low distortion. Griffin and Lim [3] presented a method based on recursively approximating the timescale modified speech in the spectral domain. This method worked quite well, but was also computationally very intensive and required substantial time to compute even a single modified sentence. More recently, Moulines and Charpentier [5] published the PSOLA [4] and related approaches which can be used to modify both the timescale and the pitch of utterances using computationally simple time domain operations. For more information about the PSOLA algorithm, see my article "Pitch Modification of Speech Using PSOLA" (page 187). The timescale modification algorithm presented in this article exploits the temporal structure of the speech signal in a way that is quite similar to the PSOLA algorithm, but is simpler because, unlike PSOLA, it is not intended for pitch modification. Before reading either this article or the PSOLA article, the reader might find it helpful to review my article on general speech acoustics, "Introduction to Speech Acoustics" (page 159).

1.1 Uses of Timescale Modification

There are a variety of reasons one might wish to alter the timescale of speech. If you have ever tried to find a particular passage in a long recording, or wished to quickly review voicemail or answering machine messages, one use of timescale modification should be fairly obvious; to scan as rapidly as possible through the recording. Of course, this can be done by simply speeding up the playback rate of the recording, but the side effect of this is to produce "chipmunk" speech which is probably better for amusement than for speech scanning. Timescale modification, on the other hand, allows equal or greater scanning rates, but without the chipmunk effect.

For scanning, speech rate can be increased uniformly, that is, all portions of the signal are changed by the same amount (up to a factor of about 2 for carefully articulated speech) with virtually no loss of intelligibility. However, timescale modification is not restricted to simple linear rate shifts. It can be used to alter rate to different degrees in different portions of an utterance. This aspect has been exploited in attempts to achieve higher compression rates than are possible with linear compression schemes [1], and to develop aids for people with speech disorders. One of the most prominent aspects of many speech disorders is distortion to speech timing. Disordered speech is, overall, slower than normal speech by a factor of two or more, and frequently exhibits very irregular timing, not at all like the rhythmic patterns of normal speech. Several research laboratories have examined the use of timescale modification to adjust disordered speech to make it more natural sounding (e.g., see [6] for one of the earliest such attempts). When one knows what the talker has said, it is possible to reconstruct the timing of the utterance to approach "natural" timing, essentially synthesizing just the temporal structure of the disordered talker's speech while leaving all other aspects unchanged. Even when the content of the speech is not known, it is possible to make some reasonable guesses about changes to the temporal structure of the utterance that generally make it more natural sounding, at least in the sense of flowing more steadily. Although there is little evidence that such adjustments to speech, even when the speech content is known, actually enhance its *intelligibility*, there is evidence that temporal changes alone can improve its perceived *naturalness* [7]. Just improving the naturalness of speech for persons with severe speech disorders may afford interpersonal social and psychological benefits by reducing the markedness of an individual's speech disorder in settings such as telephone conversations where the technology could be applied without being disruptive in itself.

Turning from socially valuable contributions of timescale modification to purely economic contributions, another recent application of time compression is to adjust the length of movies, commercials, and other prerecorded material to fit within a restricted time frame. When speech is compressed by up to 20 percent, the change in intelligibility and naturalness is barely distinguishable, but compressing 30 minutes of air time by 20% provides 9 additional minutes in each half-hour time slot for the main point of commercial television: the commercials. The amount of additional revenue that could be generated over the course of a two to three hour special feature could fund a small speech research laboratory for years.

1.2 The Problem

Speech that is read aloud by American English speakers typically contains between four and five syllables per second [2]. Of course, there is a moderate amount of variability between speakers and speech modes. Some people speak more rapidly than others and casual conversational speech tends to be faster than read speech.

One way to gain some insight into how timescale modification works is to consider what talkers do—and do not do—to speed up or slow down their speech.

What do talkers do when they change their speaking rate? It is obvious that talkers are not prone to change either their average voice pitch or the pitch range that they use solely as a function of speech rate changes (although pitch range effects may be observed when talkers slow down to emphasize a point). Such changes primarily are (a) the number and length of pauses in speech and (b) the rate at which speech is articulated. To a first approximation, talkers go through all the same articulatory gestures whether they are uttering a particular passage slowly or rapidly. If we can think of the speech source signal that embodies intonation as a carrier signal which is modulated by movement of the supralaryngeal articulators, speaking more rapidly amounts to increasing the modulation rate, but not otherwise changing the carrier signal.

It bears mentioning in this context that we perceive speech to be more discrete than it really is at the acoustic level. In particular, it is easy to imagine that there is a brief silence separating words in an uttered sentence just as there are spaces separating words in a written sentence. In fact, this is rarely true. There may be pauses between phrases or sentences in speech, but there is almost never any silence between words within a phrase unless that silence is actually part of a phoneme (stop consonants like /p/, /t/, and /k/ typically introduce brief silent intervals) and phoneme-related silences are as likely in the middle of a word as between words. Because real pauses in speech tend to be relatively infrequent, increasing or decreasing the durations of the pauses alone does not achieve effective timescale modification. When talkers increase or decrease their speaking rate, they do modify the durations of pauses, but most of the real increase or decrease in speech rate is due to modifying the durations of the speech itself, not the silences between speech.

How to approximate natural changes in speaking rate computationally. To achieve a similar effect with recorded speech, it is necessary to shift the modulation rate of the speech signal without changing the characteristics of the carrier source function. One way to do this is to consider each pitch period (or similar-sized epoch of voiceless speech) as "sampling" the talker's articulatory state at a specific moment in time. Since pitch periods—and hence our samples—typically recur at a much higher frequency than the slowly changing articulatory events they sample, articulation is effectively oversampled. Thus, one can increase speaking rate by uniformly downsampling the sequence of pitch periods. That is, by dropping pitch periods (while maintaining their individual lengths), we achieve the same effect as talkers do when they increase their rate of articulation. Section 2 outlines a simple, but effective, procedure for doing this.

2 Algorithm

The procedure for speech timescale modification can be formulated in terms of the process of copying an input waveform buffer or file to an output waveform buffer or file. In the copy process, very small pieces of the input waveform are copied one at a time to the output waveform. During the copy, some pieces of the input waveform may be discarded (to compress the speech), or duplicated (to expand the speech). The trick, of course, is to pick the right pieces for discarding or duplication. Based on our previous discussion, the obvious answer to the question, "Which are the right pieces?" is "Pitch periods," at least during voiced regions of speech. With voiceless regions, it is even simpler; nearly any small pieces will do because the temporal structure is not granular in the way that the temporal structure is for voiced speech.

The most challenging aspect of this algorithm is the problem of locating pitch periods in the speech waveform. Although pitch periods are visually quite easy to locate in most cases, algorithms for automatically locating the onsets of pitch periods seem to fail with surprising frequency. Common modes of failure include doubling or halving F0 by missing every other pitch period onset or inserting false onsets into the middle of pitch periods. Additionally, many "pitch tracking" algorithms have a tendency to correctly identify F0 but misplace the onsets of pitch periods to coincide with secondary excitation events or with some other feature of the waveform. The algorithm used in the TimeScale program presented here is based on three observations: (a) most commonly, the initial full cycle of F1 waveform following vocal cord closure at the onset of a pitch period is greater in amplitude than subsequent cycles of F1 waveform (see "Introduction to Speech Acoustics" (page 159) for a definition and illustration of F1 cycles); (b) the slope of the waveform at the onset of a pitch period is normally greater than at any time within the pitch period; and (c) the amplitude of F1 cycles just prior to the onset of a pitch period is at its weakest. Thus, in a restricted region of waveform, the best guess one can make regarding the onset of a pitch period is to choose the location where F1 cycles are largest in amplitude, steepest in slope, and following an area of very weak amplitude F1 cycles. The function `BestPt` below shows how this descriptive account is operationalized.

3 Annotated Code Excerpts for TimeScale and Function BestPt

```
/*
 * Initialize with:
 *    maxst - Maximum PP length
 *     minst - Minimum PP length
 *     srms  - Sample rate in samples per msec
 *     cut   - Lowpass filter cutoff
 *     inbuf - Buffer of input speech for
 *             compression/expansion
 *     tsc   - Timescale factor for compression/expansion
 */
```

```
/*
 * Loop from here until we reach the end of the input.
 */
lsamp = 0;
while(timein < duration) {
/*
 * Convert timein to a sample pointer. Adjust the sample
 * pointer isamp to center timein within a working window
 * of nwork samples.
 */
    isamp = (int) (timein * srms + 0.5);
/*
 * Locate the probable start of a pitch period within the
 * working window.
 */
    if (isamp > 0)
       jsamp = isamp + lap +
               BestPt(maxst, inbuf+isamp+lap, cut);
    else
       jsamp = 0;
/*
 * Locate probable end of the pitch period (i.e., probable
 * start of the next pitch period and compute pitch period
 * length in samples (nsamp). Note that ksamp points to the
 * start of the NEXT PP so nsamp = ksamp - jsamp.
 */
    ksamp = jsamp + minst +
            BestPt(maxst, inbuf+jsamp+minst, cut);
    nsamp = ksamp - jsamp;
/*
 * Do overlap blending if a lap interval was specified.
 */
    if (lap && (jsamp > lap)) {
        for (j = 0; j < lap; ++j) {
            outbuf[lsamp+j] = (short)(outbuf[lsamp+j]*wl[j] +
                                  inbuf[jsamp-lap+j]*wr[j]);
        }
    }
/*
 * Copy this chunk to the output buffer.
 */
```

```
    for (j = 0; j < nsamp; ++j) {
        outbuf[lsamp+j+lap] = inbuf[jsamp+j];
    }
/*
 * Update timeot and scale it using tsc to find new timein.
 */
    lsamp += nsamp;
    timeot = (float) ((lsamp-lap) / srms);
    timein = timeot / tsc;
}
```

Figure 1. Code excerpt from TimeScale.c illustrating the simple logic of the time compression or expansion algorithm.

Figure 1 shows a code excerpt for the general compression or expansion algorithm implemented in TimeScale. A time scaling factor `tsc`, input time pointer `timein`, and output time pointer `timeot` are initialized. The variable `tsc` provides a mapping from the output timescale to the input timescale; thus, the temporal location pointers `timein` and `timeot` are related as:

```
timeot = tsc * timein
```

A waveform epoch (pitch period or unvoiced region of short duration) is copied from the input file and appended to the output file. Given the new duration of the output file, the timescaling factor is applied to find the location within the input file from which to select the next epoch. This process is repeated until the end of the input file is reached (i.e., until `timein` is no longer less than the `duration` of the input waveform).

As each epoch is extracted from the input and appended to the output, a small amount (usually 1 to 2 ms) of prior waveform context is used for overlap blending of the epoch with the tail of the output waveform. The blending process is a weighted averaging of the samples in the overlap region with corresponding samples in the tail of the output waveform. The example uses a precomputed set of blending weights which range in value from 0.0 to 1.0 over the duration of the overlap region to increase the contribution of the new data to the average while a complementary weight is applied to samples from the tail of the output waveform. This eliminates small waveform discontinuities which might arise when epochs are either duplicated or skipped due to differences in the timescales of the input and output waveforms.

```
/*
 * First lowpass the signal (returns a floating point array
 * of length N in signal).
 */
signal = lowpass(n, data, cut);
/*
 * Now find most likely run. We do so by tracking the
 * magnitude of the difference between successive maxima and
 * minima in the filtered input. This magnitude is weighted
 * by the run slope to favor runs of steep slope, and we add
 * the difference between an adjacent pair of runs to the
 * second (later) run if the later run is larger because we
 * want to favor large runs that follow small runs.
 *
 */
ip1 = 0;
/* Default return value is left edge of the window */
ret_val = 0;

if (!irun(n, signal, &ip1, &ip2)) {
    d1 = signal[ip2] - signal[ip1];
    if (ip2 > ip1)
        d1 = (d1*d1)/(float)(ip2 - ip1);
    else
        d1 = 0.0;
    ipleft = -1;
    dmax = (float) 0.0;
    while(!irun(n, signal, &ip2, &ip3)) {
        d2 = signal[ip3] - signal[ip2];
        if (ip3 > ip2)
            d2 = (d2*d2) / (float)(ip3 - ip2);
        else
            d2 = 0.0;

        if (d2 > d1)
            dx = (float) (d2 * 2 - d1);
        else
            dx = d2;
        if (dx > dmax) {
            ipleft = ip1;
            ipmid = ip2;
```

```
            ipright = ip3;
            dmax = dx;
        }
        ip1 = ip2;
        ip2 = ip3;
        d1 = d2;
    }
    /* Proceed only if a maximum was found. */
    if (ipleft != -1) {
/*
 * Locate a positive-going zero crossing and return its
 * location.
 */
        if (data[ipleft] < data[ipmid]) {
            for (j=ipleft; j<ipmid; ++j) {
                if (data[j] >= 0) {
                    ret_val = j;
                    goto done;
                }
            }
            ret_val = ipmid;
        } else {
            for (j=ipmid; j<ipright; ++j) {
                if (data[j] >= 0) {
                    ret_val = j;
                    goto done;
                }
            }
            ret_val ipright;
        }
    }
}
```

Figure 2. Code excerpt from the BestPt function showing how pitch period onsets are located heuristically.

The selection of pitch period onsets occurs in function `BestPt`, which implements a reasonable heuristic approach to guessing where pitch periods begin and end. For most laboratory speech (i.e., good signal-to-noise ratio and stable recording channel characteristics), we have found that a simple approach based on detecting features within a lowpass-filtered copy of the input waveform performs nearly as well as more elaborate techniques, at relatively low computational cost. The input waveform is lowpass-filtered at 750 Hz so that it will be likely to include oscillations due to F1, but not F2. The filtered waveform is then searched in the region from which a segment is to be copied to locate the largest excursion between a waveform minimum and adjacent (preceding or following) maximum. From the location of the maximum, the preceding positive-going waveform zero crossing is then taken as the start of a pitch period. A second call to BestPt is used to locate the start of the immediately following pitch period (subject to parameters which constrain the likely F0 and jitter[1] for the speech), and from that the duration of the pitch period to be copied is determined. This process is restarted as an independent search each time a pitch period is to be located.

When the input speech signal is not voiced, the same logic is used to locate some waveform feature within the input which can serve as the start of a waveform epoch to be copied. On occasions where there is too little energy below 750 Hz to leave useful minima and maxima in the filtered waveform, the search returns to the center of the input sequence as the next location of a pitch period and 10 ms as the period duration.

Because this approach picks each new pitch period or voiceless epoch independently, it avoids the problem of compounding errors: One error in locating the start of a pitch period is unlikely to lead to another. The approach also avoids the need to actually track the pitch periods throughout the input utterance. These two factors make this an algorithm which can be applied as a "filter" (in the UNIX sense of the term) through which data are passed, with the output emerging as an altered version of the input.

4 Discussion

The full code for the driver program `TimeScale.c` is included on the accompanying CD-ROM. It takes a waveform as input and generates a waveform as output which can either be directed to a file or to the computer's audio output channel. A small number of command line switches determine its operation. Although the example driver program only supports uniform timescale alteration, it could be extended easily to allow

[1] Jitter is period-to-period change in duration leading to slight F0 variation. Another form of period-to-period variation, shimmer, refers to slight changes in amplitude from one pitch period to the next.

the timescaling factor to vary dynamically while a waveform is being processed.

TimeScale is an example of a speech processing application that is relatively simple and works well most of the time on the limited task for which it is intended. Nonetheless, there are a number of ways this program can fail to produce natural sounding output speech. The most prominent type of failure stems from attempting to introduce too much expansion. The human auditory system is quite sensitive to the presence of periodicity in sounds. If we sample 10 ms of a random process like white noise and then produce a longer waveform by replicating the 10 ms segment many times, the resulting longer waveform will have a perceptually strong 100 Hz periodicity. If one takes a short fricative and time-expands it using the TimeScale program, distortion related to this periodicity effect is often perceptible. A similar form of distortion occurs with voiced speech when a very short segment is over-expanded. In the case of voiced speech, the periodicity can result in a signal that sounds more like a sequence of organ notes than a human talker.

Moulines and Charpentier [5] suggest that one way to reduce this problem (for voiceless epochs where it is most perceptible) is to time-reverse the sample sequence in alternate successive repetitions of the same epoch. Another way that works for voiced or voiceless epochs is to introduce jitter and shimmer artificially into the output of highly expanded speech. By randomly varying the amplitude of repeated epochs to create shimmer, or by randomly varying the epoch length to produce jitter, the pure periodicity of the output speech is removed and the resulting signal sounds somewhat more natural. While it is fairly easy to envision how the amplitude of an epoch can be altered in the TimeScale program, the algorithm implemented in TimeScale is not well-suited to varying epoch length. The reader will find discussion of how jitter should be handled in "Pitch Modification of Speech Using PSOLA" (page 187). As we will see, the PSOLA algorithm provides an excellent solution to the problem of how to introduce jitter.

There is one other failure mode for timescaling algorithms like the present one that simply discards chunks of the original waveform when compressing speech. As mentioned earlier, changes in the speech signal that are due to articulation occur on a relatively long timescale compared to the duration of individual pitch periods. Thus, it is usually safe to discard pitch periods or voiceless epochs every so often. However, the sampling theorem applies to this process in exactly the same way it apples to digitizing sound. The timescale is more macroscopic, but the consequences of aliasing are just as real and it is possible to significantly disrupt the intelligibility of time-compressed speech by undersampling the articulatory information present in the original signal.

The accompanying CD-ROM contains a working implementation of this algorithm including C source code and examples.

Annotated Bibliography

[1] M. Covell, M. Withgott, and M. Slaney. "MACH1: Nonuniform Time-Scale Modification of Speech." *Proceedings of ICASSP* (1998), 349–352.

This paper from a recent meeting of the International Conference on Acoustics, Speech and Signal Processing reported the use of PSOLA to achieve substantial time compression of the speech signal by paying careful attention to the way talkers locally adjust speaking rate when speaking rapidly. It illustrates the advantages of respecting articulatory and perceptual constraints in optimally maintaining speech intelligibility.

[2] T. H. Crystal and A. S. House. "Articulation Rate and the Duration of Syllables and Stress Groups in Connected Speech." *J. Acoust. Soc. Am.*, 88 (1990), 101–112.

This and several other papers by the same authors (many are referenced in this article) represent one of the early efforts to characterize speech acoustic properties based on large databases of recorded utterances from many talkers. Such studies have only been feasible in recent years because of the development of reliable automatic algorithms to label massive amounts of speech.

[3] D. W. Griffin and J. S. Lim. "Signal Estimation from Modified Short-Time Fourier Transform." *IEEE Transactions on Acoustics, Speech, and Signal Processing* 32 (1984), 236–243.

This describes a method for speech compression or expansion that is based on very different principles than the time domain approaches presented here.

[4] C. Hamon. "Procédé en dispositif de synthése del parole par addition-recouvrement de formes d'ondes." Patent no. 8811517.

This is the patent document for PSOLA.

[5] E. Moulines and F. Charpentier. "Pitch-Synchronous Waveform Processing Techniques for Text-to-Speech Synthesis Using Diphones." *Speech Comm.* 9:5/6 (1990), 453–67.

This is a more accessible description of PSOLA and related techniques. It is also a well written and extensive discussion of the overall topic of altering speech prosodic properties.

[6] M. J. Osberger and H. Levitt. "The Effect of Timing Errors on the Intelligibility of Deaf Children's Speech." *J. Acoust. Soc. Am.* 66:5 (1979), 1316–1324.

[7] G. H. Yeni-Komshian and H. T. Bunnell. "Perceptual Evaluations of Spectral and Temporal Modifications of Deaf Speech." *J. Acoust. Soc. Am.* 104:2:1 (1998), 637–647.

This is a recent article describing studies of how prosodic factors influence the perceived normalcy of speech. It also describes a number of related research efforts and the signal processing techniques used for them.

Pitch Modification of Speech Using PSOLA

Tim Bunnell

1 Introduction

If the objective of timescale modification is to alter the rate or timing of speech without changing its pitch or other characteristics, its prosodic complement, pitch modification, has the objective of altering the overall pitch or intonation contour of speech without changing its timing or other characteristics. However, you should not be misled by this treatment of timescale and pitch modification to suggest that they are wholly independent manipulations of speech. Using the waveform altering techniques that we present here, you will see that the two techniques are not at all independent. In fact, changes in duration are a necessary side-effect of pitch modification when it is achieved through time-domain (i.e., waveform modification) operations. As a consequence, to change the pitch without changing the original timing of an utterance, it is actually necessary to apply timescale modification to undo the durational side-effects of the pitch changes. Readers are encouraged to see my articles on overview of speech acoustics, "Introduction to Speech Acoustics" (page 159), and timescale modification, "Timescale Modification of Speech"(page 173), before reading this article.

1.1 Uses for Pitch Modification

Pitch modification has been used extensively in speech research laboratories to study intonation. Much of the information covered in the introduction on pitch accents has involved studies in which pitch was manipulated, either by synthesis of speech or by modifying the pitch of recorded utterances.

Outside the laboratory, an increasingly common use of pitch modification is in concatenative speech synthesis (also discussed in Craig Utterback's article, "Voice Concatenation: A Stitch in Time Saves Nine" (page 123), and Debbie Yarrington's article, "Synthesizing Speech for Communication Devices" (page 143)). This type of synthesis involves concatenating short snippets of recorded speech such as words or phrases to build much longer or more complicated utterances. One challenge when attempting to use concatenation is that, for the speech to sound natural, the intonation of the concatenated segments must flow in a natural manner. To ensure that this happens, one can either record enormous amounts of speech (so that all desired intonation patterns can be "found" somewhere in the recorded speech database), or impose the desired intonation on speech that is segmentally appropriate, but did not have the correct pitch structure.

A simpler form of the concatenative synthesis application could be applied to those annoying prerecorded "variable" messages (e.g., "You have ordered FOUR tickets to see Ernest saves Christmas Showing TODAY AT two-Fifteen PM"). Adjusting the intonation of the concatenated words in such sequences substantially improves their naturalness. For sequences like phone numbers and fitting single words in phrases, this is a computationally very tractable task.

Another potential use of pitch modification is to distort a talker's pitch (say, shifting it up or down by a constant amount) to disguise the talker's identity. The software associated with this chapter will allow you to experiment with this effect. Taking an adult male voice and shifting its pitch up by an octave, into the pitch range of typical adult females, will not necessarily produce a convincingly "female" voice, but it will substantially obscure the identity of the original talker.

1.2 The Problem

As with timescale modification, the problem that we face in pitch modification is how to change the appropriate acoustic features without introducing substantial change or distortion into other speech features. At the level of the acoustic signal, pitch is related to fundamental frequency (F0) which in turn is determined by the length of the individual pitch periods within a voiced region of the signal. Thus, as with timescale modification, the acoustic "units" we must operate on to alter pitch are pitch periods.

However, unlike timescale modification, it is necessary to modify the *spacing* of pitch periods. To increase F0, we must pack pitch periods closer together, whereas to decrease F0, pitch periods must be spaced farther apart. Obviously, this requires actually changing pitch periods and notes, with timescale modification merely duplicating or deleting them in their entirety. Moreover, changes must be applied to *every* pitch period, not merely selected ones.

So, there are really two problems to solve for pitch modification: 1) accurately identifying all the pitch periods in an utterance that is to be modified, and 2) actually changing the spacing of the pitch periods by making them longer or shorter in duration. As we mentioned earlier in connection with timescale modification, the first of these problems is a surprisingly difficult problem to solve. Although pitch periods appear to the eye to be fairly well-defined features of the waveform, there does not appear to be any simple acoustic definition that infallibly selects pitch periods. Whereas we avoided global pitch tracking with timescale modification by only solving it "as needed" (i.e., when it was necessary to cut or paste a segment of waveform), it is necessary to locate all the probable pitch epochs in a sampled speech waveform for pitch modification. Fortunately, there are a number of reasonably reliable "pitch tracking" methods and we will make use of one developed in our laboratory for this program example without attempting to describe it (see the function `ptract` provided on the CD-ROM accompanying this book). With that said, we will proceed to describe one very nice solution to the second problem which has been termed Pitch Synchronous Overlap Add or PSOLA [1], [2].[1]

2 PSOLA Described

The heart of PSOLA is the manner in which pitch periods are "packaged" so that they can be readily manipulated. Given a speech signal divided into pitch periods (or similarly sized voiceless epochs), PSOLA deconstructs the speech signal into packets consisting of windowed waveform epochs centered on the onsets of the periods. The windowing function for extracting the packets is typically a raised cosine:

$$w_i = 0.5 - 0.5\cos(2\pi(i = 0.5)/I), \tag{1}$$

evaluated for i from 0 to $I - 1$ where I (the number of samples in the packet) is a variable defined as twice the number of samples in the current

[1]The acronym PSOLA is typically pronounced as a single three-syllable word spelled *Pee.so.la* with stress on the penultimate syllable (so).

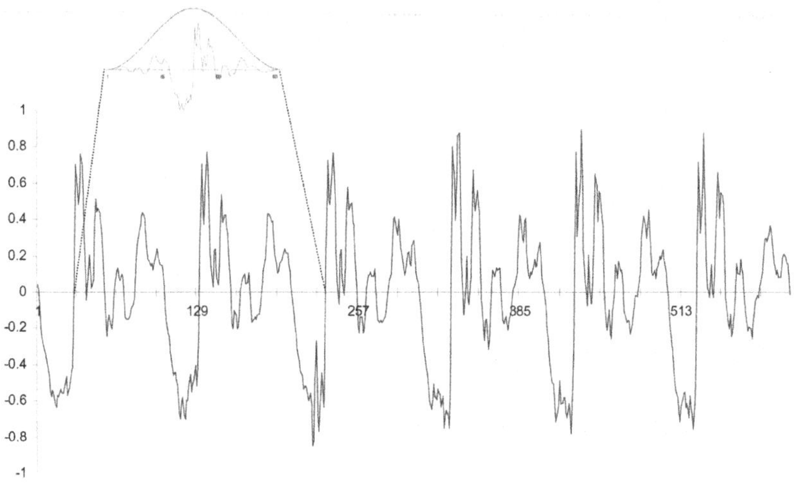

Figure 1. Illustration of extraction process for PSOLA algorithm. A raised cosine window is used to obtain a waveform packet centered on the onset of a pitch period and extending the duration of the pitch period in either direction.

pitch period. This is illustrated graphically in Figure 1, which shows the extraction of a single pitch epoch from a region of voiced speech. The extracted packet is shown with the cosine windowing function. Its length (I samples in Equation (1)) is exactly twice the length of the pitch period which fills the right half of the packet. Obviously, the left half of the packet is the trailing portion of the previous pitch period. To completely decompose a waveform, overlapping windowed packets are similarly extracted for every pitch period. For regions of voiceless speech, it is typical to treat successive the 10 ms regions of the waveform as though they were pitch periods.

To reconstruct the speech waveform almost exactly from the packets of a decomposed waveform, one simply initializes a buffer long enough to hold the entire waveform and adds each packet to the location within the buffer that preserves the temporal location of the packet in the original waveform. The right half of each packet sums in a complementary way with the left half of the subsequent packet to reconstruct the waveform from the center of one packet to the center of the next. This, of course, is why the technique is called "overlap add." The reconstruction is very close to the original, but generally not exact because the length of each packet is a function of the length of the pitch period in its right half only.

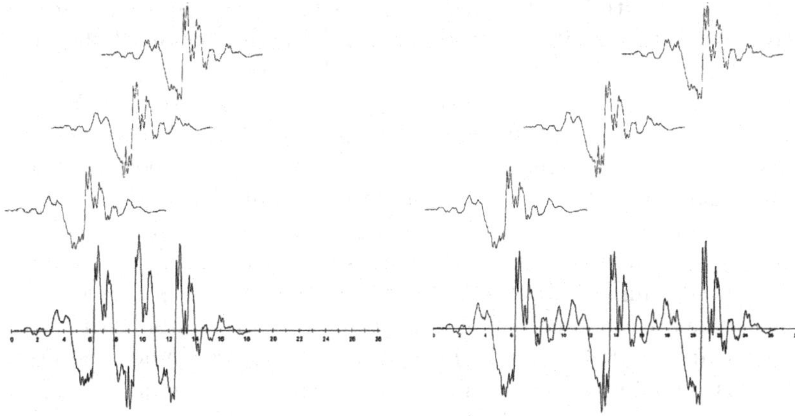

Figure 2. Reconstruction of a short segment of voiced speech using the PSOLA method. The same three pitch period packets are summed with different temporal spacing to procude speech with different F0.

So how do we use this approach to alter the pitch of the waveform? We alter the temporal relations of the packets. By increasing the amount of overlap (i.e., decreasing the distance between the centers of successive packets), we increase F0. Conversely, by increasing the spacing between successive packets (relative to their original spacing), we lower F0. This is illustrated in Figure 2, which shows the same three packets (top) overlap added with decreased spacing (left lower waveform) or with greater spacing (right lower waveform).

It is noteworthy that the lower left waveform in Figure 2 is distinctly shorter than the lower right waveform even though both were derived from the same original waveform. This means that to preserve the original duration of a region of speech that has been pitch altered, it is necessary to also apply timescale modification to compensate for the durational effects of the pitch alterations. Fortunately, the timescale modification is a fairly trivial extension of the overlap add process: if the pitch shifted waveform falls more than one half a pitch period's duration short of the duration of the original waveform up to the current pitch period, duplicate the current overlap add packet; if the pitch shifted waveform becomes longer than the original waveform, discard the current packet.

Notice that the middle pitch period in the reconstructed waveform on the left in Figure 2 is somewhat higher in amplitude than its surrounding pitch periods even though all three of the original waveform packets are of about equal amplitude. This pitch period is higher in amplitude because all three packets contributed (were summed) in this region of the illustration, but only two packets contributed substantially to the summation for the first and last pitch periods of the reconstructed waveform. Had we drawn this illustration out further, with many overlapping pitch periods, the pattern that would emerge is one in which all the pitch periods except the first and last in the waveform would be amplified by approximately a constant amount. However, if F0 was changing so that packet spacing was changing over the course of the reconstructed waveform, the amount of overlap add amplification would also be changing. Hence, changes in F0 over time are accompanied by changes in waveform amplification over time that are an artifact of the reconstruction process. When the F0 of the reconstructed waveform is greater than that of the original waveform, amplification is observed and when the reconstructed F0 is less than that of the original waveform, attenuation is observed.

To be completely transparent, the overlap add synthesis process would need to remove any amplification or attenuation in the output waveform that is due to these overlap add effects. This can easily be accomplished by maintaining an extra array with one element for each sample in the reconstructed waveform. As the waveform is reconstructed, the elements of the extra array would be updated with the accumulated sum of the weights associated with the windowing functions of each packet that contributed to the corresponding waveform sample. After the reconstructed waveform is completed, each of its samples would then be divided by the sum of the windowing weights associated with it to remove whatever amplification or attenuation effects were introduced by the reconstruction process.

In practice, this additional bookkeeping is rarely applied. The amount of distortion that is introduced by overlap addition is small compared to the normal range of amplitude variation common in speech. Moreover, there is some natural tendency for speech amplitude to increase with increasing F0 and consequently, the gross amplitude artifacts introduced by overlap addition mimic natural speech tendencies.

3 Code of PSOLA Function

The two basic functions needed to implement PSOLA are `GetPacket`, which returns a windowed PSOLA packet from a specified location in an input waveform buffer, and `PutPacket`, which overlap adds a packet at a specific location into an output waveform buffer. These functions are called by the function `psola` which implements pitch shifting.

```
/*
 * Function GetPacket extracts a PSOLA packet from an input waveform
 * array. The packet is centered at loc, with (p0-1) samples
 * preceding and following the sample at loc. A raised cosine window
 * is applied to the packet waveform as it is copied from the input
 * waveform.
 */
void GetPacket(short *waveform, long loc, long p0, short *packet)
{
  long lloc,      /* left edge of packet in waveform */
  rloc,           /* right edge of packet in waveform */
  offs,           /* offset to guard against buffer underrun */
  slop = p0 - 1; /* left tail of windowed region */
  int j;
  double rad,     /* radian measure for cosine window */
  rinc;           /* radian increment to rad for each window sample */
/*
 * Adjust start pointer to p0 samples before loc
 */
  /* window will have odd length, centered at loc */
  lloc = loc - slop;

  /* Make sure we don't underrun the output buffer*/
  if (lloc >= 0) {
    offs = 0;      /* No underrun */
  } else {
    offs = -lloc; /* Number of samples to skip to avoid underrun */
    lloc = 0;
  }
  rinc = 6.28318530718 / (p0 + p0 - 1);
  rad = rinc / 2.0;
  rloc = loc + p0;
  for (j=0; j<offs; j++, rad+=rinc)
    *packet++ = 0;
/*
 * Copy and window the data. Note that we do no error checking here.
 * We assume that there is enough data in the input and space in the
 * output arrays. These need to be checked in the calling routine.
 */
  for (j=lloc; j<rloc; j++, rad+=rinc)
    *packet++ = (short) ((double)waveform[j] * (.5 - .5*cos(rad)));
  return;
```

Figure 3. Annotated code for function `GetPacket` which extracts a windowed packet of waveform data for use in overlap add pitch shifting. A parallel function `PutPacket` is used to overlap add a packet into a waveform buffer.

```
/*
 * Function psola - Pitch Synchronous Overlap Add (time-domain
 *                  implementation)
 *
 * Synopsis
 *  int psola(short *output, short *input, long nin, int sr,
 *            float scale);
 *
 *  output   - Pointer to buffer that will receive the generated
 *             waveform as a sequence of 16-bit samples.
 *  input    - Pointer to buffer containing the input waveform.
 *  nin      - Number of sample in the input.
 *  sr       - Integer Sampling rate in samples per second.
 *  scale    - Pitch period scaling factor. Values > 1.0 decrease F0
 *             while values < 1.0 increase F0.
 */

/* This is the longest packet that we will handle. */
#define MAXPAC 8192

int psola(short *output, short *input, long nin, int sr,
          float scale)
{
  long j, jsam, ksam, ppl, lastj;
  double spm = sr/1000.0;
  double tout, duration;
  PPSDATA *pps;
  short *packet;

  packet = (short *) malloc(MAXPAC * sizeof(short));

  /* Locate pitch periods in input. */
  pps = ptrack(input, nin, (short) sr);
/*
* Initialize counters and pointers.
*/
  j = 0;
  lastj = -1;
  tout = pps->time[0];
  ksam = (long) (tout * spm);
  for (j=0; j<ksam; j++)
    output[j] = 0;
  duration = pps->time[pps->npps - 2];

  while (tout < duration) { /* Loop till the end of utterance. */
    /* Locate corresponding input PP. */
```

```
    j = pploc((float) tout, pps);
    if (j != lastj) {
      /*PP location in input */
      jsam = (long) (spm * (pps->time[j] + 0.5));
      if ((ppl = (long) (spm * (pps->time[j+1] - pps->time[j])))
          > MAXPAC)
        ppl = MAXPAC;

      /* Get the packet of waveform. */
      GetPacket(input, jsam, ppl, packet);

      /* Remember where we got it. */
      lastj = j;
    }

    /* Write it to the output. */
    PutPacket(output, ksam, ppl, packet);

    /* Calculate next Output loc. */
    ksam += (long) (scale * ppl + 0.5);

    /* Calculate progress. */
    tout = (float) ksam / spm;
  }
  free(packet);
  free_pps(pps);
  return ksam;
}
```

Figure 4. Annotated code for PSOLA function. This version implements a simple linear pitch-scaling algorithm.

4 Discussion

PSOLA is elegant in its simplicity and computationally undemanding aside from the problem of locating pitch periods in the first place. Within limits, it typically produces speech that is close to the original speech in quality, but *only* within limits, and not in all cases even when the limits are observed. While it is very effective most of the time, anyone who intends to use PSOLA extensively should be aware of several of its most common difficulties.

First, it should be fairly obvious that one can only lower F0 by about a factor of two (i.e., one octave) before there is no longer any overlap at all between successive packets. At that point and beyond, the algorithm is producing speech that is decidedly unlike that produced by human talkers and its quality begins to suffer significantly. The second problem occurs when one attempts too great an increase in pitch. As previously discussed, amplitude tends to increase when F0 is raised, but normally one does not need to adjust for this effect. However, if F0 is increased by a significant amount (say, more than a factor of two), it probably will be necessary to introduce some compensatory attenuation. Finally, in our own laboratory use of PSOLA and similar algorithms, we have occasionally observed signal distortion (heard as roughness) in pitch-altered speech. While we have not systematically studied this effect, it appears to be due to overlap adding packets wherein oscillations due to F1 are in destructive phase relation to one another.

One final note regarding PSOLA: If you intend to use this algorithm in a commercial application, please be aware that it is patented [2].

The accompanying CD-ROM contains a working implementation of this algorithm including C source code and examples.

Annotated Bibliography

[1] F. Charpentier and E. Moulines. "Pitch-Synchronous Waveform Processing Techniques for Text-to-Speech Synthesis Using Diphones." *Speech Comm.* 9:5/6 (1990), 453–467.

This is a more accessible description of PSOLA and related techniques. It is also a well-written and extensive discussion of the overall topic of altering speech prosodic properties.

[2] C. Hamon. *Procd en dispositif de synthse del parole par addition-recouvrement de formes d'ondes.* Patent no. 8811517.

This is the PSOLA patent document.

Applied Signal Processing

Audio Dynamic Range Compression

Mark Kolber and Daniel Lee

1 Introduction

This article reviews the reasons why we need audio dynamic range compression; how compressors are characterized; how they are implemented; and various audible effects in different applications. The most common dynamic range controller is the compressor. We introduce and present the basic design of an audio compressor, and then show how variations such as the expander can be created with minor modifications to the basic algorithm. Finally, several simple simulations are also presented to illustrate the behavior of the devices.

Audio compression, in this context, is short for *audio dynamic range compression*. It refers to the use of an automatic variable gain control system to reduce or compress the dynamic range of an audio signal, i.e., to reduce the difference between the loudest and quietest portions of an audio program. This is in contrast to methods used to compress or reduce the data needed to transmit or store an audio signal, which are called *data rate compression* or *coding*. Please refer to Malvar's article "Auditory Masking in Audio Compression" (see *Audio Anecdotes I*) for a discussion on data rate compression and coding.

An audio compressor is a device that is used for automatic control of the dynamic range of audio signals with a minimal alteration to the frequency composition of the signal. From a listener's perspective, a compressor is a device that is used to control the volume (loudness) of a sound. The function of a compressor is similar to that of a person whose role is to control the volume knob of an amplifier, turning it down when the music

dB	Power Ratio	Voltage Ratio
0 dB	x 1	x 1
+3 dB	x 2	x 1.414
+6 dB	x 4	x 2
+10 dB	x 10	x 3.16
+20 dB	x 100	x 10
+30 dB	x 1000	x 31.6
+60 dB	x 1,000,000	x 1000

Table 1.

is too loud. Audio dynamic range compressors are also sometimes known as "processors."

The ear responds to an extremely wide range of loudness levels, and we perceive these differences in intensity in a logarithmic fashion (see Ballas and Fouad's article "Auditory Psychophysics" (page 407)). Therefore, sound intensity is measured by the decibel (dB), which represents a ratio based on the base 10 logarithm. Absolute sound pressure levels are measured in units of pressure or Pascals (Pa), or one millionth of a Pascal—microPascals (μPa). To establish an absolute intensity of sound, a standard reference is used corresponding to the quietest sounds that can be heard (see Fouad's article "Understanding the Decibel" in *Audio Anecdotes I*). This is a sound pressure level (SPL) of about 20 μPa and is denoted as 0 dB SPL. The threshold of pain corresponds to about 100 Pa, or 140 dB SPL.

Once sound has been converted to an electrical signal, an electrical reference level is used, usually 1 mW corresponding to 0 dBm. In a 600 Ohm system, this corresponds to 0.775 Volts RMS. Table 1 relates dB to power ratios and voltage ratios. Note that power is proportional to the square of voltage.

The dynamic range of audible sound extends over 120 dB, corresponding to a power ratio of $1 : 1 \times 10^{12}$ and a voltage ratio of $1 : 1 \times 10^{6}$. For example, if 0 dBV is used to represent a nominal electrical signal of 1 Volt, then −60 dBV represents 1 mV (a very small electrical signal) and +60 dBV represents 1000 Volts (a very large electrical signal). This exceeds the dynamic range capability of most electronic audio equipment. The dynamic range of analog equipment is determined by the equipment noise floor on the low end and the clipping level on the high end. The dynamic range of digital audio equipment is established by the finite number of bits used to represent the audio signal. This sets the quantization noise floor on the low end and a definite clipping level on the high end. Exceeding the clipping level causes severe harmonic and intermodulation distortion. A signal that is too small will be noisy. For example, a 16-bit representation provides a dynamic range of about 96 dB. Even though compression can introduce its own type of distortion, the distortion caused by compression is often less objectionable when compared to clipping distortion or noise.

Compressors were originally used to reduce the dynamic range of the entire signal, as it was necessary to ensure that the signal to be broadcast or stored did not exceed the dynamic range of the medium. Compression can be used to reduce the dynamic range of the audio material before it passes through a system so that it fits within the available dynamic range. Compression is also often used in audio and video tape recording equipment to automatically set the correct recording level despite changes to the input level.

Compression is also used to modify the aesthetic characteristics of the sound. Compression contributed to the famous "wall of sound" popularized by Phil Spector in the 1950s and 60s. Today this is referred to as making the sound "thicker" or "denser." Here are some other examples of how compression is used during the recording process to modify the sound:

(1) Ensuring that the signal does not exceed the media's dynamic range ceiling.

(2) Achieving dynamic range consistencies of different sounds that can be achieved from a source (e.g., finger-style playing versus "popping" or "slapping" on a bass, or the use of a brush stick versus a wood stick on a snare drum).

(3) Modifying the characteristic of a musical instrument sound source by apparently stretching (or shortening) the sustain.

(4) Modifying the attack qualities of a musical instrument.

(5) To ensure dynamic range consistency between multiple sound sources relative to each other (e.g., to ensure that the "loudness" of each backing singer is consistent, or to ensure that the "loudness" of each unit of the drum set is not inconsistent).

(6) For smoothing effects (e.g., to ensure that the dynamic range is consistent between the strong voice (shouting) and the normal voice of a singer).

(Dan Levitin's articles, "How Music Recordings are Made I" (page 3) and "Instrument (and Vocal) Recording Tips and Tricks" (see *Audio Anecdotes I*), further explore musical recording techniques.)

Compression is also used to make the dynamic range appropriate for the intended listening environment. The full dynamic range of a symphonic orchestra would not be desirable in the home or car listening environment, even if the technology could reproduce it. For example, a naïve musical purist related that he assumed that dynamic range compression was just destroying the dynamics of the music and wanted none of it until he tried listening to Orff's *Carmina Burana* on a CD player in an automobile. He relates that ... "During a pianissimo part with just a triangle tinkling, I'd have to crank up the volume to hear it over the ambient car noise ... then, when the entire chorus and orchestra with tympani would come crashing in sforzando fortissimo, nearly deafening me, I'd have to lunge to crank the volume back down ... then, it would go pianissimo again and I'd have to crank it up again ..."

Compressor-type devices have found their way into many consumer products. Many new "portable" CD and tape players contain an electronic circuit that performs compression on the audio signal. Such systems provide the user with some protection for their long-term hearing. Compressors have also found their way into home entertainment and theatre products. These systems compress the sounds during explosive action scenes while allowing soft intimate dialog scenes to be heard clearly, minimizing the need for user intervention on the volume control.

2 Steady State Input/Output Level Characteristics

Audio compressors are characterized by their steady state input/output level characteristics which are described by *threshold* and *slope*, or *ratio*, or *compression ratio* (refer to Figure 1). The x-axis represents the steady state input level in dBm, while the y-axis represents the steady state output level in dBm. The upper line represents a system with no dynamic range compression. The slope is equal to 1:1 and the output is simply equal to the input. An ordinary amplifier or attenuation would also have slope equal to 1:1, but would simply be displaced upward or downward. For each 1 dB change at the input, there is a 1 dB change at the output.

The bottom line represents an audio compressor with a threshold of −20 dBm and a compression ratio of 2:1. (Note that by convention, the compression ratio is referred to as 2:1, even though the actual slope of the line as defined by "rise over run" is 1/2. The compression ratio is actually

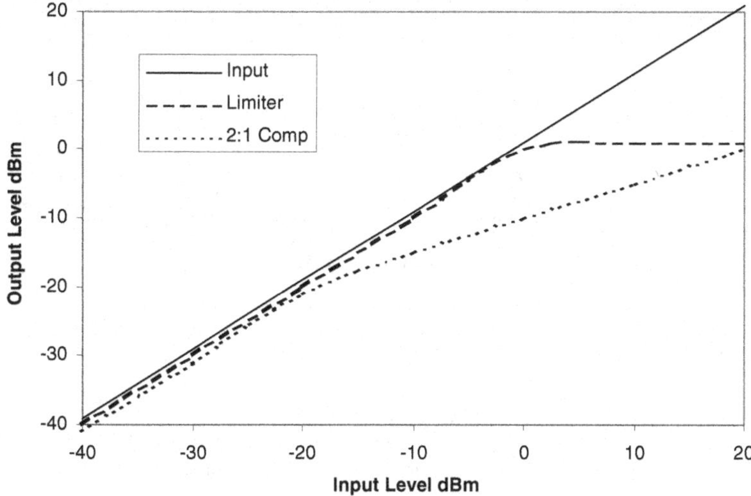

Figure 1. Input/output characteristics.

the inverse of the actual slope of the line.) For input signals above the threshold, each 2-dB increase at the input will be reduced or compressed to only a 1-dB increase at the output. For each 2-dB increase at the input, the gain through the compressor will reduce by 1 dB in order that the output increases by only 1 dB. Notice that the input signal is unaffected as long as it is below the threshold. Below threshold, the input/output characteristic has a slope of 1:1. Below the threshold, the gain is constant and does not change. Above the threshold, the gain begins to change in response to the input signal.

The middle line represents a different compressor that has a higher threshold of 0 dBm and a larger compression ratio of 10:1. A compressor with a high threshold and large compression ratio is often called a *limiter*. Above the threshold, the output increases by only 1 dB even though the input has increased by 10 dB. Notice that both the limiter and 2:1 compressor reduce the overall dynamic range but they do so in different ways. The compressor typically has a low threshold and so operates over most of the dynamic range of the input. The limiter, on the other hand, has a high threshold, so maintains a constant gain over most of the input range, but reduces gain sharply above the threshold. The limiter operates only on the loudest sounds. Notice that for a limiter to strictly enforce an upper "limit" on the level, it would need an infinite compression ratio to ensure that there would be *no* increase in output level above the threshold.

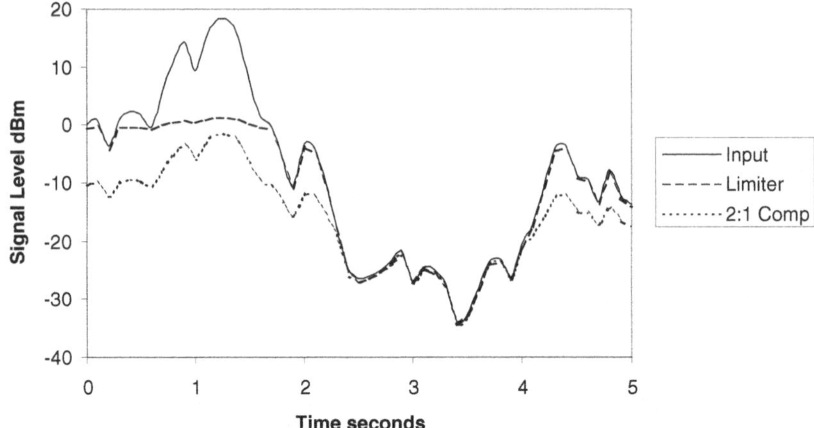

Figure 2. Input/output characteristics in time.

Most professional compressors allow the engineer to vary both the slope and threshold to suit the application, and can behave as compressors or limiters. Some compressors even provide for an adjustment of the shape of the threshold, allowing it to be varied from an abrupt transition in slope, as depicted in Figure 1, to a more gradual knee.

Note that even though the input/output characteristics appear linear on these graphs, because the scales are in dB, the actual transfer functions contain logarithmic terms.

Figure 2 shows another representation of the input/output characteristics. The x-axis now represents time and the y-axis represents both the input and output levels for some hypothetical signal of varying intensity. The top line represents the level characteristics of the uncompressed input signal with a range from below -30 dBm to almost $+20$ dBm. The bottom line shows the effect of a compressor with a threshold of -20 dBm and a 2:1 slope. Note that below -20 dBm, the output is the same as the input. Above -20 dBm, the level changes are reduced by 2:1. The middle line represents a limiter with threshold at 0 dBm and 10:1 slope. The output is the same as the input for all signals below 0 dBm, but above 0 dBm the output is nearly flat. This shows the difference in operation between a compressor and a limiter. A compressor moderately affects the signal over a wide range of signal level; a limiter, on the other hand, has no effect over a wide range of level, but then has a severe effect above threshold.

3 Dynamic Characteristics in Time

The input/output curves discussed above characterize the steady state behavior of a compressor. The dynamic characteristics *attack* and *decay times* describe how quickly in time the compressor gain responds to input level changes.

The *attack time* refers to the time it takes for the compressor to reduce gain when the output level is too high. During the attack time, the output level is larger than desired and the compressor is reducing its gain. Typical attack times range from 1 ms to 100 ms. A short attack time is desirable to avoid prolonged output signals above the desired level. If the attack time is made too short, however, the compressor gain will reduce unnecessarily in response to very short transients.

Decay time, also called *release time*, refers to the time it takes for the compressor to increase gain when the output level is too low. During the *decay time*, the output level is lower than desired and the gain of the compressor is increasing. The decay time is often slower compared to the attack time. Typical values range from 10 ms to several seconds. A long decay time is desirable to prevent the compressor from increasing gain unnecessarily during short pauses in the program material, such as between syllables or between words of speech. This is sometimes called "pumping," and can often be heard as the background noise increases during short pauses. Most professional compressors allow the engineer to vary both the attack and decay times.

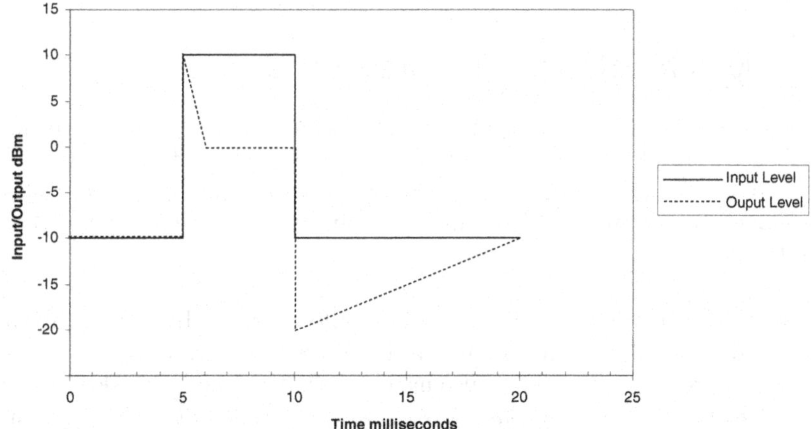

Figure 3. Compressor attack time.

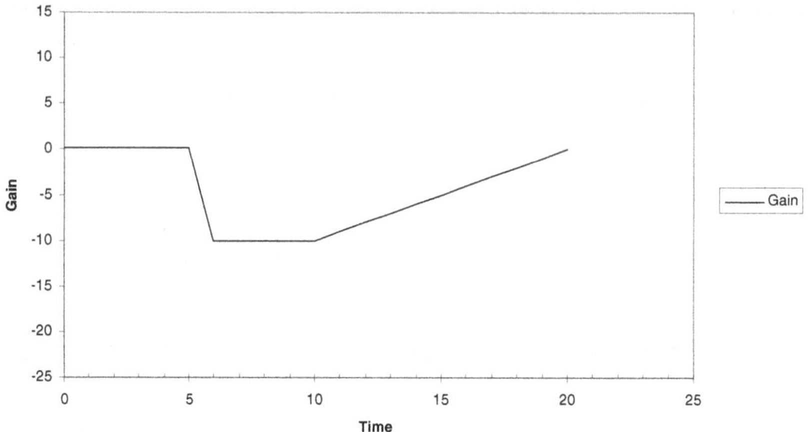

Figure 4. Compressor decay time.

Figures 3 and 4 demonstrate the attack and decay times of a compressor. In Figure 3, the input signal represented by the solid line increases from −10 dBm to +10 dBm. The output signal initially follows, but then reduces to 0 dBm after the attack time, which is 1 ms in this example. Figure 4 shows the gain of the compressor reducing by 10 dB. At 10 ms, the input reduces back to −10 dBm. Again, the output initially follows, but then gradually returns during the 10-ms decay time in this example. Figure 4 shows the gain increasing during the decay time.

4 Dynamic Range Compression Devices

The steady state input/output characteristics of a compressor are described by the slope and threshold. The dynamic characteristics are described by the attack and decay times. A shorthand terminology has developed to describe some common combinations of characteristics that are frequently used.

- *AGC (Automatic Gain Control) amplifiers* usually have their threshold set at the desired signal level and operate with a high slope or compression ratio. They also have a slow attack and very slow decay times, which usually last several seconds. They are often used in consumer recorders to automatically set the overall record level with a minimal change to the aesthetics of the program. The threshold is set near the correct recording level, and any level exceeding this is reduced to the correct level.

- *Compressors* typically have a medium-level threshold and a variable compression ratio setting with fast attack and variable decay times on the order of 100 ms to 1 second. Professional recording studios and radio broadcast stations use compressors to modify the aesthetic quality of a program and give the material more "punch." Broadcasters employ compressors to make their station sound louder, believing this improves ratings. Compression can make the program sound louder because the average level can be increased without increasing the peak level. The maximum peak level is determined by the channel (100% modulation in the case of radio), and compression allows the average to be raised without the peaks exceeding 100% modulation. To actually increase the average volume, the attack and decay times must be rather fast, corresponding to the time duration of speech syllables (typically a 10-ms attack time and 100-ms to 1-second decay time). This type of compression also sounds loud because it mimics the ear's natural compression; unfortunately, this also leads to listener fatigue. See Levitin's aforementioned article on recording tips for additional discussion of compression in professional recordings.

- *Limiters* have a high threshold and a very high compression ratio. They usually have very fast attack times, usually under 1 ms. They are used in applications where it is necessary to prevent brief, unexpected audio transients from exceeding an upper limit. These applications include radio transmission where it is important to prevent over-modulation. Radio stations typically employ compression to increase loudness followed by a limiter to protect against over modulation. Limiters are also used in high-power PA work where it is necessary to protect speakers from damage due to overloads.

- *Hard clippers* have similar slope and thresholds as limiters. Limiters and compressors are typically designed to avoid distortion of the waveform. Clippers, on the other hand, are simply nonlinear devices that severely modify and clip the waveform above threshold. Clippers have essentially instantaneous attack and decay times. This creates harmonic and intermodulation distortion. Below the threshold, however, there is minimal effect on the waveform. Clippers can be simply implemented in DSP by setting a maximum absolute value on the signal value. Clippers are very easy to implement and are effective at controlling audio transients; however, they also create severe distortion above threshold.

- *Soft clippers*, like hard clippers, have instantaneous attack and decay times. Soft clippers, however, have a lower compression ratio and therefore are less effective at holding an absolute upper limit, but they also create less distortion. They are relatively easy to implement and are a compromise between effective transient control and distortion. Soft clippers are similar to limiters with instantaneous attack and decay, but with a slope below infinity. The lower the slope, the more "soft" the limiter.

- *Expanders* have steady state input/output characteristics that are the opposite of compressors. They increase the dynamic range of the signal. When the input signal is below the threshold, every 1-dB decrease in input signal level results in a 2-dB decrease in output level. Note that the typical implementation of an expander is fundamentally different from that of the typical compressor in that there is no feedback loop in an expander. In a compressor, the OUTPUT level is used to control the attenuation of the VCA forming a feedback control loop. In the expander configuration, the INPUT level controls the VCA forming a feed-forward type system.

- *Noise gates* are similar to expanders with low input level thresholds and high ratios. They are used to gate or turn off a program during pauses in the material and are usually used to gate out excessive background noise or reverberation. See Levitin's aforementioned article "Instrument (and Vocal) Recording Tips" for an example of how noise gates are used in recording drums.

- A *compander* consists of a matched compressor and expander pair. For example, if the compression is set for 3:1 and the expander set for 1:3, and if the thresholds and attack and decay times are aligned correctly, the dynamic range of the final output will be the same as that of the original input. The signal in the channel between the compressor and the expander, however, will have 1/3 the dynamic range. Compandors are used to improve the dynamic range or reduce the noise of a channel. The Dolby Noise reduction system, commonly used with cassette tapes, is an example of the use of companding. A compressor is used during recording to reduce the dynamic range of the signal recorded on the tape. During playback, an expander restores the playback signal to its original dynamic range.

- A *de-esser* is a variation of the compressor, and is used to limit the amount of sibilance. De-essers are a handy tool to have when amplifying a voice that has strong sibilance. When amplified, the sibilance tends to become a distraction for listeners because of the "sharpness" of the sound, eventually causing irritation. The de-esser contains a pre-emphasis block that is added to allow the compressor to be sensitive to, and compress only, the high-sibilant frequencies.
- *Multiband processors.* The de-esser is a simple example of frequency sensitive compressors. Adding to frequency sensitivity are devices known as multiband compressors. In a multiband processor, the audio program is broken down into several frequency ranges or bands. Each band is compressed separately, allowing individual compression ratios, thresholds, and attack/decay times to be applied throughout the audio spectrum, hence, allowing greater control of the overall signal. Multiband compressors are popularly used in both the mastering process (to "shape" the final sound of a mix) and in the area of broadcast. In the age of "pop" music where louder is better, compressors are being used by radio stations to try to achieve a "louder" sound to compete against other radio stations.
- A *ducker* is used when two signals exist simultaneously, but where one has to take precedence over the other. The effect of the ducker is often heard on radio and in shopping centers when the piped music seems to fade away, although remaining audible, while the announcer or DJ is speaking. Similarly, the music mysteriously fades back in once the speaker has stopped (a block diagram of a ducking device is shown in the applications later on in this article).

5 Implementation of Dynamic Range Compressors/Limiters

The basic structure of a traditional compressor consists of a negative feedback control loop (see Figure 5). The control loop adjusts the gain of the variable gain cell in order to obtain the desired output signal level as measured by the level detector. If the output level is too high, the control signal reduces the gain. If the output level is too low, the control signal increases the gain. An expander does not form a closed control loop, but rather is an open loop with a feed forward structure (see Figure 6). The input signal level directly controls the variable gain cell, independent of the output.

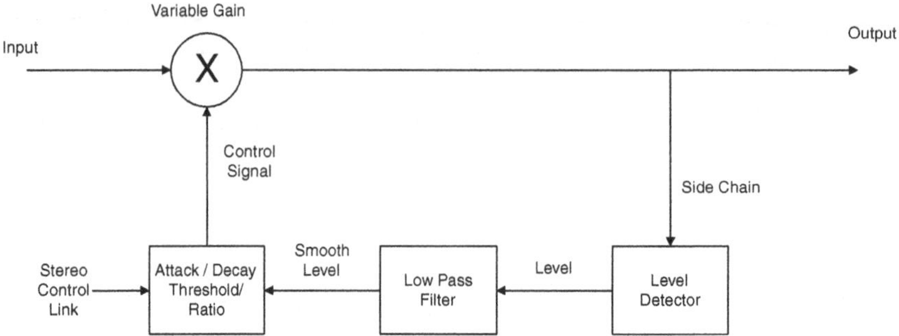

Figure 5. Compressor block diagram with feedback structure.

Using Digital Signal Processing (DSP) techniques, compressors of moderate slope can now also be implemented using the feedforward structure. The feedforward structure has the advantage that a time delay can be placed in the signal path so that the compressor can, in effect, "anticipate" changes in the signal level and have a zero attack time. However, it is difficult to implement a limiter or compressor with a very high compression ratio using the feedforward structure. This is because the characteristics of the level detector and variable gain cell need to be closely matched so that the changes in input level can be exactly mimicked by the changes in gain. This matching is not needed when using the conventional feedback structure, because the control signal will adjust itself as needed to obtain the required output.

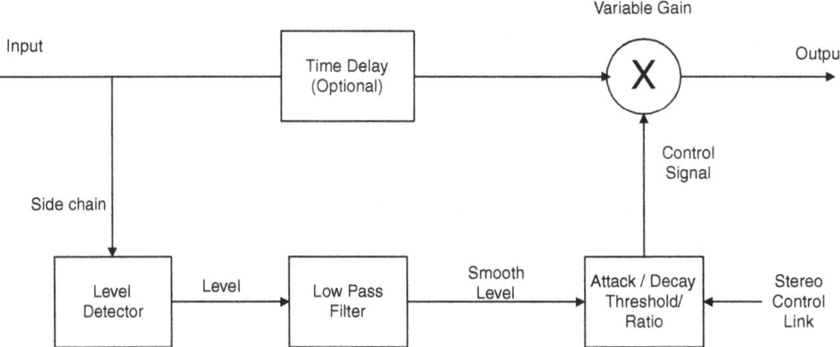

Figure 6. Expander block diagram with feed-forward structure.

The heart of any compressor or expander is the variable gain cell whose gain is varied by the control signal. In an analog system, the variable gain cell is typically implemented by a Voltage Controlled Amplifier, or Voltage Controlled Attenuator (VCA). In a DSP system, the variable gain cell is implemented simply by multiplying the audio signal by a slowly varying control number or coefficient. Since the control coefficient value changes relatively slowly compared to the audio signal value, specialized efficient multiplication algorithms may be used to reduce the complexity of the DSP hardware or software.

The level detector is another important element in the compressor. Analog implementations typically use a full wave diode or op-amp envelope detector-type circuit to convert the AC audio waveform to a DC voltage which represents the audio level or envelope of the waveform. Depending on the detector design, the DC voltage may represent the average audio level or the peak level. The Root Mean Square (RMS) value provides the best match to perceived loudness. A true RMS detector is rather difficult to implement, however. In a DSP implementation, the RMS value can be found by squaring the input signal, time averaging, and then taking the square root. In less demanding applications, the difficult squaring and square root operations can be eliminated and the time average of the absolute value of the signal can be used instead. In this case, the average level of the signal will be controlled, rather than the RMS value, and the perceived loudness may change somewhat depending on the signal waveform.

The attack and decay dynamic characteristics of the compressor are controlled by the time constants in the control signal averaging and filtering. The detection function provides a steady indication of the present signal level. If the time averaging is too short, the indication will not be steady, but rather will vary on a cycle-by-cycle basis of the low frequencies in the program material. Any cycle-by-cycle variation of the control signal applied to the variable gain cell will distort the waveform of the signal, creating harmonic and intermodulation distortion. If, on the other hand, the time averaging is excessively long, the output will be smooth, but will not accurately follow rapid changes in the program level, making it difficult to achieve very fast attack times. Since the time duration of rapid changes in the envelope can be on the same order as the cycle-to-cycle durations of the low frequencies, some compromise is necessary. An alternative is to employ multiband processing where the audio program is broken down into several frequency ranges or bands. Each band is compressed separately and the time constants of each frequency band can be individually tailored.

The DC transfer function of the circuits generating the control signal determines the steady state slope and threshold characteristics of the compressor. For example, a threshold is created by setting a lower limit on the control voltage. The control voltage will be held at this lower limit unless the detector output exceeds this level. The gain of the compressor will therefore be held constant until the detected level exceeds the threshold. The gain in the feedback control loop path determines the input/output slope. A large loop gain provides tight control of the output level corresponding to a large input/output slope.

Control loop stability is a key concern in any negative feedback control loop system. The combination of the filtering and loop gain must result in a stable feedback loop. In the "dominant pole" approach, the filter section contains one filter element whose time constant is much longer than the others in the loop.

The compressor feedback path is also known as the side chain. Placing an equalizer in the audio portion of the side chain before the detector allows the audio engineer to create a compressor that responds to only certain frequency ranges. An even more dramatic effect, known as *ducking*, is created by connecting the side chain audio to a completely different audio program. This causes the level of one audio source to control the gain of another; for example, the presence of an announcer's voice can automatically reduce the level of background music during voice-overs.

The compression of stereo material requires the use of two interlocked compressors. If the left and right channels are compressed separately, the balance between the two channels will vary as the two compressors change gain independently, causing the sound image to wander. This is resolved by tying the two control signals together so that the gain of both channels tracks each other.

6 Audible Effects of Compression

Compression can be used to fit the dynamic range of an audio program into the dynamic range of the equipment with the least audible effect. Compression can also be used to modify the dynamics of the program and intentionally change the way it sounds. The most noticeable audible effect of simple compressors occurs during pauses in the program material when the compressor increases its gain in an attempt to maintain the desired output level. The level of any background noise increases in a noticeable fashion. This undesired pumping or breathing effect can be minimized by a very slow decay time. Gating is another way to reduce breathing effects. Gating establishes another input level threshold. When the input is below this threshold, the compressor gain actually reduces similarly to an expander. Sounds that are above the gating threshold but low in amplitude are brought up in level as in the usual compressor. When the input is below the gating threshold, the compressor concludes that no input is present and reduces its gain to minimize any noise output.

Another undesired effect of compression is harmonic and intermodulation distortion. This can be caused by poor hardware implementation, particularly the variable gain cell. Inadequate filtering is another more fundamental cause of distortion. If the control signal contains not only the level information but also some of the audio waveform, the compressor gain will vary on a cycle-by-cycle basis, distorting the audio waveform creating harmonic and intermodulation distortion. Proper filtering of the control signal to eliminate the audio waveform is important in minimizing this form of distortion.

Masking is another audible effect of compression. When a complex program consisting of many elements is passed through a compressor, the loudness of one element can sometimes be heard controlling the volume of another element. For example the level of a flute may be modulated by louder drum beats. During and after each louder drum beat, the level of the flute will be momentarily reduced. The level of the flute will increase in between the drum beats, which is similar to the psycho-acoustic masking effect that normally occurs in human auditory perception. This causes the drum to be perceived as very loud when, in fact, it is not. This creates an effect known as listener fatigue, where the listener gets tired of listening for extended periods. Listener fatigue was a common problem for radio broadcasters using heavy compression. The problem can be reduced by the use of multiband processing, whereby the audio band is split into several frequency ranges and each range is compressed separately.

Audio programs often consist of stereo pairs, i.e., a left and a right channel. If compression is applied to the two channels of a stereo pair independently, the gain of the two channels may change independently. This will cause the sound image to shift back and forth as the channel balance is affected. The gain control signals for the left and right channels are usually combined into one to eliminate this undesired effect, causing the gain changes in the two channels to track each other. Figure 7 is an example of a feedforward compressor that can be implemented using DSP techniques.

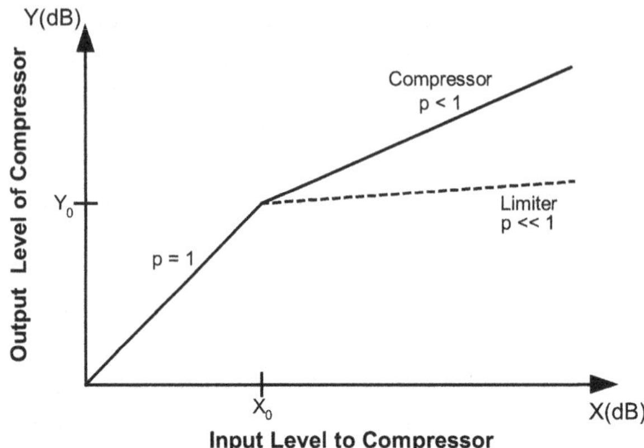

Figure 7. Relationship between the input and output level (dB) for compressors and limiters.

6.1 Compressor Description

In Figure 7, compressors determine the level of a signal (x-axis) with respect to a user-defined threshold (x_0). Compression by a ratio, $1/\rho$, occurs when the signal exceeds the user-defined threshold to produce the output level shown on the y-axis.

6.2 Compressor Structure

In Figure 8, it can be seen that the input signal $X(n)$ is sent through an envelope/level detector which determines the amplitude/power of the signal. The output of the level detector is the control signal $C(n)$, which is fed into a gain processor that determines the amount of attenuation required for the input signal. The output of the gain processor, $G(n)$, is then multiplied with the input signal $X(n)$, to give the output of the compressor $Y(n)$.

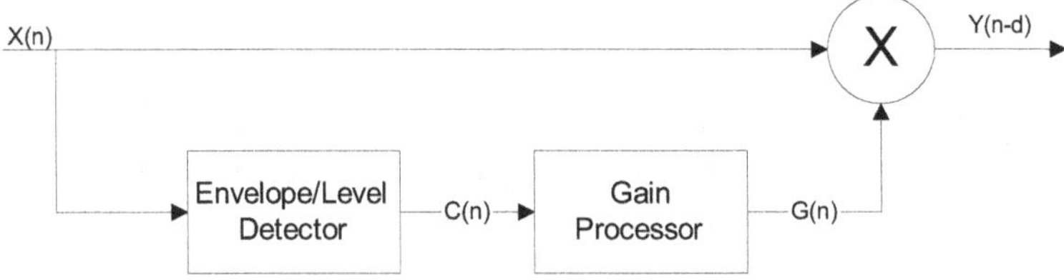

Figure 8. Basic block structure of a compressor system.

7 Compressor Algorithm

Orfanidis [2] provides the following equations for the envelope/level detector and gain processor as a basis for the development of a digital compressor. Modifications can be made to fine-tune the system's overall behavior and characteristics.

7.1 Compressor: The Level Detector

The level detector acts to rectify and smooth the input signal to provide a control signal to the gain processor. In the same way that the coefficients of a low pass filter determine the rise/fall time of the filter, the characteristics of the *attack* and *release* times can be altered by changing the parameter λ in Equation 1:

$$C(n) = \lambda C(n-1) + (1-\lambda)|X(n)|, \tag{1}$$

where $C(n)$ is the output of the level detector, $X(n)$ is the new sample (input), and λ is a user-defined parameter.

This equation may be varied to determine the mean square value of the signal by rewriting it as

$$C(n) = \lambda C(n-1) + (1-\lambda)[X(n)]^2. \tag{2}$$

Here, λ is used to define the rise time (transient) of the control signal generated, and in turn, is directly proportional to the attack and release times of the compressor.

A conditional statement can be applied to compare $C(n-1)$ with a past value of $C(n)$ such as $C(n-2)$. This will track the change of the control signal and allow different λ to be applied, thereby allowing independent attack and release times.

A special case for Equation 2 is when $\lambda = 0$. The first term reduces to 0, while the second term remains. In this situation, the level detector acts as an instantaneous peak detector.

7.2 Compressor: The Gain Processor

The gain processor uses the output of the envelope detector as a control signal to calculate the multiplier value $G(n)$. The key parameters of the gain processor are the threshold, C_0, and the compression ratio, $1/\rho$. The threshold determines when compression is applied to the sample, while the compression ratio determines the amount of compression required for the sample. For a linear response on a dB scale, the output of the gain

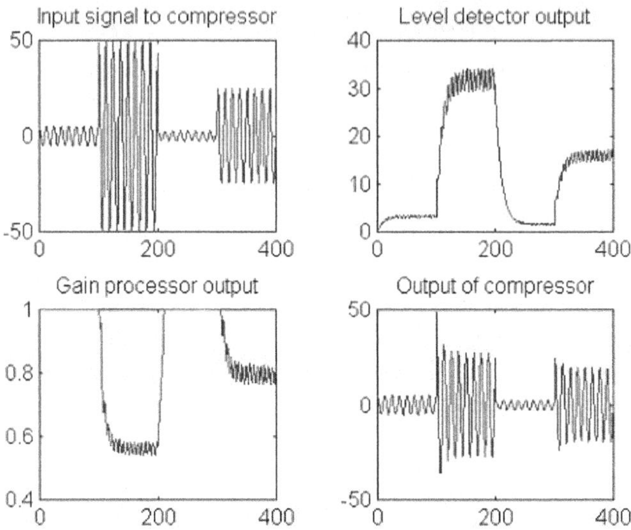

Figure 9. Simulation of basic compressor example.

processor is a log function of the control signal. The gain processor may be represented mathematically by Equation 3:

$$\begin{aligned} G(n) &= [C(n)/C_0]^{\rho-1}, \quad && \text{if } C(n) \geq C_0 \\ &= 1, && \text{if } C(n) < C_0 \end{aligned} \tag{3}$$

where $C(n)$ is the output signal of the level detector, C_0 is the threshold level (user-determined), and λ is the inverse of the compression ratio (user-determined) and is < 1.

Orfanidis [2] recommends that typical values for ρ range between 1/4 to 1/2, while for a limiter, $\rho \ll 1$ (e.g., $\rho = 1/10$).

The output of the compressor is thus represented by Equation 4:

$$Y(n) = G(n) \times X(n). \tag{4}$$

Figure 9 is a simulation of a compressor using the above equations using MATLAB. (The corresponding MATLAB and Octave scripts may be found on the CD-ROM accompanying this book.)

In this simulation, a tone burst signal was applied to the compressor with the parameters $\lambda = 0.9$, $C_0 = 10$, and $\rho = 0.5$.

Figure 9 illustrates that when the tone burst occurs, the level detect signal will increase, exceeding the threshold (10). Hence, the gain processor is then activated to calculate the attenuation according to the ratio ρ.

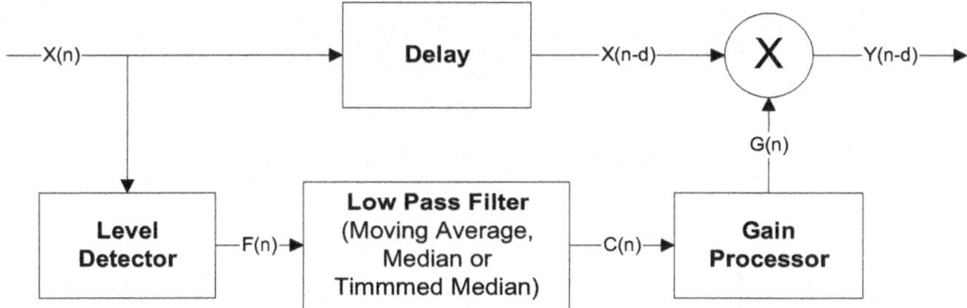

Figure 10. Alternative/improved block structure of the compressor.

Several characteristics are apparent in the simulation of the compressor algorithm.

Overshoots. Overshoots (and undershoots) in the output signal are caused by the delay introduced in the processing path (contributed by both the level detector and the gain processor).

To counter this, a delay in the straight (signal) path serves to compensate for the processing delay. Unfortunately, while this minimizes the overshoots, it is unable to eliminate them.

Distortion. The tone-burst input signal contains four discrete amplitudes that are not elegantly translated to the control signals (envelope detector and gain processor), which display a "saw-tooth" shape. When multiplied with the original signal, this creates amplitude distortion to the output. This problem may be reduced by smoothing the "steady-state" regions of the control signal $C(n)$.

Smoothing of the control signal can be achieved with appropriate filtering of the control signal. Issues to consider for the type of filter to be used are:

(1) The "step" response of the filter, i.e., the ability of the filter to switch from one state to another as quickly and accurately as possible.

(2) The "flatness" of the filter in "steady state."

A key point to note is that the insertion of another processing block (filter) into the processing path will increase the amount of delay required.

The reader is encouraged to experiment with different filter types, which may include basic types such as the Moving Average (FIR type), Median, and Trimmed Median filters. In essence, the improved structure for the compressor would be as shown in Figure 10.

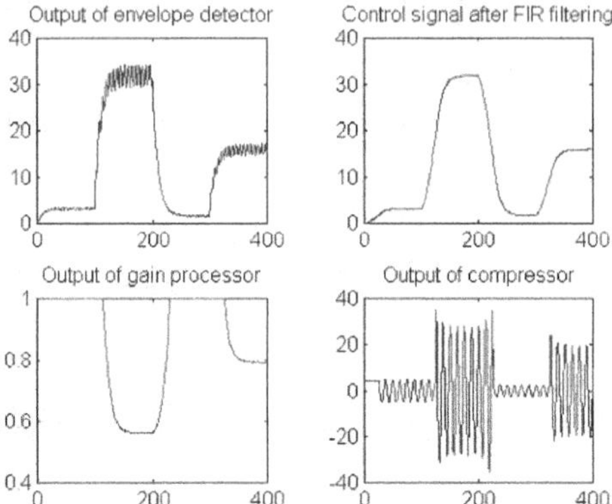

Figure 11. Simulation of the improved structure using identical parameters.

As a demonstration, a 31-tap moving average filter (uniform weighting) with a delay of 25 and all other parameters remaining the same produced the simulated results shown in Figure 11.

8 Variants of the Compressor: The Expander/Gate

With minor changes to the compressor algorithm, other types of dynamic range controllers, such as expanders and gates, can be created. While compressors are used on signals that *exceed* a threshold by reducing the amplitude, expanders and gates are used to attenuate signals that are *below* the threshold (see Figure 12).

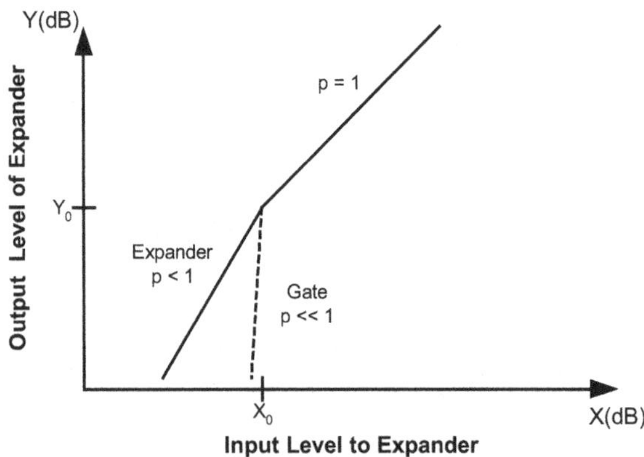

Figure 12. Relationship between the input and output level (dB) for expanders and gates.

8.1 Expanders: The Level Detector

The level detector of the expander works similarly to that of the compressor and no changes are necessary.

8.2 Expanders: The Gain Processor

In Equation 5, Equation 3 is rewritten for an expander:

$$\begin{aligned} G(n) &= 1, && \text{if } C(n) > C_0 \\ &= [C(n)/C_0]^{\rho-1}, && \text{if } C(n) \le C_0 \end{aligned} \tag{5}$$

where $C(n)$ is the output signal of the level detector, C_0 is the threshold level (user-determined), and ρ is the expansion ratio (user-determined) and is < 1.

For a signal that is less than the specified threshold, C_0, $[C(n)\ /\ C_0]$ will be less than 1. However, raising the above term to a power greater than 1 results in a number that is even smaller.

Orfanidis suggests that typical values of ρ for an expander range between 2 to 4, while for a gate, ρ is typically equal to or greater than 10.

8.3 Multifunction Compressor Using Multiple Breakpoints

The reliance of both the compressor and expander on the level detector allows the implementation of a single device that is capable of performing multiple functions of compression (at different ratios for different threshold settings), expansion, gating, and limiting.

The main change involves only the gain processor, which requires additional condition statements to specify the appropriate processing.

8.4 Ducking Device

The basic blocks can be re-arranged to achieve other effects. A block diagram for a "ducker" (described previously) is shown in Figure 13.

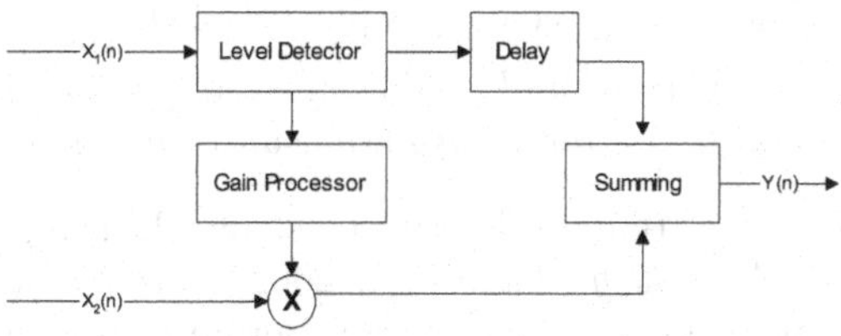

Figure 13. Block structure of a ducking device; X_2 "ducks" when X_1 is a signal that is large enough.

9 Final Word

The abuse of compression has recently become a controversial issue that has gained many supporters in recent years. Whilst popular culture appears to crave something louder (and therefore "better"), many engineers are beginning to realize that compression not only reduces the dynamic range, but can also reduce the dynamics of the sounds. Excessive compression can lead to listener fatigue that can actually cause listeners to tune away from a radio station for break from the continuous wall of sound.

It is obvious that the compressor and its variants can be used both practically and creatively. However, if abused, compression can prove to be a bane as much as it may be a boon.

Annotated Bibliography

[1] John Borwick. *Sound Recording Practice.* Oxford: Oxford University Press, 1994.

[2] S. J. Orfanidis. *Introduction to Signal Processing.* Upper Saddle River, NJ: Prentice Hall, 1996.

[3] *The ARRL Handbook for Radio Amateurs.* Newington, CT: ARRL, 2001.

[4] Scott Lehman. "Compression/Limiting" (http://www.harmony-central.com/Effects/Articles/Compression/), 1996.

This site provides a good description of Compression/Expansion basics.

[5] (http://www.alesis.com/product.php?id=49).

Go to www.alesis.com and look under Products/Signal Processors/3630 Compressor.

[6] (http://www.alesis.com/tech_notes.php?id=14).

Go to www.alesis.com and look under Support/FAQs/Technical Notes/Materlink to see the information on compressors.

[7] Tom Scheller. "Temporal aspects of hearing aid signal processing." *Audiology Insight* 3/2002, 13–19. (Available at http://www.bernafon.ch/eprise/main/Bernafon/_downloads/Publications_and_Presentations/AudiologyInsight3_2002UK.pdf).

This article provides a discussion of feed forward versus feedback technique and level estimation.

[8] "Model 166XL Compressor Gate" (http://www.dbxpro.com/ftp_mirror/PDFs/Manuals/English/166XLmanual.pdf), 1998.

Instruction Manual for a DBX166 professional audio compressor.

[9] "Compression 101" (http://www.dbxpro.com/ftp_mirror/PDFs/WhitePapers/Compression%20101.pdf), November 1998.

DBX white paper on compression.

[10] Roger Johnsen. "Detection and the Dynamics Duo (Or Why Do Some Compressors Sound Great While Others Just Plain Don't?)" (http://www.dbxpro.com/ftp_mirror/PDFs/WhitePapers/DetectionandDynamicsDuo.pdf), November 1998.

DBX white paper on RMS detection of audio levels.

Simple Speech Activity Detector

Ian H. Merritt

1 Introduction

This article describes a software-based speech activity detector that is lightweight, fast, and relatively inexpensive in terms of CPU cycles. In any packet-based voice transmission system, such a detector can significantly impact bandwidth utilization by making it possible to transmit only when the speaker is actually talking.

A fixed point implementation is discussed and a full floating point version is included on the CD-ROM accompanying this book.

1.1 A Bit of History

In the early 1980s, at the University of Southern California Information Sciences Institute (USC/ISI), working with a research group that included Billy Brackenridge and others on an early research project in the area of what is now known as Voice over Internet Protocol or VoIP, I was involved in the development of an interface device known as the Switched Telephone Network Interface[1] card (STNi). This functioned as a component of an early Packet Voice Terminal[2] (PVT) that had been developed by other project participants at the MIT Lincoln Laboratory.

[1] See *Providing Telephone Line Access to a Packet Voice Network*, ISI/RR-83-107, Ian H. Merritt, *University of Southern California Information Sciences Institute*, February 1983. This is an original research report from the project under which this detector was developed. It describes, in somewhat more detail, the interface and the broader context in which it functioned.

[2] See *A modular approach to packet voice terminal hardware design*, in *AFIPS Conference Proceedings, Vol. 50: National Computer Conference*, pp. 183–188, AFIPS Press, May 1981.

1.2 Packet Efficiency

One of the touted advantages of using a packet network to transmit digitized voice is the efficiency gain that can be realized by virtue of the bandwidth sharing inherent in packet transmission. Unlike circuit-switched systems, in which bidirectional channel bandwidth is dedicated throughout the life of the channel despite the intermittent nature of speech transmission, in theory, a packet system only uses bandwidth for the information that it has to transfer, and only in the direction of the transfer. Given the characteristics of a typical voice conversation, usually one speaker at a time, with intersyllable and intersentence pauses, it should be possible to achieve about a factor of 2.5 improvement in bandwidth utilization.

1.3 Reality Bytes

In order to realize that gain in a speech context, however, it is necessary to discriminate accurately and quickly between periods of speech activity and periods of relative silence. Complicating this problem is the fact that silence isn't reliably silent. In all real-world environments, there is background noise. Silence cannot be recognized simply as a series of bytes representing digital samples of about the same value (i.e., a flatline waveform).

1.4 Limited Resources

The hardware that made up the STNi was quite meager especially when compared to what is available now even in embedded platforms. The processor was a Z80 microprocessor running at what was then a lightning fast 3.072 MHz, nearly 4 orders of magnitude slower than CPUs or controllers commonly available today. Memory in those days was quite a bit slower, physically larger, and far more expensive than today; the entire address space of the Z80 was only 64K bytes. This seriously constrained the complexity of any software algorithms that were to run on the device. Nevertheless, it had several real-time tasks to perform simultaneously including exchanging control signals with the voice terminal, sampling speech from a codec in real time and breaking it into parcels of 180 bytes representing 22.5 ms which had to be marked as containing sound or silence, unpacking similarly encoded incoming information and feeding it out to the codec, and generating signaling tones such as MF, DTMF, and call progress (dial-tone, ring, busy, etc).

To meet this challenge, a speech activity detection algorithm was developed that could perform remarkably well despite these limitations.

Recently, Mr. Brackenridge contacted me on behalf of his colleague, Ken Greenebaum, who asked me to write a bit about this Speech Activity Detection algorithm. This is my attempt to recollect, after nearly 20 years, the algorithm, some details of the development, its performance, and perhaps to reminisce about the circumstances surrounding this work.

2 Simple Speech Activity Detector

An important part of the research project that led to the development of the STNi was proving that the touted efficiency gains were practically attainable. Speech Activity Detection, therefore, was an integral part of the STNi design.

2.1 Lincoln Logs

For this particular experiment, the MIT Lincoln Laboratory had designed their Packet Voice Terminal (PVT) to utilize a μ-law PCM codec. This is the standard used by North American telephone carriers. It consists of a logarithmically compounded encoding in which the analog data stream is sampled into a series of quantized values that are encoded into signed 8-bit byte values. These are represented in a 1s compliment format (i.e., a sign bit and an absolute value, which incidentally has both positive and negative values of zero).

2.2 Flattening Out the Logs

Early on, it was assumed that the algorithm would need to operate on the linear samples, not logs. A conversion lookup was utilized, but the Z80 processor was an 8-bit machine with limited 16-bit capabilities. This would factor into the later decision to experiment with an algorithm operating directly on the logarithmic samples.

2.3 Now to Detect Speech—Or So We Thought

A number of algorithms seemed obvious, so these were tried. A simple emulation of an analog VOX circuit was tried. This looked for any sample above an empirically selected amplitude level as a signal that speech energy had begun, and enabled transmission until a fixed period of time had elapsed without any further such samples. The performance of this method was fair in a low-noise environment and unacceptable in a noisy environment. It wasn't adaptable to differing environments, tended to be sluggish at recognizing that a speaker had begun talking, never detected intersyllabic pauses, and continued to utilize transmit bandwidth for an unnecessarily long period after the speaker was finished.

Little additional features were added to try to make it respond less sluggishly. A variety of attempts were made to make it somewhat adaptable to variable background conditions. As it seemed we were approaching a working algorithm, we ran out of CPU cycles. Because of the very slow 3MHz Z80 processor, we had a total of 384 instruction cycles per sample in which to do *everything* for which this device was responsible. When the time to process a single sample even approaches this number, other functions of the system fail to respond in a timely manner. Exceeding this number causes transmission failure.

2.4 Mean Logs?

What is the mean of a logarithm, anyway? I got to thinking about the linearization as perhaps an unnecessary step. If we could somehow operate directly on the 8-bit PCM sample values instead, we not only could save the cycles associated with the conversion, but we would no longer be operating on 16 bit values, thus saving lots of CPU cycles. But what would happen if we tried to apply our algorithms to logarithmic values directly? It seemed intuitively that this might produce satisfactory results. This would tend to apply a logarithmic curve to the algorithm itself. Perhaps this could be a good thing. Other researchers on the project were skeptical, but were willing to indulge my ignorance, if only to let me learn first-hand that it wouldn't work.

The initial result was pretty good but still needed some adjustment. Over the next few weeks, the algorithm was perfected and simplified down. Though the original algorithm was written in Z80 assembly language, it is presented here in C syntax for clarity. A complete floating point implementation is provided on the CD-ROM accompanying this book.

Once per sample:

```
// use 8bit shifts if more efficient
avg = (abs(x) / 256) + ((255 * avg) / 256);
```

Once per 22.5ms parcel:

```
thresh = minavg + 8;
if (avg > thresh) {
    sound = TRUE;
    count--;
    if (count == 0) {
```

```
            minavg++;
            count = 16;
        }
} else {
        sound = FALSE;
        if (avg < minavg) {
        minavg = avg;
            count = 16;
        }
}
```

In the sample code above, **thresh**, the threshold, always floats at 8 units above **minavg**, the minimum average value. Operating in a logarithmic domain, the range of amplitudes covered by these 8 units is relative to the threshold level. Parcels averaging in excess of **thresh** are flagged as sound and transmitted; otherwise, they are flagged as containing silence and not sent, thus conserving bandwidth. When the average amplitude level (**avg**) remains above **thresh** for 16 parcel times, **minavg** is incremented, thus increasing **thresh** by one as well. Whenever **avg** drops below **minavg**, **minavg** is immediately set equal to **avg**, adjusting for sudden drops in the amplitude. This has the effect of adapting quickly to a sudden decrease in the background noise level, and correcting for the case where a burst of speech causes **minavg** to drift up too high.

The Z80, basically an 8-bit processor with a few 16-bit registers and limited 16-bit arithmetic operations, lacks any multiply and divide instructions. It is, however, possible to move values between the 8-bit upper and lower halves of 16-bit registers, effectively multiplying or dividing by 256. Using this technique, the algorithm averages the logarithmic sample values over 256 samples. In the Z80 code, the running average is stored as a 16-bit quantity, representing a fixed-binary point number with the fractional portion in the low 8 bits. The subexpression (**255 * avg**) shown in the example is approximated in the Z80 implementation by copying the high 8 bits (whole portion) of the accumulated "average" into the low order 8 bits of another register, with the high 8 bits zero (effectively dividing by 256), then subtracting this value from the accumulated average. At the end of each parcel, a silence/sound decision is made by comparing this average with the dynamic threshold values.

Operating directly on the logarithmic values indeed performed *better* than operating on the linear values did. It seems that the resulting logarithmic response of the algorithm was better suited to the practical application than linear response. On reflection, this really shouldn't come as that much of a surprise.

The parcel time of 22.5 ms contributes something important to this algorithm as well. This works out to roughly 44 parcels per second: long enough to be a meaningful increment for buffering into a packet protocol stack, yet far shorter than a typical syllable. Because of this, the sound/silence decision is being made fast enough to detect inter-syllable pauses, and to correct its threshold drift rapidly enough to effectively prevent it from having a perceptible effect on the audio quality. Moreover, the average covers 32 ms, a time slightly longer than that of the parcel. This means that the sound/silence decision pertaining to any parcel goes back to before the beginning of the parcel. This improves the ability of the algorithm to avoid clipping off the first parcel of an utterance, while reducing false triggers due to brief spikes of noise.

2.5 Performance

So how well does all this work? Very well indeed. Unfortunately, after all these years, I no longer have access to the test data from which graphics may be generated. Originally, however, I had run an exhaustive series of tests and generated pen plots of the results. Included here are copies of these plots. Unfortunately, the color-coding is long lost, but they are adequately described nonetheless.

Charts and graphs aside, the audio quality from the point of view of a user was quite good. It degraded somewhat with the introduction of a crude echo suppression algorithm. This was necessitated by audio signals reflecting off the common imbalance in real-world hybrid networks in the 2-wire analog subscriber line interfaces to which the STNi connected.

In Figure 1, the lower of the parallel lines corresponds to `minavg` in the algorithm; the higher line is `thresh`. The left-most segment consists of background room noise and what little sound seeped through the wall from an adjacent computer room. The second segment is speech with the same background noise level. In the third segment, the door to the adjacent computer room was opened to provide a loud background noise. Note that the silence threshold climbed to eclipse this noise level completely. In the fourth segment, speech was again recorded, this time with the computer room background noise, demonstrating that the detector is still quite effective with the increased noise level. The last spike toward the end was produced by the slamming of the computer room door. Note the sudden decrease in the threshold level immediately following that event.

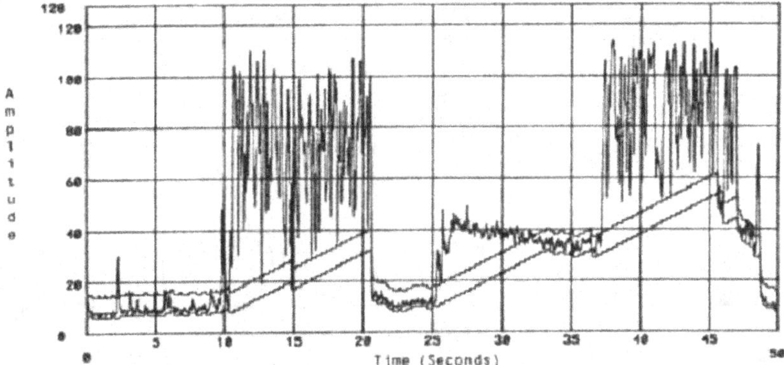

Figure 1. STNI sound detector performance with speech and background noise.

Figure 2 shows the response of the sound detector to a constant, loud tone, in this case a touch-tone. The threshold climbs slowly, eventually passing the level of the loud tone. Once it has reached this point, it ceases to climb, stabilizing at a level just above the amplitude of the tone. When the tone was removed (not shown here), the threshold dropped immediately back to its level at the beginning of the graph.

Figure 3 shows the graphic display of the #1A ESS dial tone via a foreign exchange repeater circuit and roughly 5 to 6 miles of wire. It is shown here followed by a period of silence and the off-hook "scream" tone. This was the longest of the dial tones observed: about 16 seconds.

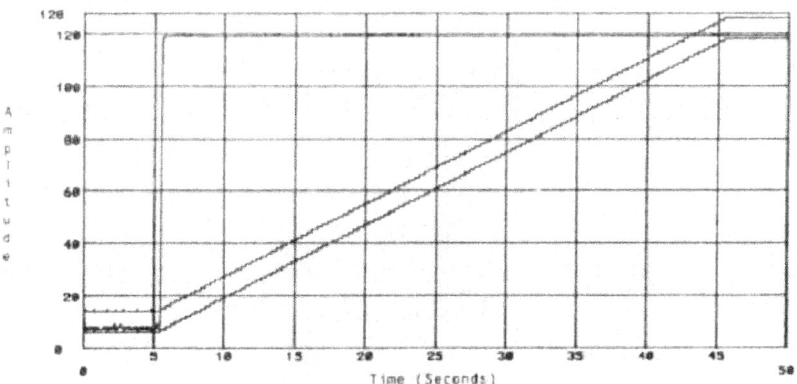

Figure 2. STNI sound detector.

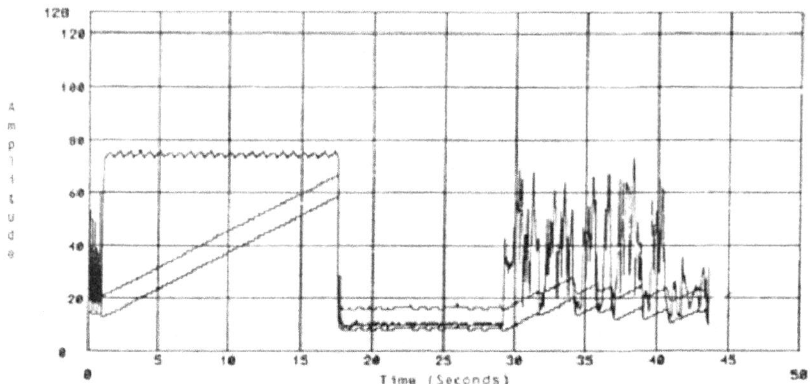

Figure 3. Bell System #1A ESS dial tone.

Figure 4 is the dial tone collected from a GTD 5 EAX switching system. This was collected from a short analog tail of no more than a few thousand feet. This particular switch does not provide any zero-battery signaling after its dial tone times out, but instead switches directly to a reorder tone which lasts indefinitely.

The sample in Figure 5 was collected from a Stromberg Carlson Crossreed PBX system. This was by far the shortest dial tone collected, lasting only about eight seconds, then terminating in an indefinite reorder tone without any battery signaling.

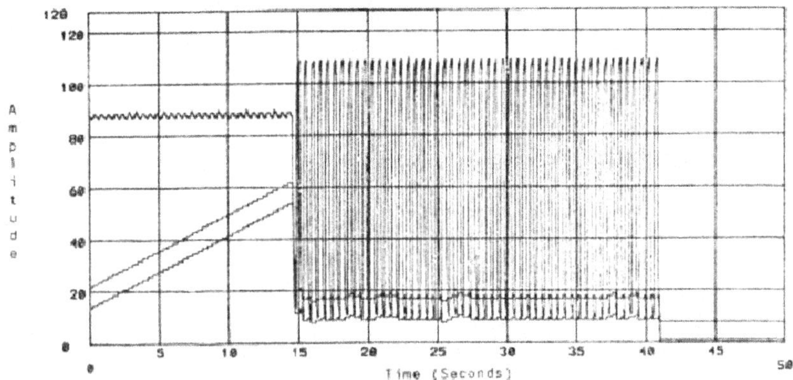

Figure 4. GTE EAX system dial tone.

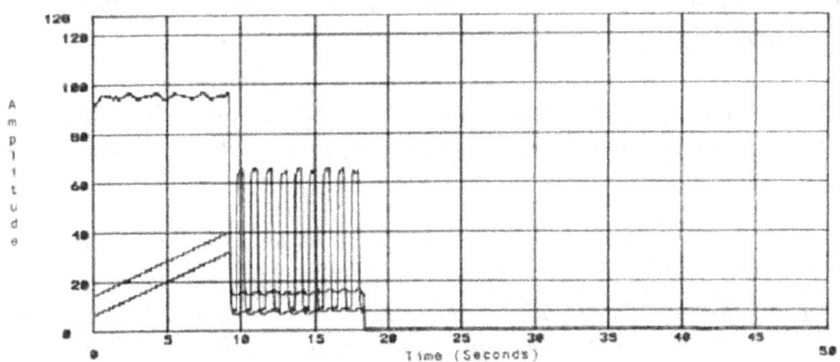

Figure 5. Stromberg Carlson Crossreed PBX system dial tone.

3 Conclusion

Many years have passed since I conducted the work that is the basis of this article and not surprisingly, much more research in the area of speech detection has been conducted in the intervening years. The algorithm presented in this article, while far from the state of the art, is surprisingly accurate and very efficient; it is well-suited for applications running on small processors with high signal-to-noise levels. More sophisticated algorithms which perform better in higher noise situations can be found in the bibliography.

4 Acknowledgments

The algorithm described herein was developed under the auspices of the *University of Southern California Information Sciences Institute* in 1982 and 1983.

Annotated Bibliography

[1] L. R. Rabiner and M. R. Sambur. "An Algorithm for Determining the Endpoints of Isolated Utterances." *Bell System Tech. Journal* 54:2 (1975), 297–315.

The classic reference describing an energy-based voice activity detection.

[2] ITU-T Rec. G.729, Annex B, *A silence compression scheme for G.729 optimized for terminals conforming to ITU-T V.70.*

The G.729 speech codec standard includes a sophisticated voice activity detector which tracks many parameters including amplitude, noise in the channel, and spectral characteristics, to determine speech activity.

[3] VoiceAge. "Open G.729 Initiative" (http://www.voiceage.com/codecsite/openinit_g729.php), 2000–2004.

Unfortunately due to patent protections and licensing issues an open source G.729 implementation is not available. However, VoiceAge participating in Cisco's vovida.org initiative makes a G.729 implementation available for non-commercial and pre-commercial development purposes.

[4] Vovida Networks, Inc. "Vovida.org: Your Source for Open Source Communication" (http://www.vovida.org).

An online, open-source, community for sharing telecommunications algorithms and advice.

[5] Jongseo Sohn, Nam Soo Kim, and Wonyong Sung. "A Statistical Model-Based Voice Activity Detection," *IEEE Signal Processing Letters* 6:1 (1999), 1-3.

A statistics-based voice activity detector which outperforms the G.729B standard in low signal-to-noise environments.

An Introduction to Sound Classification

James A. Ballas, Derek Brock, and Hesham Fouad

1 Introduction

One of the fascinating auditory abilities that we possess as humans is the capability to identify and discriminate between unique sounds in the environment. To us, this capability is so fundamental that we intuitively feel that it is a relatively simple process, one that could easily be implemented in a system of our own design.

For some sounds, there is a simple approach. For example, in the 1960s J. C. R. Licklider developed a method of recognizing the word "watermelon." This device depended on the unusually distinctive sequence of vowel sounds in the word "watermelon." Unfortunately, we have not discovered simple, robust detectors for very many sounds.

Generally, sounds cannot be identified using a simple algorithm, particularly if the algorithm needs to operate in a real (meaning noisy) environment. Current technologies for real-time speech recognition are extremely complex, and perform analysis at several levels simultaneously: acoustic, syntactic, and semantic. The processing at these levels, particularly the semantic-level processing, is domain-specific, and can require considerable effort to develop. For this article, we selected a classification task simpler than voice recognition to explore.

The algorithm that we provide demonstrates how a set of spectral features can be derived from a wave file and analyzed using a discriminant feature approach. The resulting classifier successfully classifies propeller-driven airplane sounds and has the potential to work in both real-time and noisy environments. The accompanying CD-ROM includes the classifier's source code and a set of sound files to test the program.

Acoustic pattern analysis research spans several fields with military applications having driven much of this research [2]. Specific problems, such as distinguishing between a seismic and a nuclear event, often can be addressed through acoustic pattern analysis. The problem of auditory scene analysis is now being addressed computationally [4].

1.1 Key Issues

Successful classification of sounds in a real environment must address two related issues: causal uncertainty and the performance trade-off between correct classifications and false alarms. The first issue, causal uncertainty, refers to the uncertainty about the cause of a sound that can exist because the acoustic information is not sufficient to uniquely determine its cause. Classification would be a simpler problem if dissimilar events would produce dissimilar acoustic effects. Instead, there is ample evidence that events that are thought to be dissimilar can produce similar acoustics. For example, a "click-click" sound can be generated by the use of a ballpoint pen, a stapler, or a pull-chain light switch [1]. Here, the acoustic similarity is the occurrence of two transients closely spaced in time. Other sounds will have similar long-term acoustics. For example, the sound of a small plane will produce low frequency sound similar to what is produced by wind blowing through trees, waterfalls, and even some types of frog sounds.

The challenge in designing a classifier is to find acoustic parameters that might be specific to the events of interest.

The second issue follows from the first. If causal uncertainty cannot be reduced completely, then the classification algorithm will involve a trade-off between missing the intended events (called signals), or classifying other events as signals. The relevant technical area here is signal detection theory, which characterizes classification as a binary decision-making process that produces outcomes as illustrated in Table 1. The binary decision process is based on an assumption that the evidence for a classification is noisy. Because of noise, the evidence for the occurrence of a particular sound (i.e., "A")[1] might sometimes be similar to the evidence

[1]In the traditional application of signal detection theory, there is an assumption that noise is constantly present and produces evidence that is normally distributed. The addition of a signal will shift the evidence along the axis a distance, producing a distribution called signal+noise. These distributions develop over the long term. Once they have become established, a particular instance will occur with a degree of evidence somewhere along the axis. A decision will be made about this instance depending on the setting of the threshold.

Decision	True State	
	Sound A	Not Sound A
Sound A	Hit	False Alarm
Not Sound A	Miss	Correct Rejection

Table 1. Binary decision outcomes in a simple classification task.[2]

that comes from other types of sounds. Therefore, a person has to set a threshold along a decision evidence axis, as illustrated in Figure 1, such that evidence above the threshold is called "Sound A" and evidence below the threshold is "Not Sound A." Adjustment of the threshold, in the absence of any improvement in the sound processing to increase the distance between the two distributions in Figure 1, will change the outcomes in the decision table. According to the theory, as the threshold changes to increase "Hits," "False Alarms" will also increase. As the threshold changes in the opposite manner, "Correct Rejections" will increase, but so also will "Misses." Therefore, in the development of any classifier, there is typically a tradeoff between these pairs of outcomes.

Signal detection theory is described in much greater detail in Derek DiFillipo and Ken Greenebaum's article "Introduction to the Theory of Signal Detection: Measuring Human Response" (see *Audio Anecdotes I*).

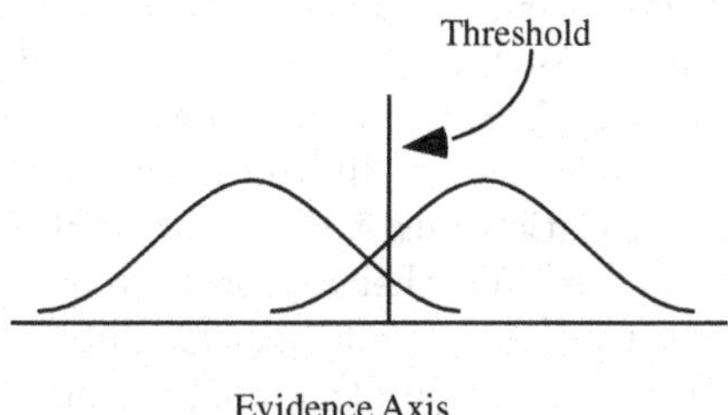

Figure 1. Evidence distributions for two classes with threshold positioned to the right of the midpoint.

2 Classification Approaches

There are several approaches that are typically used for acoustic signal classification [8]. These differ both in terms of the theory or concept of classification as well as in the computation that is used.

[2]The terms in this table are standard in psychophysics. Other fields use the term "false negative" for "miss" and "false positive" for "false alarm."

2.1 Theories or Concepts of Classification

Discriminant function. One of the easiest to understand and implement is discriminant feature classification; example code to implement this method will be given here. To implement this, you first need to identify candidate features that might be used to discriminate between the signal you want to classify and other similar signals. For example, if you were developing a frequency classifier, then the discriminant function that would separate two tones would be the mid frequency between them. Typically, the candidate features will be calculated on a training data set that includes both true and false instances. From this preliminary analysis, you can develop a discriminant function to implement the classification process. If several features were used, then the discriminant function would be a multivariate function. In simple cases, you can figure out the function by manually examining the data; for more complex cases, statistical correlation or neural network techniques can be used, as will be described below. In our example in the next section, this function will be a simple logic rule.

Similarity function. Some research on classification has supported the notion that learning produces a mental representation of a "typical" instance of the sound, which becomes a prototype. Classification will involve a comparison between the specific instance to be classified and the prototype [6]. For a frequency classifier, the prototype would be the frequency of the target tones, and the similarity function would compare the tone to be classified to the target frequency. Alternatively, if a set of examples are available, then the classification might be based on the known classification of the nearest neighbor. Whether a prototype or a nearest neighbor is used, the algorithm involves a similarity calculation along predefined dimensions. This approach might use the same features as a discriminant feature approach. In practice, a set of prototypes might be developed and used to classify signals into one of a set of classes.

2.2 Computation Approaches

The next two approaches refer to how the classification algorithm is computed. Both of these approaches will require a set of features to be used in the computation.

Threshold functions. Threshold functions are equations that calculate the value of a decision variable using either a discriminant function or a similarity function. The threshold function could be developed using statistical correlation which would produce a regression equation relating the decision variable to the set of features. The decision variable would be a binary value to mimic the classification decision. When a binary value is calculated, a decision threshold must be set to perform the classification. The regression equation computed from the training or test instances could provide a value for this threshold that minimizes the statistical error.

Neural network. This approach is similar in principle to the discriminant feature approach described above, but a neural network is used to make the classification, rather than a threshold function. Neural networks are biologically inspired models of how the brain inductively learns from examples at the level of neurons. Computationally, they are made up of a number of functionally simple nodes and a corresponding set of weighted connections for input and output. Nodes are organized in layers with at least one layer required for input and one for output. In the basic paradigm, each of a network's nodes uses the same nonlinear function to transform the weighted sum of its inputs into an activation value that is passed on to other nodes through its outputs. Connection weights are then adjusted by a process of nonlinear regression to fit a set of training data. Once they are trained, neural networks can be both accurate and fast. Kostek and Czyzewski [7] describe their successes using a two-layer, feed forward neural network as a classifier for musical instruments using a set of features of musical tone attack derived through wavelet analysis and a separate spectral and temporal set of Fast Fourier Transform-based (FFT) features as input.

2.3 Feature Analysis

All of the approaches described in the previous section will require some preliminary analysis of the acoustic information available in the sound and an assessment of the acoustic features that might best be utilized for the classification processing. This preliminary analysis of features can be very extensive, and we only cover some of the features here. The features can be categorized as spectral or temporal, and can be long- or short-term.

Spectral features refer to descriptions of the frequency properties of the sound. Calculation of spectral features will require some type of frequency filtering or frequency analysis, such as a Fourier transform. The frequency content of a signal can change very quickly and very complexly, as for example, in the formants of speech. This type of analysis, which might use cepstral coefficients, is beyond the scope of this article, but has been used on environmental sounds [5].

Sound	Mean Frequency Bin	Second Moment	Third Moment	Fourth Moment	Spectrum Skew	Spectrum Kurtosis	Total Spectral Variability	Length	Relative Spectral Variability
plane1	40.91	9.47E+05	1.05E+08	1.85E+10	1.68	1.53	101	32256	0.0031
plane2	28.13	5.88E+05	7.93E+07	1.45E+10	2.42	4.93	92.53	32256	0.0029
plane3	25.57	5.87E+05	8.13E+07	1.47E+10	2.73	6.81	84.08	32256	0.0026
plane4	30.13	2.60E+06	3.42E+08	6.23E+10	2.39	4.92	501.38	32256	0.0155
plane5	32.69	1.25E+06	1.66E+08	2.94E+10	2.46	5.09	204.06	32256	0.0063
plane6	40.29	5.83E+05	6.21E+07	1.09E+10	1.71	1.86	62.02	32256	0.0019
plane7	33.62	5.06E+05	6.26E+07	1.12E+10	2	2.82	54.48	32256	0.0017
plane8	34.82	1.20E+06	1.49E+08	2.68E+10	2.01	2.83	150.61	32256	0.0047
plane9	48.58	8.00E+05	8.12E+07	1.44E+10	1.44	0.61	61.26	32256	0.0019
plane10	37.43	8.98E+05	1.09E+08	1.91E+10	2.02	2.95	110.68	32256	0.0034
plane11	55.3	1.59E+06	1.47E+08	2.62E+10	1.27	0.09	136.29	32256	0.0042
plane12	48.24	2.33E+06	2.04E+08	3.57E+10	1.83	3.67	491.44	32256	0.0152
plane13	30.58	1.11E+06	1.42E+08	2.55E+10	2.48	5.57	215.15	32256	0.0067
plane14	37.41	1.28E+06	1.54E+08	2.72E+10	1.92	2.42	167.1	32256	0.0052
frogs1	29.86	5.69E+06	7.72E+08	1.40E+11	2.8	7.45	1284.33	32256	0.0398
frogs2	38	7.34E+06	8.72E+08	1.52E+11	2.24	4.33	1683.56	32256	0.0522
babbling brook	65.45	7.63E+06	3.45E+08	7.24E+10	0.98	1.42	2155.68	32256	0.0668
chain saw	38.9	2.46E+07	2.95E+09	5.29E+11	2.56	6.79	5106.88	32256	0.1583
16mm projector	75.68	4.73E+07	1.68E+09	4.32E+11	0.74	1.03	12683.21	32256	0.3932
saw mill	72.1	8.42E+07	4.92E+09	9.10E+11	1.14	1.14	16644.4	32256	0.516
500Hz sine wave	30.4	2.34E+08	3.15E+10	5.73E+12	2.57	5.93	16540.11	32256	0.5128
800Hz sine wave	34.69	3.02E+08	3.94E+10	7.06E+12	2.45	5.27	26971.59	32256	0.8362
waterfalls	57.09	9.16E+06	5.52E+08	9.75E+10	1.14	0.84	1688.66	32256	0.0524
wind and waves	32.78	3.68E+07	4.75E+09	8.62E+11	2.35	4.76	6500.94	32256	0.2015
wind and surf	36.6	3.79E+07	4.49E+09	8.14E+11	2.12	3.87	6461.79	32256	0.2003
wind in trees	60.98	6.10E+06	2.89E+08	5.88E+10	1.03	1.5	1452.91	32256	0.045

Table 2. Classifier output on a set of statistical features for a set of sounds.

Temporal features refer to the patterns that occur in the time plot of the wave, and might include onset and offset duration, amplitude modulation patterns, gap occurrence and duration, etc. In general, temporal features have not been as useful as spectral features in classification, if they are used by themselves. Rather, the temporal features are combined with the spectral analysis to describe complex features such as a frequency shift over a particular interval.

With any of the features, there is the option of analyzing the short-term acoustics, or analyzing the long-term, average properties of the sound. This option depends upon the type of sound event you are classifying. Long-term properties are appropriate only for sound events that have an equivalent long-term duration. Our example is a propeller driven aircraft so long-term properties would seem to be appropriate. However, a propeller sound has a short-term spectral consistency, which remains so over a long duration. Thus the critical feature turned out to require both short- and long-term analysis.

Example 1. Detecting Propeller Driven Airplanes

The following code is a simple discriminant feature analyzer, which reads a wave file, does an FFT analysis of a segment of the wave, and uses the FFT result to compute the long-term spectral distribution and the spectral differences from one FFT result to the next. The code also calculates a set of features from the long-term spectral distribution including general descriptive statistics such as its moments. Similar features have been used successfully to recognize underwater transients [3] and to discriminate between speech and music [9]. The values of these features for a variety of airplane sounds and other sounds are shown in Table 2.

According to this table, only the relative spectral variability feature is needed for this classification problem and if the threshold for this feature is set to be a value less than .02, then all of the airplane sounds are classified correctly. This feature represents the degree to which the amplitude spectrum varies and is called "flux" in [9]. An earlier version of this code, which used sounds sampled at a lower rate (16 kHz), required three features to do the classification. This code requires an FFT function; in our case we used a routine from [11].

```
// Propeller airplane classifier

#define WAVE_ARRAY_SIZE             32767      // 2^15 - 1
#define FREQUENCY_BINS              512     // 2^9

short   WaveArray[WAVE_ARRAY_SIZE];
double  FreqArrayLog[FREQUENCY_BINS];
double  FreqArray[FREQUENCY_BINS];
double  FreqArrayDiff[FREQUENCY_BINS];
double  Spectrum[FREQUENCY_BINS];
double  OldSpectrum[FREQUENCY_BINS];
double  CplxSpectrum[FREQUENCY_BINS * 2];
double  TempFreqArray[FREQUENCY_BINS];
double  BinValues[FREQUENCY_BINS];
```

```
double  WeightedBins[FREQUENCY_BINS];

short get_AIFF_sound_data(char *filename, short *buffer,
                          int buffer_size);
void initialize_arrays(void);

int main (int argc, char *argv[])
{
    short     i, j, k;
    short     half_array_size;
    short     bin_value_offset = 1;
    short     length, analylen;
    double    deviation, freqskew, freqkurt;
    double    fsum = 0.0, fcount = 0.0;
    double    mean = 0.0, variance = 0.0, sd = 0.0;
    double    var_squared = 0.0, sd_cubed = 0.0;
    double    kurt_numer = 0.0, kurt_denom = 0.0;
    double    moment2 = 0.0, moment3 = 0.0, moment4 = 0.0;
    double    total_spectral_variability = 0.0;
    double    relative_spectral_variability = 0.0;

    if (argc < 2)
    printf("Usage analyze <waveform file>\n");

    // Read wave file for processing.
    length = get_AIFF_sound_data(argv[1], WaveArray,
                                 WAVE_ARRAY_SIZE);

    if (length <= 0) return -1; // error check

    initialize_arrays();//  Zero the analysis arrays

    // Compute FFT.
    // This analysis is iterative.  The wave samples are
    //   extracted for FFT processing in groups of 512
    //   samples.  The extraction steps in increments 256 so
    //   that overlapping analysis occurs.  This helps to
    //   reduce the effects of analyzing samples that have
    //   been arbitrarily segmented.

    // Reset file length to a modulus of the FFT analysis
```

```
//   window.
length = (short)(length / FREQUENCY_BINS)*FREQUENCY_BINS;
analylen = length - FREQUENCY_BINS;
half_array_size = FREQUENCY_BINS / 2;

for (i = 0; i < analylen; i += half_array_size) {
     k = i;

     // Convert 16 bit wave data to float in
     //   CplxSpectrum because the FFT routine four1()
     //   expects to see complex numbers.
     for (j = 0; j < FREQUENCY_BINS * 2; j += 2, k++) {
         CplxSpectrum[j] = (double)WaveArray[k]
                         / (double)WAVE_ARRAY_SIZE;
         CplxSpectrum[j+1] = 0.0;
     }

     // Apply FFT
     four1(CplxSpectrum - 1, FREQUENCY_BINS, 1);

     // Calculate magnitude of complex numbers returned
     // by four1().
     k = 0;

     for (j = 0; j < FREQUENCY_BINS; j += 2, k++) {
         Spectrum[k] = sqrt(pow(CplxSpectrum[j], 2)
                     + pow(CplxSpectrum[j+1], 2));
     }

     // Add result to FreqArray.  We want a running
     // total of the spectral values.
     add2(FreqArray, FreqArray, Spectrum,
          half_array_size);

     // Calculate the absolute difference between
     //   successive spectra.  This will provide
     //   information about how much the spectra is
     //   changing.  This is a short term analysis of
     //   the spectral consistency.
     if (i > 255) {
         sub2(TempFreqArray, Spectrum, OldSpectrum,
```

```
                half_array_size);

            for (j = 0; j < half_array_size; j++)
                TempFreqArray[j] = fabs(TempFreqArray[j]);

            add2(FreqArrayDiff, FreqArrayDiff,
                 TempFreqArray, half_array_size);
            }


            memcpy((void *)OldSpectrum, (void *)Spectrum,
                half_array_size * sizeof(double));
    }

    // Calculate a single number from the array that has
    //   been used to tally the spectral changes.
    total_spectral_variability
      = integ(FreqArrayDiff, half_array_size);

    // "Normalize" this number for the length of the sample.
    //   This number will reflect the degree of spectral
    //   variation from one "moment" to the next.  Here is
    //   the long term analysis of the short term spectral
    //   consistency.
    relative_spectral_variability
      = total_spectral_variability / length;
    printf("%s:\n", argv[1]);

    // Compute moments of the long term spectrum.  First
    //   compute the mean.  This value will be in units of
    //   the FFT analysis.
    for (i = 0; i < half_array_size; i++)
        BinValues[i] = i + bin_value_offset;

    mul2(WeightedBins, BinValues, FreqArray,half_array_size);

    fsum = integ(WeightedBins, half_array_size);
    fcount = integ(FreqArray, half_array_size);
    printf("\tfcount = %lf\n \tfsum = %lf\n", fcount, fsum);

    mean = fsum/fcount;
```

```
printf("\tMean = %f\n",mean);

// Using the mean, calculate the 2nd, 3rd, and 4th
//   moments about the mean.
for (i = 0; i < half_array_size; i++) {
     deviation = i + bin_value_offset - mean;
     moment2 = moment2+pow(deviation, 2)*FreqArray[i];
     moment3 = moment3+pow(deviation, 3)*FreqArray[i];
     moment4 = moment4+pow(deviation, 4)*FreqArray[i];
}

// Calculate the variance from the 2nd moment.
variance = moment2/(fcount-1);

sd = sqrt(variance);

// Skewness and kurtosis are measures of the tails of the
//   distribution.  Calculate these from the 3rd and 4th
//   moments, respectively.
sd_cubed = pow(sd, 3);
freqskew = (fcount * moment3) / ((fcount - 1)
         * (fcount - 2) * sd_cubed);

kurt_numer
  = (fcount * (fcount + 1) * moment4)
  - (3 * pow(moment2, 2) * (fcount - 1));
var_squared = pow(variance, 2);
kurt_denom = (fcount - 1) * (fcount - 2)
           * (fcount - 3) * var_squared;
freqkurt = kurt_numer / kurt_denom;

// Print out the features.
printf("\trelative spectral variability = %lf\n",
relative_spectral_variability);
printf("\tMoment^2_%1.0f = %lf\n", fcount, moment2);
printf("\tMoment^3_%1.0f = %lf\n", fcount, moment3);
printf("\tMoment^4_%1.0f = %lf\n", fcount, moment4);
printf("\tSkewness = %lf\n", freqskew);
printf("\tKurtosis = %lf\n", freqkurt);

// Do the classification.
```

```
    if (relative_spectral_variability < 0.02)
        printf("Airplane Detected\n");
}

//  Zero the analysis arrays.  Some of these arrays could be
//    doubly used, are separately defined in this example to
//    help illustrate the analysis.
void initialize_arrays(void)
{
    short i;

    for (i = 0; i < FREQUENCY_BINS; i++)  {
         FreqArrayDiff[i] = 0.0;
         FreqArrayLog[i] = 0.0;
         FreqArray[i] = 0.0;
         Spectrum[i] = 0.0;
         OldSpectrum[i] = 0.0;
    }
}
```

3 Conclusion

We have only scratched the surface of this rich subject. After experimenting with this code example please be sure to read Derek DiFilippo and Ken Greenebaum's article "Introduction to the Theory of Signal Detection: Measuring Human Response" (see *Audio Anecdotes I*); Al Bregman and Wieslaw Woszczyk's article "Controlling the Perceptual Organization of Sound: Guidelines Derived from Principles of Auditory Scene Analysis (ASA)" (see *Audio Anecdotes I*), which explores applications of Audio Scene Analysis to gain further insight into the challenges of sound identification; and Hal Chamberlin's article "Floating Point Fast Fourier Transform" (see *Audio Anecdotes II*) for details on the Fast Fourier Transform. The following references provide suggestions for further study.

4 Acknowledgment

Preparation of this paper was sponsored by the Office of Naval Research (ONR). The opinions herein are those of the authors and do not necessarily represent the opinions of ONR.

Annotated Bibliography

[1] J. Ballas. "Effect of Event Variations and Sound Duration on Identification of Everyday Sounds." In *Proceedings of the Second International Conference on Auditory Display*, pp. 77–81. Santa Fe, NM: ICAD, 1994.

How does the identification of an ordinary event, such as a stapler, vary when some of the properties of the event are changed, such as the type of stapler, the type of push, and the type and amount of paper? This is the subject of this paper. In addition, variations of a light switch, which can be similar in acoustics to a stapler event, are used as well as stimuli in an identification task, and the analysis includes what types of stapler events are thought to be light switches, and visa versa.

[2] G. Becker and A. Güdesen. "Passive Sensing with Acoustics on the Battlefield." *Applied Acoustics* 59 (2000), 149–178.

This paper addresses ways that passive, unattended acoustic sensors might be used by the military. It describes the general detection problem, aspects of sound propagation that are particularly important for acoustic detection on the battlefield, and selected types of sensing technology and applications of this technology for particular problems.

[3] C. H. Chen. "Recognition of Underwater Transient Patterns." *Pattern Recognition* 18:6 (1985), 485–490.

The recognition of short duration sounds is important in submarine warfare, and this short paper describes ways that the sounds can be segmented and classified.

[4] D. P. W. Ellis. "Prediction-Driven Computational Auditory Scene Analysis." Ph.D. diss., MIT, 1996.

This dissertation describes ways to perform analysis of auditory scenes and extract the events that occur in the scene.

[5] R. S. Goldhor. "Recognition of Environmental Sounds." In *Proceedings of the 1993 International Conference on Acoustics, Speech, and Signal Processing (ICASSP)*, pp. 149–152. Los Alamitos, CA: IEEE Press, 1993.

Goldhor applies statistical techniques to classify a set of environmental sounds using cepstral coefficients.

[6] J. H. Howard, Jr. and J. A. Ballas. "Perception of Simulated Propeller Cavitation." *Human Factors* 25:6 (1983), 643–655.

Underwater propeller sounds can be used to determine the types of ships that are present. The human perception of these types of sounds is examined using simulated sounds that vary in attack, decay, and rate.

[7] B. Kostek and A. Czyzewski. "Representing Musical Instrument Sounds for their Automatic Classification." *Journal of the Audio Engineering Society* 49:9 (2001), 768–785.

This technical paper describes how separate feature vectors of FFT-based and wavelet-based, time-frequency parameters for selected classes of musical instruments can be chosen, modeled, and used as input for a feed-forward neural network whose output layer is matched to the number of instrument classes. The authors also discuss the relevance of their work to the goals of the MPEG-7 open standard.

[8] W. S. Meisel. *Computer-Oriented Approaches to Pattern Recognition.* New York: Academic Press, 1972.

This book provides detailed descriptions of basic concepts and mathematical methods that can be used in recognizing patterns in phenomena such as visual images and speech.

[9] E. Scheirer and M. Slaney. "Construction and Evaluation of a Robust Multifeature Speech/Music Discriminator." In *Proceedings of the 1997 International Conference on Acoustics, Speech, and Signal Processing (ICASSP)*, pp. 1331–1334. Los Alamitos, CA: IEEE Press, 1997.

This paper describes a system developed to distinguish music from speech, providing detailed information on the derived features that they used and evaluated, including some that represent the "variance" in the sound.

[10] C. C. Spicer. "Algorithm AS 52: Calculation of Power Sums of Deviations about the Mean." *Applied Statistics* 21 (1972), 226–227.

This paper provides algorithms to calculate moments of the mean.

[11] W. H. Press, B. P. Flannery, S. A. Teukolsky, and W. T. Vetterling. *Numerical Recipes in C.* New York: Cambridge University Press, 1988.

This is a popular source for mathematical routines encoded in C.

HRTF Spatialization

Why 3D Sound through Headphones?

Bo Gehring

1 What, Exactly, Does "3D" Sound Mean?

It's what you're hearing right now. If a plane flies overhead, you hear it up there even though it's outside. You don't need to turn around to know a door slammed in the back of the room. If someone just behind you whispers, you hear it coming from behind. At a concert, you hear each player in his location as well as clapping and other sounds from the audience which come from all around at the same time. In a restaurant, you can focus on different conversations even though the noise level is high and many people are talking. A recent smash-hit movie suggests that a big dinosaur might even come roaring up from behind or a kid might secretly whisper in your ear.

This is all three-dimensional sound. This article describes 3D "binaural" sound, its role on the desktop and specifically in immersive gaming, and why 3D sound is best reproduced using headphones. Binaural examples recorded by the author are included on the CD-ROM accompanying this book. For details on the psychophysics of how people localize sound please refer to Jens Blauert's classic text *Spatial Hearing.* Frank Haferkorn's article, "Head-Related Transfer Functions and the Physics of Spatial Hearing" (page 269), explores the mathematics of the head and derives the Head-Related Transfer Function (HRTF), an important element for synthesizing spatial sound.

Like the study of gravity, the study of 3D sound, which scientists call binaural sound, has a long history. There are published papers about it

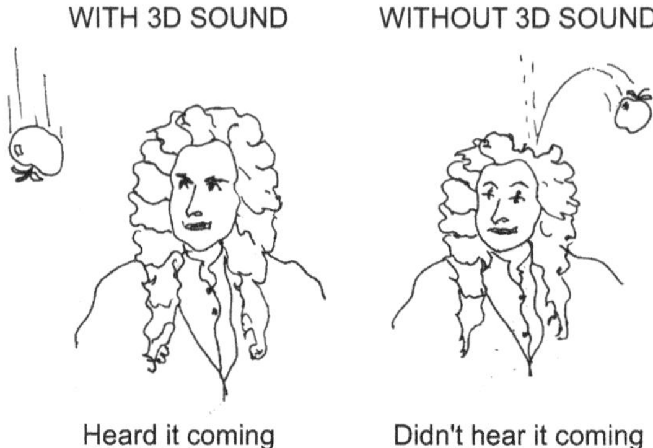

Figure 1. The benefits of 3D sound.

going back more than three centuries to the time of Newton. Compared to gravity, or at least to Newton's gravity before Einstein arrived on the scene, binaural sound requires a lot of math. That may be why it has taken so long to get to the point where lots of people will have it on their desktops. But they will, and soon. It will likely be games which bring binaural sound to the desktop the same way that games have already popularized 3D graphics technology.

In this paper 3D sound means scientifically correct binaural sound as opposed to some techniques which only attempt to approximate the phenomena. The idea is simple enough in concept. Binaural sound is created from an unlocalized free-field sound by either putting it through a pair of actual, physical, ear shapes configured like a head with ears (like the configuration Hempton describes in his article "Listening to Nature: Hearing is More Than Meets the Eye" (see *Audio Anecdotes I*)), or signal processing it to simulate the same thing for the sound location you want.

What arrives at your ear drums, and what you hear, is what you would have heard if you had been in the original experience. Since it's now possible for a game to reposition binaural sound interactively, it's also called *positional* sound.

2 How Does Binaural Sound Compare to Vision?

Diving into the numbers a little, the part of the horizon people can see is 120 degrees, more or less. The game player's world on the screen is only part of that, say 30 degrees. That's only about one twelfth of the horizon. Binaural sound, on the other hand, gives the gamer the full 360-degree

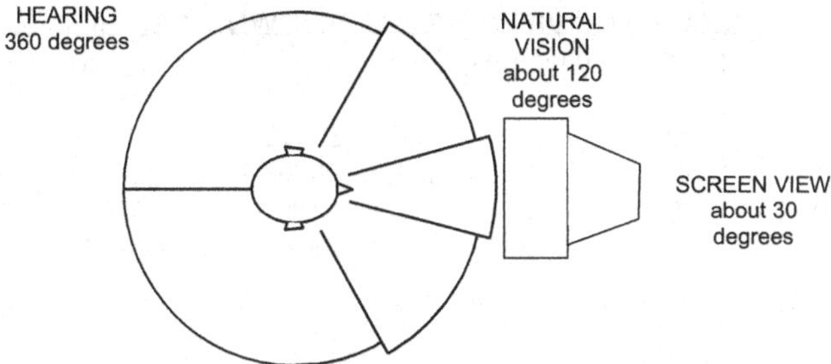

Figure 2. A comparison of the relative field of vision and hearing.

horizon and the whole sphere. It's the only way to sense things in the part of the world that's outside vision.

Another aspect of the "part of the world that's outside vision" feature is that, as any radio drama fan knows, well-produced sound is pretty good at evoking graphic images. Probably this is because sounds act as triggers in the listener's subconscious. For games, this is a good idea because the graphic images that the user provides from subconscious memory can be powerful and they don't have to be rendered.

Binaural sound does something else that vision can't. Vision is made to work at a distance. When things get close to the eyes, they lose focus. That's just the point where binaural sounds, getting closer, are at their most compelling—most threatening or friendly—or most intimate. They work all the way from infinity to the ear canal. Intimately close sounds can probably trigger very strong emotions including primitive "fight or flee" reactions, just as they do in real life. Game designers will probably find interesting things to do with this.

A thing to remember is that binaural sound doesn't compete with vision, but makes vision better. It makes objects on the screen more life-like and easier to find. But where it really comes into its own is doing what can't be done at all with vision, projecting a threat or friendly gesture into the part of the world that the gamer can't see or putting it up close, inside the personal "sacred space."

3 The Hardware to Deliver Realistic Binaural Sound Is Already in Place

Most of us are familiar with the idea that vision dominates. It is safe to say that more of a game platform's hardware cost is tied to visual display

DISPLAY	REFRESH (Hertz)	VIEW (Degrees)	COST TO OWN	CPU HIT (Percent)	REALISM
Visual:					
Baseline CRT	60	30	BASELINE	1	6
Bigger CRT	72	45	INEXPENSIVE	8	10
Commercial VR	60	90	EXPENSIVE	32	15
Military VR	100+	120	$250K+	UNKNOWN	30
Sound:					
8-bit	11,025	N/A	BASELINE	1	15
16-bit stereo	44,100	45 (pan)	INEXPENSIVE	4	40
16-bit binaural	44,100	360	INEXPENSIVE	8	80+

Table 1.

than sound. Most of today's game production budget goes into visuals. But there's a good reason why sound, binaural sound in particular, should get more attention in the future.

The best game visual displays and even the most advanced wide-field military virtual reality displays are nowhere near the bandwidth of the human visual system. There isn't much chance the gamer will mistake his visual display for reality. Table 1, based on rough estimates, compares display types. "REALISM" is estimated real-world fidelity assuming motion is included.

The point is how much easier it is to add to reality with binaural sound. There is already a growing installed base of hardware (16-bit stereo soundcards) which can deliver near real-life binaural sound. Visual displays with the same degree of realism are probably years away. Maybe sound is the easiest place to give reality a boost because the delivery bandwidth is already there. Stahlman's article, "Why the Audiocomputer is Inevitable" (page 419), and Hempton's aforementioned article provide other perspectives on the role of sound in a visually dominated culture.

4 Headphones versus Speakers

Until direct neural audio stimulation technology is developed, we will continue to rely on the venerable speaker transducer to push air molecules around to create the waves that we hear as sound. As with conventional stereo, two transducers are required to deliver binaural sound. These are called headphones when the transducers are mounted in a headset directly over our ears, and speakers when the transducers are away from our head.

The type and configuration of transducer used has a larger effect on how binaural recordings are perceived than when the same set-up is used for traditional stereo material.

5 Headphones and Out-of-Headedness

Are you hearing sounds inside your head? Welcome to the club. Users listening to conventional stereo sound played back through headphones experience the sound as being inside the head. All the sound seems to come from somewhere between the two headphone speakers.

Seriously, for 3D sound to work at all, and for sounds to come from a direction, they need to be heard outside the head. For once, the scientific description is perfectly clear. It's called having "out-of-headedness" and in this case, it is a good idea.

When properly recorded or synthesized, binaural sound on headphones is out-of-head, so when you hear a binaural sound through headphones, it seems to come from outside where it should, not from inside the headphones and especially not from between your ears. Out-of-headedness happens because the left and right binaural signals are precisely correlated with each other. The brain's auditory cortex, which is wired to look for this kind of correlation, thinks, "A-ha! Guess it's real!" and you hear it out where it's supposed to be.

There really is a subtle, but surprising, understanding that something is definitely different the first time someone experiences binaural sound. I suggest taking a moment now to find a pair of headphones and to listen to the binaural sound files on the CD-ROM. You will find a number of recordings that I have made and might find Hempton's binaural nature recordings compelling, too (see his article in *Audio Anecdotes I* and his files on that volume's CD-ROM).

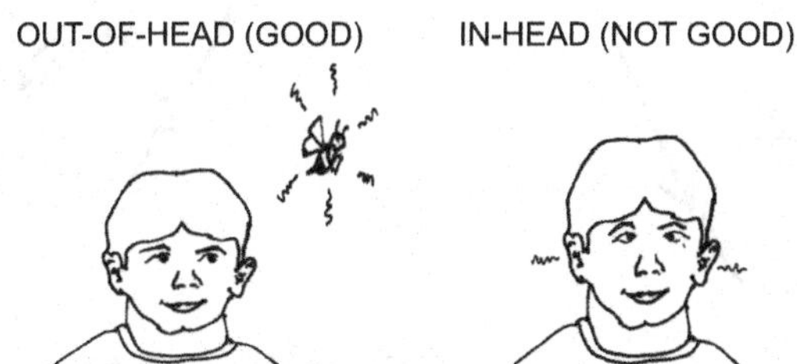

Figure 3. Binaural sound creates out-of-head experience, while stereo is experienced as in-head.

6 What about Loudspeakers?

Loudspeakers naturally provide out-of-headedness. Unfortunately, when we play binaural material on speakers, new problems come up. One issue goes under the general heading of "image stability." To produce a stable image, a clean binaural signal needs to be delivered to each ear. With speakers, almost anything can happen to the signal between the speaker and eardrum, and the listener can and will move around. If the signal isn't clean, or confusing noise has been added, the image may lose stability or collapse.

Life would be much easier with loudspeakers if the left loudspeaker only sent its sound to the left ear and the right only to the right. What actually happens is that the left speaker sends a lot of unwanted sound to the right ear and vice versa. This is called crosstalk. Obviously, if only the, say, left speaker was playing, you would hear this sound in both ears.

Loudspeaker crosstalk corrupts the clean signal that we would like each ear to have for binaural sound to work. It's very difficult to get rid of, mainly because there isn't much acoustic separation between the ears.

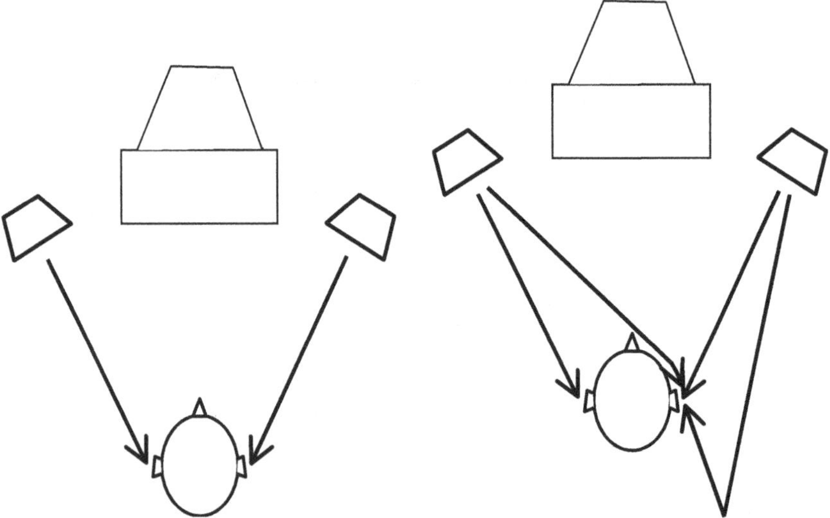

Figure 4. Idealized speaker without crosstalk.

Figure 5. Sound from each speaker reaches both ears, sometimes delayed by bouncing off other objects in the room.

Anything aimed at one side tends to also find its way to the other ear. Reverberation in the listening space, which acts like crosstalk coming from multiple sources, can have damaging effects on localization. The next drawing demonstrates the impossible situation that we would need for loudspeakers to reproduce binaural sound without sophisticated crosstalk cancellation techniques (the output of the given speaker would go directly to the appropriate ear without being reflected off objects or reaching the other ear). See Figure 4.

Figure 5 demonstrates crosstalk and reverberation, two of the many problems speaker set-ups have delivering binaural sound.

Headphones easily provide clean binaural signals directly to each ear without crosstalk or reverberation (additionally, headphones, being connected to the listeners head, will not change their relative position were the listener to move). See Figure 6.

A very sophisticated and complicated technique does exist for canceling crosstalk when using special speakers called near-field monitors whose location and sonic parameters are very well known. Mathematically special L′ and R′ signals are computed that when played back through the near-field monitors interact in such a way that two very small sweet spots are created, a head's distance apart, where only the desired left signal may be heard by the left ear, and correspondingly, the right ear may only hear the desired right signal.

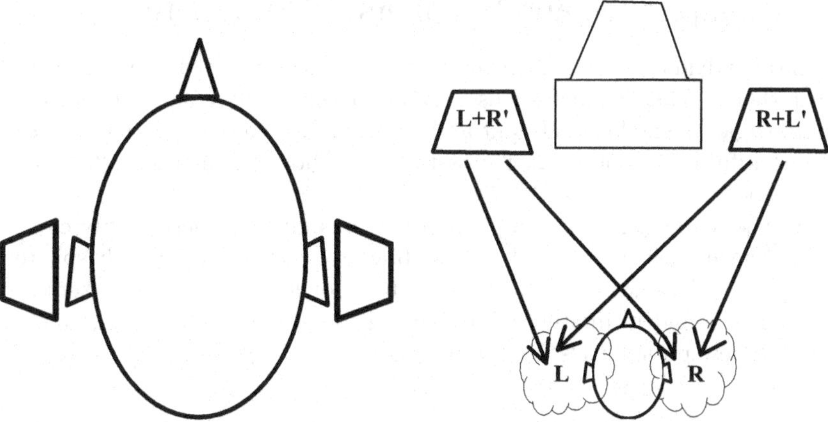

Figure 6. Headphones provide high-quality binaural sound without crosstalk.

Figure 7. Near-field monitors running crosstalk cancellation producing small sweet spots of pure right and left channel sound.

Binaural sound can effectively be reconstructed using crosstalk cancellation techniques. It is uncanny to be looking forward at the speakers producing a sound and to perceive the sound as coming from behind you! Unfortunately, it is unrealistic to have well-characterized speakers positioned at precisely known orientations necessary for this configuration to work. Furthermore, crosstalk cancellation only produces a very small sweet spot requiring the listener to be carefully positioned. See Figure 7.

A positionally stable binaural sound image comes mostly from a wavelength-based interaction of the arriving sound with the head and the visible part of each ear. This is especially true for higher frequencies, say from 1500 Hz up. A stable image may not be possible if the listener's head moves by more than part of a wavelength. At 12 kHz, for example, a wavelength is about an inch.

There's a common-sense way to see why head position change can have an effect. Take a look at the smaller features on anyone's ear, the whorls and twists. These features are necessary for binaural localization to happen. It's reasonable that a head position change larger than their detail size (which would blur or destroy their acoustic effect) could also blur localization in a loudspeaker sound field. There doesn't seem to be much practical hope of stabilizing the listener's head this accurately short of using a laboratory bite bar. Headphones deliver a stable binaural signal even if the listener's head moves.

7 Headphones and Speakers, in Summary

A major advantage of loudspeakers is that the listener doesn't have to wear them. They're easy to use. Also on the positive side: There are technologies, some fairly elegant and based on known science, that reduce the harmful effects of speaker crosstalk and allow binaural sounds to be experienced.

But loudspeakers, for the physical reasons given earlier, simply can't deliver accurately positioned, stable binaural sounds in the full sphere the way headphones do. And there is no known method for speakers to position a sound intimately close to the listener's head, one of the most exciting new possibilities for game design.

8 The Coming Headphone Market

Since today most gamers choose loudspeakers rather than headphones, it's worth mentioning how the growth of 3D sound content in games may

Figure 8. Intimate sound (if the vampire bat is a problem, substitute a kiss in the ear).

affect the headphone market. Up to now, in a market using conventional stereo at best, gamers might buy headphones for privacy or the desire for meltdown volume, but probably not because headphones actually make the game experience better. As game designers bring more binaural sound content into the marketplace, the gamer has a compelling reason to buy headphones. They immediately and dramatically improve the game experience.

9 Combining Headphones and a Subwoofer for the Ideal Game Audio System

The part of the real world audio headphones can't deliver is the part which comes in through the skin as much as through the ears—those energetic roars, rumbles, and booms that shake the furniture and give that certain something to the disaster movies we all love.

These low frequencies aren't directional (the wavelengths are too big to interact with the head and ears), so the gamer can use headphones and a subwoofer together without hurting positional quality. Together, this could be the ideal game audio system.

Annotated Bibliography

References are provided in my article "Interactive Entertainment with Three-Dimensional Sound" (page 259).

Interactive Entertainment with Three-Dimensional Sound

Bo Gehring

1 Introduction

Dynamic three-dimensional, spatialized audio or binaural audio, perhaps because of its former expense, is most often associated with very serious simulation or military applications, not with entertainment. Binaural recordings (nondynamic) have never gained mass acceptance, although pioneers like Gordon Hempton are still drawn to the medium and produce incredible results (See "Listening to Nature: Hearing is More Than Meets the Eye" in *Audio Anecdotes I*). The march of increasingly powerful and inexpensive computers to the market has allowed these techniques to begin appearing in computer games that represent most users' first exposure to the technology.

This anecdote explores an unprecedented application for binaural audio: interactive entertainment at the dance club!

Although there are limitations in the presentation of binaural audio over loudspeakers, interactive control of three-dimensional sound motion creates interesting results in the dance club and potentially in other applications. Frank Haferkorn's article, "Head-Related Transfer Functions and the Physics of Spatial Hearing" (page 269), and Ville Pulkki's "Spatialization with Multiple Loud Speakers" (see *Audio Anecdotes II*) describe three-dimensional spatialization theory; this article explores an entertainment application using the Focal Point 3D Audio technology to place sound position under control of a performer utilizing a pointing glove, wand, or touchpad. Future possibilities, including interaction via individual headphones, are discussed.

2 An Overview of Three-Dimensional Sound

In natural hearing, it is readily observed that sounds are heard from specific locations. Humans clearly hear in three dimensions: sounds are localized above, below, in any direction, and at any distance. Binaural hearing, as natural three-dimensional hearing is known, also uniquely conveys intimacy or urgency when sounds come close. Sounds in the listener's "sacred space" can be impossible to ignore: Binaural hearing is the body's natural sensor at very close range.

Historically, binaural sound has been recorded with a *kunstkopf,* i.e., a dummy head with microphones in place of eardrums as Gordon Hempton describes in his article. A number of astonishing recordings have been made using the *kunstkopf* (we include a few on the CD-ROM accompanying this book, including a live visit to the dentist by this author): Unfortunately, the technique doesn't allow repositioning the spatial position of sounds in real time.

Binaural hearing, like normal stereo, is a two-channel process: Normal stereo equipment will play binaural sound. A binaural signal is different from everyday stereo in that the left and right signals have complex signal shaping which causes the listener to imagine the sound to be three-dimensional and in the correct location. This is a *psychoacoustic* effect: On headphones, binaural sounds can be so compelling that the acoustic experience seems entirely real. The listener experiences the sound in the same way they would had they been listening to the original soundscape from the position of the *kunstkopf* used to make the recording.

3 Developments in Binaural Processing

Advances in signal processing technology together with improved understanding of binaural hearing have made it possible to artificially create the perception of natural, three-dimensional hearing. Basically, this is achieved by processing a monaural source signal to create new left and right signals which include localization information. The signal is transformed from a free-field monaural sound without localization to a binaural sound in the desired three-dimensional location.

Multiple sounds, for example, multiple musical instruments, can be processed in separate three-dimensional locations and then mixed to make binaural program material which can be reproduced on any stereo playback system.

Binaural processing, like equalization, works by adjusting gain and phase by frequency band. However, binaural processing is considerably more complex: Thinking of the processor as an equalizer, each ear's signal would require about *two hundred* sliders for gain and *another two hundred* for phase shift, all under program control and capable of varying continuously with motion. Modern processors have enough computational capacity to spatialize a number of sounds simultaneously while leaving most of the processor's resources available for other tasks.

Binaural processing technology, now economical, allows three-dimensional sound to be created and changed in real time. This has many applications including music, performance, teleconferencing, and aviation. Binaural sound is essential to immersive virtual reality. Despite the common emphasis on graphics in virtual reality, sound, not vision, is the human sense which naturally "wraps around" to the rear. Now it can be used interactively, placing and moving sounds responsive to the user's experience, rather than as a "canned" recording.

4 Binaural Sound and Loudspeakers

The effectiveness of binaural sound depends on the ability to deliver clean signal with embedded directional cues to each ear. As discussed in my other article "Why 3D Sound through Headphones" (page 249), headphones ensure this by delivering the correct signal to each eardrum, unaffected by room acoustics or speaker layout and without conflicting signals—in particular the one intended for the opposite ear.

This suggests that there are at least three reasons why the same degree of realism is not likely to be possible with two stereo speakers. First, even assuming for a moment that there is no crosstalk between the left and right loudspeakers, room acoustics can modify or override any binaural processing already applied to the signals. Second, stereo systems in public venues such as dance clubs usually have multiple speakers which can blur the acoustic image. Third, there is *always* crosstalk between left and right binaural channels.

Crosstalk between the channels can be reduced by well-known means usually involving mixing of phase-modified signal from the other channel. This tends to narrow the acceptable listening area (sweet spot) to a single line centered between the loudspeakers. Undesirable phasing and timbre effects are likely to occur outside the reduced sweet spot. For these reasons, crosstalk reduction is not used in the system described here.

Comparing psychoacoustics to more basic physics, perfected spatially stable three-dimensional audio via two loudspeakers is like antigravity. No one would dispute its value as a concept, but there appears to be no way to achieve it within the fundamental laws of physics. In this context, airplanes, which operate under known physical laws, are useful even if not as exciting as antigravity.

Similarly, playback through loudspeakers, even constrained by known physics and wildly variable acoustics, can "fly" sounds dramatically. Even in spaces with poor acoustics, binaural processing almost always expands the width and height of the acoustic image and the entire mix or elements of a mix can be moved spatially in real time, immediately responsive to the user's control

When improved playback means become available, the experience will only improve.

5 More Detailed Knowledge of Psychoacoustics

The preceding overview of binaural sound is an informal one. Frank Haferkorn's article, mentioned earlier, offers a good introduction; [2] is the definitive text in the field; and another good reference is [1].

6 Focal Point 3D Audio

Focal Point 3D Audio is a pioneer company in real-time binaural processing. It grew out of the author's early work in three-dimensional audio displays for USAF combat aircraft. One of its first products was a binaural processing system on a single PC circuit card, using a dedicated DSP to process localized sound without loading the computer's CPU. Another Focal Point technology (US Patent 5521981) was the first interactive binaural technology for PC games and is still the only such technology which works across the entire Microsoft Windows platform.

Mathematically, the Focal Point system uses a technique called *convolution* to process the source signal, a 44.1 kHz stream of 16-bit monaural samples, into new left and right binaural signals with built-in three-dimensional information. The computed location of the sound can be changed at least 500 times per second under interactive control.

One way of controlling the system's three-dimensional position is with a computer mouse, where left-to-right motion of the mouse causes the sound to move around in azimuth, the horizontal plane, and front-to-back motion causes the sound to move in elevation. By tracking the controlling motion at more than 500 Hz, the sound can move as fast as the mouse.

7 Focal Point's First Use in a Dance Club

The first use of Focal Point in a dance club setting came about when a dance event promoter, Wes Thomas, heard Focal Point demonstrated at a virtual reality conference in New York City. He proposed using the system at Limelight, a New York dance club where he was producing an event. Focal Point was demonstrated on headphones; at the time it wasn't known whether the effect would work through very high-powered loudspeakers in a large space. The Limelight club is in a converted church.

The speakers at Limelight were in two banks of about 30 speakers each plus floor subwoofers, all powered by amplifiers totalling several thousand watts. Rushing to get the system installed, it was necessary to connect directly between the main console and the amplifiers rather than in a separate effects loop which could have provided a safety net. During the dances, sound position was controlled by an assistant, Craig Kanarick, who watched the disc jockey's moves and moved the mouse with the beat. The techno dance music was loud and percussive with many broadband, nonmusical sampled elements.

The feedback was positive from the dance floor: three-dimensional sound moves were clearly heard by the crowd. When Craig Kanarick changed the move rhythm, a different mood appeared to be felt. If the sound moves were very animated, it seemed to "warm" the crowd and the dancing tended to be more active. The general impression was that the sound mix flew over the dance floor very much like the club's moving computer-controlled lights.

8 Lessons Learned

This first trial was successful, but there were obvious shortcomings. First, the stereo program feed from the console had been combined with the permission of Dmitry Brill, the evening's DJ, to monaural and processed to the same location and motion as though they were only one sound. Even though Focal Point output was three-dimensional stereo and the moves were dramatic, the stereo effects in the original mix were lost.

This suggested that an improved system could use two binaural channels, one for each side of the stereo program feed. The two left outputs could be combined to program left and the right outputs to program right. This way, the original stereo effects mix would be preserved. In addition, each side could have its own three-dimensional motion, so that the three-dimensional mix spread could be varied as part of the control. Each side of the original mix would be like a flying loudspeaker which could be independently controlled to widen or narrow the mix, still keep the three-dimensional move, and preserve the stereo engineering of the original recording.

Second, it appeared that there could be a better way of controlling three-dimensional position. Using the mouse was tiring. There was no way to record and play move sequences, so full-time operation was required. After a few hours, it was obvious that the mouse motion, basically sawing back and forth on a tabletop, had become monotonous to the operator if not to the dancers. The mouse is inherently a two-dimensional control, and its ability to naturally control spherical motion in three dimensions was limited.

Even though the first results were dramatic, another aspect later realized to be a shortcoming was that the three-dimensional sound position control (the mouse) couldn't be seen by the audience: There were no visual cues which could reinforce the perceived sound motion.

9 An Improved System

The system that we created to add these improvements included an important additional control device.

In virtual reality systems, it's desirable to have three-dimensional sounds stabilized with regard to the listener's head. A tracking device is attached to the helmet or headphones: virtual reality audio systems simply subtract head orientation angles from the desired angular location, causing the processed sound to stay in the same location as the listener's head turns or moves.

A tracking device often used in virtual reality installations is the Polhemus Isotrak™, a six-degree-of-freedom magnetic tracker which reports orientation and position to the computer 60 times per second. The Isotrak sensor is about the size of a sugar cube with a wire lead and is usually attached on top of the helmet to virtual reality applications. The device measures orientation as roll, pitch, and yaw: Location is reported as x, y, and z coordinates. The sensor can be used within a six-foot radius from a small fixed transmitter.

For an improved interactive dance club system, we adapted the Isotrak sensor by stitching it into the index fingertip of a white silk glove. The program mathematics set the sound's azimuth and elevation according to the Isotrak orientation, so the sound simply went where the finger pointed.

In addition, the spatial location of the Isotrak sensor controlled spread of the three-dimensional mix, with the effect of controlling spaciousness as well as location. The gloved sensor was usually worn by a dancer. When the music started, her fingertip's starting position was recorded. Then, during the music, the three-dimensional spread of the mix was changed according to how far she moved her finger from the original position. When this was done in motion it had the effect of wildly "throwing" the sound across the acoustic space and it was easy to do intuitively. The original mix stereo effects were also preserved by presenting the left and right original mix channels separately instead of forcing them to mono.

Since the Isotrak update rate is 60 times per second, control motions can be very fast; in fact, the three-dimensional position accurately tracks any humanly possible hand motion. The direction and "focusing" of the mix are under very close-coupled interactive control.

The adapted Polhemus tracking device is ideal to be used by a live dancer. It provides facile control of location and mix spread and is completely natural to use. The dancer provides much more interesting (and accurate) visual cues to the audience than the former "mouse-and-computer" control. The tracking system can be placed remotely, so that the dancer can be on a pedestal out on the dance floor, visible to the crowd and away from the DJ.

The improved system was first tested under control of a live stage dancer at a dance event in Toronto: The results were dramatic enough that footage of the dancer taken by a local TV station was featured on CNN's *Future Watch*.

One unexpected result using the system with a live stage dancer is that the dancer, who is highly empowered by having control of the entire three-dimensional audio environment on her fingertip, is likely to be very responsive to the crowd. The interaction is very rich: In the system's first outings, this has led to some extraordinary performances by the dancers.

10 Who Has Control?

The disc jockey controls music presentation at dance events. Using the Focal Point glove system to put the three-dimensional mix under control of a stage dancer could take control away. This potential problem had to be handled carefully: The stage dancer is out on the dance floor away from the console.

To provide an easy means to keep the DJ in control, a touchpad (two-dimensional mouse replacement pad) was added to allow the DJ to either give control to the dancer or to control three-dimensional sound location himself from the console. In addition, the touchpad can cause moves to be recorded and played back on command.

Since the touchpad provides complete control, the host computer, monitor, and keyboard can be put out of sight. This seems pleasing to the disc jockeys: Dance clubs aren't known to be computer-friendly. A future version is likely to be packaged so it doesn't even look like a computer.

11 The "Magic Wand"

After the glove tracking system was used successfully several times, we made a pointing wand from a sleeved flashlight with the Isotrak sensor attached, used at an event at the Limelight club. It was handled by the DJ at the console and had the advantage of being visible throughout the club. This concept was expanded further by Mark Ginocchio of Virtual Reality Productions in St. Petersburg, Florida, who created a clear plastic wand about 40 inches long filled with flashing lights. The wand provides a dramatic visual cue, but is heavier and more tiring to use than the glove. The system now provides for three-dimensional position control by wand, glove, or touchpad.

12 Possible Future Developments

One observed deficiency is that, depending on the space acoustics, sound projection to the front, top, and rear may not work well. This is consistent with the known shortcomings of binaural playback through loudspeakers. A future system could include additional speakers placed for better three-dimensional presentation rather than the typical stereo arrangements in most clubs. Although it would mean a more complex system, it could be very powerful to combine the psychoacoustics of binaurally processed motion with multispeaker panning.

For dance events, the audience could wear headphones—infrared coupled or suspended by coiled cord from the ceiling. Although public safety considerations would arise, the experience of close sounds and full spherical motion via headphones could be dramatic.

An interesting possibility is to link three-dimensional audio motion to matching visual effects. For example, three-dimensional sound location and computer-controlled lights could be moved together under glove or wand control. Physical effects including pyrotechnics could be triggered by pointing the glove or wand.

The Polhemus Isotrak and other existing tracking products require a wire connection to the sensor. Future tracking sensors may be linked by radio, infrared, or other remote means. This development would allow the dancer or performer to move freely and thus open up many new possibilities for interaction.

In a related application, the glove sensor could be attached to, for example, a percussionist's drumstick. Then the drum's hits would move in the hall according to the drumstick's instantaneous direction. This would have the effect of projecting the drum set's geometry and dynamics out over the entire hall. The same technique could be used with any instrument.

Another interesting possibility, perhaps a little further in the future, is that each member of the audience wears headphones with an individual tracker and Focal Point processor. The listener's own rhythms could then interactively control sound motion, either alone or together with control from a DJ or performer.

13 Other Uses

The system presented here was developed for dance club use. The reaction to it in the clubs was usually one of astonishment. The first appearances resulted in invitations and many successful visits to dance events, as well as a featured appearance on CNN. But because there was no clear business model, interactive three-dimensional audio has yet to find its market in the thousands of dance clubs. Clearly, there are many other applications for the technology. Interactive three-dimensional sound motion effects could be used in live performance: individually, as part of a personal stereo player: in large-audience stadium events such as baseball games (where the "Steeerike!" call could fly with the umpire's arm). In the world of presentation and multimedia, the system could "fly" a speaker's voice: move sounds with animated three-dimensional graphic objects; provide unusual interactive experiences in public spaces. These and other uses are likely to be realized eventually.

This article was originally presented at the 134th SMPTE Technical Conference November 1992 and has been adapted for use in *Audio Anecdotes.*

Annotated Bibliography

[1] Durand Begault. *3-D Sound for Virtual Reality and Multimedia.* Cambridge, MA: AP Professional, 1994.

Another great reference.

[2] Jens Blauert. *Spatial Hearing.* Cambridge, MA: MIT Press, 1983.

The definitive text in the field.

Head-Related Transfer Functions and the Physics of Spatial Hearing

Frank Haferkorn

Many articles in this series relate to hearing and specifically to the ability to localize the origin of sounds in space. Those articles briefly refer to *binaural hearing* and the *head-related transfer function* (HRTF) when explaining the phenomena of spatial hearing. In this article, I explore the physics of hearing using the methods that Lord Rayleigh developed more than a century ago and apply the resulting model to synthesize our own HRTF.

Most HRTFs are proprietary data sets measured using proprietary techniques. While the numerical algorithm presented here for the purpose of demonstration uses a highly simplistic model, it is useful to generate and visualize HRTF data based on first principles. More subtle elements may be added to make the model and its corresponding synthesized HRTF more realistic.

Abridged code examples are provided with the full versions available on the CD-ROM accompanying this book.

1 What Is a Transfer Function?

A *transfer function* is a mathematical formula that describes how frequency response and phase is changed by any acoustical, electrical, or abstract system influences. Let's say that an acoustical "system" such as a megaphone takes sound at its input and amplifies the sound multiple times at the output.

The transfer function of any system inserted into a signal path (such as the megaphone in Figure 1) describes the change in sound from input to

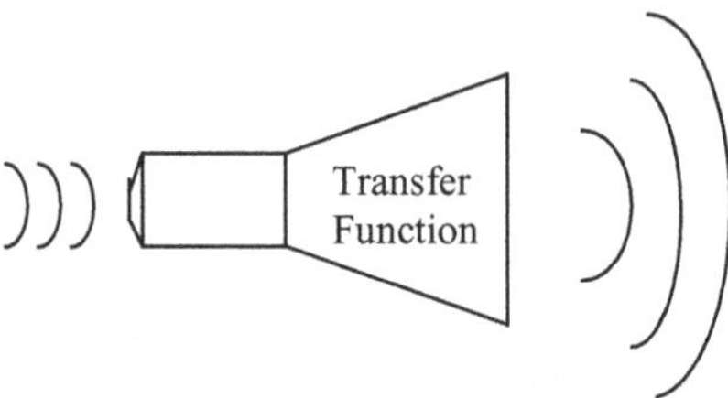

Figure 1. Example of a transfer function.

output. In this example, the amplification factor and all frequency specific changes are part of the acoustical transfer function of the megaphone.

2 What Is a Head-Related Transfer Function?

The HRTF describes the acoustical transfer function that is related to a person's head. It is measured by actually putting an artificial head or a test subject in a sound field, then measuring the sound field at the head and comparing it with the sound field without the head. This measurement is only possible within special reflectionless rooms called *anechoic chambers.*

The head's HRTF is measured in a sound field or plane waved with varied directions and frequencies (see Figure 2).

The microphone is located at the head's eardrum, which is the end of the physically modeled ear channel. The measurement is be performed only at one lateral side. The incoming plane wave is varied in frequency and incoming direction. So, the HRTF of the complete data of the two hemispheres can be gathered, using one "eardrum microphone."

The HRTF of the measured (artificial) head is compared to the sound field without the head present at the center of where the head would normally be (see Figure 3).

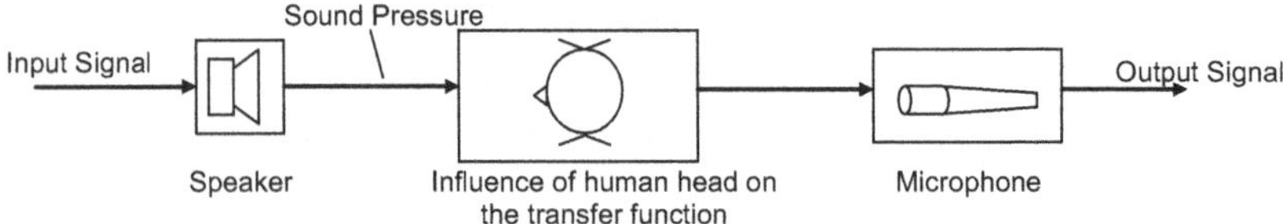

Figure 2. First part of measuring HRTF.

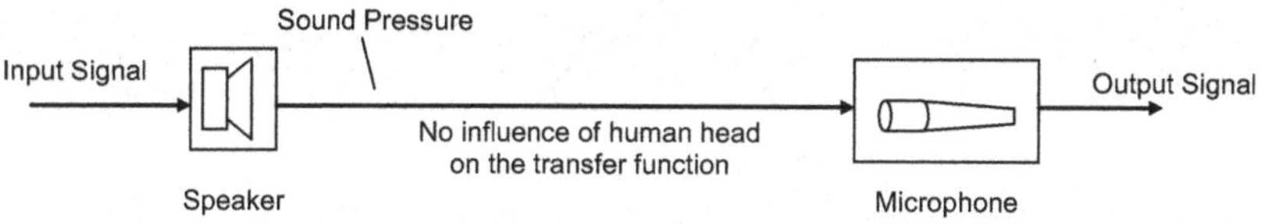

Figure 3. Second part of measuring HRTF.

Be aware that even slight differences in the set-up of the measured realistic/artificial will produce strong differences in the result of the HRTF.

3 Why Do We Gather an HRTF?

The gathered HRTF data is used from research up to end-user consumer electronics that implements binaural sound.

Using the HRTF, the sound can be computed so that the listener hears, when the sound is presented by headphones, what he would hear if he were at the position of the recording, as long as the headphone HRTF does not differ much from the listener's HRTF.

4 Idealization of the Head

Since measured HRTF data is hard to come by, we want to synthesize an HRTF based on a simplified model of the head in order to acheive a greater understanding.

Herein will be computed a (synthesized) generic HRTF for any direction and frequency of the plane incoming wave as physically modeling the influence of an *acoustically hard* head onto the undistorted, free wave.

The so-computed information of the generic HRTF contains a spectral dependent runtime, increasing the incoming wave for a reduced and very simple head.

Lord Rayleigh was able to work out his theories of hearing in the nineteenth century, as the understanding of physics had become sufficiently advanced by that time. Since then, scientists have been able to build on that work and increase our level of understanding of the basic physical principles of hearing.

Sound travels in acoustical waves and can be imagined as traveling pressure fluctuations; the so-called "waves." Analysis of how the head affects the transfer function can be reduced to dealing with objects larger than the wavelength of the acoustical wave. For most frequencies (wave-

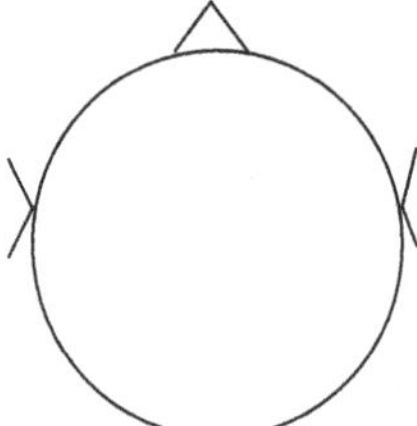

Figure 4. A simple reduced-model head.

lengths), the analysis model may be reduced to a head with two ears, one on each side.

Let's look at a simple reduced-model head without most of its features like hair, eyes, and a chin. The view in Figure 4 is from the top onto a model head consisting of a sphere, a nose, and left and right ears on the side of the modeled head.

The approach Lord Rayleigh used is a mathematical and analytical one. In order to calculate the influence on the sound field, it is necessary to model the surface of the head as precisely as possible. Using this simplified model leads to enormous difficulties in a purely mathematical analysis. These difficulties become obvious as you try to find the necessary mathematical description of the surface of this simplified head *with* a nose and ears, as shown in Figure 4.

Lord Rayleigh was bound by the numerical methods of his time. He went a step further in simplification and reduced the model in Figure 4 to an idealization of a man's head similar to a bowling ball shown in Figure 5.

The *bowling ball* idealization goes so far, that the head remains only as a hard sphere like a bowling ball. The surface of this bowling ball can be well described using the mathematics of the well-known Legendre polynomial and spherical Bessel functions. The acoustical model at the ears is modeled at the left and right side directly on the surface.

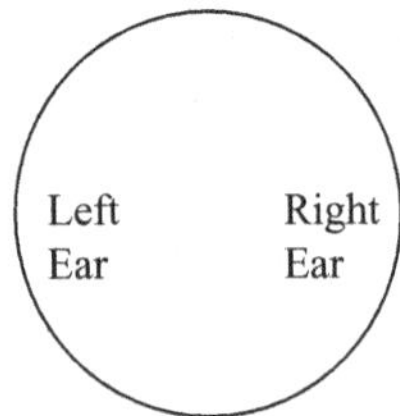

Figure 5. Lord Rayleigh's head model.

5 Used Symbols and Functions

The symbols shown in Table 5 are used in the following analytical calculation process.

i	Imaginary Unit $i = \sqrt{-1}$
t	Time
ω	Frequency
φ, ϑ	Azimuth and elevation
$\mathbf{x}$	Position of observed point in space
r	Distance of $\mathbf{x}$ to the center of the sphere
a	Radius of the sphere that idealized the head
θ	Angle between wave and $\mathbf{x}$
$\mathbf{k}$,k	Wave vector $\mathbf{k}$=(k,0,0) for plane wave from left
c	Speed of sound
Φ_{RES}	Acoustical potential of the resulting wave
Φ_S Φ_I	Acoustical potential of the scattered wave Acoustical potential of the initial plane wave
P_m(x)	Legendre-Polynom of order m
j_m(x)	Spherical Bessel-function of order m
J_r(x)	Bessel-function of order r
n_m(x)	Spherical Neumann-function of order m
$h_m^{(2)}$(x)	Spherical Hankel-function 2.kind of order m
m	Index of a sum
p_{ac}; p_{sound}	Acoustic pressure; soundpressure

Table 1. Symbols used in analysis.

In detail:

$$j_m(r) := (\frac{\pi}{2r})^{\frac{1}{2}} \cdot J_{m+\frac{1}{2}}(r),$$

$$n_m(r) := (-1)^{m+1} \cdot (\frac{\pi}{2r})^{\frac{1}{2}} \cdot J_{-m-\frac{1}{2}}(r),$$

$$h_m^{(2)}(r) := j_m(r) - i \cdot n_m(r).$$

Notice that, in some of the referenced publications, the direction of the incoming plane wave is from right to left. This is equal to defining $i = -\sqrt{-1}$ (watch for a different sign).

6 Influence of a Sphere onto a Plane Wave of Sound

The following discussion describes the calculation of an idealized head transfer function by reducing the model of the head to a hard sphere with the diameter of a typical head radius. These steps describe the transformation of the acoustical potential of a plane wave into spherical coordinates, introducing the resulting wave as a superposition of the initial incoming wave together with the scattered wave. These calculations also describe the parameters of the scattered wave. By using these parameters for the model head, the resulting influence of the model head will be determined.

6.1 Some Basic Formulas

The fundamental equation of acoustics, the wave equation, is:

$$\nabla^2 \Phi = \frac{1}{c^2} \frac{\partial^2 \Phi}{\partial t^2},$$

with the acoustic potential Φ_S. That gives us the sound velocity by $\mathbf{v} = -\text{grad}\,\Phi$ and the acoustic pressure $p_{\text{ac}} = \rho_0 \frac{\partial \Phi}{\partial t}$. The acoustic pressure p_{ac} is the real physical pressure corrected by the surrounding, static pressure p_0:

$$p_{\text{ac}} = p - p_0.$$

The wave equation has a solution as a plane wave:

$$\Phi\,(t, \omega, \mathbf{kx}) = \Phi_0 \cdot e^{\,i \cdot\, (\mathbf{kx} - \omega t)}.$$

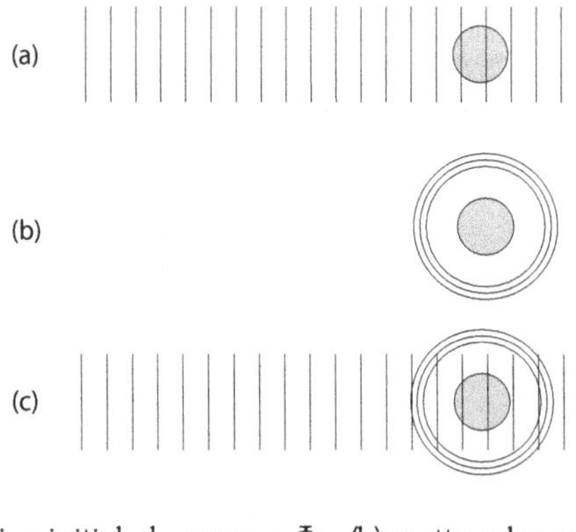

(a)

(b)

(c)

Figure 6. (a) Incoming initial plane wave Φ_I, (b) scattered wave g Φ_S, and resulting wave $\Phi_{RES} = \Phi_I + \Phi_S$.

A reduction of the complex mathematical description of the average human head to a hard sphere allows for a simplified calculation of the sound pressure at every point on the surface of the sphere. An incoming initial wave Φ_{I} produces a border condition of the surface of the scattering sphere, creating a scattering wave Φ_S. The resulting wave Φ_{RES} is the sum of both acoustical potentials. (See Figure 6.)

6.2 Plane Wave in Spherical Coordinates

Now the plane wave will be transferred into the spherical coordinates.

$$\begin{aligned}\Phi_{\text{I}}(t,\omega,kr,\theta) &= \Phi_0 \cdot e^{\,i\cdot\,(\mathbf{kx}-\omega t)} = \Phi_0 \cdot e^{\,-i\cdot\omega t} \cdot e^{\,i\cdot\, kr\cos\theta} \\ &= \Phi_0 \cdot e^{-\,i\omega t} \cdot \sum_{m=0}^{\infty} (2m+1)\cdot i^m \cdot P_m\,(\cos\theta)\cdot j_m(kr).\end{aligned}$$

6.3 The Resulting Wave and Its Scattering Condition

The resulting wave is a superposition (sum) of the incoming and the scattered acoustical potentials:

$$\Phi_{\text{RES}} := \Phi_{\text{I}} + \Phi_S.$$

The basis of this approximation is the reduction of the mathematically complex geometry of the "human head" to a hard sphere of radius a, with left and right ears. Because the sphere is an acoustical hard sphere, we can introduce a border condition of the acoustical potential on the surface of the sphere. This condition forces the radial part of the sound velocity to vanish across the whole surface. This produces a clue for the resulting wave $\Phi_{\text{RES}}(t,\omega,kr,\theta,a)$.

$$\begin{aligned}\mathbf{v}_{\perp}\big|_{r=a} &= \tilde{\mathbf{0}} \\ -\text{grad}_r\,(\Phi_{\text{RES}})\,\big|_{r=a} &= 0 \\ -\left.\frac{\partial\,(\Phi_{\text{I}}+\Phi_{\text{S}})}{\partial r}\right|_{r=a} &= 0.\end{aligned}$$

Unlike the sound velocity, the sound pressure won't vanish on the given surface.

This produces a physical connection between the initial incoming wave and the scattered wave:

$$\left.\frac{\partial\;\Phi_{\text{S}}\,(t,\omega,kr,\theta,a)}{\partial r}\right|_{r=a} = -\left.\frac{\partial\;\Phi_{\text{I}}\,(t,\omega,kr,\theta)}{\partial r}\right|_{r=a}.$$

Like Lord Rayleigh and later I. Malecki, for the basic approach for the scattered wave $\Phi_S(t, \omega, kr :, \theta, a)$ we use is

$$\Phi_s\,(t, \omega, kr, \theta, a) = \Phi_0 \cdot e^{-i\omega t} \cdot \sum_{m=0}^{\infty} C_m \cdot h_m^{(2)}\,(kr) \cdot P_m\,(\cos\theta). \tag{1}$$

Let's have a look at the structure of Malecki's approach [6]:

> The more common Fourier analysis method uses an (infinite) sum of weighted sin()/cos() terms to realize any given 1-dimensional signal. Above we did the equivalent for any spherical, 3-dimensional Potential Function. We could do this by using terms of Legendre-Polynomials/Spherical-Hankel functions instead of sin()/cos() terms.

The border conditions, which have a solution for all points on and outside the surface of the sphere, will lead us to the missing Equation (1) coefficients.

6.4 The Solution of the Scattering Condition

Let's work it out now.

First, we transform the equation for the incoming wave into spherical coordinates.

$$\begin{aligned}\Phi_{\mathrm{I}}(t, \omega, kr, \theta) &= \Phi_0 \cdot e^{\,i\cdot\,(\mathbf{kx}-\omega t)} = \Phi_0 \cdot e^{\,-i\cdot\omega t} \cdot e^{\,i\cdot\,kr\cos\theta} \\ &= \Phi_0 \cdot e^{-\,i\omega t} \cdot \sum_{m=0}^{\infty} (2m+1) \cdot i^m \cdot P_m\,(\cos\theta) \cdot j_m(kr)\end{aligned} \tag{2}$$

We already know an approach for the scattering wave:

$$\Phi_s\,(t, \omega, kr, \theta, a) = \Phi_0 \cdot e^{-i\omega t} \cdot \sum_{m=0}^{\infty} C_m \cdot h_m^{(2)}\,(kr) \cdot P_m\,(\cos\theta). \tag{3}$$

The scattering condition connects scattered and incoming waves:

$$\left.\frac{\partial\;\Phi_S\,(t, \omega, kr, \theta, a)}{\partial r}\right|_{r=a} \equiv \; -\left.\frac{\partial\;\Phi_{\mathrm{I}}\,(t, \omega, kr, \theta)}{\partial r}\right|_{r=a}. \tag{4}$$

Inserting Equations (2) and (3) into Equation (4) and using the deviation rules gives the following result:

$$\sum_{m=0}^{\infty} \Phi_0 \cdot e^{-i\omega t} \cdot C_m \cdot h'^{(2)}_m(ka) \cdot k \cdot P_m(\cos\theta) \equiv$$
$$- \sum_{m=0}^{\infty} \Phi_0 \cdot e^{-i\omega t} \cdot (2m+1) \cdot i^m \cdot j\,'_m(ka) \cdot k \cdot P_m(\cos\theta).$$

This equation has to be valid for *all* frequencies (occurring in k or ka). The complete summation over all terms of summation has to be identical, if *each* term (for all indices m) is identical. This physical method is very common and is called: *The comparison of coefficients method.*

So we have, for all m,

$$\Phi_0 \cdot e^{-i\omega t} \cdot C_m \cdot h'^{(2)}_m(ka) \cdot k \cdot P_m(\cos\theta) \equiv$$
$$- \Phi_0 \cdot e^{-i\omega t} \cdot (2m+1) \cdot i^m \cdot j\,'_m(ka) \cdot k \cdot P_m(\cos\theta).$$

We easily see that the solution for the required coefficient is when C_m is set to

$$C_m := -\frac{(2m+1) \cdot i^m \cdot j\,'_m(ka)}{h'^{(2)}_m(ka)}.$$

By inserting the coefficient C_m in Equation (3), we get an expression for the acoustical potential for the scattered wave Φ_s:

$$\Phi_s(t, \omega, kr, \theta, a) =$$
$$\Phi_0 \cdot e^{-i\omega t} \cdot \sum_{m=0}^{\infty} -(2m+1) \cdot i^m \cdot \frac{j\,'_m(ka) \cdot h^{(2)}_m(kr)}{h'^{(2)}_m(ka)} \cdot P_m(\cos\theta).$$

Together with the previous equation, the resulting wave Φ_{RES} is

$$\begin{aligned}\Phi_{\text{RES}}(t, \omega, kr, \theta, a) &= \Phi_{\text{I}}(t, \omega, kr, \theta) + \Phi_s(t, \omega, kr, \theta, a)\\ &= \Phi_0 \cdot e^{-i\omega t} \cdot \sum_{m=0}^{\infty} (2m+1) \cdot i^m\\ &\quad \cdot \left[j_m(kr) - \frac{j\,'_m(ka) \cdot h^{(2)}_m(kr)}{h'^{(2)}_m(ka)} \right] \cdot P_m(\cos\theta).\end{aligned}$$

The sub term in square braces may be evaluated on the surface (r=a) of the sphere by using the expression

$$j_m(x) \cdot n'_m(x) - j'_m(x) \cdot n_m(x) = -\frac{1}{x^2},$$

setting the wanted surface to the head's sphere ($r = a$), we get the following simplification:

$$\left[j_m(ka) - \frac{j'_m(ka) \cdot h_m^{(2)}(kr)}{h'^{(2)}_m(ka)} \right|_{r=a} \Bigg]$$

$$= \frac{j_m \cdot h'^{(2)}_m - j'_m \cdot h_m^{(2)}}{h'^{(2)}_m} \Bigg|_{ka}$$

$$= \frac{j_m \cdot (j'_m - i \cdot n'_m) - j'_m \cdot (j_m - i \cdot n_m)}{h'^{(2)}_m} \Bigg|_{ka}$$

$$= \frac{-i \cdot (j_m(ka) \cdot n'_m(ka) - j'_m(ka) \cdot n_m(ka))}{h'^{(2)}_m(ka)}$$

$$= \frac{-i \left(-(ka)^{-2}\right)}{h'^{(2)}_m(ka)} = \frac{i}{(ka)^2 \cdot h'^{(2)}_m(ka)}.$$

The resulting formula of the acoustical potential is

$$\Phi_{res} = \Phi_0 \cdot e^{-i\omega t} \frac{1}{(ka)^2} \cdot \sum_{m=0}^{\infty} \frac{(2m+1) \cdot i^{m+1}}{h'^{(2)}_m(ka)} \cdot P_m(\cos\theta).$$

With the help of the equations for sound pressure and sound velocity, the influence of the sphere on an acoustical field of sound correlated to the undisturbed field of sound gives

$$\underline{A}_{CALC}(ka, \theta) = \frac{p_{RES}}{p_I} == \frac{1}{(ka)^2} \cdot \sum_{m=0}^{\infty} \frac{(2m+1) \cdot i^{m+1}}{h'^{(2)}_m(ka)} \cdot P_m(\cos\theta).$$

See also [10][1].

7 How to Implement the Calculation of an Idealized HRTF

The following code is offered for demonstration purposes.

[1]Note: If the above formula is compared with the literature, the correct orientation of the system of coordinates has to be remembered. As in [10], the direction of the incoming wave is the other way around; this is equal to the complex value j as: $j_{MORSE} := -i = -\sqrt{-1}$.

Due to the current lack of good free (open source) code to calculate the spherical Bessel/Hankel functions and/or the Legendre polynomials, the (commercial) Numerical Recipes in C (NRC) package is used.

I chose to implement the example code in C++ to provide a "complex" type abstraction, hopefully making the code more understandable. The complex calculations could have been realized with NRC complex-arithmetic.

The implementation of the algorithm is shown in the following C++ code listings. The comments within the code describe what is happening below that line in the source code. Due to the complexity of the code, some parts were left out of the printed code listing.

```
/**********************************************************
//Rayleigh.cpp
//calculate's an Idealized Head Related Transfer function
-------------------

begin : Sept 1994
copyright : (C) 1994-2001 by Frank Haferkorn
**********************************************************/
///------------------ some declarations;
const double SoundSpeed=33;

//easy change of single/double FLOAT precision possible
#define FLOAT double
const FLOAT TauTimeMaximum=1.0/SoundSpeed;
const FLOAT eps=EPS*1000;

#include <complex.h>
typedef complex<FLOAT> Complex;
///------------------- some assisting functions
// return real geodesian angle, if using azimuth and
// elevation
FLOAT Angel(FLOAT HeadRadius, FLOAT phi, FLOAT theta,
            FLOAT *xear)
{
//phi:=Azimuth
//theta:=Elevation
  FLOAT x[3];
  x[0]=HeadRadius*cos(PI/180*theta)*cos(PI/180*(phi+90));
  x[1]=HeadRadius*cos(PI/180*theta)*sin(PI/180*(phi+90));
  x[2]=HeadRadius*sin(PI/180*theta);
```

```
// cos(alpha) = R*R_ear/(|R|*|R_ear|)
  return acos((x[0]*xear[0]+x[1]*xear[1]+x[2]*xear[2]) /
    sqrt(x[0]*x[0]+x[1]*x[1]+x[2]*x[2]) /
    sqrt(xear[0]*xear[0]+xear[1]*xear[1]+xear[2]*xear[2])
);

FLOAT Zero(FLOAT x, FLOAT epsilon)
{ if(fabs(x)<epsilon) return 0; else return x;};

#include <math.h>
// all units in metric (SI-) units
// all angles measured in counter-clockwise (mathematical)
// direction!!!
const char tab='\t'

int main(int argc, char *argv[])
{
  FLOAT PhiBegin, PhiEnd, PhiOffset;
  FLOAT EarAzimut, EarElevation, HeadRadius, rbya, Drbya;

// use these defaults
// start angle of calculation, measured in Azimuth
// from PhiBegin to PhiEnd using PhiOffset in degrees
  PhiBegin=0
  PhiEnd=360
  PhiOffset=15
  EarAzimut=90 // Azimuth and Elevation of Ear Position
  EarElevation=0
  Head Radius=0.0875 // 8a=,75 cm
// when using a radius R outside the sphere (Rbya!=1
// may lead to a nonconvergent algorithm and can lead to
// runtime errors.
  rbya=1; Drbya=0.5 // only calculation on the heads surface
                    //itself

// or work out your own argument parsing ........ here
  int i;
// work out the calculated frequencies here. Fill 'em into
// the array F[nFreq]
  const int nFreq=40;
  FLOAT F[nFreq];
```

```
  for(i = i; i<nFreq; i++)
    F[i]=i*20000/nFreq;

// initial ear variables
  FLOAT phi, theta;
  FLOAT frequency, angleR, angleL;
  FLOAT xearL[3],xearR[3];

// calculate ear coordinates in cartesian coordinates
  xearL[0] = HeadRadius*cos(PI/180*EarElevation)
             *cos(PI/180*(EarAzimut+90));
  xearL[1] = HeadRadius*cos(PI/180*EarElevation)
             *sin(PI/180*(EarAzimut+90));
  xearL[2] = HeadRadius*sin(PI/180*EarElevation);
  xearR[0] = -xearL[0];
  xearR[1] =  xearL[1];
  xearR[2] =  xearL[2];

  FLOAT k0,k 1;
  FLOAT dW;
  FLOAT dPhaseL,dPhaseR;
  FLOAT tauL,tauR;
  Complex paL0,paL1, paR0,paR1;
  FLOAT ps=-1;
  theta=0;
  FLOAT phase,phase1;
  FLOAT Inclination, ITD, KuhnITD, KuhnPiL, KuhnPiH

// Print out comment at top of output to identify the
// following columns
  cout<<"{\#}"<<"phi" <<tab <<"Theta"   <<tab <<"f[kHz]"
    <<tab <<"ka"      <<tab <<"r/a"     <<tab <<"L_left"
    <<tab <<"dL"      <<tab <<"p_left"  <<tab <<"ps_left"
    <<tab <<"arg(A)"  <<tab <<"T_l_ns"  <<tab << "ITD_ns"
    <<tab <<"ITDKuhn" <<tab <<"dT_ns"   <<tab <<"PiL"
    <<tab <<"PiH"     <<tab <<"T_l[ms]" <<tab <<"ITD[ms]"
    <<tab <<"ITDKuhn" <<tab <<"dT_[ms]"
    <<tab <<endl;
```

The following Main Calculation Loop writes some status information to `stderr` and the desired data output to the Standard output (`stdout`).

```
// Loop thru surfaces above the head // usually not used
// NOTE: RbyA may be different from 1.0, beware of numerical
// instabilities
  for(FLOAT RbyA=1.0;RbyA<=rbya;RbyA+=Drbya)

  // Loop thru frequencies
  for(frequency=F[ifrq=0]; ifrq<nFrq; frequency=F[++ifrq])
  {
    // Loop thru angles
    for(phi=\textit{PhiBegin}; phi<=PhiEnd; phi+=PhiOffset)
    {
      angleR=Angle(HeadRadius, phi, theta, xearR);
      angleL=Angle(HeadRadius, phi, theta, xearL);
      k0=TWOPI*frequency/SoundSpeed;

      // Calculate HRTF Pressure differential
      paR0  = press(k0*HeadRadius,RbyA,angleR,eps);
      paL0  = press(0*HeadRadius,RbyA,angleL,eps);
      dW    = TWOPI*frequency*1E-2;
      k1    = (TWOPI*frequency+dW)/SoundSpeed;
      paR1  = press(k1*HeadRadius,RbyA,angleR,eps);
      paL1  = press(k1*HeadRadius,RbyA,angleL,eps);
      phase = arg(paL0);

      // retrieve phase
      phase1 =arg(paL1);
      dPhaseL =arg(paL0/paL1); // =arg(paL1)-arg(paL0);
      dPhaseR =arg(paR0/paR1); //=arg(paR1)-arg(paR0);

      // detect phase jump from 2PI --> 0;}}
      if (dPhaseL/dW< -TauTimeMaximum) dPhaseL+=PI;
      else if (dPhaseL/dW> TauTimeMaximum) dPhaseL-=PI;
      if (dPhaseR/dW< -TauTimeMaximum) dPhaseR+=PI;
      else if (dPhaseR/dW> TauTimeMaximum) dPhaseR-=PI;

      // Retrieve runtime tau
      // Group-runtime tau:=dPhase/dOmega
      tauL=dPhaseL/dW;
      tauR=dPhaseR/dW;
```

```
// Comparison with G. F. Kuhn's
// "Localization in the Azimuthal Plane"
// in J.A.S.A, Vol. 62, No.1 , July 1977
// get Theta_inc
if(angleR<angleL) Inclination =PIby2-angleR;
else Inclination =PIby2-angleL;

ITD      =(tauL-tauR);
KuhnPiL = ITD
          /(HeadRadius/SoundSpeed*sin(Inclination));
KuhnITD = HeadRadius/SoundSpeed
          *(Inclination+sin(Inclination));
KuhnPiH = fabs(ITD)/KuhnITD;
if(KuhnITD<1E-8) KuhnPiL=KuhnPiH=0;

// Printout the calculated data in a sing
cout << setprecision(3)
     << Zero((phi==360)?360:fmod(phi,360)) <<tab
     << theta                              <<tab
     << frequency/1000                     <<tab
     << k0*HeadRadius                      <<tab
     << RbyA                               <<tab
     << P2dB(abs(paL0))                    <<tab
     << P2dB(abs(paL0)/abs(paR0))          <<tab
     << abs(paL0)                          <<tab
     << abs(ps)                            <<tab
     << arg(paL0)                          <<tab
     << setprecision(0)
     << Zero(tauL*1E9)                     <<tab
     << Zero(ITD *1E9)                     <<tab
     << Zero(KuhnITD*1E9)                  <<tab
     << Zero((ITD-KuhnITD)*1E9)            <<tab
     << setprecision(4)
     << KuhnPiL                            <<tab
     << KuhnPiH                            <<tab
     ;
cout << setprecision(4)
     << Zero(tauL*1E3)                     <<tab
     << Zero(ITD *1E3)                     <<tab
     << Zero(KuhnITD*1E3)                  <<tab
     << Zero((ITD-KuhnITD)*1E3)            <<tab
```

```
            <<endl;
    }
  } cout<<endl;
  return 0; // main()
}
```

The basic numeric calculation happens in the function `press()` as presented here. It is a simple translation of the formula for `A_calc` as discussed below.

```
/************************************************************
Morse.cpp - description
-------------------
begin : Sept 1994
copyright : (C) 1994-2001 by Frank Haferkorn
************************************************************/

#include <math.h>
#include <iostream>
#include <fstream>
#include "Morse.h"

FLOAT plgndr(int m,int l, FLOAT x);
void sphbes(int n, FLOAT x,
            FLOAT *sj, FLOAT *sy,
            FLOAT *sjp, FLOAT *syp);

Complex press(FLOAT ka,
              FLOAT rbya,
              FLOAT theta,
              FLOAT eps,
              Complex *pplane,
              Complex *pscatter)
{
//Declarations
  FLOAT kr=ka*rbya;
  FLOAT costheta=cos(theta);
  Complex I(0.0,1.0),factor;
  FLOAT ja, jpa, jr, jpr;
  FLOAT ya, ypa, yr, ypr;
  Complex h2r, h2pa;
```

```
Complex termpnew,termsnew;
Complex termpold, termsold;
int m=0,im=0;
Complex ps(0,0),pp(0,0);
termpnew=termsnew=Complex(0,0);
do
{
  termsold=termsnew;
  termpold=termpnew;
  termsnew=Complex(0,0);
  termpnew= termsnew

  //SPEEDUP at initi of 'factor'
  for(im=0;im<4;im++)
  {
    switch(m%4) {
      case 0: factor=1;break;
      case 1: factor=I;break;
      case 2: factor=-1.0;break;
      case 3: factor=-I ; break;
    }
    factor*=(2*m+1)*plgndr(m,0L,costheta);

    sphbes(m,ka,&ja,&ya,&jpa,&ypa);

    // h2'(ka) := j'(ka)-I*y'(ka)
    h2pa= jpa-I*ypa;
    sphbes(m,kr,&jr,&yr,&jpr,&ypr);

    // h2(ka) := j(ka)-I*y(ka)
    h2r =jr-I*yr;

    // j'(ka)/h2'(ka)*h2(kr)*I;
    termsnew+= -factor*jpa*h2r/h2pa;
    termpnew+=  factor*jr;
    m++;
  }
  // sum over all terms
  pp+=termpnew;
  ps+=termsnew;
}
```

```
  while(m<1000&&
  (  abs(termsnew)>eps
   ||abs(termpnew)>eps));

  if(m>1000)
    std::cerr<<"more than "<<m<<" iterations !!!"<<endl;

  if(pplane!=NULL)
    *pplane=pp;
  if(pscatter!=NULL)
    *pscatter=ps;
  return (pp+ ps);
}
```

Remember that the functions to compute Legendre polynomials and or any equivalent (`plgndr/sphbes`) and all depending functions are *not included in source* on the CD-ROM that accompanies this book. You will need the "Numerical Recipes in C" or an equivalent package that includes computation of Spherical-Bessel/Legendre polynomial.[2]

Due to the licensing policy of the Numerical Recipes in C, only non-NRC source files are on the CD-ROM, *but* we are able to include the compiled *Win32/ELF binaries* for Windows/Linux-i386.

In the remainder of this article, we will have a look at various plots of properties of the HRTF that we have computed, which we will refer to as the idealized cases. We use a head size of a = 8.75 cm, the same used by Blauert [1]. We will also compare our computed HRTF with some well-known measured HRTFs, including Shaw's study of people [13] and Neumann's artificial head [3].

7.1 Let's Have a Look: Idealized Pressure Difference (IPD-haf95)

In the following discussion, the value ka is equivalent to frequency.

ka a=8.75 cm =3.41 inch	0.1	0.5	1	2	5	8	10	12	15	20	25	30
f/Hz	60	300	600	1200	3000	4800	600	7200	9000	12000	15000	18000

Table 2. Translation table: wave vector to frequency.

[2]Using the NRC package, look for the sources beschb.c, bessjy.c, chebev.c, nrutil.c, plgndr.c, and sphbes.c and the header files, nrutil.h, and precisn.h.

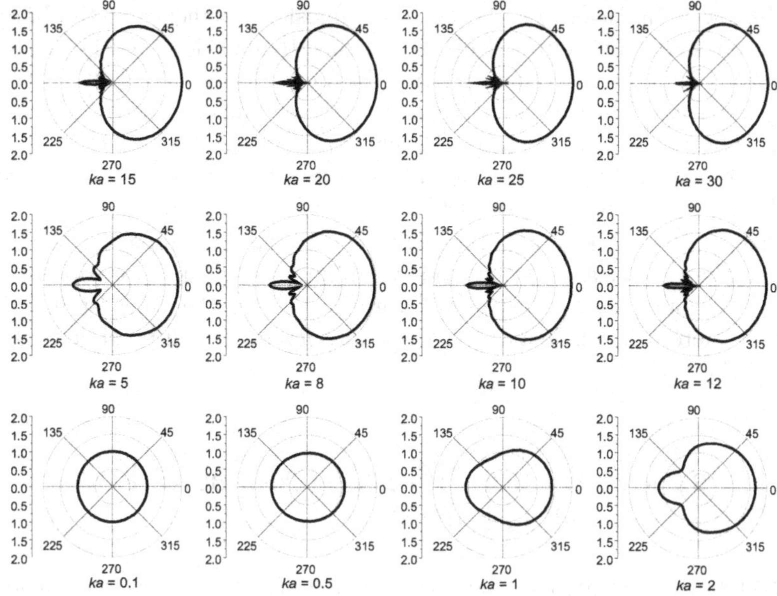

Figure 7. For various k, pressure on the surface of a scattering acoustical hard sphere by a plane wave (0°).

The diagrams in Figure 7 show the resulting pressure compared with the undisturbed pressure P_{RES}/p_I on the surface of a scattering acoustical hard sphere by a plane wave coming from the right side at an angle of 0°.

The sphere has radius a and wave number $k = 2p : f/c$, where c is the speed of sound. The absolute value of the pressure is drawn in radial direction. The scale at the left side of each diagram is a linear scale. The product of the wave number and the radius is proportional to the size of the scattering object compared to the wavelength of the incoming plane wave.

The corresponding frequency at the sphere with radius $a = 8.75$ cm can be determined from Table 2.

Hint: It is best to imagine the scattering sphere at the origin and a sound source at the right edge of the diagram.

Example: Please watch the top-left diagram: For $ka = 15$ ($a = 8.75$ cm $\rightarrow f = 9$ kHz), the wave that comes from the right side (0°) is shadowed away at the backside of the idealized head. The peak at 180° is a relic of the extreme symmetric idealization.

For low frequencies ($ka<1$), there is almost no influence of the hard sphere on sound pressure. While for higher frequencies ($ka>1$) at the front side (0°) there is higher pressure. In the backside (90°–270°) of the head, the sound pressure is increasingly reduced with frequency. In this diagram or at higher frequencies (bigger ka), a pressure peak increases to a maximum at 180°. This can be imagined as a constructive interference of all sound paths with identical phase around the sphere.

This is due to modeling the head as an exactly symmetric sphere (bowling ball idealization) that leads to an intensity peak at the opposite side of the sound source. With real-world heads and their corresponding HRTFs, there will not be a constructive interference on all possible paths around the head.

8 Let's Have a Look: Idealized Monaural Level Difference (MLD-haf95)

In the following discussion, the value ka is equivalent to the frequencies listed in Table 2.

The monaural level difference (MLD) is the amplitude (in decibels) of the microphone-head-eardrum transfer function. Sound pressure at the left ear is compared to the pressure of the undisturbed field of sound at the center of the sphere calculated for a radius of 8.75 cm. The position of the left ear is φ=100° and ϑ_R=0° in the horizontal plane. (See Figure 8.)

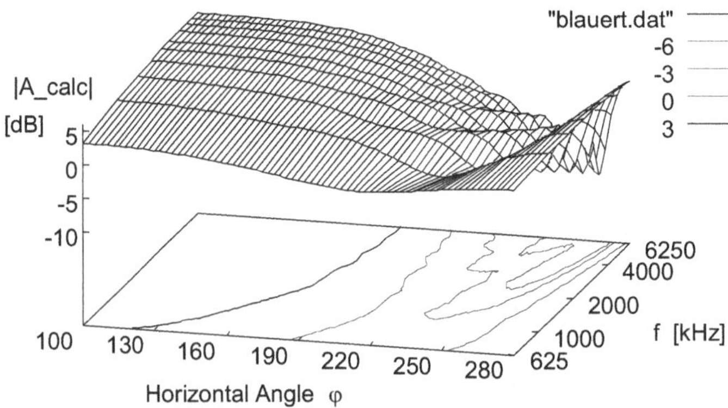

Figure 8. Calculated monaural level difference. 0° = frontal, 90° = at side of left ear, 180° = behind, 270° = at side of right ear, 360° = frontal.

9 Let's Have a Look: Idealized Interaural Level Difference (ILD-haf95)

The interaural level difference (ILD) shows the sound level difference between the left and right ear.

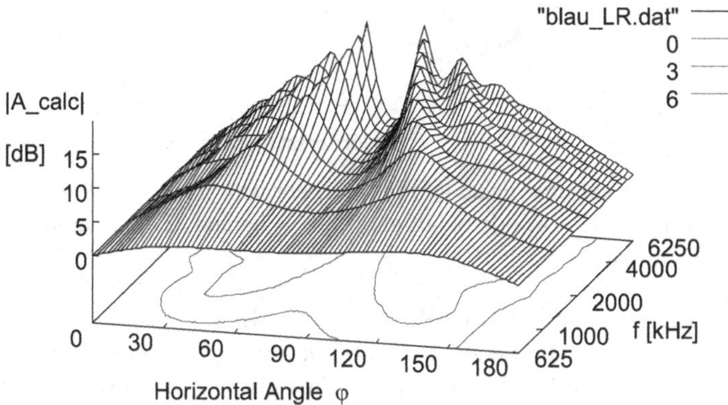

Figure 9. Calculated interaural level difference (ILD): the ILD between left and right ear as a function of the direction of the incoming wave with a sphere of radius 8.75 cm. The position of the observed ears is φ_L= 100°, φ_R= 260° ϑg 0°. 0° = frontal, 90° = at side of left ear, 180° = behind, 270° = at side of right ear, 360° = frontal.

10 Let's Have a Look: Idealized Monaural Time Delay (MTD-haf95)

Equal to the MLD, the monaural time delay (MTD) is the *time delay* of the idealized head up to the eardrums. In order to observe the results of the numerical calculation of the transfer function, we use a sphere of radius of 8.75 cm. The time delay can be calculated by using the equation

$$\tau_{group} = -\frac{d}{d\omega} \cdot \arg\left(\underline{A}_{CALC}\right).$$

The numerical processing gives the result shown in Figure 10.

At lower frequencies, the time delay can be modeled by a simple SINUS-LAW, which simply ignores the presence of the head in the sound field. For high frequencies, ($f > 4$ kHz), the time delay behaves like the model of creeping waves. This model propagates in the case of direct

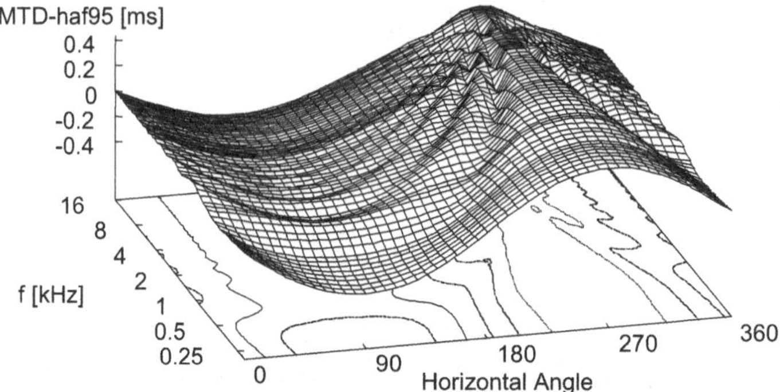

Figure 10. Monaural time delay (MTD) of an ear with $\varphi_{ear} = 90°$ and $\vartheta_{ear} = 0°$. 0° = frontal, 90° = at side of left ear, 180° = behind, 270° = at side of right ear, 360° = frontal.

sound approach the SINUS-LAW (0°–180°). In the case that the sound has to move around the head (180°–360°), a creeping wave which travels on the surface of the head is assumed. This gives a MTD in the shape of an attic around 270°.

11 Let's Have a Look: Idealized Interaural Time Delay (ITD-haf95)

The interaural time delay (ITD) is the *time difference delay* of any signal received by the idealized head up to the eardrums. It can be retrieved from the MTD as described above. Using $\text{ITD}- = (\text{MTD}_{\text{left}} - \text{MTD}_{\text{right}})$, we get the result in Figure 11.

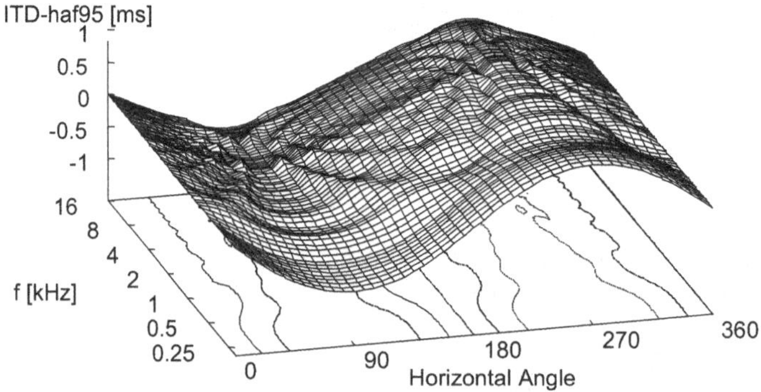

Figure 11. Calculated interaural time delay.

12 Measured Data: E. A. G. Shaw's HRTF from 1986 (SHAW-haf95)

Shaw took measurements of 100 people in 1986 and averaged their head-related transfer function in order to get a representative result of the HRTF of an average head. While it is true that the contemporary practice of structural averaging is much better, Shaw was limited by the capabilities of the technology available in 1986.

Shaw presented his average head-related transfer function in 1986 in numerical form. Figure 12 shows this HRTF data in a graphical presentation.

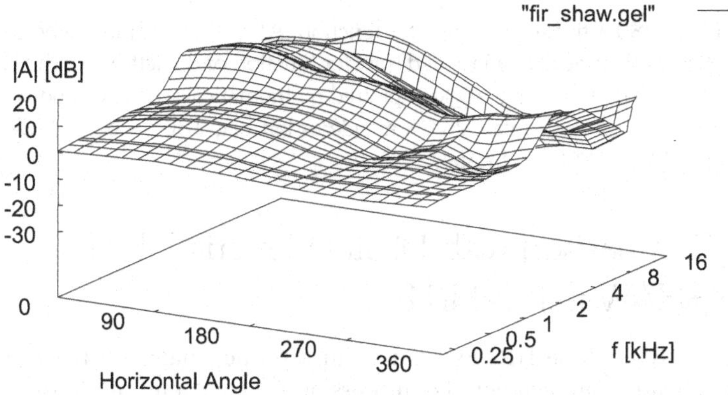

Figure 12. Head-related transfer function by Shaw in the horizontal plane: the average head-related transfer function of more than 100 people at the left ear. The horizontal angle is plotted mathematically positive and is equal to the directions: 0° = frontal, 90° = at side of left ear, 180° = behind, 270° = at side of right ear, 360° = frontal.

13 Measured Data: Neumann KU80 Artificial Head HRTF (KU80-haf95)

The Neumann KU80 is a reliable tool for measuring the influence of the head on a sound field. The KU80 is certainly not a realistic human head, but its advantage is that it reduces the head to the simplest form without hair, etc. Although this artificial head isn't the modern one, the diagram in Figure 13 shows that it gives useful measurements.

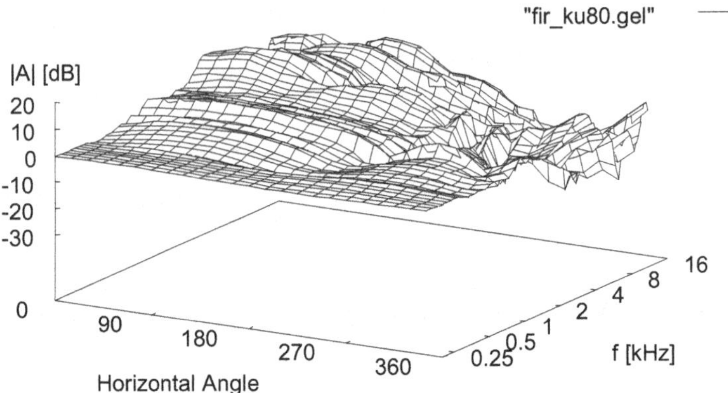

Figure 13. KU80 artificial head transfer function $|\underline{A}^{KU80-haf95}|$ in the horizontal plane. Measured artificial head related transfer function of the left ear of the KU80 artificial head. The horizontal angle is plotted mathematically positive and is equal to the directions: 0° = frontal, 90° = at side of left ear, 180° = behind, 270° = at side of right ear, 360° = frontal.

14 Comparison with Digital Generic HRTF (SHAW-haf95-FIR16)

How can any of these HRTFs be used in a proper manner? If you want to give a headphone listener the impression that a sound originates from the left side, the "only" task is to simulate a real-world (or an artificial head's) HRTF.

This can be done using digital filters. They are called *finite impulse response* (FIR) filters. The main task is to produce adequate and precise filter coefficients using nonlinear regression methods. Because this method, together with the usage of FIR filters, is a far too complex topic, it won't be presented herein. See also Allman's article "Finite Impulse Response Filters" (see *Audio Anecdotes II*).

The transfer function given by Shaw's averaged HRTF $|\mathrm{A}^{SHAW-haf95}|$ is used to construct a set of digital finite impulse response filters; one filter for each horizontal 15° step. The simulation software is included as a binary. It is compiled for Linux-i386 and Win32 and is included on the CD-ROM. It can be used to simulate the influence of the KU80-haf95 and SHAW-haf95 HRTFs on any mono audio signal to provide localization when listening to the result over headphones. Follow the instructions in the file README.TXT.

WAV format IO is used. Direct audio output is not implemented, but using a computer faster than a PentiumII-350 together with Linux, there are ways to listen to the spatially mixed output sound in real time.

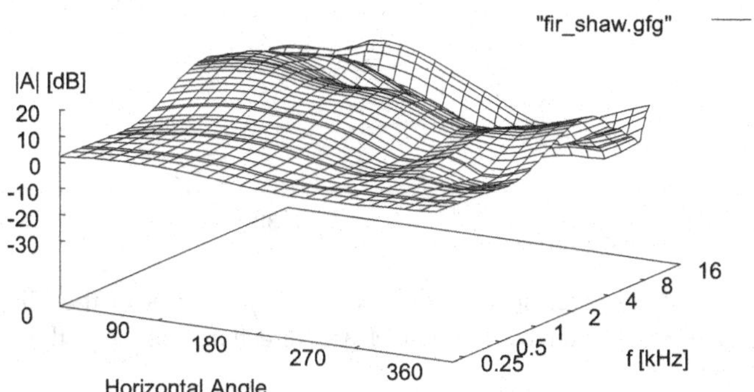

Figure 14. FIR-Head-Related Transfer Function FIR- $|A^{SHAW-haf95}_{FIR16}|$. $|\underline{A}^{SHAW-haf95}_{FIR,16}|$ using 16 FIR coefficients fitting to get similar the HRTF of Shaw $|\underline{A}^{SHAW-haf95}|$.

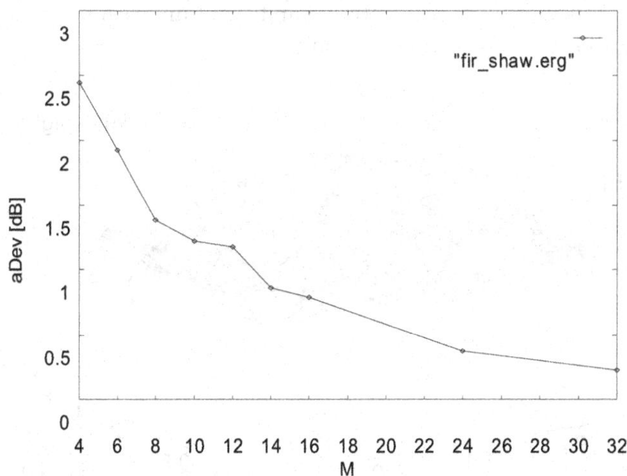

Figure 15. Absolute Error by order of fit $aDev^{SHAW}_{FIR}(M)$. This graph shows the dependency of the absolute error of the FIR method on the number of filter coefficients M. Averaged over all directions in the horizontal plane, fitted to get the HRTF of $|\underline{A}^{SHAW-haf95}|$.

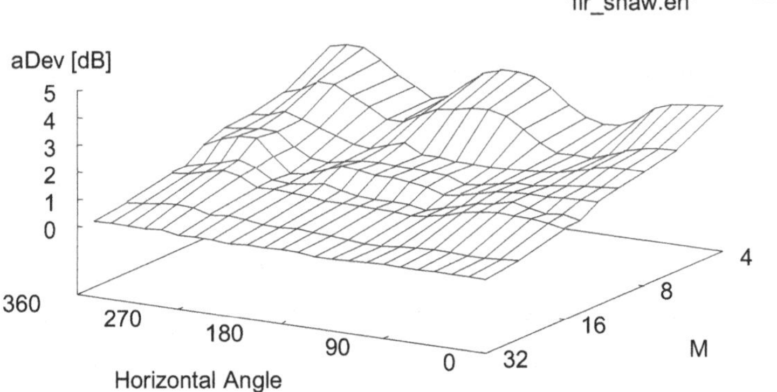

Figure 16. Absolute Error split $aDev_{FIR}^{SHAW}(M, \varphi)$. Error of the FIR Method versus the number of filter coefficients M and directions, fitted to the HRTF of Shaw $|\underline{A}^{SHAW-haf95}|$.

15 Comparison with Digital Generic HRTF (KU80-haf95-FIR16)

When the KU80-haf95 artificial head HRTF data is used to design a set of FIR filters, considering a good nonlinear fitting algorithm, the following data in Figures 17–19 will be the result.

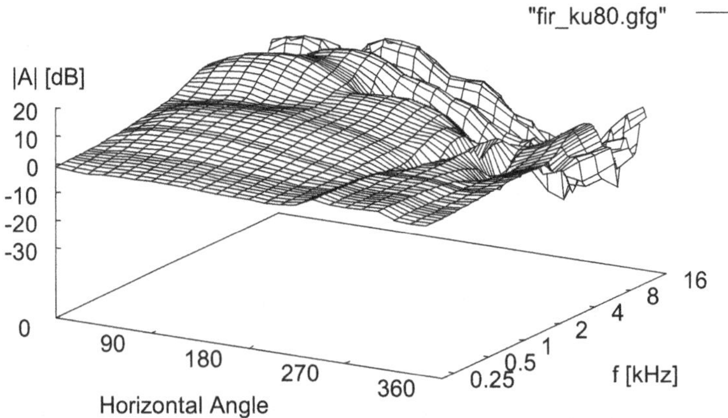

Figure 17. FIR-head-related transfer function $|\underline{A}_{FIR16}^{KU80-haf95}|$. Result of the FIR method using FIR Filter with 16 filter coefficients in order to represent the measurement of the HRTF of the KU80 Transfer Function $|\underline{A}^{KU80-haf95}|$. See for comparison the measured data $\underline{A}^{KU80-haf}$ | as presented before.

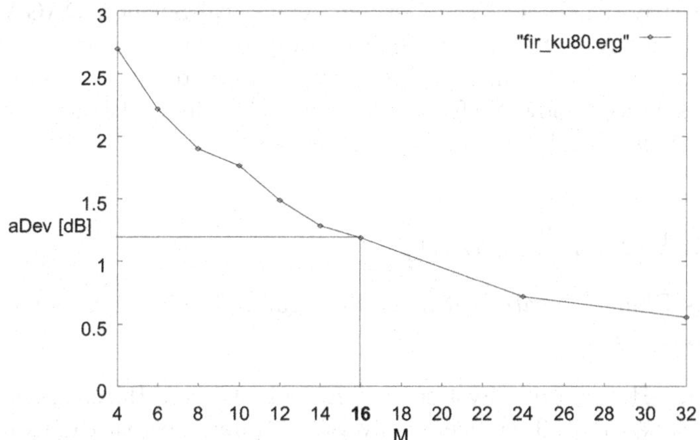

Figure 18. Absolute Error by order of fit $aDev_{FIR}^{KU80-haf95}(M)$. This graph shows the dependency of the absolute error of the FIR method on the number of filter coefficients M. Averaged over all directions in the horizontal plane, fitting to get HRTF of the KU80 $|\underline{A}^{KU80-haf}|$. The error of M = 16 coefficients is marked. This error of 1.2 dB is smaller than the interpolated error of the measured HRTF of the KU80 (1.5 dB).

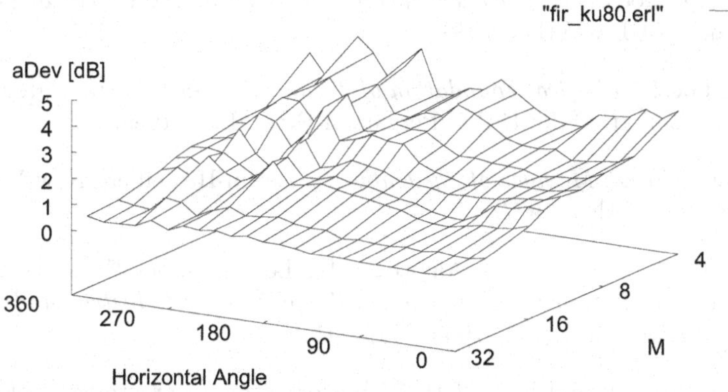

Figure 19. Absolute Error split $aDev_{FIR}^{KU80-haf95}(M, \phi)$. This graph shows the dependency of absolute error of the FIR method on the number of filter coefficients M, split by directions, and fitting to get HRTF of the KU80 $|\underline{A}^{KU80-haf}|$. For the position around 270 degrees (behind the measured ear), the error is a bit greater.

This article is based on the author's prior publication in the twenty-second yearly congress of the German Acoustical Society; DAGA 1996, Bonn (Germany). In a short article, there is barely room to scratch the surface of this fascinating, but complicated, topic. Please see the references listed below to further research this field. Blauert's *Spatial Hearing* [1] is considered to be the classic text.

Annotated Bibliography

[1] Jens Blauert. *Spatial Hearing.* Stuttgart, Germany: S. Hirzel Publishing, 1974.

[2] Frank Haferkorn. "System zur Erzeugung von Hörereignisorten." Diploma thesis, Technichal University Munich, Institute of Computer Interface, 1995.

[3] Frank Haferkorn. "System zur Erzeugung von Hörereignisorten." In *Proceedings of the 22nd Yearly Congress of the German Acoustical Society*, 1996.

[4] John David Jackson. *Classical Electrodynamics.* Berlin-New York: Walter de Gruyter, 1983.

[5] George Joos. *Lehrbuch der theoretischen Physik.* Wiesbaden, Germany: AULA-Verlag, 1989.

[6] I. Malecki. *Physical Foundation of Technical Acoustics,* translated by Irina Bellert. Oxford, UK: Pergamon Press, Ltd., 1969.

[7] Hans Marko. *Methods of Systemtheory.* Berlin-Heidelberg-New York: Springer Verlag, 1977.

[8] D. W. Marquardt. "An Algorithm for Least-Squares Estimation of Nonlinear Parameters." *Journal of the Society for Industrial and Applied Mathematics* 11 (1963), 431–441.

[9] S. Mehrgardt and V. Mellert. "Transformation Characteristics of the External Human Ear." *Journal of the Acoustical Society of America* 61:6 (1977), 1567–1576.

[10] Phillip M. Morse. *Vibration and Sound.* New York-Toronto-London: McGraw Hill Book Company, 1948.

[11] W. H. Press, S. A. Teukolsky, W. T. Vetterling, and B. P. Flannery. *Numerical Recipes in C – The Art of Scientific Computing.* Cambridge, UK: Cambridge University Press, 1992.

[12] Lord Rayleigh. "On the Acoustic Shadow of a Sphere." *Phil. Transact. Roy. Soc. London* 203:A(1904), 87–99.

[13] E. A. G. Shaw. "Earcanal Pressure Generated by a Free Sound Field." *Journal of the Acoustical Society of America* 39:3(1996), 465–470.

[14] E. A. G. Shaw. "Transformation of Sound Pressure Level from the Free Field to the Eardrum in the Horizontal Plane." *Journal of the Acoustical Society of America* 56:6 (1974), 1848–1861.

[15] E. A. G. Shaw. "Transformation of Sound Pressure Level from the Free Field to the Eardrum Presented in Numerical Form." *Journal of the Acoustical Society of America* 78:3 (1985), 1120–1123.

Synchronization

Synchronization Demystified: An Introduction to Synchronization Terms and Concepts

Ken Greenebaum

Synchronization is a subject that can be difficult to approach and even more challenging to achieve. There are many reasons for this, but it doesn't help that the term is rather ill defined. Dictionary definitions for synchronization commonly include: *to cause to occur with exact coincidence in time or rate.* Computer folk generally agree that the term synchronization has something to do with maintaining the correct relationship in time between streams of media, most often audio and video, which is the connotation that we will be exploring in this article and chapter.

Synchronization is commonly regarded as critical; simultaneously, it is also commonly regarded as inherently ephemeral and thus difficult to measure. I only agree with the first half of that. Synchronization is inherently measurable, and I further suggest that if "what can't be quantified can't be achieved" is true, then it is critical to begin any digital media project with the tools necessary to measure the degree of synchronization achieved. Only in this way is it possible to understand if any given change brings a project closer to meeting its synchronization goals and to know when success has been achieved.

Ironically, many developers new to digital media either assume that synchronization is trivial to achieve or simply take it for granted that robust synchronization is both a solved problem and a service provided by the underlying multimedia framework or operating system (this changes once they have had an opportunity to test their first application).

The naïve developer might reason: what could be easier than starting the audio and video at the same time, perhaps with back-to-back calls to functions such as `StartAudio()` and `StartVideo()`? These developers quickly discover that this seemingly obvious approach leads to inconsistent performance in which the audio and video only loosely line-up at the beginning of playback and often drift further out of sync over the length of a feature film, with each invocation achieving different results. What often follows are a series of attempted quick fixes such as running the processes as high-priority or attempting to lower the latency of the start calls that change, but never seem to improve, the fundamental issues.

This article attempts to demystify synchronization beginning with synchronization terms and concepts as well as common related topics such as *time code* or *edit decision lists.* Fundamental techniques such as *start* and *dynamic synchronization* are introduced. Engineering tradeoffs for synchronization quality are put into context, stressing that the primary consumer of media is the human user and that the resulting requirements can be evaluated by studying human perception. Finally, degrees of synchronization from *catch-as-catch-can* to *subsample accuracy* are discussed with detailed phasing and edit scenarios used to motivate the need for higher standards.

The articles that follow in this chapter present a historic context for synchronization and analyze specific techniques for achieving (and measuring) synchronization.

1 Differing Views of Synchronization

Synchronization is considered very differently by the film, consumer electronics, and computer industries.

To film and video professionals, synchronization is essentially a solved problem. Precise synchronization (for their application) can be consistently achieved when the appropriate gear (supporting features like SMPTE *time code*, *house-sync*, and defined/calibrated *pre-roll*) is used, and accepted production protocols are rigorously adhered to. After all, film production has been refined to such a degree that it is almost considered a science. Modern film production began with the talkies in the 1920s: they have had a long time to refine their craft.

Consumers are accustomed to (and demand!) inexpensive devices that *just work.* Consider the consistently excellent degree of synchronization long achieved by most any consumer device: televisions, DVD players, camcorders, etc., or the experience of synchronization in the *real* world: clap your hands and the sound always coincides with the collision (at least when observed at close range). Consequently, consumers take synchronization for granted, unless it was lost, and then they would consider the affected product to be defective (that is broken, not just in need of a reboot).

Compared to film or even video, computer manipulation of digital media is a much newer and still-evolving phenomenon. Although there are earlier examples, many consumers' first introduction to computer-based video was QuickTime videos that Apple Computer debuted in 1991. The computer industry has made considerable progress in the intervening years; those first twenty-second *postage stamp*-sized videos by which we were once so excited have been replaced by capabilities we take for granted, like being able to play DVDs on modern PCs.

New capabilities enable new applications, and often these applications, and their users, become increasingly demanding. For instance, those early 20 second video clips didn't have much opportunity to drift out of sync when compared to a 1.5 hour DVD movie, and the consumers of those early clips weren't very demanding at all—they were thrilled just to see moving pictures on their computers. Modern consumers, on the other hand, expect their DVDs to play as well on their laptops as they do on their dedicated DVD players. Actually, most consumers don't recognize it, but they want the computer to play considerably better than the DVD player/TV combo; for instance, they expect a high-quality full-screen video playback on a much higher resolution display (latest laptops have screens with up to 1920×1200 pixels, almost eight times the size of NTSC TV) than their television (with square-pixel NTSC being 640×480). Computers must use sophisticated interlaced-to-progressive scan, line-doubling techniques to fill those large screens.

The latest applications have raised the stakes even higher. PCs have, for some time, been used in the *offline* production of both films and video (Pixar's animated features are *rendered* using large arrays of general-purpose computers, and PC-based *nonlinear editors* have replaced many of the fabulously expensive dedicated solutions from companies like Quantel). General-purpose computers are also beginning to be used for live broadcasts, such as Al Gore's current TV cable network, formerly considered to be the domain of *broadcast quality* professional video gear. Not only are *real-time* live broadcasts more challenging, but they are also *mission critical*; a botched offline edit can be immediately repeated only irritating the engineer, but it is considered unacceptable for a glitch to make it into a broadcast where it is seen by a wide audience.

2 Synchronization in Motion Film

Given the success and maturity of the motion film industry, it is worth examining its history and development of synchronization, looking for techniques that might be applied to similar problems in the computer domain. These solutions didn't come easily or quickly to the film industry. The development and commercialization of *talkies*—films with spoken dialogue and sound, as opposed to silent films—was a long-time goal that took years to be realized, largely due to the limitations of early-1900s technology to solve problems related to synchronization.

At one time, due to technological limitations, it was necessary to record sound and moving images using different devices. This created physically-distinct media without direct timing correlation, presenting a large challenge to resynchronizing these media at playback. Sound and image tracks are, to this day, largely captured separately by independent devices, although this is now due to process more than technical necessity.

To present a film in a theater, there are some fundamental requirements: the sound has to come from near the screen at the front of the theater to maintain the illusion that the sound is coming from the actors and other action in the scene. The projector needs to be some distance from the screen, usually at the rear of the theater. In the era before electrical amplification, this required the sound reproduction gear (something similar to a Victrola) to be placed at the front of the theater and the projector to be at the rear. It took twenty years to find a viable solution to synchronizing the sound and image playback devices from across the theater, a distance too great for mechanical linkages.

Early, and commercially unsuccessful, attempts at talking motion pictures used human beings to overcome the limitation of technology; synchronization was achieved manually using two technicians (one by the sound system, and one by the projector). The technicians would signal each other and attempt to start the sound and film playing at the same time. Thereafter the projectionist would closely watch the film and would adjust the playback speed of the projector to attempt to maintain synchronization with the soundtrack. If the synchronization was allowed to drift more than a split second apart (a syllable or more) then it might be impossible for the technician to bring the film back intro synchronization again. As a result many film presentations would end with the sound or images ending not only out of sync but also significantly before the other completed.

Two inventions were required to transform talking films from curiosities to the modern art form film has become. The first was the electrical encoding, amplification, and transmission of sound (what we today think of as an amplifier, speaker cables, and speakers). *Electro-accoustic* sound reproduction both allowed the sound and image reproducing equipment to be physically co-located where they could be successfully integrated and also freed sound reproduction from using direct *mechano-acoustic* mechanisms that severely restricted both amplitude and fidelity. The second invention, optical audio encoding, allowed the soundtrack to be physically printed on the same film as the images, physically establishing the synchronization relationship of the tracks.

Today, the film industry uses long-established processes to manage all aspects of sound and image syncronization from filming, to post-production, and finally, to printing the media for distribution and eventual playback. Many people are familiar with the clapboard and its signature sound used to mark the beginning of a film take. However, some might not realize that in addition to identifying the specific take, the clapboard also serves as synchronization aid. The impulse in the sound track from the slamming clapper's "CLAP" and the frame where the clapboard closes correspond to the same moment in time and are used to establish the alignment of the audio and image media in editing and post-production.

3 All a Matter of Degree

I believe it is useful to consider five degrees of synchronization which roughly correspond to synchronization strategies:

(1) *Catch-as-catch-can* (the most simple attempt to synchronize). This is where only a naïve attempt is made to start the media, say a movie's audio and video tracks, at the same time. Often, this is attempted by using VCR-like interfaces that are supposed to *play* or *stop* a given media stream *as soon as possible.* This is the degree of synchronization found in many applications that treat event notification as an afterthought. Ever notice that the sound your email client plays when you have new mail only roughly corresponds to when the graphics are updated?

(2) *Best attempt.* In *best attempt* the developer goes to longer lengths to attempt synchronization, often thinking that they are using the best practices on the platform (with the implicit assumption that low-latency, precise synchronization is not possible on general-purpose machines). Best-attempt techniques often include using large, high-latency buffers, running as much code in the operating system's ker-

nel (ring 0) as possible, exploiting real-time operating system support such as non-degrading high-priority run levels, and demanding low-latency VCR controls (stop, play, etc.) for their media interfaces. Consider the increasingly popular *video chat* teleconferencing software, where it almost looks like the lips might sync to the voice.

These first two categories are very similar and differ more in effort than in quality of results. I have found that catch-as-catch-can quickly leads to best attempt as developers discover issues and struggle to understand and fix them.

(3) *Frame accurate.* Synchronization is performed to video frame granularity. For instance, sounds or events are started within the desired frame's duration (from 1/60 s to 1/24 s depending on frame rate). This level of synchronization is adequate, even optimal for many situations, such as for sounds with related graphics in a video game that don't correspond to a players input (i.e., an explosion, but not a shot being fired).

(4) *Sample accurate.* Digital media including audio and video streams are synchronized to the finest granularity available, the audio sample, perhaps by using the techniques similar to those described in my pipeline synchronization article (page 331). At the 48 kHz professional audio sample rate, sample accurate means that all streams are aligned to ± 1 sample time or within approximately ± 21 μs of the intended time. Similarly, frame accurate synchronization aligns to the closest video frame, or about ± 17 ms (17,000 μs) for 29.97 frames per second NTSC video. (See also my article "Count in Frames!" in *Audio Anecdotes II.*)

    Sample accurate audio is highly precise and is an adequate degree of synchronization for many applications; however, it should not be mistaken to be the highest degree of synchronization possible on a digital system.

(5) *Arbitrary precision* (subsample accuracy). By taking sample accurate techniques one small, but somewhat computationally expensive, step further, nearly arbitrary precision synchronization can be achieved. Essentially, streams can be re-sampled (using signal processing techniques involving super sampling) to shift the signal in subsample time increments. In this chapter, Eric Lee's article on dynamic sync introduces the concept of *resampling* an audio signal to change its time base.

4 Perception of Synchronization

Earlier, we stated that this article concerns itself with the concept of synchronization, of maintaining a time sense primarily between the audio and video media streams on a PC. For the moment, let's broaden that definition to include other events such as human interactions: for example, squeezing a joystick trigger, clicking on a PLAY button, or sliding a volume control. Ideally, each of these actions results in a reaction from the computer that the user would perceive as having a causal relationship. For this to occur, the reaction must closely follow the original action within a short time window for the user to perceive causality, and a smaller critical window for the user to perceive the actions as being simultaneous.

Most of us expect a movie's sound track to closely correspond to the image track, but few of us have a clear idea of how close in time the sound and image tracks need to be synchronized for the user to have an optimal experience, or alternately how far the timing of the tracks have to diverge before the latency first becomes noticeable, then apparent, and finally unbearable.

It is important to understand the engineering tradeoffs in any design. Specifically, it is important to know the required precision of the end product of your process as well as that of the precision of the inputs, calculations, and intermediate values.

Significantly, the ultimate consumer of almost any media systems is a human. Consider a telephone, TV, CD, DVD, teleconferencing system, etc. (an exception would be scanning a document to be translated to text by an optical character recognition (OCR) system). Consequently, human perception provides a basis for determining the optimal degree of synchronization (as well as determining most other parameters such as resolution, dynamic range, etc.).

The human perception of time has been well studied for the senses of vision and hearing and somewhat for touch. Specifically, for any set of media events, we are interested in the *just noticeable difference* (JND) in time. That is the smallest time delay between events that is perceivable. Time delays between events of less than the JND are all perceived as being simultaneous, and time delays of greater than JND are perceived as being increasingly noticeable, potentially irritating, or worse. Thus, it is critical to achieve a degree of synchronization that meets the JND criteria; however, it adds no value to exceed this, since the difference can't be perceived (though finer synchronization can help provide the ability to chain multiple systems together without accumulating too much error).

For more information on this topic, see Derek DiFilippo and my article, "Perceivable Audio Latencies," from *Audio Anecdotes I*, which extensively explores the relationship of latency (time difference between event and effect) and the resulting perception of causality for a wide variety of stimuli. The other articles in this chapter explore how to programmatically achieve this level of synchronization.

5 Start and Dynamic Sync

There are two components critical to achieving the synchronization of multiple streams: they must be started at the same time, and they must thereafter be kept in synchrony. This might seem obvious, however the second component is often forgotten or neglected, especially since it involves the challenge of adjusting the rate of an arbitrary stream.

I refer to the first component as *start synchronization*: ensuring that presentation of a media stream begins together at a precise time. In the pipeline synchronization article (page 331), I describe a simple and effective method for achieving highly precise start synchronization, loosely based on the use of film leaders by projectionists.

The naïve reader may fail to realize that it takes planning and preparation to begin multiple streams at the same time. First, a *rendezvous time* has to be decided on. This time can't be "now" because all devices or algorithms have latency variously described as group delay, priming, inertia, pre-roll, etc. Then, the intention to meet at a rendezvous time has to be communicated to all devices, so that when that time arrives all streams will be just beginning.

The second component is what I call *dynamic synchronization*; however, it is also referred to by other names, including *drift sync.* Whatever the name, it refers to the process of periodically monitoring and adjusting the streams to remain closely synchronized over time. Eric Lee's article (page 347) describes dynamic synchronization and introduces the important subjects of resampling and control theory to the reader.

It is also easy to fail to grasp the importance of dynamic synchronization, perhaps by assuming that media streams are inherently *locked* on modern computers and thus don't require any extra monitoring or control. Unfortunately, this is not the case. Digital media facilities on computers today are implemented using a collection of I/O hardware modules that hardware engineers select and integrate without much thought about how these might be integrated and later controlled by software systems. These

I/O modules might include ethernet, high-speed serial I/O (FireWire or USB), audio CODECS, high-resolution displays, video I/O (NTSC or PAL), MIDI I/O, etc. Shockingly, each of these modules usually independently derives a clock from its own inaccurate crystal oscillator—which drifts with respect to every other clock on the system.

However, even if the media systems on future PCs shared a master clock, and thus didn't drift with respect to each other, dynamic synchronization techniques would still be useful in many situations, such as when recovering from dropped samples (basically, recovering synchronized audio/video after a glitch caused by the computer failing to meet its real-time media commitments), when playing back media originally recorded using clocks running a little fast or slow (two hours of audio captured on a device running just one half of a percent slow would run 36 seconds longer than the video captured at the correct rate), or when streaming media across a network (with unsynchronized clocks and unexpected media dropouts).

Please consider that while we concentrate on providing audio examples of start and dynamic synchronization for the purposes of this book, both the pipeline and the drift compensation techniques are easily extended to elegantly handle the synchronization of other types of media streams.

6 Two-Way and N-Way Synchronization

Dynamic synchronization requires a media stream to be sped up or slowed down. In the analog realm, speed changes are relatively straightforward to manage (often involving changing the physical speed of motors driving the media), but changing the speed of a digital media stream is complicated and involves a process known as *resampling.*

Digital streams are really representations of the equivalent analog stream with instantaneous values recorded at precise time intervals. The process of digitization is called *sampling.* It is critical that the analog signal being sampled is bandwidth limited such that all frequencies higher than one half the sampling rate are first filtered out.

To slow a digital signal by, say 10%, somehow 10% more samples have to be "constructed." This may be accomplished using multirate digital signal processing techniques that are introduced in Eric Lee's article (page 347) and described in depth in Tor Ramstad's article "Rate Conversion" in *Audio Anecdotes I.*

For discrete media like video, it is possible to "cheat" and change the length of time an individual frame of video is displayed. Because it is difficult to change the rate of a continuous signal like a digital audio stream, it is often convenient to synchronize by cheating the video to match the audio. (These manipulations are only possible for video displayed on a computer screen and will not work for actual video signals.)

In the scenario that I call *two-way* sync, the nonvolatile stream, usually audio, is used as the *master clock*, and the other stream, usually video, is modified to match the time of the master. This is how almost all audio and video are synchronized on PCs today. It works pretty well in the narrow but common case where one audio stream and one video stream are being played back on the computer; however, it breaks if the situation becomes more complicated.

For instance, let's add an additional audio stream to the existing audio and video stream *mix:* perhaps one portable audio deck was used to record the vocalist and a second to record the band. Let's say that the second stream was recorded (sampled) on a device running faster than the device used to sample the first audio stream. Over time, the two audio streams will drift apart, even if the individual samples from each were presented at the same time.

The solution to this problem, and the general solution to all such problems, is what I call *N-way synchronization.* N-way sync involves resampling all streams against a common, high-resolution time base. While neither the start synchronization nor the dynamic synchronization articles specifically address the N-way case, both of the algorithms scale and together are sufficient to implement robust N-way synchronization.

7 Keeping Time: Time Codes

A timekeeping mechanism is important both for achieving synchronization and for describing more complicated media interactions in time, like edits. While it is easy and obvious to keep track of time by keeping track of the number of audio samples or video frames played, it can also be problematic. The largest problem is that counting frames provides only a relative time sense. For instance, there would be no way to determine absolutely where in a sequence you were if you didn't begin counting from the beginning. Also, the all-too-common problem of dropped frames would both be undetectable and undermine the time sense. Consequently, schemes have been developed to explicitly add time signatures, called *time codes,* to individual pieces of media. Ancillary data such as time codes are considered *metadata* (data about data) and are most often encoded *out of band* so that they don't obviously change the source signal.

The Society of Motion Picture and Television Engineers (SMPTE) defined the standard timekeeping scheme used in many industries including film and video. It is simply referred to as SMPTE time code. Time codes are nothing more than a colon-separated string of the current hour, minute, second, and frame (HH:MM:SS:FF) that is recorded with each video frame as metadata for keeping track of time. Digital representations maintain this eight-element structure by encoding the time code as eight four-bit, binary-coded decimal values. The "frame" field usually refers to the video frame number, although time codes are used to keep track of time for audio as well. Because of different video standards, many variations exist, including 24, 25, 29.97 drop frame (useful for making this compromise frame rate match wall-clock time), 29.97 non-drop frame, and 30 frames per second.

For many media types, time code is typically written to blank media as a pre-pass before actual content is recorded, in a process called *striping*. As a convention, time code is often striped such that the content will begin at time one hour, time code 01:00:00:00.

There are a number of encodings commonly used for SMPTE time code:

- LTC, Linear Time Code, pronounced "*litsee*," encodes time code as audio that is often recorded on an extra audio track on analog video tape recorders (VTRs). LTC time code can only be recovered when the tape is playing.

- VITC, Vertical Interval Time code, pronounced "*vitsee*," encodes time code as video data on an unseen scan line during the vertical interval, the normally blank time provided for televisions to retrace the electron gun to the beginning of the raster. VITC adds a SPMTE time code stamp to each individual frame of video. VITC can be seen as a line of flashing segments if the vertical hold is adjusted to show lines above or below the actual image. VITC time code may be recovered from a still frame of video.

- BTC, also known as burn-in, displays the eight-digit SMPTE time code in the video content itself where it can be observed without any special gear.

- MTC, MIDI Time Code, encodes SMPTE time code as a series of eight quarter-frame MIDI messages.

- Digital audio and video formats such as AES/EBU or S/PDIF audio, DV or 1394/Firewall video, etc. embed time code in headers in the digital audio stream.

Time code is a very convenient way to identify video media content for edits and is used in edit decision lists (EDL) as described in the next section. Time code is also used as a way for devices to track time, such as when they are to begin recording or playing.

In a studio environment, time code is usually centrally computed then distributed and is often called *house-sync.* In recent years wiring devices to a common time code source may be avoided by using individual devices that directly derive time code from the satellite global positioning system's (GPS's) high-precision clocks.

8 A/B Roll Example: Frame-Accurate Synchronization

In professional editing suites, the final video is created by essentially cutting and pasting portions of video and sound together from raw footage. The director or editor describes the clips of video that will comprise the final edited video in what is known as an *edit decision list* (EDL) or cut list. Before nonlinear editors, which store and manipulate video streams on a hard disk, video was recorded on videotape and a very common edit was called the *A-B roll.* In its simplest form, an A-B roll requires three frame-accurate video tape decks (VTRs).

A (human) editor might construct a table such as Table 1 to designate the desired edit.

In this case three frames from the tape in deck A beginning at time 01:07:08:03 will be recorded onto the tape in deck C at location 01:00:02:03 and will be immediately followed by 2 frames from deck B location 01:05:02:06. To accomplish such an edit, a set of operations must be carried out at precise times. The decks must be cued to the desired locations, started, and stopped (see Table 2).

Source	Source Time	Duration	Destination	Destination Time
A	01:07:08:03	00:00:00:03	C	01:00:02:03
B	01:05:02:06	00:00:00:02	C	01:00:02:06

Table 1. Example edit decision list.

Time	Deck	Operation
01:00:00:00	A	Cue 01:07:08:03
01:00:00:00	B	Cue 01:05:02:06
01:00:00:00	C	Cue 01:00:02:03
01:00:01:05	C	Record
01:00:01:05	A	Play
01:00:01:08	A	Stop
01:00:01:08	B	Play
01:00:01:10	B	Stop
01:00:01:10	C	Stop

Table 2. A-B roll operations.

The first deck's tape is cued to the beginning of one piece of desired footage (A), the second decks's tape is cued to the beginning of a second footage (B). The third deck is used to *lay down* what will become the final edited video, and its tape is cued to the insertion point where the new footage will be recorded. For the edit to be successful, VTR A must begin playing the desired video footage at exactly the time that the record deck begins recording. Then, VTR A must stop and VTR B must begin playing at precisely the time that the desired portion of clip A has finished. Finally, the record deck must stop recording at precisely the time the desired portion of clip B has completed, so as not to overwrite video that might already have been recording to the tape after where this new footage is being inserted. The edit looks something like Figure 1 from the perspective of the media itself.

While the A-B roll as described clearly illustrates the need to very accurately be able to control the start synchronization of media recording and playback, the process is actually a little more involved than described. Due to the physical inevitabilities, a tape deck has inherent latency; the mechanism has mass and inertia, and correspondingly takes time to come up to speed and be able to begin recording or playing from a stop.

In professional decks, pre-roll—the time a deck takes to come up to speed and be able to play or record—is both predictable and fixed. Predictable pre-roll does come at a cost; the "inexpensive" frame-accurate VHS decks I used were $10,000 apiece (D1 uncompressed digital component video decks were one hundred thousand dollars). Fortunately digital *prosumer* decks are now available for around a thousand dollars (my mini-DV camcorder is frame accurate and costs less than $800).

For the edit to work, the tape in each deck must be cued to a specific position before the desired insert point by an amount corresponding to

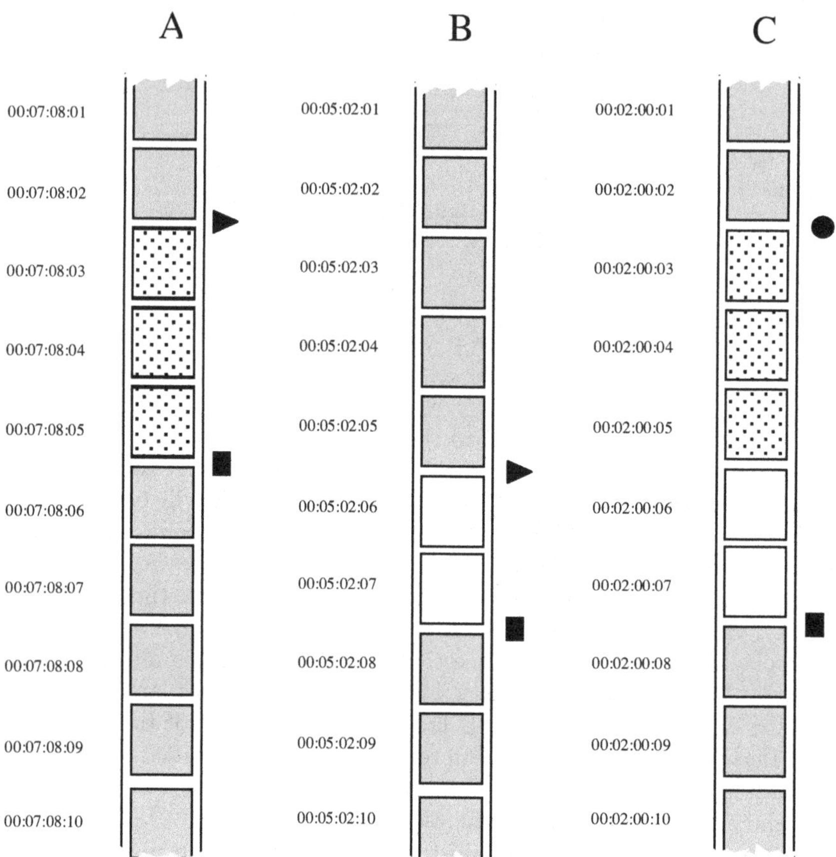

Figure 1. A-B roll media perspective.

each deck's individual pre-roll time. Additionally, each deck needs to be commanded to play or record early by the deck's pre-roll time. For instance, in the edit described in Table 1, decks A and C might be cued to a different number of frames before the intended frame. Then, one deck might be started before the other, so that when both decks are up to speed, the decks will be at the intended frames at precisely the correct time.

Table 2 assumes "magic" decks with no inertia, which correspondingly have a pre-roll of zero frames. (Even digital computer based solutions have latency, although it might be less than a video frame in duration.) The instructions in Table 3 factor a pre-roll of three frames for deck A, six

Time	Deck	Operation
01:00:00:00	A	Cue 01:07:08:00
01:00:00:00	B	Cue 01:05:02:00
01:00:00:00	C	Cue 01:00:02:01
01:00:01:03	C	Record
01:00:01:02	A	Play
01:00:01:08	A	Stop
01:00:01:02	B	Play
01:00:01:10	B	Stop
01:00:01:10	C	Stop

Table 3. A-B roll operations factoring pre-roll times of three, six, and two frames for decks A, B, and C, respectively.

for deck B, and two for deck C. (Notice that all the media are cued to locations earlier than desired and decks A and C are no longer started at the same time.)

9 Concatenation and Looping Example: Sample-Accurate Synchronization

Concatenation is the process of sequencing media such that the next piece begins immediately after the previous ends without any gap or overlap. In our digital world this means that the first sample of m_{n+1} is presented one sample period after the final sample of m_n.

On a macro level it does not sound or look very good if one piece of media begins before the previous ends. Imagine television where commercials sometimes overlap the program that they are to follow. This overlap would be disconcerting if not confusing depending on the degree of overlap. In Figure 2 the beginning of media clip m_2 (represented by frames containing pluses) overlaps the end of media clip m_1(represented by circles).

While overlap, usually in the form of a cross-fade or a wipe, is sometimes desired, overlap can also be confusing, especially as the length of the overlap increases. More subtly, these inaccuracies add up and lead to cumulative timing errors such that one cannot predict the time of the end of a sequence by adding the length of each media element:

$$\sum_{x=0}^{n} \overline{m_x}.$$

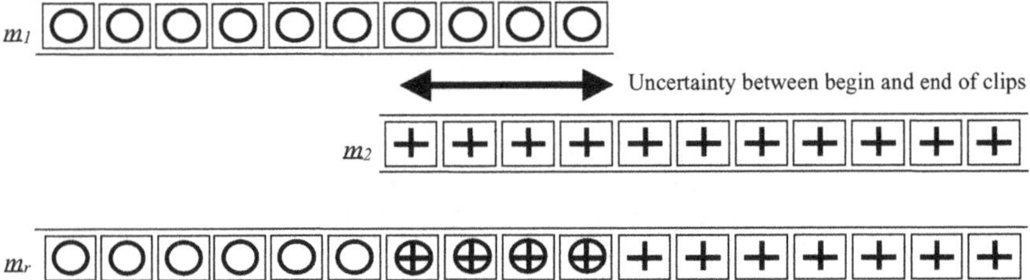

Figure 2. Beginning of m_2 overlapping end of m_1 yields a confused result m_r.

Another example of concatenation, on a micro scale, is *concatenative synthesis*, a technique to synthesize complicated sounds by concatenating a sequence of simple sound elements. Concatenative synthesis is similar to some of the voice synthesis techniques described by Craig Utterback ("Voice Concatenation," page 123) and Debbie Yarrington ("Synthesizing Speech for Communication Devices," page 143) but differs from granular synthesis described in Ross Bencina's article (see page 55) in that granular synthesis overlaps or mixes together the sound elements called grains. A simple example of concatenative synthesis is the attack, looped sustain, and decay sequence used to create musical notes of different length. Figure 3 is an example of a struck sound: please notice the rapid onset (attack), the period of constant amplitude (sustain), and the exponential attenuation (decay).

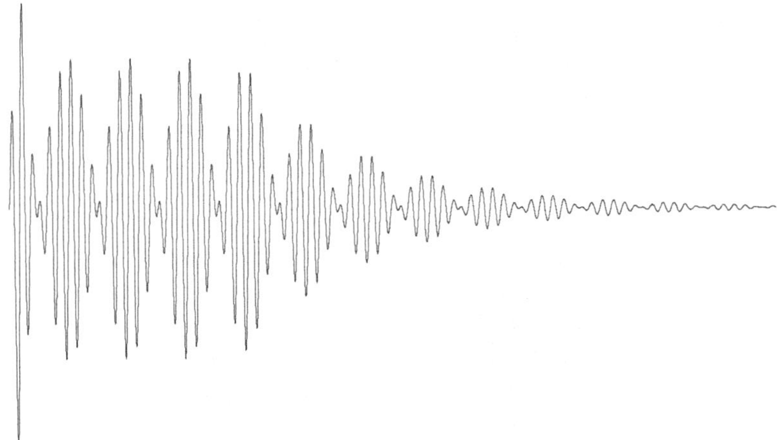

Figure 3. Struck sound consisting of attack sustain and decay elements.

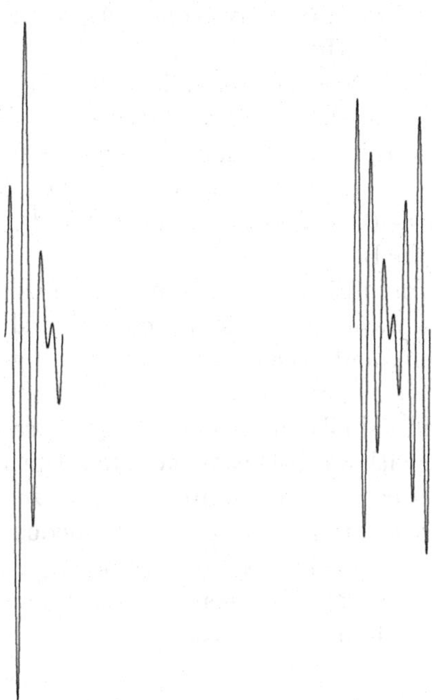

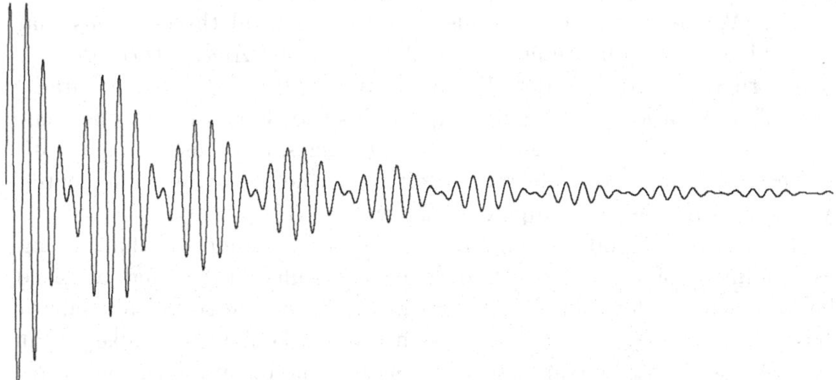

Figure 4. Discrete attack, (one period) sustain, and decay sounds.

Attack corresponds to the rapid onset of sound such as when a piano key is struck, sustain to the (mostly) constant sound emitted while the key is held, and decay to the rapid damping of the note after the key has been released. Those readers unfamiliar with the piano's mechanism might enjoy peeking under the cover while striking, holding, and releasing a key to watch the interplay of felt dampers being removed from a set of strings, strings being struck by a hammer, and then the dampers being restored to the strings (the mechanism in a grand-piano is fabulously refined and sophisticated).

While the waveform in Figure 3 was synthesized using a mathematical expression, a similar waveform could be constructed by concatenating discrete attack, sustain, and decay waveforms (see Figure 4).

The sustain waveform may be looped to easily change the length of the sound. Each of the individual component sounds are carefully constructed to assemble and loop without discontinuity: often this is accomplished by beginning and ending each sound component at a zero crossing. Recall that discontinuities in the form of large instantaneous changes in sample values, energy, etc. are perceived as loud, annoying clicks or pops. Discontinuities such as tiny gaps between looping instances of the sustain sound cause obvious and annoying artifacts.

10 Phasing Example: Sample-Accurate Synchronization

Some synthesis algorithms require a strict phase relationship between sounds. While it may be obvious that the binaural three-dimensional positioning algorithms described by Hempton (see *Audio Anecdotes I*), Haferkorn (page 269), and Gehring (page 249) require phase accuracy, "trivial" applications like mixing require this too. For instance, one common type of synthesis is called *additive synthesis*, often used to generate the percussive sounds of collision. Additive synthesis may be implemented by mixing a number of damped resonators together.

Recall from "Sound Propagation" (see *Audio Anecdotes I*) that mixing two instances of the same sound together results in a sound of twice the amplitude. However, if the two instances of the sound are out of phase, then some degree of cancellation results. While it is unlikely that a signal would ever be completely attenuated due to mis-synchronization (complete cancellation would require the two signals to be precisely 180° out of phase, which would be unlikely to arise from shifting the sounds by an integer number of samples), significant attenuation, especially of

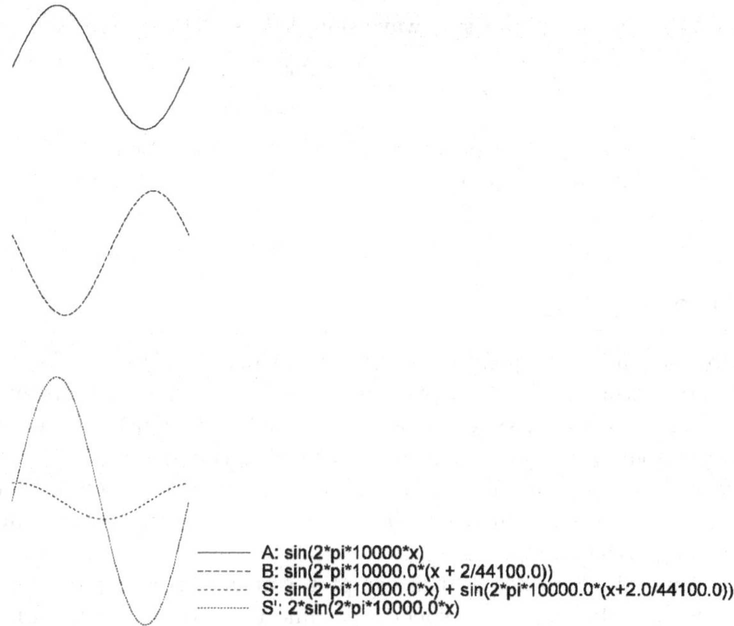

Figure 5. Two-sample mis-synchronization causes dramatic phase shift and attenuation of 10-kHz sine waves sampled at 44,100 Hz. Signal A: first 10-kHz signal. Signal B: second 10-kHz signal mis-synchronized by two samples. Signal S: the dramatically attenuated result of adding signals A and B. Signal S': the sum of signals A and B if B had not been mis-synchronized (superimposed on the actual sum).

higher frequency sounds, is likely: each period may be represented by only a small number of samples, making even only a small mis-synchronization very significant.

For instance, one period of a 10 kHz sine wave is represented by fewer than 5 samples at the common 44,100 samples per second CD sampling rate:

$$4.41 = \frac{44,100 \text{ Samples Per Second}}{10,000Hz}.$$

Consequently, the phase shift caused by synchronization errors of a small number of samples results in substantial attenuation. Each sample time by which the signals are mis-synchronized contributes approximately 82°

of phase shift of our 10 kHz sine wave sampled at CD audio rates:

$$81.63°/\text{sample} \approx \frac{360°}{4.41 \text{ samples}}.$$

A seemingly modest two-sample synchronization error would result in about a 163° phase shift and a dramatic attenuation if the two signals were added instead of a two-fold amplification (see Figure 5).

11 Conclusion

Synchronization is a deep subject with a great deal of history. I have attempted to introduce the concepts of start and dynamic synchronization and two-way and N-way synchronization, as well as demonstrate the relationship between precision of synchronization and the requirements of the consumer of the resulting media. I hope that placing these requirements in a historical context can better help us understand the opportunities and challenges that we now face.

The remaining articles in this chapter continue this exploration of synchronization by providing specific techniques and examples. Please be sure to examine the interactive code examples on the accompanying CD-ROM.

I hope that these articles will collectively help dispel some of the confusion that has grown around this important subject and help lead to better designs and products.

Annotated Bibliography

[1] Anders Askenfelt, editor. "Five Lectures on the acoustics of the Piano," WWW edition. Available from World Wide Web (http://www.speech.kth.se/music/5_lectures/), 2000.

This website provides the content of the book, now out of print, and describes the evolution of the earliest 1720 piano to the modern concert grand. It provides a introduction to the physics and mechanisms involved and is both wonderful for appreciating the mechanics of the modern piano and useful as a guide to begin synthesizing a piano using physical modeling techniques. Many photos, illustrations, and recordings are provided.

[2] John Watkinson. *The Art of Sound Reproduction.* Woburn, MA: Focal Press, 1998.

John, the author of the classic texts Introduction to Digital Audio and Introduction to Digital Video, does a nice job of illustrating and describing mechanical, and electro acoustic reproduction of sound, among many other topics. I especially like the historical context he provides for devices and technologies.

[3] Keith Jack. *Video Demystified*, Fourth edition. Woburn, MA: Newnes, 2004.

The latest update of the classic tells you much of what you need to know about video before attempting to decipher the actual video standards.

[4] John Ratcliff. *Timecode: A User's Guide*, Third edition. Woburn, MA: Focal Press, 1999.

This is a thorough, and perhaps the only, book dedicated to the subject of time code. I have personally created software-based timecode encoders and decoders based on the information in this book.

Synchronization in Film: Birth of the Talkie

Ken Greenebaum

My article "Synchronization Demystified" (see page 301) introduced many synchronization concepts that will be explored in the following two articles on start and dynamic sync. Before diving into those subjects, however, it might be helpful to examine an actual example of synchronization to help make these otherwise abstract concepts concrete. Let's explore synchronization in film since sound-image synchronization was first applied to motion picture technology.

The creation of the *talkie,* adding synchronized sound to the *silent movie*, wasn't an easy or a rapid transition. Rather, it took over twenty years of research and experimentation to create a commercially viable system; this system has since evolved into the motion picture that we recognize today and take for granted. I feel that the computer industry can learn much from this process.

1 An Overview

Even without formally attending film school, most of us have soaked up enough film references from watching popular movies and TV to understand the basics of motion picture production. From *Singing in the Rain* to *The Aviator*, the film industry has been more than a little narcissistic, and often features elements of its favorite industry in its own productions. Some claim that the rest can be learned from watching DVD extras.

As an oversimplification, live action is shot using motion picture cameras that capture a series of consecutive images on long rolls of film stock (imagine a 1000-foot long roll of film very similar to that used in a 35mm still camera). Each discrete image is called a frame. The film is developed and edited (requiring the film to be physically cut and spliced back together in a different sequence) to create a master of the final film that is then duplicated and distributed to theaters, where it is eventually projected. The projector displays each frame for a fraction of a second resulting in a reproduction of the original action that we recognize as a *movie*.

Things become a little more complicated when we consider the sound track. Unlike a consumer video camera, a motion picture camera only captures images and does not record sound. On a motion picture *shoot*, microphones and audio tape recorders are used in parallel with film cameras to record both the audio and motion images. This captured sound track is commonly called *production sound* and is subsequently *sweetened* in post-production by removing unwanted *wild sound* (such as coughs, airplanes, honks, etc.) and radically embellished by adding extras such as sound effects, extra or replacement dialogue, and music. Although not much if any production sound recorded outside of a studio sound stage makes it into any given soundtrack, it does help guide editing, automated dialog replacement, and Foley sound creation processes.

Because sound and image tracks are captured on distinct devices, there is no innate time reference available to establish the time relationship between the media that can be used to synchronize the tracks. The film industry uses the *clapboard*, a very pragmatic technology, to establish this timing relationship. Simply, the specifics of the current *take* are both chalked onto the clapboard's slate and read aloud; then, the clapper is slammed shut. In production, the "CLAP" impulse on the sound track is aligned to the frame where the clapper appears to close.

2 Early Attempts at Talking Pictures

Silent films were an art form distinctly different from what we think of today as the movie. However, silent movies weren't silent because silent films were considered artistically ideal, nor because it never occurred to anyone to add sound to movies. Rather, adding sound to motion pictures was an obvious, but difficult, technological challenge, somewhat similar to adding color to black and white photography or adding motion to still photography. Over a thirty-year period, engineers from around the world, including this likes of Thomas Edison, experimented with adding synchronized sound to motion pictures with initially far from satisfactory results.

Figure 1. Frames from an early Edison experimental sound motion picture illustrate how performers were forced to play directly into the horn of the insensitive wax-cylinder-based recording machines of the 1890s.

Early attempts to add a soundtrack to the then silent pictures kept sound on the recording media of the day: initially Edison wax cylinders and eventually gramophone disks (similar to the vinyl LP records that are themselves quickly receding into history). For instance, 1889 marked the first attempt with the kinetophonograph, which somehow attempted to connect a gramophone, for sound, to the Edison kinetograph, for motion images, in a synchronized manner.

Warner Brothers' 1926 *Don Juan* was the first commercially released film to include even a rudimentary soundtrack (the soundtrack basically contained music and *ambient* sound but no dialogue or sound effects requiring precise synchronization). Their release the following year of *The Jazz Singer* featured a much more ambitious soundtrack and contained sound effects and even a little dialogue. This production used a technology branded Vitaphone (named after Vitascope, the 1895 device that perhaps was the first motion picture projector) developed by Bell Telephone. The sound track was provided on a wax disk with the projector synchronized to the phonograph. Interestingly, the audio disk was recorded in a studio long after the motion picture itself was filmed, by actors and musicians playing directly into the horns of the insensitive recording devices of the day.

3 The Challenges of Synchronizing Separate Media

Technologies that store the sound track on a medium separate from the images are referred to as *sound-on-disk*. Distinct sound and image media were necessary early on, before technology made it possible to combine the media. Having the sound and image media physically separated necessitates the creation of a system to keep the tracks in sync. While today successful sound-on-disk systems work well thanks to modern electronic techniques, early attempts had to make due with the challenges presented by the technology of the day, resulting in systems both that were initially impractical and provided poor performance.

For instance, in Edison's time, state-of-the-art audio reproduction and amplification were accomplished *mechano-acoustically*. A needle tracked the waveforms encoded in the disk's serpentine groove. The needle's movements were transformed to audible vibrations (sound) by a mechanically coupled diaphragm, and finally a large horn acoustically directed the sound to the listener.

Such a sound reproduction system has many issues, including severe limits to the possible loudness, fidelity, and noise floor. However, for the purpose of adding sound to film, the largest limitation might have been the inability to be able to physically separate the sound medium from the sound emitter. Edison's sound player had to be placed at the front of the theater to create the illusion that the dialogue came from the actors located on-screen. The projector by necessity was located at the rear of the theater (physically distant from the audio device).

Edison attempted to physically couple the Victrola to the projector via long silk belts to provide synchronization between the physically distant sound and picture reproduction units. When these attempts failed to work outside the lab, Edison resorted to using human intelligence to make the system work. Edison employed a pair of technicians to initially start the picture and sound playing at the same time (start sync). Thereafter, the technicians had to vigilantly watch the movie and dynamically adjust the speed of the film playback to keep the sound and picture roughly synchronized (see Lee's article "Dynamic Synchronization" on page 347).

If the audio was allowed to drift more than a split second out of sync, it became nearly impossible for the human operators to restore sync. Many a movie presentation either ended with a mute-figure soundlessly mouthing their lines, or with the soundtrack playing on after the film itself had gone dark. To make matters worse, the sound fidelity was so poor that it was very difficult to understand the dialogue. Problems such as these soured audiences to sound motion pictures, and it took roughly 20 years for inventors and investors to return to the concept and create a viable system.

Indeed, no sound-on-disk based strategy succeeded until Bell Telephone introduced Vitaphone, which featured electrical amplification, making it possible to keep the audio and image reproduction physically synchronized at the back of the theater, with wires running to speakers next to the screen. (Electrical amplification had initially been applied to magnetic wire audio recorders by the German inventor Kurt Stille in the early 1920s using Lee De Forest's *audion* vacuum tube. Interestingly, for home use, experimenters added electrical amplification to their gramophones using *wireless* units, i.e., radios, long before commercial amplified phonographs were introduced.)

4 Sound-on-Film: The Birth of the Talkie

As already mentioned, the first successful talking films were Warner Brothers' 1926 and 1927 releases of *Don Juan* and *The Jazz Singer,* using sound-on-disk technology.

However, most modern films have been distributed using an approach called *sound-on-film*, which physically places the sound and corresponding images on the same piece of film media. Indeed, it was the invention of optical sound encoding that made adding synchronized soundtracks to (previously) silent pictures commercially viable. The revolutionary new films with synchronized sound and images were initially known as *talkies* and caused the pre-existing films to forever be remembered as *silent films.*

For sound-on-film, the soundtrack is optically encoded (first analog, now digitally) along the length of the film itself next to the corresponding image frames. Sound-on-film has a number of advantages over techniques that encode sound on a second media. Not only does sound-on-film make it difficult to separate, lose, or confuse the audio and video components of

Figure 2. Academy tracks: 35mm Optical Monophonic sound and Picture Tracks (standard since 1927).

a film, but perhaps more importantly, it physically locks the time relationship of the sound and image tracks, ensuring consistent synchronization. By 1930, with the introduction of MovieTone, sound-on-film became the dominant format because it is simply so cost-effective to reproduce films using the conventional film printing technology. In 1938, equalization associated with the mono optical encoded soundtrack was made the official standard now sometimes referred to as the *Academy Curve.*

But, having the sound recorded on the film media causes a playback challenge: the film projector needs to simultaneously smoothly pass the audio track over an audio pickup and advance the image track in single frame increments of 24 times a second.

The pragmatic solution allows both actions to occur. The sound that is supposed to play during a frame isn't recorded next to the corresponding image: instead, the soundtrack precedes the image track by a precise distance. Over most of the projector's film path, especially including the audio pickup area, the film smoothly advances (which is also important for maintaining the film); however, in the region of the optical shutter, the film is advanced in a stuttering manner. Anyone who has ever threaded film into a projector in high school remembers the small loop of film required somewhere deep in the film path. This film loop is the physical embodiment of a *buffer;* it absorbs the moment-to-moment different film speeds before and after the stuttering step of the shutter.

This clever solution unfortunately causes the audio track to be physically displaced along the length of film from the corresponding image frames. In practice, this isn't a problem, since the *post-production* facility knows the appropriate correspondence between the sound and image tracks and creates the film accordingly; however, it does complicate attempts to edit or splice production films.

There have been many improvements to sound in motion pictures in the intervening years: stereo optical soundtracks, surround sound, magnetic and digital optical encodings, to name just a few; however, an Academy format film may still be projected in any modern movie house.

5 Conclusion

While promoters of digital "filming" and distribution of motion pictures tell us that film may soon be relegated to the history books, it is both interesting and educational to learn how these systems work and were initially developed. This article provides just a bare introduction to a system that has been refined to a true art.

Annotated Bibliography

[1] Scott Eyman. *The Speed of Sound: Hollywood and the Talkie Revolution, 1926–1930.* New York: Simon & Schuster, 1997.

This telling of the story of how the talkie eclipsed the silent film industry that preceded it provides a nice perspective on the technologies and economics involved. Oh yes, it also tells the sometimes-tragic stories of the individuals involved, too.

Sample Accurate Synchronization Using Pipelines: Put a Sample in and We Know when It Will Come Out

Ken Greenebaum

1 Introduction

Historically it has been felt that sample accurate synchronization is not needed on the PC, that consumers can make do with *good enough* (whatever that means). While this may have been true at a time in the rapidly receding past when multimedia consisted of short, jerky, postage-stamp-sized video clips, consumers now expect to be able to use their multimedia equipped PCs in their living rooms to play back feature film length video, at least as well as on their inexpensive DVD player, or to edit their own digital video and burn the results to DVD.

Many developers are under the false impression that sample accurate synchronization is, in fact, impossible to achieve on the PC, that synchronization requires a *hard real-time* operating system and is correspondingly impossible on general-purpose, preemptively multitasking operating systems such as Windows, UNIX, or Mac OS X. They feel that all media applications would have to (impractically) reside in the operating system's kernel or that synchronization requires dedicated hardware or hardware that is faster than what is commonly available today. Consequently, systems are designed as a best effort and are not expected to fully *work*, and media performance is often not even measured or used as a release criteria.

The industry has attempted to improve synchronization and reduce latency. One approach has been an attempt to minimize the latency of the `play()`, `stop()`, `rewind()`, etc. VCR-like calls commonly exposed by PC media APIs, for instance, by reducing the time it takes for the media to begin after an application calls `play()`. This approach is flawed.

On a multitasking operating system, the media application's process might not even be running at the moment the low-latency "PLAY" command would need to be executed. Well-meaning developers believing that there is no other solution to reducing latency and improving synchronization attempt to move more and more of the audio system into the operating system's kernel, where it can not be preempted. This approach has increased code complexity and difficulty to debug while undermining the system's stability. Unfortunately, this approach does not significantly increase the quality of the performance achieved by media applications since even a theoretically impossible zero-latency call will not solve the synchronization dilemma.

In this anecdote, we will explore a technique that is straightforward to implement and also delivers sample accurate synchronization. Embracing predictable latency in the form of a pipeline is the key element making synchronization, presenting media at precisely the desired time, straightforward to achieve. Specifically, we demonstrate how to schedule audio to play at a sample accurate time in the future. Code examples are provided, and their performances are quantified and evaluated using a simple timing routine, the code of which is also presented. Please see my article on quantifying media performance ("RampTest" in *Audio Anecdotes I*) for more examples.

2 Start Synchronization

As described in "Synchronization Demystified" (see page 301), I break robust synchronization into two components: *start synchronization*, starting a media stream at the precise time it is needed (discussed in this article), and *dynamic synchronization*, the complimentary process of keeping media streams synchronized in the face of drifting timebases and dropped samples (described in Eric Lee's article(see page 347)).

Please consider that while we only consider start synchronization of a single media type and stream in this article, these pipeline techniques may be extended to elegantly handle the start synchronization of multiple media streams and even dynamic synchronization if resampling techniques such as those presented by Tor Ramstad in his article "Rate Conversion" from *Audio Anecdotes I* are applied.

2.1 Why Is a Deterministic Start Time Desirable?

Predictably starting a media stream at a desired time is a fundamental element of any media presentation. For there to be a noon matinee, the film strip and the soundtrack must both start precisely at 12:00:00. In this series, for Hesham Fouad's environmental synthesizer (see *Audio Anecdotes II*) or Ross Bencina's Granular synthesizer (see page 55) to function, they need to be able to accurately schedule and present the sounds that comprise them. Please refer to those articles for details. We will briefly explore one example here.

In professional editing suites, the final video is created by essentially cutting and pasting portions of video and sound together from raw footage. The director or editor describes the clips of video that will comprise the final edited video in what is known as an *edit decision list* (EDL) or *cut list.* Before nonlinear editors, which store and manipulate video streams on a hard disk, video was recorded on video tape, and a very common edit was called the *A-B roll.* In its simplest form, an A-B roll requires three frame accurate video tape decks (VTRs).

A-B roll and other applications of sample-accurate start synchronization are discussed in further detail in "Synchronization Demystified" (see page 301).

2.2 What Is a Pipeline?

The *pipeline* is simply an implementation of the Silo or FIFO (first in first out) data structure (see my article "Introduction to the Ring Buffer FIFO" from *Audio Anecdotes II* for an efficient and flexible implementation). Conceptually, a pipeline is a conveyor belt with discrete bins consistently placed along its length. In the digital world the conveyor belt moves discretely by one bin per time unit instead of moving smoothly as it would in the analog world we normally inhabit. Samples enter the pipeline at one end, progress down its length, then finally exit at the other end.

Think of an automotive assembly line, where a stream of, perhaps, transmissions moves in lockstep, one station at a time, to have a single new part fitted at each station. Completed transmissions emerge at the far end of the pipeline. In our pipelines the objects moving in lockstep are frames of audio samples, and, unlike the transmissions, they will not

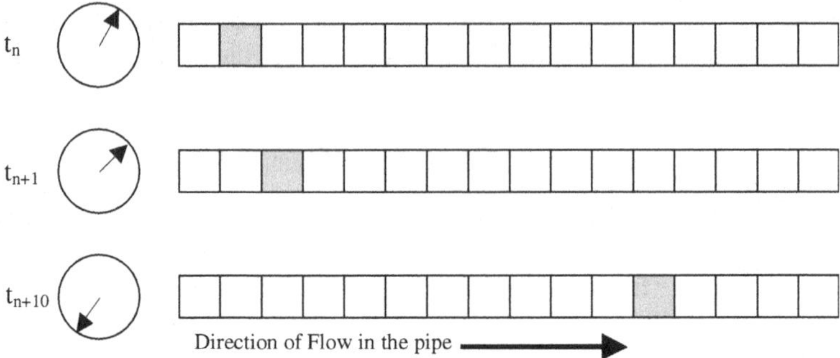

Figure 1. Three snapshots of a pipeline showing a marked data's progress through the pipeline.

necessarily be modified or inspected as they pass each station; the pipeline serves other purposes that will be explored below.

Most importantly, the pipe has a known length (number of stations/samples), and samples progress through the pipeline at a predictable rate. Hence, we can accurately predict the time at which a given sample will emerge at the far end of the pipeline (be presented) by simply knowing two values: the sample's position, p, relative to the end of the pipeline and v, the rate of the pipeline. Recall from high-school physics that time is equal to position over velocity: $t = \frac{p}{v}$.

Figure 1 demonstrates a piece of data progressing step by step through the pipeline (the position of the data is predictable as long as the pipeline progresses at a steady rate).

3 The PC Audio System

In this article we consider pipelines governed by the *pull model*, where the advancement of samples in the pipeline is caused by the consumer at the far end of the pipeline removing samples.

For example, consider the hardware in a typical PC sound card. A rather small FIFO (hardware pipeline) containing, perhaps, tens of samples is connected to the card's DAC (digital-to-analog converter), the consumer. A crystal oscillator circuit accurate to a small number of ppm (parts per million) causes the DAC to *pop* the next sample to be output from the FIFO, causing the pipeline to advance by one position. It is important to realize that this is a hardware process which once configured by the audio driver will continue without any intervention.

It is the responsibility of the audio driver, the producer, to ensure that the hardware FIFO is not allowed to empty. To overcome, somewhat, the unknowns of running software on a multitasking operating system, the audio driver is likely run by at a precise interval by a timer-based interrupt (or theoretically from an interrupt generated by the FIFO emptying). The device driver itself will likely employ a software-based pipeline to receive the streams of audio samples that applications would like to output.

In the case of a stereo sample stream, the left and right streams are multiplexed, and two samples are removed at a time. For simplicity we will only consider mono streams in this example.

3.1 It Is a Buffer!

buff-er, (bŭf′ ər) *noun.*

2. One that protects by intercepting or moderating adverse pressures or influences.

The American Heritage® Dictionary of the English Language, Fourth Edition

A FIFO is referred to as a buffer for a reason; it decouples the processes of adding or removing samples, making these operations somewhat independent from each other. The ring-buffer implementation described in my articles in this book even include a mechanism to allow the data structure implementing the buffer to be accessed by the producer and consumer threads simultaneously without requiring a mutex for serializing access.

For instance, the buffer allows the consumer, say the DAC, to pop samples steadily one at a time and the producer to infrequently add a large number. Thus, the buffer relieves the producer of needing to adhere to hard real-time obligations like synthesizing a new sample every 21 μs (assuming a 48 kHz sample rate) as long as the producer inserts samples often enough to not allow the buffer to empty. If the buffer were 60 seconds long (contained 60 s $\times$ 48,000 samples/s, which is 2,880,000 samples or around 5.5 MB of 16-bit samples), the producer process would only have to wake up and add new samples once a minute—a task that hardly anyone would classify as being a challenging real-time obligation to meet. Being romantic, I like to imagine the producer shoveling coal into the boiler of a steam locomotive, racing to keep the coal from being fully consumed and the fire going out.

It is not important when shovelfuls of coal are added to the boiler, nor how much coal is contained in each shovel full, so long as the boiler never is allowed to go empty. Shovelfuls of coal are usually added long before they are needed, but it is allowable, if risky, to add coal just before that coal is required, which would be considered low-latency, or just-in-time, shoveling. A critical element of this system, however, is the requirement that the system should be able to shovel coal (produce samples) at a rate faster than they are consumed, otherwise the system would never be able to run for an indefinitely long period of time.

A subtle point is that it takes a small but finite amount of time for the producer to create and enqueue new samples. For instance, it takes time for the fireman to add more coal to the boiler after being told to do so (or baker time to bake fresh bagels and add them to the empty(ing) display case).

Underflow is the state where the buffer is empty when it is time for the consumer to pop the next sample, leaving the consumer high and dry—in our example when the coal is all consumed. Obviously, underflow is to be avoided! Consequently, systems are designed to request new samples from the producer while there are still enough samples in the buffer to last long enough for the producer to create and add new ones.

To avoid underflow, the system must be designed such that the producer is told to start generating and adding samples before the buffer empties past the point where the remaining samples won't last long enough. If it takes 10 seconds to scoop up a new shovelful of coal and add it to the boiler, then the boiler operator must begin shoveling the next batch of coal before the boiler consumes all but the last 10 seconds worth.

3.2 How Much Buffering Is Necessary to Avoid Underflow?

A complicated analysis is needed to determine the size of the buffer required to provide a certain degree of certainty that underflow will not occur. It is important to remember that it is a statistical game and that no amount of buffering can provide absolute certainty that underflow will not occur, since many of the parameters themselves are probabilistic in nature.

Theoretically, calculating the required buffer length is based on the required underflow avoidance confidence and the combination of statistical time factors such as the length of time necessary to generate a new sample (based on the complexity of the algorithm, speed of processor, memory bandwidth, etc.), statistical length of time necessary to fetch the next sample if it is coming from a network, disk, or other source, the statistical scheduling delay imposed by the operating system to allow the synthesis algorithm to run again (this needs to include the possible requirement of paging its code or data space back into main memory from secondary storage), as well as other factors!

While these calculations are made when designing single purpose machines like DVD players, realistically a PC environment is so variable that the modeling and calculation is never explicitly made. Instead, the performance of actual systems are observed, and the buffers are tuned heuristically.

The PC does contain one parameter that is assured: the audio codec. Being controlled by a crystal oscillator, the output circuit represents a hard real-time machine guaranteed to consume audio samples at the predetermined sample rate.

3.3 Buffer Provides an Opportunity!

Samples belonging to a new sound don't have to be inserted into the end of the FIFO but rather may be inserted at contiguous locations anywhere within the buffer. This may seem like an unusual practice, but it actually affords a wonderful benefit: by selecting how *deep* we insert samples into the pipe, we can precisely control how long those samples take to traverse the pipeline, directly controlling when those samples will be output by the DAC, causing the new sound to be heard. Since the pipeline is initially "primed" with zeros, which are silent when output, the new sound's samples may be inserted anywhere by overwriting the zero values.

This situation is analogous to being able to precisely control when in the near future a ball will strike the ground by deciding how hard to throw it upward. The harder the ball is thrown, the higher it will rise and the longer it will take to finally hit the ground. In the case of the buffer, the shallower the samples are placed into the buffer, the longer they will take to progress through the buffer and eventually be played.

Our analogy continues with physical limits. Just as an individual can only throw a ball so high, a buffer has finite length and can only provide so much of a delay. What is important is that in both cases we can precisely control when an event will occur in the near future by using a deterministic mechanism, whether that is gravity or a crystal oscillator driven pipeline.

For a pipeline of n samples and a sample rate r a given sample n_s will be presented at time t:

$$t = \frac{n - n_s}{r}.$$

Thus, we may schedule a sound to play within one sample time of an arbitrary time in the future provided that the pipeline is deep enough to contain samples that extend that far into the future. To schedule a sound a greater distance into the future than the depth of the buffer, one must in turn use the operating system to put the process to sleep and wake it back up within a buffer's distance of time to the desired start and then schedule the sound's samples by inserting them at the appropriate depth in the buffer.

For example using the CD sampling rate of 44,100 samples per second, a liberal 250ms (1/4 second) buffer would contain 11,025 samples (or a modest 21.5 KB assuming a 16-bit mono stream). If a process determines that a sound is to play at precisely 12:00:00 noon, it would first determine the time between now and noon and use an operating system resource, like UNIX's `sleep(time)`, to put itself to sleep for current-time minus start-time minus 1/2 buffer length (to allow for scheduling jitter for the OS waking the process up). Once the process wakes up, it will once again determine the current-time (preferably using a microsecond-accurate clock) and subtract this time from the desired start time to determine how deep into the buffer to schedule the new sound.

Let's say that the operating system woke the process up 108,000 μs or 0.108 s before the desired start time. The process would begin writing the samples that belong to the new sound at the buffer location calculated as 0.108 s $\times$ 44100, which is 4,762.8. So, sample 4,763 would yield the closest playout time theoretically within 0.2 samples or 4.5 μs of the desired time. Not too shabby!

3.4 System Requirements for Sample Accuracy

While the system doesn't have to provide hard real-time guarantees to allow sample accurate scheduling using pipelining, there are other requirements that must be met. The first is fundamental: the producer has to be able to provide samples faster than they are consumed. If this was not the case, then the system would not be able to output an infinite stream but would eventually exhaust any pre-buffered cache of samples, not being able to keep up with demand.

Secondly, for our system to work, there needs to exist a solid audio foundation. To be able to predict when a sample in a pipeline will be output, we need to be able to rely on the assumption that there are no "bubbles" in the pipeline; that samples are never dropped or repeated. See my article on audio system testing ("RampTest" in *Audio Anecdotes I*) to evaluate how solid your audio system actually is. Many audio systems occasionally drop, repeat, or have other sample errors especially when the system is loaded. I was surprised to learn that many commercial audio systems are only tested to "sound good" and for their applications not to crash—the audio system itself is never tested for dependability.

Finally, for this technique to work, the buffer must never be allowed to experience buffer overflows or underflows, or at least these conditions must be detected and accounted for. Underflow/overflow must be handled differently depending on the situation. For instance, in a professional edit suite an underflow should be detected and the edit halted so that it can be reset and repeated since it is both repeatable and must be perfect. In a real-time presentation it might be preferable, say in the case of an audio underflow, for the video to continue without audio then have the audio resume in synchrony with the video effectively having a portion of the audio dropped; this is an extreme example of dynamic synchronization. Another possibility in the case of an audio underflow would be to have the video also stop then the audio and video resume in synchrony, not missing any of the audio or video content.

4 Code Examples

The following code examples demonstrate three approaches to the problem of playing a small sound, or chirp, at a precise interval. While this example may be a little contrived, it does allow us to try different techniques and actually quantify the results.

The naïve attempt of producing a chirp every second uses the operating system's `sleep()` system call for timing, and while it generally works, it falls orders of magnitude short of sample accuracy. This example is similar to the approach and results many PC applications take to synchronization.

The next approach uses the timing properties of pipelines described in this article; it inserts silent samples into the pipeline to affect precise delays. This example does achieve sample accuracy, however, at the expense of constantly outputting samples: outputting silent samples during the delay period between chirps.

The final version uses a combination of the first and second techniques and is both sample accurate and more efficient than the second example. The final version also more closely approximates real-world situations than the highly simplistic second version.

4.1 Measuring Results

While an oscilloscope is the instrument commonly used to measure periodic signals such as our chirp, they are expensive and unfortunately not commonly found in software development labs. Fortunately, we can use our very own computers and sound cards to build very specialized tools.

I present a small piece of code called **trigger** that analyzes a signal presented on the audio input. **trigger** emulates an oscilloscope's analog trigger and will measure the time distance between events, in this case, our chirps. **chirp** and **trigger** may be run simultaneously, on the same machine, provided that the machine supports *full-duplex* audio and the system's audio out is wired to the audio in, the microphone is in proximity to the speaker, or an internal mixer provides this loopback. This analog solution is highly dependent on input and output audio levels; please experiment with the levels until you receive a single clear trigger for each chirp. For best results always use a digital loopback. Unfortunately, many systems lack digital S/PDIF I/O. Please refer to my article "Ramp Test" on testability and quantification in *Audio Anecdotes I* for more information on these techniques.

5 Trigger

```
int main(void) {
   float buffer[NUM_FRAMES];
   PABLIO_Stream *inStream, *outStream;
   int x;
   double      time = 0.0;
   double lastTime = 0.0;
   double     delta = 1.0 / SAMPLE_RATE;
   double lastSample;

   OpenAudioStream(&inStream, SAMPLE_RATE, paFloat32,
                   PABLIO_READ|PABLIO_MONO);

   // initialize last sample
   ReadAudioStream(inStream, &lastSample, 1);

   while(1) {
      ReadAudioStream(inStream, buffer, NUM_FRAMES);
      for(x= 0; x < NUM_FRAMES; x++) {
       if((lastSample<TRIGGER_LEVEL)
       && (buffer[x]>=TRIGGER_LEVEL)) {
          printf("%f (%f)\n", time, time-lastTime);
          lastTime = time;
```

```
        }
        time+=delta;
        lastSample = buffer[x];
        }
    }
}
```

5.1 First, Naïve Example

Here is the inner loop from a naïve attempt that uses the operating system's `sleep()` call as a time source:

```
while(1) {
    // output chirp
    WriteAudioStream(outStream, chirpBuffer,
                     chirpBufferSamples);

    sleep(1); // sleep for one second
}
```

Listening to the output of this program, `chirp1.c`, all seems well; there is a click that occurs once a second as expected. Unfortunately, when we examine the audio output on an oscilloscope or our `trigger` application, we learn that the time between chirps vary from the desired one-second interval by amounts on the order of 0.02 seconds. This may seem to be an impressive feat of precision but is actually orders of magnitude off from achieving sample accuracy.

The operating system's `sleep()` call is at best only accurate to a single quantum (the length of time that the operating system will allow a process to run before it is preempted if another process is ready to run, often as long as 0.05 seconds). The performance of `sleep()` is affected by the scheduler used by the operating system and the load and process mix on the system, including the priority of the processes and the number of computationally bound versus I/O bound processes.

As described in Derek Difilippo's article "Perceivable Auditory Latencies" in *Audio Anecdotes I*, humans can't easily detect relatively small time differences such as the timing variance in this code example. The `trigger` code produced the output in Figure 2 on my Windows XP laptop running a light process load (using the built-in microphone and speakers):

```
3.300249 (1.021723)
4.275510 (0.975261)
5.297256 (1.021746)
6.272540 (0.975283)
7.294308 (1.021769)
```

Figure 2. The `chirp1` microphone experiment: time of each chirp and (time since the previous trigger).

5.2 Second Example Is Sample Accurate

The following example is more sophisticated; it outputs a precise number of silent samples to accurately control the time chirps. The number of silent samples to "stuff" is easily computed:

```
int chirpBufferSamples; // number of samples contained in the
                        // chirp
int stuffSamples = SAMPLE_RATE - chirpBufferSamples;
```

The inner loop is simply

```
while(1) {
    // output chirp
    WriteAudioStream(outStream, chirpBuffer,
                     chirpBufferSamples);

    // stuff enough samples to complete one second
    WriteAudioStream(outStream, stuffBuffer, stuffSamples);
}
```

To my ears, the output of `chirp2.c` sounds the same as `chirp1.c` but the chirps appear rock steady on the oscilloscope. `trigger` provides the results in Figure 3 on my SGI Indy (with the microphone positioned in front of the speaker and levels carefully set).

```
83.837800 (1.000023)
84.837800 (1.000000)
85.837710 (0.999909)
86.837710 (1.000000)
87.837755 (1.000045)
88.837755 (1.000000)
```

Figure 3. The `chirp2` microphone experiment: time of each chirp and (time since the previous trigger).

The **chirp2** code provides orders of magnitude improvement in precision over the first technique. At 44,100 Hz each sample lasts for about 22.6 μs, so in the results from Figure 3, each chirp is measured within two samples of the desired one-second interval. As you may suspect, the uncertainty is in the analog coupling of the speaker to the mike and the trigger mechanism. This assumption can be verified by running the same code on the SGI using digital loopback (digital audio output is looped back to the digital audio input) that generates the boringly consistent results in Figure 4.

```
11.988685 (1.000000)
12.988685 (1.000000)
13.988685 (1.000000)
14.988685 (1.000000)
15.988685 (1.000000)
16.988685 (1.000000)
```

Figure 4. The chirp2 digital loopback experiment: time of each chirp and (time since the previous trigger).

5.3 A Hybrid Approach

Finally, this last code example uses a hybrid of the two techniques to both efficiently use the operating system's **sleep()** call to block its execution until there is actual work to be done and also make use of the audio library to keep track of when the operating system wakes the process up relative to when it intended:

NOTE: This is pseudo code. PABLIO doesn't presently include the sample counting required to implement this example.

```
const double period = 1.0; // play tone every N seconds
double bufferTime = SizeOfBufferInSeconds();
double nextFrameTime = getFrameTime(outStream) + period;

// output the first chirp
WriteAudioStream(outStream, chirpBuffer, chirpBufferSamples);

while(1) {  // synthesize and output samples forever
   // sleep for most of time + leave margin for jitter
   sleepSeconds(nextFrameTime - getFrameTime()
                  - 0.5 * bufferTime);
```

```
   deltaFrameTime = nextFrameTime - getFrameTime(outStream);
   if(deltaTime < 0) { // oops, the OS woke us up late,
                       // we missed our click
      exit(-1);
   }
   else if(deltaTime < bufferTime) { // need to chirp within
                                     // the buffer
      nextFrameTime = getFrameTime(outStream) + period;
      writeSilence(outStream, deltaTime);
      writeTone(outStream);
   }
   else { // the OS woke us up too early and the can't write
          // to the buffer just sleep again
   }
}
```

If we could execute this code, chirp3.c, with trigger, we would see results similar to those of the second example. If the load on the system increased too far, the sleep() call might wake the process up too late to chirp in time, a condition that the code detects.

Ironically, this process wouldn't consume much less CPU time than chirp2 even though chirp2 outputs samples unnecessarily. Audio sample rates are very low compared to the speed on modern computers, causing chirp2 to also spend most of it's time blocked by the OS in blocking calls to WriteAudioStream() after it has filled its buffer.

This example is provided to explain how to determine timing relationships in more complicated situations where a sound is to be played asynchronously but with a sample accurate timing relationship to other sounds.

6 Implementation Considerations

The pipeline described in this article is actually a different use of the ring buffer described in my article "Introduction to the Ring Buffer Queue" from *Audio Anecdotes II*. The major distinction is that, in the classic ring buffer, samples are added strictly at the tail pointer, but, in the pipeline, samples may be added anywhere in the buffer depending on when they are to be eventually presented.

It is important to carefully select the length of the pipeline buffer; the more samples the pipeline contains, the longer the timeline it represents and ultimately the farther into the future it "sees." The longer the pipeline, the lower the requirements for the operating system to provide accurate process scheduling. The process can schedule itself to wake up earlier and then insert samples into the deep pipeline wherever appropriate based on when the OS actually woke it up.

7 Conclusion

Very precise start synchronization is realizable using commonly available mechanisms if we approach the problem in a consistent way. In Derek Di-Filippo and my article "Introduction to the Theory of Signal Detection" from *Audio Anecdotes I*, we present the concept that latency is unavoidable and perhaps even helpful. This article presents just one technique that takes advantage of latency to allow very precise scheduling of sounds based on pipeline delays. Accurate start synchronization should be married to dynamic synchronization as described in Eric Lee's article (see page 347) to keep your media presentation synchronized once it has begun in (start) sync.

Executables and source code for the `trigger` and various versions of `chirp` programs used in this article are provided on the CD-ROM accompanying this book.

Annotated Bibliography

[1] Jon Bentley. *Programming Pearls*, Second edition. Reading, MA: Addison-Wesley, 1999.

Jon's articles, originally published in the Communications of the ACM, inspired a generation of programmers to evaluate the performance of their applications and to constantly search for a better algorithm or a refinement to the algorithm that they are already using. I attempted to channel Jon when writing this article.

[2] Derek Difilippo and Ken Greenebaum. "Perceivable Audio Latencies." In *Audio Anecdotes I*, edited by Ken Greenebaum and Ronen Barzel, pp. 65–92. Natick, MA: A K Peters, 2004.

As mentioned in the conclusion, this article not only provides an extensive list of stimuli and latencies but it also attempts to demonstrate the engineering opportunities in embracing and using non-perceptible latency.

[3] Ken Greenebaum. "RampTest: Quantified Audio Performance." In *Audio Anecdotes I*, edited by Ken Greenebaum and Ronen Barzel, pp. 295–311. Natick, MA: A K Peters, 2004.

This article makes a case for deterministic testing for digital media applications that are often only subjectively tested. A trigger-like test could be used to quantify some forms of synchronization.

Dynamic Synchronization: Drifting into Sync

Eric Lee

The previous article (page 331) introduced the pipeline algorithm, a method for achieving *sample accurate* start synchronization. However, this technique solves only half the problem: even if the individual media streams *start* synchronously, they will still drift apart over time, unless there is another mechanism in place to detect and correct this drift. As was discussed in more depth in Ken Greenebaum's article "Synchronization Demystified" (see page 301), a number of factors contribute to drift, with a primary one being the inaccuracies of the time sources that clock the individual media streams.

In most general-purpose computer platforms, the audio and video hardware are independent devices that provide their own clocks for timing (this is also true in the case where multiple audio cards are added to a system). These clocks are usually implemented using a device called a *crystal oscillator.* Crystal oscillators contain a piece of quartz precisely lapped to dimension, so that they resonate at a specific frequency, and can thus be used as a time source. Quartz crystal is often used because it exhibits the piezoelectric effect required to couple the physical resonance to an electrical circuit, and quartz has a small thermal expansion coefficient (it changes little in dimension and resonance as its temperature changes).

However, any physical device has only finite accuracy and is subject to influence from outside factors including manufacturing tolerance, temperature, age, and vibration. Mil-spec crystal (crystals manufactured to military specification) oscillators are hand-lapped to dimension and contain sophisticated stabilization measures like temperature-regulated enclosures. Unfortunately, most of the two billion crystal oscillators manufactured a year intended for use in inexpensive consumer devices, including desktop computers, are notoriously inaccurate.

As an example, let us examine the specifications of a commonly-used oscillator in PCs. According to its technical specification sheet, this oscillator has an accuracy of ± 300 ppm (parts per million), which means in the time that we expect the device to produce a million oscillations, the actual number of oscillations can be off by as many as 300. Since the particular device that we are considering nominally oscillates at 400 MHz, the actual clock rate could be anywhere from 399.88 to 400.12 MHz, an error of roughly $\pm 0.03\%$ or one second every hour. If we were watching an hour-long movie, we would definitely notice if the audio gradually drifted ahead or behind the video by one second, as this error is more than enough to completely destroy lip-sync (see Derek DiFillipo's article "Perceivable Auditory Latencies" in *Audio Anecdotes I*). This error is also equivalent to about 13 audio samples per second for audio sampled at 44.1 kHz (which could result in continuous pops and clicks if these extra or dropped samples were naïvely dealt with).

Compounding this problem, the crystal oscillator is not the only source of drift in the final system: the oscillator is often used to simply drive a *phase-locked loop* (PLL) to generate a clock at a much higher frequency to drive the device. The PLL also introduces non-linearities such as drift and wander in the clock signal.

Thus, for the reasons described above, each clock source is effectively different from all others. In many systems, including home entertainment setups and personal computers, this results in multiple, distinct *timebases.* This phenomenon is more pervasive that one might imagine—you may observe this yourself by synchronizing your watch to your computer by manually setting your watch to match the time displayed on the computer. Comparing the values over time, you will likely notice that the times will noticeably diverge after a modest period of time. Alternatively, you might be surprised by the results of the following experiment: point a video camera attached to your computer at your watch and capture, say, an hour of video. Play this video back with your watch synchronized to the beginning of the video. Again, you will likely notice that the time on the watch and the video of the watch deviates over time.

1 Clocks Separated by a Distance

The problem of multiple drifting clocks is exemplified when those clocks aren't located in the same machine, the machines themselves are distant from each other, and media needs to be streamed between the machines.

Let's take the example of streaming video over the Internet: most of these systems support multiple clients simultaneously. These systems allow the client to begin playing content at any time. The server sends the client data faster than required, and the clients notify the server using a *back channel* when its buffer is full so that the server stops sending data for a while. When the client's buffer drains past a certain point, the client tells the server to resume sending data. Such a *flow control* arrangement is very common, and as long as the server can source data, and the channel can carry data faster than real time, the system works well and can easily compensate for clock drift. Such a system can also support advanced functionality, such as allowing clients to pause and, potentially, rewind content. What it doesn't do well, however, is scale; while such servers may be able to support tens, or even hundreds, of simultaneous flow-controlled streams, the number of clients remains limited by the server's ability to handle so many individual video streams and by the network bandwidth required to transmit each of those streams and still service the individual back channels.

Broadcast streaming is used to serve, far more efficiently, media content to a large number of clients by eliminating the back channel and providing only a single stream for all clients. Companies often use broadcast streaming to provide employees in their, sometimes off-site, offices access to company meetings or other presentations in real time.

Unfortunately, while efficient, broadcast streaming exposes the problem of clock drift. Specifically in this case, the server has to stream data at precisely the rate that each of the client's different audio and video clocks consume data. If, for instance, the client machine's clock runs slightly faster than the server's clock, then it will be consuming the data at a faster rate than the server is sending it—even if there is a *jitter buffer* in place to compensate for unpredictable delays in network transmission at the client machine, the buffer will still eventually underflow, resulting in unwanted pauses and pops in the audio until the jitter buffer fills up again, at least partially. On the other hand, if the client's clock runs slower than the server, then the buffer will eventually fill and cause overflow, data loss, and potentially more pops.

To solve this clock drift problem, the clocks of the client and server must be kept synchronized. The Network Time Protocol (NTP) was created as a way of keeping the clocks on individual computers connected to the same network synchronized [6]. NTP works by the client computer periodically sending a timestamped packet to the server, which then sends a reply timestamped with when it thinks the request was received and when the reply was sent out. Upon receiving the reply and examining when it arrived, the client is able to determine a relatively accurate estimate of what the time should be.

NTP was designed to keep clocks accurate enough to compare log information and to make distributed revision control and other, similar applications work. Consequently, NTP can keep machines' clocks synchronized to within a small number of milliseconds of each other, which is an impressive feat. Unfortunately, most digital media applications require synchronization to be many orders of magnitude more precise.

2 Drift Synchronization for Multimedia

Unlike NTP, the dynamic synchronization algorithm introduced in this article is designed to resolve clock drift in a single system with multiple timebases. As a result, the clocks can be synchronized to within microseconds of each other, which is usually within one audio sample or less.

For clarity, our discussion will be limited to *two-way synchronization*, where one track is slaved to the time represented by a second track. Normally, in a digital media system, the audio track is used as the reference timebase and the video as the dependent timebase, and we will stick to this example. When necessary, we will also use the example of synchronizing one audio track to another. Note, however, that the algorithm naturally extends to the more general *n-way synchronization*, where every track is slaved off a common, independent time reference.

We will divide our discussion into three topics: first, we will discuss how to calculate an adjusted rate to compensate for clock drift. Then, we will discuss how often one needs to correct for this drift. Finally, we will touch on how to apply rate conversion to PCM (pulse code modulated, i.e., digital and uncompressed) audio streams.

3 A Little Bit of Control Theory

Before we move on to the topic of synchronization itself, it makes sense to introduce some basic concepts of *control theory* [7, 5]. The simple approach of starting devices synchronously and letting them run independently is called an *open loop* system (see Figure 1). Open loop systems cannot adapt to changes—going back to our example of crystal oscillator-based clocks, our open loop system would not be able to, for example,

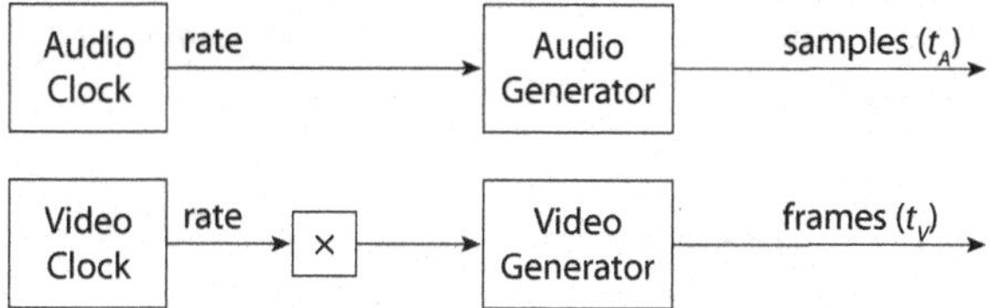

Figure 1. Open loop control of video play rate to maintain synchronization. A constant multiplier attempts to compensate for any differences in the video and audio clocks.

compensate for temperature changes that cause the clocks to oscillate at slightly different frequencies.

When talking about a control system, there is always one *independent variable* and one or more *dependent variables.* If we are synchronizing the video to the audio as mentioned earlier, the audio timebase would be our independent variable, and our video timebase would be our dependent variable. The control task is then to keep the video timebase synchronous with the audio timebase, which involves making sure they tick not only at the same rate, but also in phase (that is, if we are currently one second into the audio track, then we should also be one second into the video track). In an open loop system, the problem would be limited to starting the audio and video at the same time, using, for example, the pipeline algorithm in Greenebaum's article "Sample Accurate Synchronization Using Pipelines" (page 331). As a further improvement, we could measure the difference in oscillation frequencies of the audio and video clocks before starting playback and adjust the play rate of the video accordingly such that the two should theoretically remain in sync. For example, if we know that the video clock runs 1% faster than the audio clock, we could set the audio play rate to its nominal 1.0 value, but the video play rate to 0.99.

This open loop system is, unfortunately, not able to adapt to changing environments. If, for example, the temperature in the room were to change, or as the oscillators age, the clock rates of the two devices will be affected differently, resulting in the audio and video gradually drifting out of sync over time, despite our efforts to sync them when we began playback. To detect and correct this drift, we must implement *feedback*: in our case, the difference between the two outputs, the current audio position and the current video position, is used to estimate the drift, which is then used to adjust the dependent variable (video play rate). A system with feedback control is referred to, unsurprisingly, as a *closed loop* system (see Figure 2).

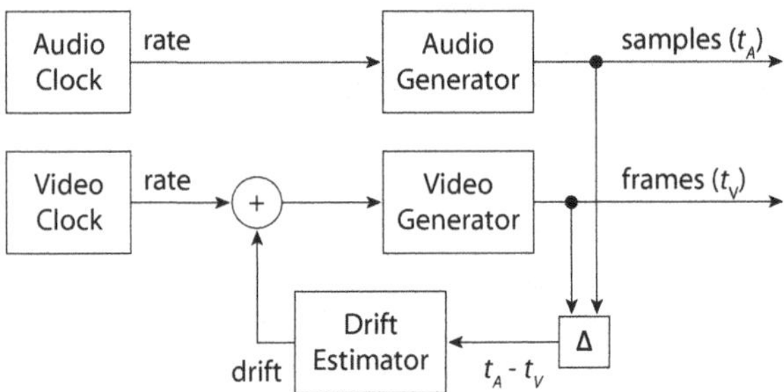

Figure 2. Closed loop control of video play rate to maintain synchronization. The measured difference between the audio and the video positions is fed back into the system, and the adjusted video play rate compensates for any drift.

We will revisit control theory in Section 5 as we progress in our discussion of drift synchronization.

4 Computing an Adjusted Play Rate to Compensate for Clock Drift

One of the first problems we need to address is how to go about utilizing the feedback that we get from this closed loop sync system. As changes to our environment are happening all the time, it is not surprising that we need to periodically examine where we are in the video timebase, compare it to where we are in the audio timebase, and adjust accordingly. What "periodically" means, exactly, will be discussed in the next section. For now, let's concentrate on how to compute an adjusted video play rate given the feedback input.

At first glance, one might be tempted to do a position-based adjustment. If we are falling behind, we could simply skip ahead to the correct position, or if we are ahead, skip back. While this simple adjustment works in principle, it is undesirable for most practical applications because of the resulting discontinuities in an otherwise continuous timeline. Especially for time-based media such as audio and video, discontinuities are extremely noticeable, and disturbing, to the user. In audio, for example, the discontinuities caused by jumping around the audio stream will produce very audible and annoying pops and clicks due to instantaneous changes in energy (see Figure 3).

Even in the case of a more generic clock, discontinuities can cause a host of problems. Usually, there is an implicit understanding that time

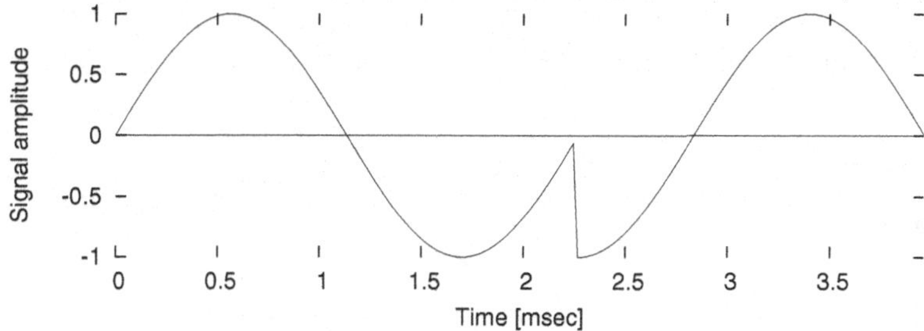

Figure 3. Effect of an instantaneous correction to audio position on a single 440 Hz tone sampled at 44.1 kHz. The correction at $t = 2.27$ msec results in a sudden jump in the audio signal that sounds like a "pop."

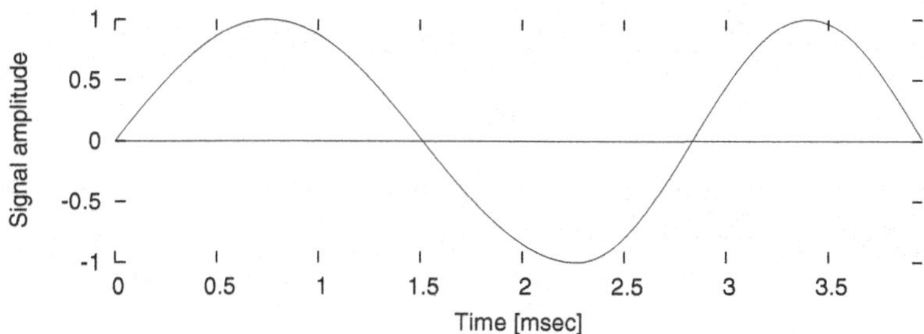

Figure 4. A 440 Hz tone using rate adjustment to compensate for drift, resulting in a distorted but overall much smoother signal, compared to Figure 3.

moves along smoothly and forwards, and often this is an intuitive assumption that is taken for granted when writing software that depends on time. If we now have a clock that unpredictably shifts around in time, this assumption no longer holds, resulting in chaos: for example, timers that are set to fire at a particular time instant may be executed multiple times or even not at all.

A much better solution is, rather than instantaneously adjusting position, to adjust the speed of the dependent timebase such that it will sync up with the reference timebase at a future point in time. This way, time remains continuous and always progresses forwards (but at the expense of introducing rate distortion, see Figure 4).

To compute the adjusted play rate, let's examine the scenario illustrated in Figure 5. The horizontal axis represents real time, and the vertical axis shows the progression of the audio and video over time. Let's assume that the audio and video tracks start perfectly synchronous but

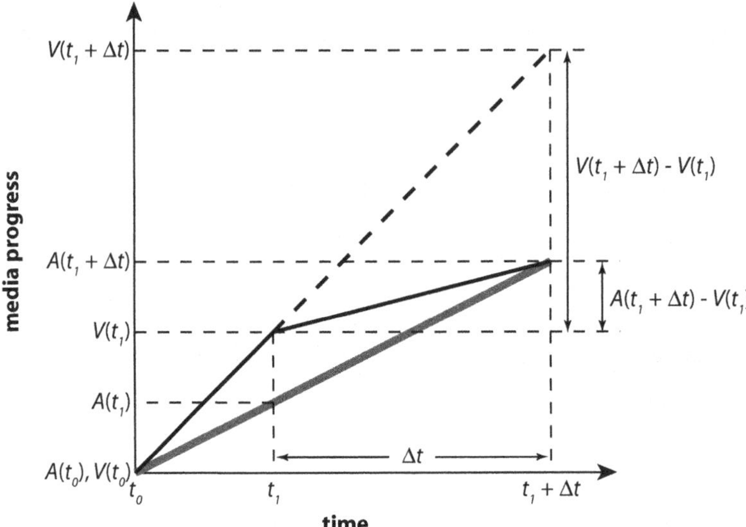

Figure 5. Synchronization scenario. The thick line shows audio progress over time, and the thin line shows video progress.

at slightly different rates. It's important to keep in mind that we do not know what these rates actually are, since the clocks are separate entities; we just know that they're *supposed* to be ticking at the same rate. Let t_0 denote the start time of the audio/video. After a certain time, which we'll denote t_1, let's again examine the current position of the audio, $A(t_1)$, and video, $V(t_1)$, and see how far they've drifted apart. We would like to compute a new video play rate, r_{v1}, such that the audio and video will sync up again at time $t_1 + \Delta t$. The play rate, r_v, is expressed as a percentage of its uncorrected speed (e.g., 0.5 is half speed, 2.0 is double speed, etc.).

Let's denote $V(t_1 + \Delta t)$ as the expected video position at time $t_1 + \Delta t$, were it to progress at its current rate, r_{v0}, and $A(t_1 + \Delta t)$ as the expected audio position at $t_1 + \Delta t$. Then, the following relationship holds:

$$\frac{r_{v1}}{r_{v0}} = \frac{A(t_1 + \Delta t) - V(t_1)}{V(t_1 + \Delta t) - V(t_1)},$$

which leads to

$$r_{v1} = r_{v0}\frac{A(t_1 + \Delta t) - V(t_1)}{V(t_1 + \Delta t) - V(t_1)}.$$

Intuitively, this formula states that we need to scale the current video rate by the ratio of how much we *want* the video to progress and how much we *expect* the video to progress.

Assuming that the clocks for these timebases are relatively stable, we can approximate

$$A(t_1 + \Delta t) \simeq A(t_1) + \Delta t \frac{A(t_1) - A(t_0)}{t_1 - t_0}$$

and

$$V(t_1 + \Delta t) \simeq V(t_1) + \Delta t \frac{V(t_1) - V(t_0)}{t_1 - t_0}.$$

Let us now examine how we could implement this in code. The full source example is on the accompanying CD-ROM; here, we will include only the interesting snippets. In this example, one audio stream is synchronized to another, but for consistency the A and V notation is retained (i.e., we are syncing the V audio track to the A audio track). We keep track of time by counting the number of audio samples that we've processed; we also need to keep track of the adjusted video rate, initially set to 1.0.

```
int aFrameCount = 0, vFrameCount = 0;
float adjustedRate = 1.0;
```

At the beginning of every correction cycle, we convert this frame count to seconds simply by dividing by the sample rate:

```
At1 = aFrameCount / SAMPLE_RATE;
```

If we define the adjustment interval $t_1 - t_0$ as NUM_FRAMES, expressed in samples, then we can compute $A(t_1 + \Delta t)$:

```
At1deltaT = At1 + deltaT * (At1 - At0)
          / (NUM_FRAMES / SAMPLE_RATE);
```

We can then compute the adjusted video rate as per the equation for r_{v1} given above. We will want to guard against overly large or small (or even negative!) rates.

```
adjustedRate *= (At1deltaT - Vt1) / (Vt1deltaT - Vt1);
if (adjustedRate < MIN_RESAMPLE_RATE)
   adjustedRate = MIN_RESAMPLE_RATE;
else if (adjustedRate > MAX_RESAMPLE_RATE)
   adjustedRate = MAX_RESAMPLE_RATE;
```

The last thing we need to do is apply the adjusted rate to the dependent audio track:

```
numVFrames = (int)ceilf(NUM_FRAMES * adjustedRate);
GetVBuffer(vBuffer, vFrameCount - RESAMPLE_WINDOW_SIZE_HALF,
           numVFrames + RESAMPLE_WINDOW_SIZE);
Resample(vBuffer, numVFrames + RESAMPLE_WINDOW_SIZE,
        vBufferResampled, NUM_FRAMES, adjustedRate);
```

Details of what goes on inside the `Resample()` function will be discussed later in this article.

Choosing an appropriate adjustment interval, `NUM_FRAMES`, and catch-up interval, `deltaT`, will be the topic of the next section.

5 Choosing an Appropriate Interval between Corrections

Now that we've discussed how to calculate an adjusted play rate to account for drift, let us take a more careful look at a couple of parameters that we glossed over in the previous section, namely the adjustment interval, $t_i - t_{i-1}$, and the catch-up interval, Δt.

If the clocks are fluctuating widely, and if a smaller variance between the audio and video is required, it makes sense to select a smaller adjustment interval to be able to react as quickly as possible to these fluctuations. On the other hand, changing the play rate too often results in a lot of overhead that is best avoided whenever possible. Moreover, there may be other constraints on how often the play rate can be adjusted. Changes to video frame rate may be limited to the video clock, and changes to the audio play rate may be constrained by particular processing algorithms. It is usually the case that audio is processed in blocks of a few hundred or even thousand of samples at a time, in which case play rate changes are limited to once per processing block. For audio sampled at 44.1 kHz, the maximum number of adjustments per second is 86 for a block size of 512, 43 for a block size of 1024, etc.

For the purposes of our discussion here, where we are primarily concerned about inaccuracies of crystal oscillators, neither the clock drift nor the clock rate fluctuations are that large. Thus, it may not be necessary to be correcting continuously. When the audio is initially started, it may make sense to adjust once per processing block until the play rate stabilizes. Once our play rate has stabilized, we can gradually increase

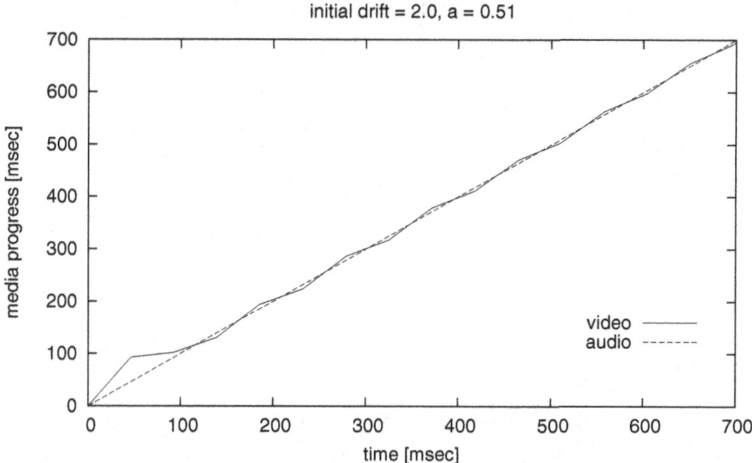

Figure 6. Asymptotically stable system. Even though we are overshooting our synchronization point, the amount that we overshoot is small, so the initial ringing will eventually settle down.

the correction interval, settling at once per second or every few seconds to account for fluctuations due to temperature changes or other external factors.

The other parameter to consider is the catch-up interval, which we defined previously as Δt. When talking about this parameter, we must again turn to a bit of control theory. Let's define $\Delta t = a(t_i - t_{i-1})$ and analyze what happens for various values of a. If a is less than 1, then the catch-up interval is less than the adjustment interval ($\Delta t < t_i - t_{i-1}$), and we will overshoot the desired synchronization point by the time we are given another opportunity to adjust, resulting in a "ringing" effect. This ringing effect is caused by continuously overshooting the desired synchronization point, followed by over-correcting on the next adjust cycle, and so forth. If we don't overshoot by *too* much ($0.5 < a < 1.0$), then the ringing will still eventually settle down (see Figure 6); in control systems theory, the system is *asymptotically stable.* If $a \leq 0.5$, then the ringing will not stop at all and might even get worse as time goes on (see Figure 7); the system is *unstable* (*marginally stable* if $a = 0.5$, because the ringing does not worsen, although it doesn't get better either). In any case, this ringing will create an undesirable "warbling" in the resulting audio, and so we will not consider values less than 1 as a wise choice for a.

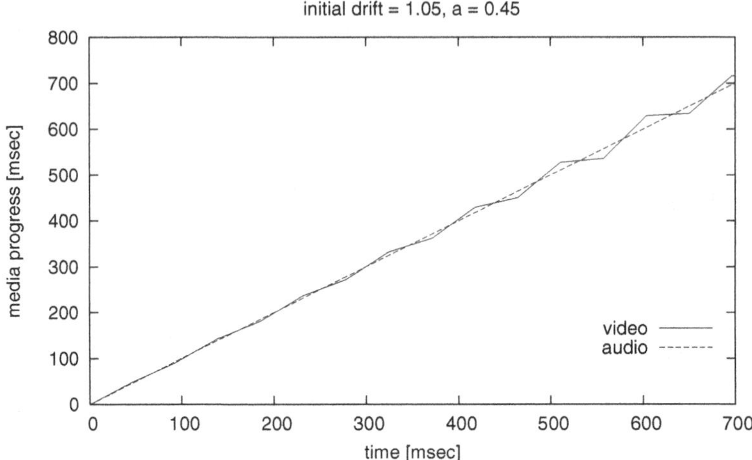

Figure 7. Unstable system. Even though our initial drift is small (5%), we are overshooting our desired synchronization point by too much, resulting in a ringing effect that worsens over time.

If $a = 1$ ($\Delta t = t_i - t_{i-1}$), the system is still said to be asymptotically stable, even though convergence happens exactly when expected in the ideal case when our estimates of $A(t_1 + \Delta t)$ and $V(t_1 + \Delta t)$ are accurate, and we are not over-correcting or under-correcting (see Figure 8). However, since there will be, in practice, an error associated with the estimation of $A(t_1 + \Delta t)$ and $V(t_1 + \Delta t)$, this scenario is unlikely to occur.

The final scenario, where $a > 1$ ($\Delta t > t_i - t_{i-1}$), is again asymptotically stable, because sync will occur, albeit gradually (see Figure 9). The two timebases will converge exponentially at a rate that depends on the value of a that is chosen.

Let us attempt to characterize this convergence more precisely: the rate at which convergence occurs is $\frac{1}{a}$, which we can then use to calculate how fast the dependent timebase will converge to the reference timebase. For example, let's say that we would like to determine the amount of time required before the drift is compensated to within 1% of the detected difference. This is defined by $(1 - \frac{1}{a})^n = 0.01$, where n is the number of corrections required. If we use $a = 2$, n comes out to 6.64. If we are correcting every 512 audio samples and our audio is sampled at 44.1 kHz, then it will take about 77 ms to reach the desired accuracy. Exactly what value of a to choose will depend primarily on two factors. For reference clocks with higher jitter, a higher value of a is more desirable to smooth

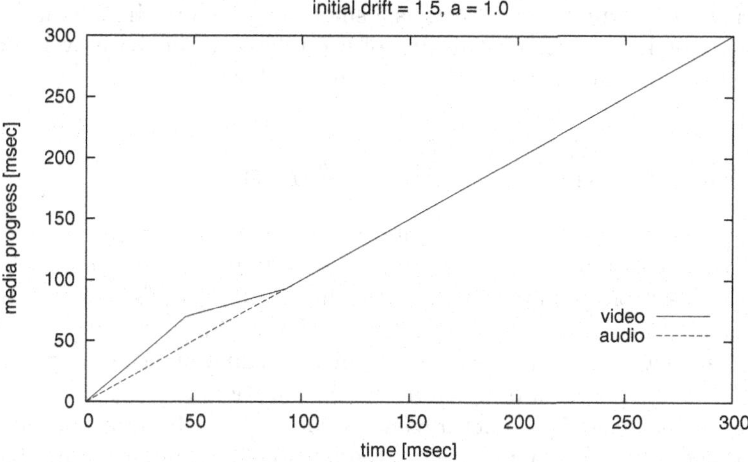

Figure 8. The video play rate is adjusted such that the audio and video are perfectly synchronous at the next correction cycle, and no further adjustments are required.

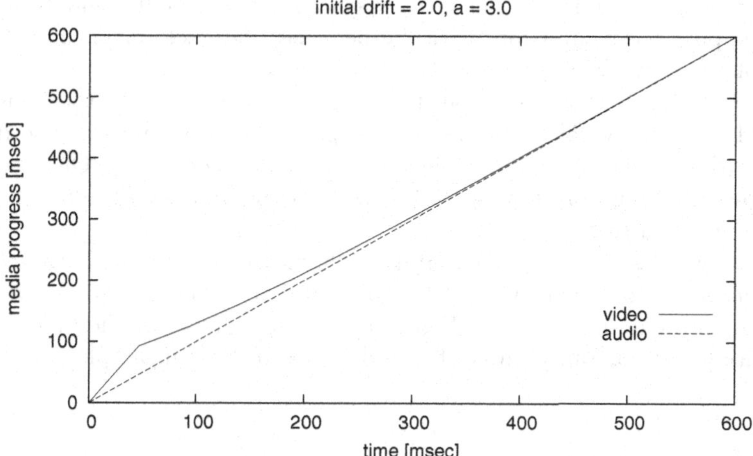

Figure 9. Asymptotically stable system. Convergence to the desired play rate is exponential, without the ringing effect of Figure 6.

out these irregularities. On the other hand, a lower value of a will allow the dependent timebases to more closely follow the reference. As a general rule, values of a between 1.0 and 2.0 are probably a reasonable choice for most situations.

Another interpretation of a is as a smoothing factor. Higher values of a will result in a smoother tracking of the reference timebase over time, at the expense of taking longer to respond to sharp changes.

6 Altering the Play Rate of Audio

The last issue to address is a method for altering the play rate of audio. This process is known as *resampling* or *sample rate conversion*, and although this topic is discussed in detail in Tor Ramstad's article "Rate Conversion" in *Audio Anecdotes I*, as well as in other literature [1, 8, 9], we will review some of the basic mechanisms behind audio resampling to complete our discussion of dynamic synchronization.

Let us begin with a quick review of some of the basic properties of digital audio: we obtain a digital representation of an analog audio signal by a process called *sampling*, which is essentially taking "snapshots" of the audio signal at regular intervals (see Figure 10). To change the play rate, we essentially need similar snapshots of the original audio signal, but at different intervals. Thus, the *resampling* problem amounts to how to compute the values for these "in-between" samples, given only the samples that we currently have.

For clarity, let's take the specific example of increasing the total number of samples by 25% (also known as *upsampling*—if we wanted to decrease the number of samples, that would be *downsampling*). One could imagine a number of approaches for determining values to use for these newly inserted samples.

The simplest and most computationally inexpensive method is a *nearest neighbor* approach, where we simply use the existing sample value closest to the desired one (see Figure 11). Although this method requires essentially no computation (just rounding the fractional sample index to

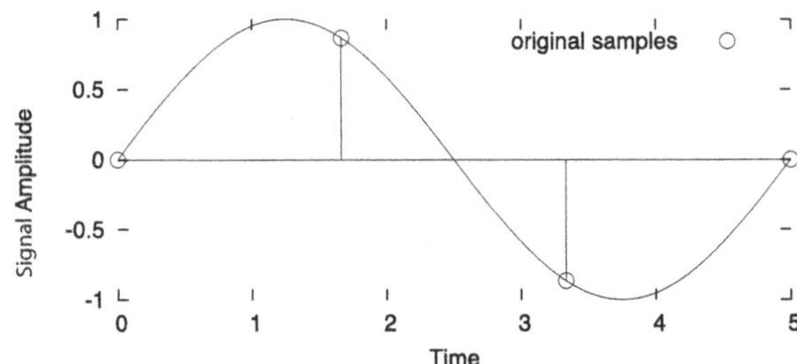

Figure 10. One period of a sine wave with four samples.

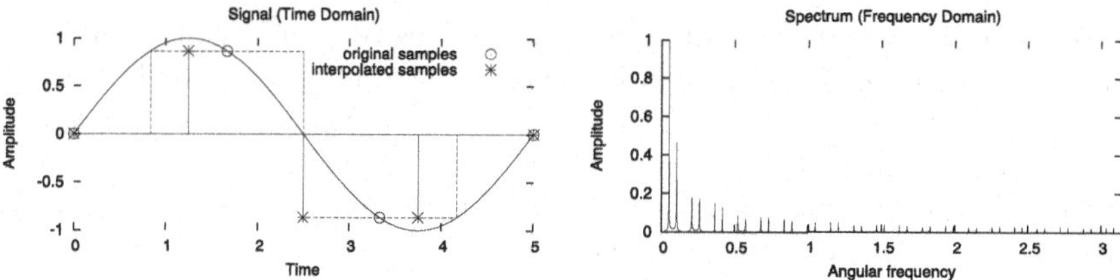

Figure 11. Nearest neighbor resampling. This interpolation scheme produces a lot of unwanted frequencies in the signal's spectrum.

the nearest integer), we can see that it doesn't yield very satisfactory results relative to the theoretically "correct" answer. A plot of the spectrum of this signal further illustrates just how poor this approach is.

A second, slightly better approach is *linear interpolation*, where we reconstruct the in-between sample value by taking a weighted average of the two samples to its immediate left and right. The resulting waveform is somewhat better (see Figure 12).

Linear interpolation is achieved by using the following formula: given the fractional sample index x, let $x_l = \lfloor x \rfloor$ and $x_r = \lceil x \rceil$. The weighting coefficient is $\eta = x - x_l$, and the interpolated sample is $s(x) = (1 - \eta)s(x_l) + \eta s(x_r)$.

To further improve upon linear interpolation, we can do *polynomial interpolation*. This involves fitting a polynomial of some order N to the data points and using that to interpolate the values. Common types of polynomial interpolation include quadratic interpolation ($N = 2$) and cubic interpolation ($N = 3$).

The techniques described above (nearest neighbor, linear interpolation, and polynomial interpolation) are often used in computer graphics to, for example, resample texture maps or construct continuous paths from a set of discrete control points (splines).

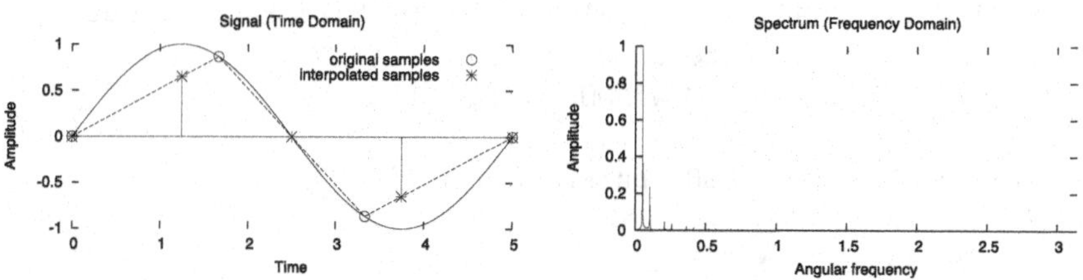

Figure 12. Linear interpolation. The unwanted frequencies are significantly reduced, compared to Figure 11.

We can do better resampling for audio, however, with a little understanding of digital signal processing theory. Let us go back to how our sampled signal was constructed to begin with: the *Nyquist-Shannon sampling theorem* states that a sampled signal can be perfectly reconstructed if the sampling frequency is twice the highest frequency in the signal. Real-world, digitally-sampled signals are in fact *bandlimited* to half the sampling frequency to prevent *aliasing* artifacts, so in theory we should be able to achieve perfect reconstruction of the original audio signal without resorting to the approximation techniques described above. In practice, of course, issues such as quantization and the non-ideal nature of sampling prevent perfect reconstruction, but we can at least come much closer to the ideal. The sampling theorem tells us to use the sinc function to interpolate the in-between sample values. The sinc function, which is zero at integer values (except 0), is used to compute a set of weighting coefficients that is then used to weigh and sum the neighboring samples to produce the desired output sample (see Figure 13).

The sinc function is mathematically defined as $\mathrm{sinc}(t) = \frac{\sin(\pi t)}{\pi t}$, which extends out infinitely in either direction over time t (see Figure 14). This, of course, presents a problem for us, since it means that we would need to multiply an infinite number of samples and the reconstruction would have an infinite delay. Thus, we need to time-limit the sinc function by *windowing* it. Simply truncating the sinc function at some point is equivalent to the simple rectangular window; non-trivial window functions gradually taper to zero at either end.

Here is a very simple (albeit naïve) implementation of sinc interpolation:

```
#define RESAMPLE_WINDOW_SIZE_HALF 16
void Resample(float *inBuffer, float *outBuffer,
              int numOutputFrames, float rate) {
   int i, j;

   // The first and last RESAMPLE_WINDOW_SIZE_HALF frames
   // are used for interpolating.
   inBuffer += RESAMPLE_WINDOW_SIZE_HALF;

   for (i = 0; i < numOutputFrames; i++)
   {
      float x = i * rate;
      int xInt = (int)x;
      float frac = x - xInt;
```

```
        // Accumulate output sample frame using neighbouring
        // samples weighted by a sinc.
        outBuffer[i] = 0.0f;
        for (j = -RESAMPLE_WINDOW_SIZE_HALF;
             j <= RESAMPLE_WINDOW_SIZE_HALF; j++)
        {
            outBuffer[i] += sinc(-frac + j)
                          * inBuffer[xInt + j];
        }
    }
}
```

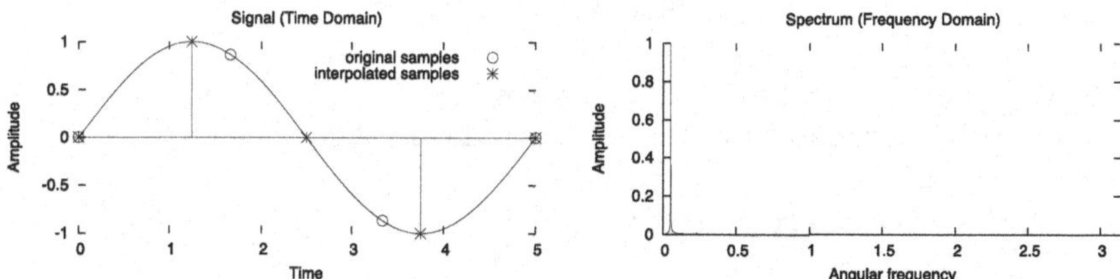

Figure 13. Sinc interpolation. We are able to get perfect reconstruction, with an almost perfect spike in the frequency amplitude plot corresponding to the input tone, especially when compared to Figures 11 and 12.

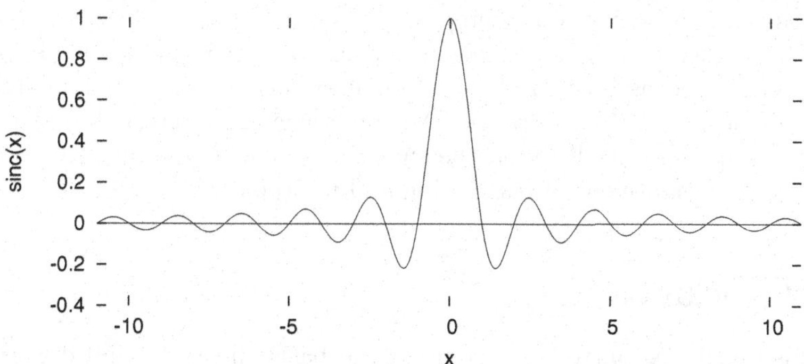

Figure 14. Plot of the sinc function.

And here is a code example showing how `Resample()` could be used (recall that `Resample()` is also used in our code example for sync in Section 4):

```
float playRate = 0.9; // Can be anything you want

while (1) {
   // Get the input samples.
   int numInputFrames = (int)ceilf(NUM_FRAMES * playRate);
   GetInputBuffer(inBuffer,
                  inFrameNum - RESAMPLE_WINDOW_SIZE_HALF,
                  numInputFrames + RESAMPLE_WINDOW_SIZE);

   // Resample it to get the desired play rate.
   Resample(inBuffer, numInputFrames + RESAMPLE_WINDOW_SIZE,
            outBuffer, NUM_FRAMES, playRate);

   // Output it to the audio device.
   WriteAudioStream(outStream, outBuffer, NUM_FRAMES);

   inFrameNum += numInputFrames;
}
```

The astute reader will no doubt observe that this implementation of sinc interpolation is horrendously inefficient and thus impractical for any sort of real application. Tor Ramstad's article on sample rate conversion in *Audio Anecdotes I* describes the theory behind a polyphase interpolation structure, which is essentially a much more efficient implementation of the same idea (and also one that produces better results, for reasons that are described in detail there).

The theory behind how and why ideal sinc interpolation is able to give perfect reconstruction of the original audio signal is, unfortunately, beyond the scope of this article. We encourage the interested reader to refer to the references listed at the end of this article for a more in-depth and rigorous treatment of resampling and interpolation.

7 Conclusion

In this article, we introduced some of the basic theory behind dynamic synchronization (also called drift synchronization).

We began our discussion with a distinction between a system that only starts the media in sync (open loop system) and one that not only starts in sync but periodically adjusts to correct for drift (closed loop system). We determined how the current position of the dependent timebase and the reference timebase can be used to compute an adjusted play rate to gradually compensate for this drift, and the trade-offs between choosing an appropriate interval between adjustments (faster convergence vs. higher overhead) and catch-up interval (more closely following the reference clock vs. ability to absorb jitter in the system). Finally, we offered a brief discussion of approaches to changing the play rate of audio via resampling.

A more thorough discussion of the theory behind this topic would involve aspects of control theory and digital signal processing that are beyond the scope of a single article. As our aim was to provide a more practical perspective of synchronization, we introduced aspects of control theory and digital signal processing only as needed and dispensed with the fancy mathematical derivations wherever possible, perhaps at the expense of some mathematical rigor. And while we used audio for many of our examples, the concepts that we introduce in this article also apply to other forms of digital media, such as video.

We hope that this article is helpful to the reader and do encourage the interested reader to dig deeper into these subjects for more information, beginning with the provided references.

The author would like to thank Julius Smith, Ken Greenebaum, and Thorsten Karrer for their feedback and input on early drafts of this article.

Annotated Bibliography

[1] R. E. Crochiere and L. R. Rabiner. *Multirate Digital Signal Processing.* Englewood Cliffs, NJ: Prentice-Hall, 1983.

A classic text on digital signal processing, this book is an excellent reference for engineers and scientists working with digital signal processing.

[2] Integrated Circuit Systems, Inc. "ICS954101: Programmable Timing Control Hub™ for Desktop P4™ Systems." Available from World Wide Web (http://www.icst.com/datasheets/ics954101.pdf/), 2005.

Data sheet for an off-the-shelf crystal oscillator component. The specifications for this particular device are typical for the inexpensive crystal oscillators used in computers and other consumer electronics for time keeping.

[3] L. Lamport. "Time, Clocks, and the Ordering of Events in a Distributed System." *Communications of the ACM* 21:7 (1978), 558–565.

The classic paper on time-keeping and ordering of logical clocks in a system.

[4] E. Lee, T. Karrer, and J. Borchers. "Toward a Framework for Interactive Systems to Conduct Digital Audio and Video Streams." *Computer Music Journal* 30:1 (2006), 21–36. The video for this article appears in the *Computer Music Journal Sound and Video Anthology* 29:4, 2005.

An example of how the drift sync algorithm can be used in a different context. We present a variation of the algorithm described in this article, used to synchronize an audio/video recording of an orchestra to a person's beating patterns with a digital baton. This allows us to create the illusion that the user is conducting the virtual orchestra with their movements.

[5] F. L. Lewis. *Applied Optimal Control and Estimation: Digital Design and Implementation.* Englewood Cliffs, NJ: Prentice-Hall, 1992.

A more advanced book on control systems theory, with an emphasis on digital systems. The first chapter of this book, "Introduction to Modern Control Theory," is available online: http://www.theorem.net/theorem/lewis1.html.

[6] D. L. Mills. "Network Time Protocol (Version 3) Specification, Implementation and Analysis." RFC 1305, IETF, 1992.

The definitive reference documentation for the Network Time Protocol, version 3. Although version 4 is in the works, its RFC is not yet publicly available, and NTP v3 is still the most widely used.

[7] N. Nise. *Control Systems Engineering,* Fourth edition. New York: Wiley, 2004.

A well-recommended introductory text on control systems theory, with MATLAB examples.

[8] R. W. Schafer and L. R. Rabiner. "A Digital Signal Processing Approach to Interpolation." *Proceedings of the IEEE* 61:6 (1973), 692–702.

An early paper on the theory behind interpolation, this article discusses resampling in great detail from a digital signal processing perspective.

[9] J. O. Smith and P. Gossett. "A Flexible Sampling-Rate Conversion Method." *Acoustics, Speech, and Signal Processing, IEEE International Conference on ICASSP '84*, pp. 112–115. Los Alamitos, CA: IEEE Press, 1984.

This article describes an efficient resampling method that also supports varying resampling factors over time. This algorithm has been implemented in programs such as SoX, *a set of cross-platform audio processing utilities (included on the CD-ROM accompanying this book). An expanded tutorial and associated free software are also available on Julius Smith's homepage: http://ccrma.stanford.edu/~jos/resample/.*

Music Composition

Music Composition Techniques for Interactive Media

Evan Buehler

1 Introduction

The incredible computational power of inexpensive computers today promises an unprecedented level of rich interactive experience. While offering state-of-the-art three-dimensional graphics and AI, many designs fall far short of their potential by failing to exploit interactive music. The potential, however, is there to make every interactive experience a custom-scored cinematic experience.

This article explores the concept of interactive music comparing it to traditional linear music, details the process of composing for interactive media, including the nontraditional skills and tools the composer will need to master this new medium, and is followed by a walk-through of the design process of the interactive music for a level from the game *SWAT 3: Elite Edition.*

While games represent both the most common and one of the earliest adopters of interactive media, the techniques described in this article are applicable to many other applications.

Music performance has traditionally been a linear noninteractive experience. A symphony begins and ends. A song is sung and is completed. It is not common practice to experience a musical performance where, through the listener's action, the music is altered. Imagine a concert where the act of standing up caused the music to change in some way or an interface where a user could intelligently alter the music to their own taste simply by pressing a button. While still quite uncommon in live performance (unless you happen to be the conductor), these situations are becoming commonplace in interactive media.

Interactive media is any medium in which the audience member is an active participant in the work itself.

2 Point of Departure

Conventional musical composition presupposes the audience to be passive. These pieces are also generally written to create a linear experience. While sections of music can repeat, it is almost always written to lead to a conclusion. With interactive media, we are presented with a different set of challenges than with standard musical composition. Often, the music in an interactive project needs to able to repeat or continue for indefinite periods of time without drawing too much attention to itself. The music needs to be able to quickly evolve to become relevant to the participant's present situation, for example, when a new character enters the scene, or the level of danger or anticipation changes.

Let's consider the situation where a character in a game walks from one contrasting environment to the next. If the person playing the game (the user) is only able to go from one environment to another in one direction and in a set period of time, a musical transition using standard composition is suitable. But, if the user can easily traverse the environments in a nonfixed time period and can go either direction, the relationship between the environments and therefore the music must be carefully considered. The music for each environment must be made to fit with one another in a logical way. The music must also be designed so it can continue for an indefinite period of time until the user decides to change locations in the virtual world. This kind of music needs to be composed in such a way that the end result is seamless to the user.

3 Questions to Consider

When first undertaking the task of composing music for any interactive media, I find it essential to ask a set of questions which help define the role that my music will play in the overall project. These design considerations will be essential in helping me define what kind of composition is needed. Please keep in mind that these are rhetorical questions that have no right or wrong answers, but are meant to lead to a better understanding of the music that you will write.

The first question to consider is what is the nature of the project, in which the music is going to be included? Is this a game, an educational product, a productivity application, etc.? Knowing the specifics of the project that you are working on can help you narrow down your choices. Music used in a productivity application will likely function quite differently than in an arcade-style game.

The next question that should be asked is who is the audience of the project? Knowing who your audience is and what they might be expecting from you is a key ingredient in both performance and composition. If you were working on a game that is geared towards small children, the kinds of compositions would be different than if you are writing for a game that is geared toward adults.

What style of music is appropriate? If you have thought about the previous questions, this one should be easier to answer. Developing a consistent style for all pieces of music can also be very helpful in the compositional process. Often for computer games, the style of music is dictated by the game. A game that involves gangsters in the 1930s will likely require a different style of music than a game that is set 200 years in the future.

What resources are available? You can only create music with the instruments that you are given. If you have the opportunity to compose for a symphony orchestra, you will have more options available to you than if you have only a piano at your disposal. Knowing your limitations will also help you decide what you realistically will be able to produce. It is also important to consider what effect the lack of means of production will have on your project. If you believe that a symphonic score is appropriate to the project, but do not have the budget to hire an orchestra, you will have to make your compositional choices accordingly.

What format(s) will the music need to be authored in? The end file format can also affect your composition as well. If your piece must be delivered in 22 kHz, 8-bit, monophonic, you will undoubtedly need to take this into account. This is usually more relevant when mixing. If your music is only going to have monophonic output, then it is useless to compose a piece with stereophonic elements. Also, many subtle high-frequency elements can be distorted or lost if your final output is in a low sample rate. Additionally, low quantization levels, such as 8 bits per sample, only afford 256 sound levels and require the music to not have a wide dynamic range. The softest passages have to be closer in volume to the loudest passages or else all detail would be lost in the softer passages. For example, rock music, while often played loud, tends to have a narrow dynamic range when compared to classical music. The need to record classical music is one reason 16-bit quantization, yielding a very wide 96 dB dynamic range, was selected for the CD format.

How is the music going to be used within the project? This is an important question, because it can help define what role your music is going to play. Often in games, music is used to convey emotions or provide added drama to situations or events. There also might be different roles that music is meant to fill in a project. Music could be used to establish an ambient setting or it could be the background for a grand introduction to the game. The music composed for each section will most likely need to be different. Thom's article "Designing a Movie for Sound" (see *Audio Anecdotes I*) and Back's article "Designing the Auditory Narrative: A Methodology for Sound Design" (see *Audio Anecdotes II*) elaborate on the topic from different perspectives.

What does the music add to the project? Obviously, music is being included for some purpose. If there were no music in the project, what would it be like? Specifically, what is the overall effect that your musical piece adds to the project? Does it provide a mood or ambiance to a setting? Is it only heard when a specific task is completed? This is a question that you should be constantly referring back to during the composition process. It will help give you focus on what you are writing.

Is there a relationship that needs to exist between the various musical pieces used in the project? This is a more technical composition-oriented question. If you need to create three musical pieces for three different environments and three additional pieces that can be activated by the user at any given time when they are in the environments, you will need to plan out the structure accordingly. In addition to this, let's say that each environment needs to represent different emotions such as happiness, sadness, and anger. Now in addition to each piece needing to work with each other, you will need to convey each emotion in the music. Knowing the exact nature of this relationship will greatly aid in the compositional process.

4 Creating the Composition

Hopefully, after pondering these questions, you have become inspired to create the composition. While there are many different methods or tools of composition, I would like to focus on a few that I have personally found to be helpful.

The first tool is imagination, plain and simple, which is simply the process of attempting to imagine the piece that you are going to create. This works best when you have some other reference available such as a complete game level or a screen. Try to imagine what kind of music would be playing in this area. I find it helpful to take notes when imagining or visualizing music. If you imagine a string section playing, or a specific synthesizer patch that would be used, write that down. Also, if possible, note any melodies or harmonic progressions you might be imagining. This method often does not actually end with a fully notated piece, but it can result in a good sketch.

The next method I find useful is chance or random music generation. Random sequences are nothing new in music composition, but I use this method really only as a starting point and not as the end result. This method consists of taking randomly generated musical elements and then arranging them in a way that the piece is coherent and works within the design constraints of your project. There are many ways to begin the process: rolling dice, creating a random number sequence on a computer, or even asking people to pick numbers off the top of their head, the point being that the initial musical idea is going to be generated by chance. Most often I pick notes off the top of my head until I have a sequence that seems useful. Say I pick A, C, D flat, G, A. This sequence could be the beginning notes of a melody or they could represent the relationships between notes to create a harmonic structure.

The ways that random sequences can be used is really limitless. However, realize that this is only a starting point. By starting with a random series of notes, I can begin to build some sort of musical structure with them.

A common and very effective way to begin composing is to start with a set harmonic structure. The structure of your musical piece can be derived from the structure or arrangement dictated by the integration of the piece into the overall project. For instance, if this is a piece that is in C minor and needs to transition into a G major section for a different environment, the harmonic structure needs to be constructed accordingly. After your harmonic structure is set up, all other musical components can be composed. I usually will write out all melodic components over the harmony and then go to the task of orchestrating the composition.

Another traditional method is to compose a melody first and then create a harmonic structure from the melody. This is a contrast to the previous method. Here, the melody of your composition will decide the harmonic structure. Of course, there are many ways to harmonize a melody. The choices that you make should ultimately be made so that the harmony accentuates the meaning of the melody in your interactive piece. It is also a good idea to create a melody that is ambiguous or suggests multiple harmonies. Such a melody is more easily transformed than one that suggests a specific harmonic progression.

Blocking out the composition is very similar to our imagination technique, only it is much more defined. Blocking a piece of music is often done by first mapping out what must take place first (i.e., modulations, meter changes, etc.). If this piece needs to align with or change into another section, then this should also be taken into account. The next step is to write out what each section of the piece should consist of. For example, this could be: an introduction with strings only, followed by a timpani solo, a grand pause that immediately starts into a waltz section. In a way, this is a more specific form of visualization in that each small section is imagined in relation to the whole work.

The composition technique that I use most frequently is improvisation which is broadly defined as instantaneous composition. There are a couple of principles of improvisation, which I believe are necessary for it to be beneficial to composition. First, you should be fairly fluent on the instrument that you are using to improvise and second, you establish the parameters for your improvisation before you begin. Without any technical facility on your instrument, your ideas will most likely be limited by your lack of ability to express your ideas on the instrument. It's also important to improvise over a set of parameters. Often an improvisation is done over a set meter, tempo, and harmonic structure. When improvising something for an interactive piece, your set parameters can be directly related to other aspects of the piece that do not incorporate improvisation. The great advantage of improvisation is that you can create many variations on common set-up parameters.

The last method is using another piece of music as a guide to composition. This is very common, especially when writing music for games. Often you need for a piece to match an exact style or specific piece. This method can be the most difficult in that a great amount of research is needed to match a specific composer's style. If one needs to create ragtime music, an analysis of the musical components that exemplify ragtime music is needed. However, this does make the composition process easier in that your structures and orchestration are usually already dictated before composing the piece.

5 Pause to Review Your Composition

After the initial round of composing, I feel that it is best to then immediately review what you have done so far. Usually, I find the initial burst of creativity to be the most rewarding and usually not too far from the final product. At this point, ask yourself all of the rhetorical questions that I suggested at the beginning of the process. If you are satisfied with the results, then continue on the process. Most likely, there will need to be either technical or aesthetic changes. Do not be afraid to really edit your composition or even abandon what you have done so far. Sometimes, the first composition leads you to a better composition later on.

6 Rendering the Music

After the initial composition process, the piece then needs to be recorded, edited, and mixed. Depending on the kind of music that you are writing, there are many different ways to go about this process. When you realize the music, keep in mind whatever sections are going to be looping. I would recommend recording at least three repetitions of the loop so that when you edit the file, it is much easier to get a loop that is seamless.

Once I have realized my music, I then go about getting ready for implementation in the project. At this point, you will need to convert it to the right format, edit the digital file to the correct lengths, and most likely create files that are able to loop.

Implementation of your interactive music is just as important as the compositions themselves. When the music that you have created for an interactive experience is actually used in the project, you will finally have the ability to see how the interactive piece functions. Many elements, which before were abstract, are now a reality. At this point, it becomes important to do something that is rarely done in linear or traditional composition: test the composition.

You will want to test the interactive components of your music and its implementation to verify that they work. Testing all of the interactive elements also gives a good understanding of the composition that you have created. Interactive music is really only first realized when it is integrated into the project itself. I would recommend checking all of the elements that you know the user will experience, then attempting some more unusual interactions. For instance, if the user has two buttons that change their game state and the music changes with that, try changing rapidly between each button. Does this ruin your composition? Some users may frequently use many interactive elements which you envisioned would be used rarely. The unpredictability of interactive music is probably the most interesting aspect of the music, but also can be a great pitfall.

"Playing" with the music is the best way to ensure that your music is implemented the way you intended.

Does the musical piece fit with the overall project? This question should be answered after reviewing the piece and before it is integrated in the project. Often this is done in the last phases of development. However, the musical pieces can be reviewed earlier on in the project. It is important that when the musical piece is reviewed in a project, the other relevant material (such as artwork) is also present and final. Otherwise, your musical piece could possibly be out of context with the rest of the project.

It is important that dynamic levels are set within the project as a whole so that none of the ambient music is too present and nonambient is at reasonable levels. The music will most likely need to balance with the other audio in the project. In games, music is often secondary to the dialogue and sound effects. In some situations, the music will be the focus. It is important that your levels reflect this. One way that I help balance this mix is by establishing the loudest and softest sound events (music, sound effect, or dialog). Use these as references when setting all of the levels for your music.

Transitions are another important factor to keep in mind when reviewing the interactive elements in your music. Each piece will need to smoothly transition from piece to piece. Depending on the elements, there may be several triggers which cause transitions to occur. Test all of the transitions that you can in context and verify that the musical ideas work.

7 Evaluate the Results

The last step is an objective review of your interactive piece and its implementation in the project. This can be a difficult process since the composer can never truly be objective about his or her own work. The ideal solution is to have someone that you trust give you constructive criticism about your music. Ideally, this person will have some musical background so that they can provide informed and specific feedback. I would also recommend that you ask whoever is criticizing your work to provide you with specific feedback. General comments can provide an overall impression of the composition, however, without specific musical examples, you will likely do entirely too much revision. I also recommend that the composer review the work at the same time. Ideally, take at least a day away from the project before going back and listening to it again. I find the more time away from the music, the more objective I become.

8 Composing *SWAT 3: Elite Edition*

To concretely illustrate some of the techniques described earlier, I will share the process that I used to create music for one level in a recent gaming project, *SWAT 3: Elite Edition.*

SWAT 3 is a subtler example of the first-person shooter genre made famous by ID's *Doom* and *Quake.* The player sees a three-dimensional world as if looking though the eyes of the character that they are controlling. *SWAT 3* allows the player to lead a five man SWAT team through a series of levels of increasing complexity and difficulty. Each level of the game is a scenario that presents your SWAT element with the task of resolving a different crisis ranging from hostage rescue to VIP protection.

There are two basic modes of play for your SWAT element: stealth and dynamic. When in stealth mode, your team moves slowly and is trying to remain undetected. Dynamic mode is used when a threat is present: a gunman, a hostage, or gunshots fired. Stealth and dynamic modes are controlled by the player as well as triggered by events in the game.

The sound engine used in this game has a number of specific limitations: All sounds, including the music, must be 22 kHz, 16-bit mono. There are severe limitations on file size of the music; hence, all music needs to have a memory footprint of less than 2 MB. We utilize a compression scheme that allows us to get three times as much music into the same footprint which helped quite a bit considering the size limitations. Our engine also allows the specification of fade-in and fade-out times for the music enabling smooth crossfades between different pieces. Music selections may be designated to play in specific locations. The game engine supports portals between sections of the map to allow faster rendering and to allow the AI to navigate the map. Finally, for each section, both stealth and dynamic music selections are specified.

The scenario for this particular level is a high risk warrant. Your SWAT team is required to deliver a warrant to a suspected bank robber in the Hollywood Hills. The level takes place at night and consists of an outdoor location, a house, and an underground bunker.

With our game, the music has a specific function, to manipulate the mood of the players! When in stealth mode, the music needs to be engineered to cause tension. When in dynamic mode, the music needs to convey the feeling of action and excitement. The music also functions to help delineate different areas of the level.

The first step when creating music for a level is to become familiar with the level itself. Usually, I look for areas of the level where I want the music to create a specific effect in the player. The game designer is also an important reference, being the one who creates the story and the overall objectives for the mission. The designer also acts as kind of a director for the level design. After playing the level and getting some direction from the game designer, I was able to create a couple of guidelines for what music was needed. This particular level was divided into three distinct sections: the outdoor area, the house, and a maze-like underground bunker. These were the three sections for which I wanted to have different music. Also, all of these areas could interconnect. All of the musical pieces that I would compose would need to fit with one another. In addition to this, I needed to have dynamic music that would be able to be instantly played in all three areas. Having such a small amount of memory allocated to music, I needed to write short pieces. I also decided to write a piece of music for stealth mode for each area and create just one piece of music for dynamic mode.

I also wanted each piece of music to represent the overall look of the level. The house, the central location in the level, was built in the Hollywood hills in the 1970s. I wanted the music to be evocative of that era. Also, each piece of music for stealth mode needed to elicit a specific reaction from the player. I wanted the outdoor music to give the sense of sneaking up on the main structure, the interior music to make the player feel a sense that something is wrong or out of place and lastly, I wanted the music in the underground bunker to feel cavernous and spooky. These concepts helped me decide on the instrumentation for each piece.

As I explained earlier, improvisation is my preferred method of composition. I began writing by improvising several ideas on electric piano. I wanted each piece of music to have the same tonal center so that it would be easy to transition from one to another. For the outside music, I came up with an ostinato bass line that would be the central idea. I then took this idea for the second piece and created a piece with a thicker orchestration and with a more defined sense of meter and rhythm. Improvising a couple of different ambient synthesizer pads created the third piece of stealth music. I also included some electric piano sounds to try and tie the overall feel to the stealth music. For the dynamic music, I wanted to evoke the feeling of music from a 1970s cop show and wound up writing the piece for a small string ensemble and rhythm section. Since the dynamic music needed to be played instantly and transition from each piece of stealth music, I made sure the opening section of the music didn't suggest any specific tonal center and included a couple of sweeping string runs suggesting the same tonality as the stealth music.

After composing and recording the music, I then added the music to the level to see how each piece would work for each area. I also evaluated how each composition would flow from one area to the other and how everything worked when changing modes of play. Fortunately, each piece fit quite well in this particular level after adjusting the cross fades from one area to another and tweaking the overall volume levels of the files.

The game designer and I then reviewed the level for any changes that would need to be made. After listening to the music in the level with her, I decided to make some small changes to the mix and instrumentation. I had used a snare drum sample for several of the pieces which tended to stand out too much when playing the game. I changed this sample to a less dramatic snare drum with brushes. I also changed some volume levels of the strings since they were a little too prevalent. After making my changes, we reviewed the level with music and decided everything worked well.

To create the music for this particular level of our game, I followed some of the methods mentioned earlier in this article. At first, I needed to ask myself specific questions that would help me focus on exactly what was needed for the level and how it would fit in aesthetically. I also needed to take into account the constraints that I had working with this particular game engine.

Ideally, after going through this process, compositions for interactive media will be more successful than if one muddled through composing with no planning. By following a process which allows you to understand who is going to interact with your music, how the music is going to be implemented, and the problems that can arise, you can more effectively compose music that works in the unpredictable environment of an interactive project. The way you generate your musical ideas should also be taken into consideration and always reflect the interactive nature of the music you are writing. The great fun of writing interactive music, especially for games, is that each user will receive a unique experience based on how they individually interact with the game. Instead of just hearing background music that conventional linear music provides, the user feels as if they are starring in a movie with their own scored soundtrack!

Annotated Bibliography

[1] Kent Kennan and Donald Grantham. *The Technique of Orchestration, Fifth edition*, Englewood Cliffs, NJ: Prentice Hall, 1996.

This is a great reference for writing any orchestral or chamber music. Even if you are using samplers to replicate classical instruments, it is handy so that you can get the correct instrument ranges and general advice on orchestration.

[2] Curtis Roads. *The Computer Music Tutorial.* Cambridge, MA: MIT Press, 1996.

This is another great reference that deals with many different aspects of electronic music from synthesis to psychoacoustics.

Polyrhythm and Musical Culture

Bob Brozman

1 Introduction

This article discusses various interesting and fundamental aspects of rhythm. It is meant to be an overview of some basic cultural and perceptual ideas about how different rhythms are conceived. Many of the concepts herein are part of the extant body of musical knowledge, and some of the ideas have been developed through direct observation and participation by the author in the music of dozens of countries around the world over the last few decades. Much published research of a more comprehensive nature has been done in these areas, and there is much yet to be done. The bibliography at the end of this article has suggestions for further reading. Readers are also referred to Tomassetti's articles "Basic Music Theory: Notation, Scales, and Chords" and "Basic Music Theory: Rhythm and Meter" (see *Audio Anecdotes II*) for the basics of Western musical pitch and rhythm theory

Since prehistoric times, the human race, with its huge range of cultures, has been involved in exploring sounds through pitch and rhythm, the two musical parameters which are abundant in nature already. As with other animals, our bodies and brains seem to be built to interpret sound in this manner in the natural world. The reasons for the seemingly universal drive to explore and utilize sound are unclear, though certainly may be related to the evolutionary value of birdsong and whale-song, i.e., "showing off" better DNA for memory and intelligence in order to attract mates. When the human intellect is added to this biological drive, external cultural factors come into play, altering and refining the sounds to create more complex and subtle musical art.

Historically, European musical culture focused on harmony as the primary pursuit of musical art, whereas African-based music found its artistic expression in rhythm. There are exceptions to this general statement, more so in recent times, since the spread of music through recordings and other mass media have clouded this distinction somewhat.

The European concept of rhythm is normally conceived as being in one meter (a set number of beats per measure) at a time, either 2, *or* 3, *or* 4, etc. African-based music normally has as the fundamental meter *both* 2 and 3 *at the same time.* This opens the door to much syncopation, polyrhythm, and rhythmic creativity. It is acknowledged that Europeans developed harmony to a higher point than any other culture, but rhythmically, their culture is among the planet's most primitive. Rhythmically speaking, European-based music is like working on a computer with one window open, whereas in African-based music, there are always *two* windows open, and you are working in both of them at once, continuously. The "work" is really simple multiplication and division, all based on 2 and 3. The layers of rhythmic complexity can get dizzying in African-based music, and these ever-changing layers stimulate the mind and body, inspiring the tradition of dance that often accompanies African music.

2 Grouping Single Beats in the Mind

The way in which the human brain processes and perceives rhythm is a book-length subject, and is fascinating indeed. Here we shall explore the basic concept of grouping. A simple set of terms will be used herein. Let us use the term pulse to mean any single pulse which can be a beat or subdivisions of a beat. Let us use the term beat for a unit of time which can be divided into pulses. Let us use the term meter to indicate a system of creating measures of a set number of beats. It can be said that all rhythms could be counted as "1,1,1,1,1,1,1,1 ..." assuming simple pulses of equal length. It is the mind that causes the sensation of grouping.

There are two basic causes of grouping, involving two stimuli: internal and external. The internal stimulus is created by merely deciding that the series of "ones" are counted in groups, whereas the external stimulus is caused by sound coming into the brain, which may affect the grouping. For example, the internal stimulus may arbitrarily decide that a series of 1,1,1,1,1,1,1,1,1,1,1,1 is to be grouped as 1,2,3,1,2,3,1,2,3,1,2,3. A musician or listener will support and strengthen this "illusion" by boosting the external stimulus—by accenting the "1," or perhaps tapping the foot on each "1," creating $\underline{\mathbf{1}}$ 2 3 $\underline{\mathbf{1}}$ 2 3 $\underline{\mathbf{1}}$ 2 3 $\underline{\mathbf{1}}$ 2 3. By the same token, the musician can change the external stimulus by accenting **1** 2 **1** 2, or **1** 2 3 4 **1** 2 3 4, or back to 1,1,1,1,1,1,1, thus altering, creating tension against, destroying, or demanding increased strength of the internal stimulus. This is the essential creative activity of the African rhythm esthetic.

Thus, a major part of the art form of African-based music involves literally "playing" with different external stimuli, which creates an exciting tension for musician and listener alike, as the internal stimulus (the count) must be stronger and more "resolute" as the external stimuli change. A simple example would be as follows: Let's say that we have a four-beat measure, each beat divided into three pulses; thus, 12 pulses per measure. The internal count of pulses (1, 1, 1, 1, etc.) for all the players and listeners is felt as **1** 2 3 **1** 2 3 **1** 2 3 **1** 2 3. Think of this as a measure of four subdivided beats (**1** 2 3 **2** 2 3 **3** 2 3 **4** 2 3) counted as "1 and-a 2 and-a 3 and-a 4 and-a." One musician, in creating an artistic statement during a fleeting moment, will accent quite loudly once every four pulses, creating a strong external stimulus that sounds like **1** 2 3 4 **1** 2 3 4 **1** 2 3 4. Clearly, four sets of three pulses are the same as three sets of 4: 12 single pulses. They come back together every 12 pulses. If we superimpose the two sets, we see:

1	2	3	**1**	2	3	**1**	2	3	**1**	2	3
1	2	3	4	**1**	2	3	4	**1**	2	3	4.

This creates an exciting syncopation when all accents are heard together, sounding much like the cadence created by the words "play the doggone rhythm." The other players who are supporting the illusion of **1** 2 3 **1** 2 3 **1** 2 3 **1** 2 3 must be more firm in their "insistence" that the pulses are in groups of three. The fellow playing the groups of four is stretching the abilities of the other players, while of course stretching his own ability, because he must maintain the internal sets of three in his mind in order to enjoy playing the sets of four successfully and to return to the groove at the right time. The soloist can then create higher level "tricks" by temporarily making four his "internal" stimulus, and creating new "external" stimuli against that. All of the resulting syncopations are still mathematically "legal" with the original tempo, though the "coming back together" points will be farther apart (perhaps every 24, 36, or 48 pulses).

The creative possibilities are nearly limitless, and again the art form involves constantly changing and playing with the listener's brain state. It is scientifically fascinating and something of a miracle that the listeners' internal and external stimuli can be adjusted by the player's decisions in this creative process.

3 The Importance of the "and"

The function of the "and" (the pulse between primary pulses) in music cannot be overstated. It is used as a tempo regulator, a jumping-off point for all syncopation, and can be used to understand the difference in perception between European and African music. In normal counting of rhythm, the "and" is placed between the "1, 2, 3, 4" primary count, yielding "1 and 2 and 3 and 4 and." This "and" stroke represents a division of the beat.

There are three types of "ands"—the difference being in the way the beat is divided. The most common is the duple division created by placing the "and" between the "1, 2, 3, 4" primary count, yielding:

1 and 2 and 3 and 4 and.

This divides the beat in half, so that every "and" equals 50% of one beat. This is commonly heard in march, polka, disco, and techno music, all rhythmically identical, and perhaps the least interesting way to divide the beat.

The two other "ands" are based on dividing the beat into three parts (triplets), saying the "and" as "and a":

1 and a 2 and a 3 and a 4 and a.

It is also commonly counted 123 123 123 123. Each division represents 33.333...% of the beat. In a blues shuffle, the "2" of each triplet, or the "and" of each "and a," is silent, leaving:

1 – a 2 – a 3 – a 4 – a.

Thus, the "and" is sounded at 66.6666...% of the beat. The least known "and," where the "3" of each triplet is silent, still divides the beat into thirds, but yields an "and" which occurs at the 33.333...% position of the beat. This "and" is sounded quite forcefully, and can be very surprising to the uninitiated listener. This rhythm seems to be exclusive to the Indian Ocean islands of Madagascar, la Réunion, Mauritius, and Seychelles, with faint hints of its use in certain South American cultures as well:

1 and – 2 and – 3 and – 4 and – .

4 Downbeat and Backbeat

The "and" also has another important function, which is that of verifying and regulating the overall tempo of a piece of music. In blues, jazz, and swing music, measures of four beats (1, 2, 3, 4) are often felt as measures of two, with "ands" ("1 and 2 and"). In these types of music, the 2 and the 4 of the 1, 2, 3, 4 are felt more strongly, yielding 1 2 3 4. This is commonly referred to as the "backbeat," with the 1 and the 3 usually called the "downbeat." The roots of the naming convention are unknown to the author, but certainly when you march you put your feet DOWN on the beat, and pull BACK up for the backbeat. In theory, each of the four beats occupies 25% of the measure—at the following positions: 0, .25, .50, .75. Interestingly, in practice, the timing position of the backbeat is variable. In fact, to gain the quality of swing, it is critical to delay the "2" and the "4," perhaps pushing them back as late as .30 and .80. Therefore, while the "1" and "3" beats always fall at 0 and at 50% of the measure, the "2" and "4," which function as separators of "1" and "3," can be adjusted each measure, thus regulating the overall tempo. One of the greatest American masters of this art was Louis Armstrong. His ability to be "late" was so elastic, and yet so controlled, that it gave his music an undeniably compelling quality. Pretty much any solo or vocal he recorded from 1928–32 is a great example.

5 Cultural Context of Downbeat and Backbeat

Worldwide, the author has seen a strong fundamental difference between colonizing and colonized cultures in the way the downbeat/backbeat relationship is perceived, and in the priority given to the backbeat in this relationship. Put simply, marching (colonizing) cultures see the downbeat as something to follow, and the "marched-upon" (colonized) cultures see the downbeat as something to react to, using the backbeat. This is not at all a racial issue of black and white, as Japan and its colony Okinawa also bear out this theory. It is simply that the function of the downbeat in marching and organizing troops is critical. In "backbeat" cultures, dancing is usually far more important than marching, and most observers will find that dancing to the backbeat is far more sensual than marching along to the downbeat.

For the musician playing, reacting as opposed to following the beat feels quite different physiologically. Playing reactively means that the beat becomes something to jump away from. For example, in blues music, all of the important events—the basic groove, the timing of vocal entrances, the starting and ending points of musical riffs—all begin on an "and." The beat itself is constantly implied, but blues players avoid placing any important event on the beat. Even nonmusicians will hear something humorously "wrong" if a blues line is sung beginning on the downbeat.

The music of the Indian Ocean islands seems to be the strongest "re-active" style of rhythm in the world, because the accented "and" at 33% is so close to the quietly played downbeat. The "loud thing" happens in an unexpected place, and on initial exposure to this music, the untrained ear wrongly perceives this accent as the downbeat. Learning to hear it correctly actually causes a perceptible physiological change in the body.

6 Basic Triplets

The first simple rhythm every musician should learn is the triplet (sets of three) played with alternating hands. This involves setting your internal clock to **1** 2 3 **1** 2 3 **1** 2 3, while your hands play right-left-right-left, etc. If you don't support the internal count by accenting every **1**, then the external stimulus will sound like **1** 2 **1** 2 **1** 2. Therefore, the accented **1** will necessarily change sides every time **1** occurs.

The goal of the following exercises is to strengthen your sense of the internal stimulus clock (which is counting **1** 2 3 **1** 2 3 **1** 2 3), by challenging it with increasingly stronger external stimuli (in this case, **1** 2 **1** 2 **1** 2). To strengthen your internal "resolve," you can increase the external stimulus of **1** 2 **1** 2 **1** 2 incrementally as follows: First, play triplets with alternating hands on your legs. Next, play each hand on two different sounding surfaces, for example the leg and the chest. This boosts the external **1** 2 **1** 2 **1** 2 sound, causing you to need increased "resolve" that the real beats are **1** 2 3 **1** 2 3 **1** 2 3. The next step would be to "play" one of the hands in the air, silently, again effectively increasing the external stimulus and driving you to be stronger still. Finally, alternate one hand and one foot to further boost the external stimulus and further strengthen the internal count.

To review these steps:

(1) Count and maintain the internal clock of **1** 2 3 **1** 2 3, etc., Always.

(2) Then play this triplet rhythm with both hands always alternating on legs.

(3) Play same movement and pattern but with one hand on leg and one on chest.

(4) Play same movement and pattern but with one hand silent playing in the air.

(5) Play same pattern using one hand and one foot.

All of this will quickly make any musician much stronger rhythmically.

7 Basic Polyrhythms

Learning a little bit about playing polyrhythms will enhance musical perception and increase musical coordination for any musician playing any instrument. The basic polyrhythms are easy to learn, when understood conceptually. Simply put, a polyrhythm is two (or more) different meters at the same time, i.e., 2 and 3 both occupying the same length of time. In the case of 2 and 3, the most basic polyrhythm, the common multiple, 6, is the basis for understanding the pattern. However, immediately after hearing the sound of the simple pattern, it will no longer be necessary to count.

In order to play 2 against 3 with the hands, start by counting 1 2 3 4 5 6. The "3" hand will play **1** 2 **3** 4 **5** 6, and the "2" hand will play **1** 2 3 **4** 5 6. Superimposing the two patterns yields the following:

Right hand:	**1**	2	**3**	4	**5**	6
Left hand:	**1**	2	3	**4**	5	6.

Begin by counting all six beats as you play, saying the played notes of 1, 3, 4, 5 LOUDER than the 2 and 6—as **1** 2 **3 4 5** 6. Note that when playing the pattern, the '2' and the '6' pulses are silent. Using the cadence of spoken word to illustrate this effect, it is: "both, rest, right, left, right, rest." Assign equal value to rests and struck notes. Another way to count and feel it is "One two and 3."

Left-handed people often find it easier to play "both, rest, left, right, left, rest." However, it is beneficial to train oneself both ways (some teachers recommend first training the harder side, and from there the easy side will be a simple transition; but if the easy side is learned first, transitioning to the hard side can be daunting).

The next step in increasing coordination would be to begin separating the sounds and body parts, to emphasize the sonic differences between the "2" and the "3" which, as before, boosts the external stimulus and helps you confirm and strengthen the internal stimulus. The goal would be to be able to walk in 3 while clapping in 2, then walk in 2 while clapping in 3. If you can reach a point where you can do this, or any of the skills above, and *hold a conversation,* then you will know you have integrated it into your body, and no longer require your intellect to do it.

A higher level of polyrhythm involves placing 3 against 4. The common multiple here is 12:

Right hand:	**1**	2	3	4	**5**	6	7	8	**9**	10	11	12
Left hand:	**1**	2	3	**4**	5	6	**7**	8	9	**10**	11	12.

With a phase of this length, it is easier to use a verbal mnemonic device: "both- -left-right-left-right-left." A verbal phrase for this is "play the dog-gone rhyth-m" (as mentioned earlier) or:

Right hand:	**play**		**dog-**		**rhyth-**	
Left hand:	**play**	**the**		**-gone**		**-m**.

This 3-against-4 pattern should be practiced with increasing levels of sonic and body-part contrast, to strengthen the internal clock: Start with hands tapping legs (producing the same sound), *then* move to hands tapping leg and chest, to boost the external stimulus. This procedure, used previously with 2-against-3, of changing body parts to increase the external stimulus' power should be followed, with the only difference being the pattern played. It is important to begin with tapping hands on both legs, which will yield the whole pattern. Separating body parts to contrast the tone reveals the separate elements of this polyrhythm, thus demanding greater awareness of the whole pattern.

8 Development of 6/8 Time

The waltz meter is 3/4, which is to say, three beats per measure. 6/8 meter is a way of expanding 3/4 time, so that a measure of 6 pulses can be felt *either* as 2 beats or 3 beats per measure. This opens the doors to 2-against-3 syncopation possibilities, and this type of rhythm is employed and enjoyed by many of the world's cultures, for example, across Africa, Central and South America, the Middle East, and Asia. The player and listener can enjoy a sense of "multitasking" the simple arithmetic involving 2 and 3.

This mentally rich "play" is taken a step further in Madagascar, Réunion, and other Indian Ocean islands. The two-beat feel of the 6/8 time is retained, but the accent is flipped, by *displacing* it by an eighth note. Thus, the accent that was on **1** and **4** now gets moved to **2** and

5. The chords and measures still start on 1, but the unexpected "loud thing" happens on the 2 and 5. Taken as two triplets (123 123), we see that we have an accent on the 33% "and," as previously described.

The time perception of 6/8 can be organized in steps of increasing complexity, from Europe to the Indian Ocean islands.

1		**2**		**3**		The standard European waltz.
1	and	**2**	and	**3**	and	The standard European waltz with eighth-notes.
1	2	3	4	5	6	The standard European waltz with eighth-notes counted in six.
1	2	3	**4**	5	6	Six felt as two main pulses, as in Africa and Central and South America.
1	**2**	3	4	**5**	6	Flipped accent six, as in the Indian Ocean islands.

9 Rhythm in the West

Generally, African-American music is less polyrhythmic than African music. While there are brief, isolated events of a polyrhythmic nature in African-American music, there are very few examples of blues, swing, rhythm and blues, soul, or funk music that could be accurately described as truly having more than one basic meter. It is believed by the author that this is a direct result of two social phenomena. First, with the exception of New Orleans, black slaves in America were forbidden to have drums, because the slave owners were afraid of their potential use in communication. Second, the abundance in America of diatonic European instruments such as piano and guitar caused many attempts by African-Americans to adapt to the European forms and systems of music, emphasizing harmony and melody.

There was also a social trend toward assimilation and "proper" (read, European) music training. As a result, we hear many aspects of polyrhythmic thinking in short riffs, phrases, drum fills, etc., but never two musicians continuing to play 2 against 3 or other more complex polyrhythms.

10 Conclusion

Musicians who observe carefully can find the little moments of polyrhythm in this music, and then mentally extend them into continuous polyrhythms. Next time you hear any standard 4/4 pop music—that is music that is counted 1, 2, 3, 4—simply tap along and start counting the beats as 1, 2, 3, instead; it will educate your mind.

As a guitarist, the author has observed that four European traditions have had negative impacts on modern guitar-playing, causing most contemporary guitarists to be quite weak rhythmically. The first tradition is the hierarchical way of organizing groups of musicians, with rhythm delegated to the lower ranks, and "lead" melody considered more important. The second tradition is the focus on notes and scales, considered to be far more important than rhythm. The third is the "sports" attitude, which considers speed to be the primary measure of musical virtuosity. The fourth tradition is attempted standardization of what is considered a "good tone" (timbre) for one's instrument. These four ways of handling music contribute to the fact that most guitarists spend 95% of their time practicing scales and 5% or less practicing groove and timbral changes. Ironically, manipulation of groove and tone provide far greater range of expression and create so much more impact on listeners that rapidly played scales start to seem like a lot of work for little gain.

In every language thus far encountered by the author, people do not say "work music"; they say "play music." This is essential for musicians to realize. Using ideas of polyrhythms and timbres is an easy way to get more "play" from the music.

With large corporations commercializing "rock" music, the 4/4 rhythms of American pop music are taking over the world. In the same sense that biological species and human languages are rapidly disappearing, musical cultures are also dying out under the commercial onslaught of "globalization" of pop culture. Music is getting *less* complex and evolved, in order to reach wider and wider markets.

Listening to music from other, particularly non-Western, countries can be a wonderful musical education in and of itself. Tapping along in various ways as you listen will improve your appreciation of the music. Generally, only the best musicians get to record in non-Western countries, so that you are nearly always guaranteed to hear virtuosos playing on most non-Western recordings. In the West, the fully privatized media tends to marginalize artists who are not part of the corporate system. It is important to maintain one's own individual taste in music and freedom of choice.

11 Appendix

Current Releases		
2003	MAHIMA with Debashish Bhattacharya	WORLD MUSIC NETWORK (Global)
2003	Metric Time	private label
2002	DIGDIG Rene Lacaille Ensemble and Bob Brozman	WORLD MUSIC NETWORK (Global)
2001	LIVE NOW Recorded live on tour in the USA and Australia	private label
2001	NANKURU NAISA Takashi Hirayasu and Bob Brozman	RESPECT RECORD, LTD. (Japan)/WORLD MUSIC NETWORK (Global)
2001	IN THE SADDLE Ledward Kaapana and Bob Brozman	DANCING CAT/ WINDHAM HILL (USA)
2000	TONE POEMS 3: RESONATOR INSTRUMENTS David Grisman, Mike Auldridge, and Bob Brozman	ACOUSTIC DISC RECORDS (USA)
2000	OCEAN BLUES Djeli Moussa Diawara and Bob Brozman	MÉLODIE DISTRIBUTION (France)
2000	GET TOGETHER Woody Mann and Bob Brozman	ACOUSTIC MUSIC RECORDS (Germany)
2000	JIN JIN Takashi Hirayasu and Bob Brozman	WORLD MUSIC NETWORK (Global)
1999	THE RUNNING MAN	private label
1999	FOUR HandS SWEET & HOT Cyril Pahinui and Bob Brozman	DANCING CAT/ WINDHAM HILL (USA)
1998	KOSMIK BLUES & GROOVES	RDS-MUSIC (Germany)

Table 1. Bob Brozman's discography (most available at www.bobbrozman.com).

1998	SUNRISE Debashish & Subashish Bhattacharya with Bob Brozman	SAGARIKA (India)
1997	KIKA KILA MEETS KI HO'ALU Ledward Kaapana and Bob Brozman	DANCING CAT/ WINDHAM HILL (USA)
1997	GOLDENSLIDE	SKY RANCH/ VIRGIN EUROPE
1995	BLUES 'ROUND THE BEND	SKY RANCH/ VIRGIN EUROPE
1994	SLIDE A GO-GO	SKY RANCH/ VIRGIN EUROPE
1993	SLIDE CRAZY (compilation)	SKY RANCH/ VIRGIN EUROPE
1992	EVERYBODY SLIDES (compilation)	SKY RANCH/ VIRGIN EUROPE
1991	TRUCKLOAD OF BLUES	ROUNDER/ VIRGIN EUROPE
1989	REMEMBERING THE SONGS OF OUR YOUTH The Tau Moe Family and Bob Brozman	ROUNDER/ VIRGIN EUROPE
1988	DEVIL'S SLIDE	ROUNDER/ VIRGIN EUROPE
1985	HELLO, CENTRAL... GIVE ME DR. JAZZ	ROUNDER/ VIRGIN EUROPE
1983	SNAPPING THE STRINGS	KICKING MULE/ VIRGIN EUROPE
1981	BLUE HULA STOMP	KICKING MULE/ VIRGIN EUROPE
1978	CHEAP SUIT SERENADERS NUMBER 3	YAZOO/SHANACHIE
1974	YOUR PAL	(bootleg)

Table 1. (cont'd).

Annotated Bibliography

[1] Simon Broughton and Mark Ellingham. *The Rough Guide to World Music 01: Africa, Europe, and the Middle East.* New York: Penguin Books, 2000.

[2] Simon Broughton. *The Rough Guide to World Music 02: Latin and North America, the Caribbean, India, Asia, and the Pacific.* New York: Penguin Books, 2000.

[3] Bob Brozman. *The History and Artistry of National Resonator Instruments.* Anaheim, CA: Centerstream Publishing, 1994.

[4] Bob Brozman. Instructional video: "Rhythm in Your Riffs." Homespun Tapes. Available from World Wide Web (http://www.bobbrozman.com/), 2000.

[5] John Miller Chernoff. *African Rhythm and African Sensibility.* Chicago: University of Chicago Press, 1979.

[6] Jared Diamond. *Guns, Germs, and Steel.* New York: W. W. Norton & Co., 1999.

[7] Adam McGovern, editor. *Music Hound World: The Essential Album Guide.* Canton, MI: Visible Ink Press, 2000.

[8] Steven Pinker. *The Language Instinct: How the Mind Creates Language.* New York: Perennial, 2000.

[9] Kay Kaufman Shelemay. *Soundscapes.* New York: W. W. Norton & Co., 2000.

Human Experience

Spatial Emphasis of Game Audio: How to Create a Theatrically Enhanced Audio Experience

Richard Bailey

1 Introduction

Adding a few simple techniques to our games can help create an aural illusion of space, greatly enhancing the game's virtual environment.

In this article I will discuss such techniques including ways in which volume levels and Doppler shift of sounds can be boosted or cut to provide a theatrical (if physically inaccurate, unrealistic) effect. I will also explore a system that allows for automatic tuning and management of these volumes (mix levels) based on camera and player positions.

The term *spatialization* describes the ability to discern an object's position and velocity (its change in position). Sound travels at fairly constant speeds, and our ears have the ability to discern very slight changes in arrival time, phase, frequency, and amplitude. This sense gives us the ability to recognize the direction from which a sound comes and the rate at which it is moving relative to us.

Other articles in this volume describe how the sophisticated Head Related Transfer Function (HRTF) technique is used to physically simulate how the human perceives sound as it arrives and interacts with their head, shoulders, and pinnae, for the ultimate in spatial realism. Game players are, however, more likely to compare the game audio experience to that of an action movie rather than reality; after all, how many of us have ever jumped a speeding car off a bridge or shot fully automatic weapons?

In movies, sound mixers adjust levels to emphasize the hero's car or the villain's footsteps behind us. These mix levels are tested and tweaked until the desired effect is achieved. In games, we desire to achieve a range of mixes that dynamically vary in response to real-time *gameplay*.

2 Distorted Reality

During gameplay, the volume levels of every sound contributing to the mix are determined, mostly by physics formulae, based on the distance and relative position of the sound and player (listener). How these levels change can make a huge difference in how the player perceives the game. By further adjusting the levels of sound sent to the players beyond the values determined using physics, we can exaggerate the perception of distance and position. For instance, by adjusting the Doppler calculations and rate of change in volumes, we can exaggerate the perception of speed and change in position.

The addition of speakers behind the player, as found in the increasingly common surround sound systems, allows movies and games to extend our perception of the space beyond the visual screen that displays the action. However, even in this situation it may be desirable to deviate from the laws of physical reality to improve gameplay. For instance, in a racing game it can be advantageous for the car behind the player to be louder than the car in front. Since the player can already see the cars in front of them, providing an audio emphasis of the same cars by boosting their volume contributes little to the gameplay. It is much more useful, however, to boost the volume of the cars behind the player. Boosting the level of cars behind the player provides additional information that is not visually apparent, thereby enhancing both gameplay and immersion in the game world. An additional technique is to exaggerate the panned location of the sound of the car behind the player. This will enhance the player's perception of the car's position as it moves from one side to the other, thus improving the ability of the player to determine the position of the other car/player even when out of sight. (See Figure 1.)

Unfortunately, the sound library software interfaces provided to game developers to control HRTF spatialization, Doppler, and distance rolloff features are not flexible enough to accommodate the use of the theatrical exaggeration techniques discussed in this article. Current audio systems are designed to implement straightforward physics, and a game developer's desire to selectively exaggerate reality was not anticipated.

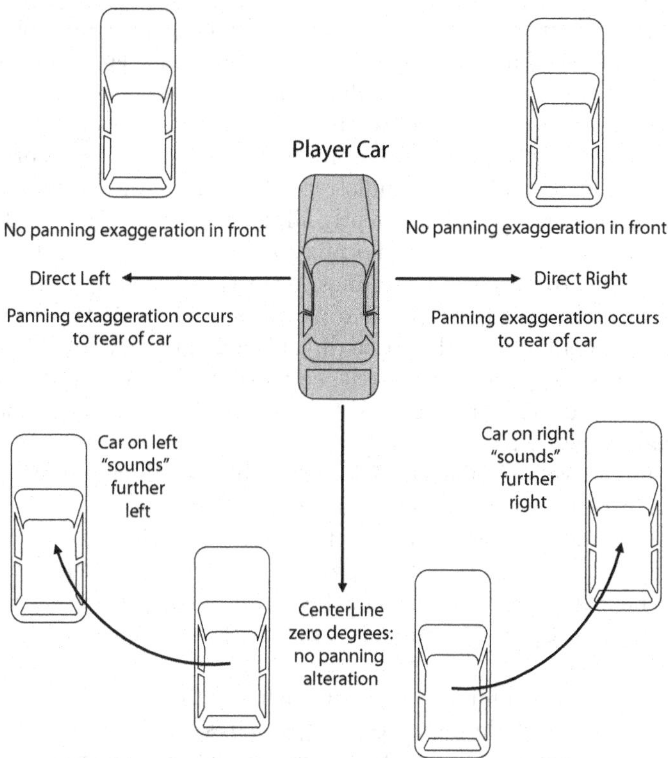

Figure 1. Rear emphasis of lateral panning: how the volume level of other players can be boosted based on relative position and angle from the player in order to emphasize and exaggerate the horizontal movement of the player.

3 Camera vs. the Listener

Let's consider what often changes in a movie soundtrack when the camera pans during a scene. The director often uses audio to draw the movie-goer's attention to the desired action in the picture. For instance, the soundtrack in a scene depicting two people conversing in a noisy crowded room might emphasize the focus of scene, the conversation, by raising its level in the mix and deemphasize other unimportant sonic elements by attenuating and filtering them. The technique and resulting effect may be obvious or very subtle.

During the filming of a movie, directional microphones are hoisted on booms to capture sounds from specific parts of a scene. For instance each actor might have their own microphone and another microphone might be used to capture the ambient sound of the location such as a brook, breeze, or café buzz. The signal from each microphone is recorded on its own track of the multitrack audio recorder so that the contribution of each microphone may be independently adjusted or even eliminated in the final mix. To create the final audio mix for the film, the sound designer combines sound from these recordings, adjusting the levels throughout the scene and mixing in additional sound effects. It is at this time that the multi-channel levels of the three-dimensional sounds are authored. If we want to raise the gaming experience to that of a Hollywood feature film, then game developers will need to implement similar audio facilities in their game engines.

We can achieve a similar effect in games by introducing a few simple concepts. First we need to include a notion of *camera focus.* Here I am referring to camera focus not as the focal length of the lens, but rather as the target or subject that the camera is intending to keep in frame. This may be a single player currently being followed by the camera. This notion of camera focus may already exist in the camera system of your game.

Next, create a volume control for each type or category of sound. Categories might include Guns, Footsteps, Tires, Collisions, Engines, or Exhaust. Additionally, we create the set of volume controls for every category of sound for objects having camera focus, as well as objects *not* having camera focus. So, for instance, we might have volume controls for FocusGuns, FocusTires, as well as for NonFocusGuns, and NonFocus-Tires. A gun shot sound occurring on a gun that currently is the focus of the camera would play at the FocusGun volume level. Other Guns not in focus would play at the NonFocusGun volume level. This simple and tunable feature is a great resource to sound designers as they tune the game's audio experience.

For added flexibility, if the game supports multiple camera angles, allow these levels to be set for each camera angle. This now becomes the primary audio identity for camera angles. I call this set of mix levels for each camera definition the *Listener Perspective.* (See Figure 2.)

Note that a Listener Perspective can include any parameters that your audio system supports such as filters to muffle non-focus players sounds or exaggerate Doppler.

Volume emphasis is one way to change the game audio spatialization to deliver an improved gameplay experience. Doppler emphasis can create

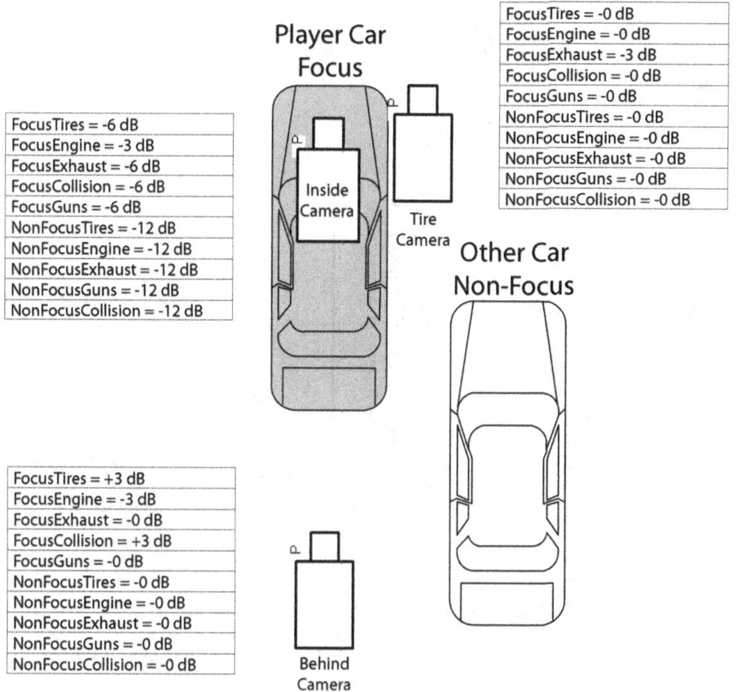

Figure 2. Listener perspective: how a systems can allow audio designers to "tune" the levels of each type of sound for each camera angle.

an increased sense of velocity. The Doppler pitch shift is a direct representation of the difference in velocity of a sound source from the listener hearing the sound. In movies, Doppler pitches have been increasingly exaggerated in order to make things seem like they are moving ever faster. Because of this, many games deliver Doppler pitch shifts of 1.5 to 2 times the physically correct real-world amounts in order to create the desired sense of speed.

The emphasis applied to effects like Doppler can also be accentuated such that a car passing at 10 MPH might be accompanied by the physically correct Doppler shift, but as the car passing approaches 90 MPH we desire it to sound as though it is traveling at a much higher speed, perhaps 170 MPH. As previously stated, most sound systems do not provide a convenient way for game developers to override the Doppler calculation, without completely disabling Doppler calculation and manually applying the pitch shift to each sound. (See Figure 3.)

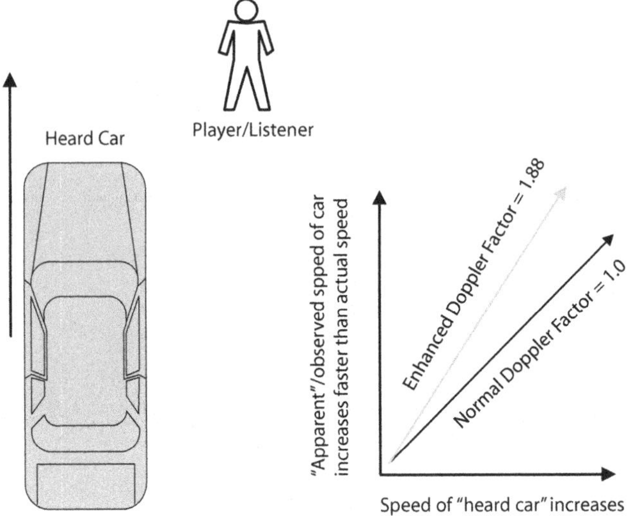

Doppler factor is ratio of observed speed compared to actual speed

At 10 MPH, observed speed is 10 MPH; Doppler factor is 10 MPH/10 MPH = 1.0

At 90 MPH, observed speed is 170 MPH; Doppler factor is 170 MPH/90 MPH = 1.88

Figure 3. Dynamic adjustment of Doppler factor: how Doppler pitch shift can be exaggerated to emphasize speed of other players.

4 Conclusion

It is important to experiment. Listen carefully to the soundtracks of movies you know well to learn how that director and sound designer managed audio. Take notes. Pay special attention to movies of a genre similar to that of your game. Imagine what effects could improve immersion or add excitement to your game. For instance, try boosting the Doppler shift of a car approaching from behind to create a sense that the player is going to be passed suddenly. Or try attenuating the game's ambient sounds as the villain sneaks up on the player to create the "calm before the storm" creepiness of silence commonly used in movies. Try a few simple ideas, and add tunable controls to allow the audio designer to play with the concept.

As mentioned, creating a theatrically enhanced audio experience often is at odds with audio system features designed to accurately recreate reality such as HRTF, standard distance volume roll-off, and standard static Doppler shift. Future audio systems may start to recognize the need for theatrical perception of audio rather than realistic perception of audio. Until then, it is up to us as game audio programmers to empower audio designers to deliver the rich experiences they strive for while at the same time working around the limitations of existing systems.

Annotated Bibliography

[1] Ken Greenebaum and Ronen Barzel. *Audio Anecdotes I: Tools, Tips, and Techniques for Digital Audio.* Natick, MA: A K Peters, 2004.

I value this text for the pragmatic approach used to describe the concepts of spatialization in audio.

[2] P. Horowitz and W. Hill. *The Art of Electronics.* Cambridge, UK: Cambridge University Press, 1990.

This text has the best description of the Decibel of any I have seen. It thoroughly describes dB amplitude, dB power, and dB Sound Pressure Level (SPL) as well as giving formulas for each.

[3] D. Resnick, R. Halliday, and K. S. Krane. *Physics.* New York: John Wiley & Sons, 1992.

As is common in many basic texts on physics, this one has good chapters describing sounds and acoustics.

[4] Thomas D. Rossig. *The Science of Sound.* Reading, MA: Addison-Wesley, 1982.

This text has excellent chapters on sound propagation, Doppler, absorption, and psycho-acoustics.

[5] Carl E. Seashore. *Psychology of Music.* New York: Dover, 1967.

This text began to shift the way that I would think about audio away from the physics and more toward the human factor. Though the text specifically focuses on music, it covers much in the area of perception of sounds. It also covers a significant amount of terminology to describe how sounds are similar and different from each other.

Auditory Psychophysics: Basic Concepts and Implications for DAC Quantization

James Ballas and Hesham Fouad

1 Introduction

This article provides an introduction to auditory psychophysics, which is the study and understanding of how certain aspects of auditory perception are related to the measurable properties of sound. Understanding these relationships can help an engineer or software developer know when to be highly precise about sound computation, and when precise computation might not matter. It should help to explain instances when what you hear doesn't seem consistent with what you have programmed. It might even help you separate the chaff from the substance in commercial advertisements. However, there is a caveat. The relationships between auditory perception and quantifiable aspects of the sound are very complex, and a short overview such as this can only provide an introduction and one detailed example of how DAC quantization might relate to intensity perception, especially intensity difference perception.

The reader will want to explore the articles in this series that deal with other aspects of auditory psychophysics: Henrique S. Malvar's article "Auditory Masking in Audio Compression" (see *Audio Anecdotes I*) provides a detailed treatment of another psychophysical phenomenon, auditory masking, and how it is used in audio compression algorithms; Derek DiFilippo's articles (the first of which is co-authored with Ken

Greenebaum), "Introduction to the Theory of Signal Detection: Measuring Human Response" and "Perceivable Auditory Latencies" (see *Audio Anecdotes I*), discuss perceptual latency as well as signal detection; and Al Bregman and Wieslaw Woszczyk's articles, "Controlling the Perceptual Organization of Sound: Guidelines Derived from Principles of Audio Scene Analysis (ASA)" (see *Audio Anecdotes I*) and "Creating Mixtures: The Application of Auditory Scene Analysis (ASA) to Audio Recording" (page 39), discuss guidelines based on Audio Scene Analysis. Also, readers not comfortable with decibels (dB) should read Hesham Fouad's introduction, "Understanding the Decibel" (see *Audio Anecdotes I*).

2 A Brief Overview of Auditory Psychophysics

Psychophysics has a long history, having been founded by Gustov Fechner in the nineteenth century. The field is concerned both with the description of psychophysical principles and with the experimental methods for studying them. Here, the emphasis will be on the principles, rather than the methods. For additional information on methods, see [1] or [5].

Psychophysics is defined as *"the science that deals with the quantitative relationship between physical and psychological events"* [11]. It is a science that addresses all the senses, but the focus here is on auditory psychophysics and the relationships between physical auditory events and psychological auditory events. Even so, this definition is very broad because there is an immense number of psychological events that might be of interest. For example, we might be interested in aspects of musical perception, such as rhythm, style, melody, etc. Each of these is a psychological event in that a listener, upon hearing a musical selection, can have an experience with each of these and describe it to others. To develop a psychophysical principle, you have to define precisely the psychological event of interest. Because the development of the quantitative relationships is quite difficult, only a few psychological events have been studied in sufficient detail to be able to define quantitative relationships. There are four of them and they can be simply defined as follows:

- Can you hear the sound at all? (Detection)
- Can you hear the difference when the sound is changed? (Discrimination)
- How does your judgment or experience of magnitude change as the sound is changed? (Scaling)
- What is the sound? (Identification)

These four questions have been the focus of psychophysics; answers to these have both practical and theoretical significance. For example, detection (and to some extent discrimination) psychophysics is employed in audiometric tests for hearing loss. Psychophysical research in detection and discrimination processes is the foundation for theories of auditory mechanisms. Answers to all questions are specific to the type of auditory dimension being investigated, such as loudness, pitch, or timbre. Each of these has been studied intensely, and controversy still exists about the basics. To simplify the further description of psychophysics, only one dimension will be covered here in additional detail. This is the dimension of sound intensity, which leads to the perception of loudness. Malvar's article covers the perception of frequency and what it means for masking and the design of compression algorithms.

3 Detection

The detection question takes up the issue of absolute sensitivity to the intensity of a sound, when there are no other sounds, or with other sounds present (e.g., see Malvar's article). Finding quantitative relationships between sound intensity and detection is a complex task for several reasons. First, the auditory system is incredibly sensitive. The nominal absolute threshold is 0dB SPL, or 0.0002 dyne/cm^2, when the sound is about 3 kHz. This is within 20 dB of the pressure that would be exerted by Brownian motion of air molecules [7]. At this pressure, the eardrum is only moving the diameter of a hydrogen atom.

A second reason for the complexity of determining detection relationships is that many factors will affect the outcome, including the sound parameters. For example, maximum sensitivity depends on the frequency of the sound, as illustrated by the lowest of the Fletcher-Munson curves (see Malvar's article), which shows threshold levels as a function of the frequency of the sound.

A third reason is that noise is prevalent in many of the components including the sound generation devices and the human auditory system, and these noise levels will affect the threshold measurements. Therefore, detection decisions are influenced by the properties of the noise, and the quantifiable relationships must reflect these influences. The theory of signal detection was developed to model the effects of noise on detection decisions, and its components, such as the Receiver Operating Curve (ROC, sometimes called the Receiver Operating Characteristic), are well-established in the field. This subject is beyond the scope of this article, although some further details are provided in "An Introduction to Sound Classification" (page 233). Finally, procedures used to assess the relationships may have subtle influences on the outcomes. Several procedures have been developed, several by the founder of psychophysics, Gustov Fechner (e.g., method of limits, constant stimuli and adjustment), and others more recently (staircase, forced choice) which minimize or quantify experimental effects such as bias to produce a particular result (e.g., hearing loss for disability reimbursement, hearing normal for continued employment). Some procedures have been adopted as standards (e.g., [12]) and it is a good idea to use these wherever possible.

4 Discrimination

Once above threshold, the psychological event for intensity perception is discrimination. Perceived intensity differences are called Just Noticeable Differences (JNDs) or Difference Limens (DLs). The general psychophysical relationship is that the JND depends on the level of the sound; as the level increases, larger intensity differences are required to be noticeable. This relationship is known as Weber's law:

$$k = \Delta I / I, \tag{1}$$

where I is the intensity of the sound at the base or background level, ΔI is the amount of increase or decrease in intensity that must occur to be noticed, and k is a value that is generally the same for the middle ranges of I. The constant k is called the Weber fraction and it is the proportionate change that must occur to be noticed.

The Weber fraction for a 1000 Hz tone is about 0.1. This means that the JND for intensity is about 10% of the level. But empirical studies [9] indicate that the fraction increases as I decreases and is about 0.5 near the threshold of hearing. This decrease is called the near miss to Weber's law, and is incorporated in the following equation from [9]:

$$\Delta I / I = 0.463 (I / I_0)^{-0.072}, \tag{2}$$

where I_0 is the intensity in dB at the threshold of audibility.

An approximation of the JND in dB [9, 10] is given by

$$DL = 1.644 dB - 0.0141 * SL, \tag{3}$$

where SL is the intensity in dB above the threshold of audibility.

It should be noted that experimental data on intensity discrimination are expressed in different ways, and different experimental procedures give somewhat different results (see [9], [10] for examples of different measures and paradigms for measuring intensity discrimination).

5 Scaling

Once a threshold and perceptible steps above the threshold are known, a numeric scale can be developed. The form of this scale is the critical issue. Fechner assumed that a geometric increase in the physical stimulus was accompanied by an arithmetic increase in the resulting sensation. This is known as Fechner's law:

$$\Psi = k\log I. \tag{4}$$

where Ψ is the psychological magnitude.

While empirical research on intensity perception (both in audition and vision) and perception of weights are consistent with a logarithmic function, not all psychophysical relationships are explained by a logarithmic function (i.e., pain perception); and Stevens proposed a power law instead:

$$\Psi = kI^n. \tag{5}$$

Here, the exponent varies with the phenomena. For loudness judgments, the exponent is about 0.6. Exponents for other phenomena are given in nearly any book on psychophysics (e.g., [1]).

6 Identification

With identification, one is interested in measuring how many different sounds a person can consistently identify. Given the large dynamic range of intensity that a person can perceive, one might expect that a listener could learn to identify a large number of sounds using intensity alone. However, in a classic paper, Miller [13] argued that there was a limit of about five to nine in the number of identifiable levels for phenomena like loudness. There are obvious exceptions to this rule, such as perfect pitch. But for untrained, ordinary listeners, the number of sounds that can be identified by listening to the level of a single property is remarkably small. Durlach and Braida [4], in an important series of papers, concluded that two types of noise account for this limitation: sensory and memory noise. For intensity and loudness perception, their papers provide a comprehensive approach that can integrate the data from detection to identification experiments into a single theory. Both sensory and memory factors are important in the identification of everyday sounds [2].

7 Practical Implications of Psychophysics: DAC Quantization and Intensity JNDs

Psychophysics can help in understanding how to design and use audio hardware and software. For example, one might be interested in knowing the capabilities and limitations of current sound cards. Many of these use 24 bits to encode the level of a sound; 24 bits can represent a large dynamic range of sound (~120 dB) which may seem to be adequate. However, can the dynamic range of intensity perception be properly represented using 24-bit PCM coding? Using psychophysics, we will show how 24-bit quantization will produce level differences larger than the JND for intensity especially at low intensities, and what happens with amplification.

The type of system that we are considering is illustrated in Figure 1. We are using a DAC to produce waveforms, which are amplified and drive a speaker. This is a notional, hypothetical system which has a DAC that can produce a 1-volt, peak-to-peak output, and an amplifier that can translate the peak DAC output to about 140 dB SPL. A sound level meter measures the output in order to translate the output into units that can be compared to psychophysical data. We assume that the system is linear throughout. Hartmann [8] says that this assumption is reasonable, especially with the improving technology. With this assumption, the voltage changes from the sound card will produce equivalent changes in the sound level meter [3]. For example, a doubling of the DAC output will produce a +6 dB in voltage and +6 dB in sound pressure.

A 24-bit DAC can produce a maximum value of 16,777,216, which is comparable to 144 dB in relative change if translated to voltage level, so theoretically, a 24-bit DAC can replicate the immense dynamic range of human hearing. The range of human hearing is quite large. At the

Figure 1. Illustration of notional system.

maximum, when one starts to feel pain, sound levels approach 140 dB SPL. The psychophysical question we ask is whether the DAC can produce changes smaller than the JND throughout this range and in particular at the threshold of hearing.

Assume that we have a 1-bit change. What will this produce in sound pressure level and how does it compare to the JND near the threshold of hearing? The first bit change would be a single step above the combined noise level of the sound card, the amplifier, and the speaker or headphone equipment. This calculation will vary by equipment, so to simplify the calculation, let us assume that there is no voltage loss in the system, that the noise is very small, and consider a single bit increase above setting the first bit. This would double the voltage output and produce a +6 dB increase in sound pressure level. Thus the first step is quite large in terms of dB. Is this change greater than the JND at the threshold of hearing? Yes, definitely, since the JND at threshold is about 2 dB. Perhaps this approach is too simple. Would an increase of 1 bit above the first bit really produce this type of change?

An alternative analysis confirms this result. Davis and Davis [3, Figure 3-31] provide a figure illustrating relationships between different scales, including the notional relationship between dB SPL (with a range of 80 dB to 150 dB) and the effective voltage across 600 ohms (.00775 to 24.5 volts). Using the data in their table, the following equation is obtained:

$$\text{dB SPL} = 150.169 + \log_{10}(\text{voltage}). \qquad (6)$$

From this equation, if we set the amplification in the notional system so that a 24-bit DAC will produce at its maximum setting of 24 bits 150 dB SL from 1 volt, then the voltages produced by the first two binary steps would be 5.96 E-08 and 1.19 E-07, and the dB SL for the these two levels would be 5.32 dB and 11.35 dB, respectively, a difference of about 6 dB. This is illustrated in Figure 2, which shows the notional output of the system in sensation level as the bits setting is increased, the differences with each bit change, and the approximated JNDs at each output level using Equation (3). Note that at the threshold of hearing, one can discriminate about a 2 dB change in intensity, but the output of the notional system is well above this, so even a 24-bit DAC, if mapped to the full output range of human hearing, cannot reproduce step changes at the lowest levels that are less than what can be discriminated.

Obviously, reduced amplification levels will effectively compress the dynamic range and correspondingly the single-bit intensity differences potentially to sub-JND levels.

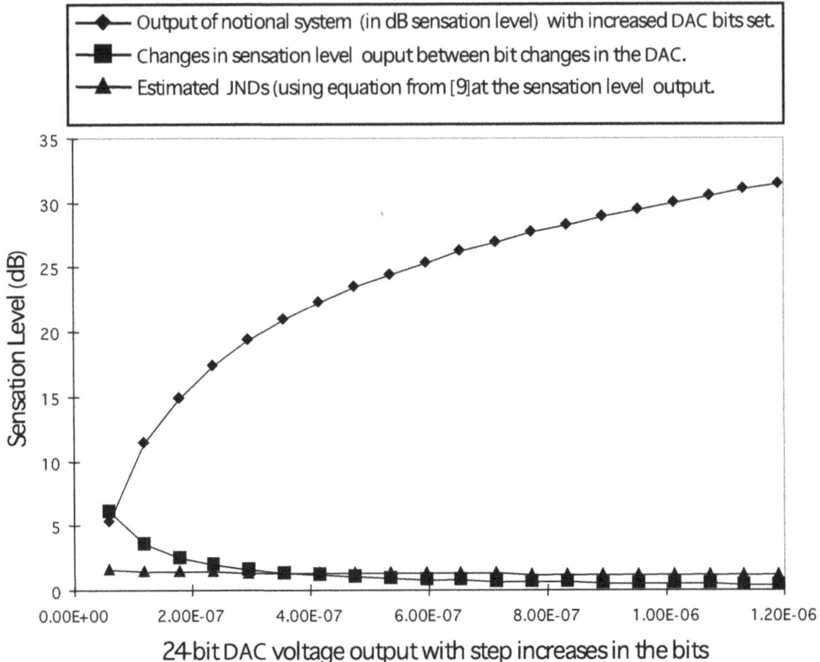

Figure 2. Quantization steps (in dB sensation level) for the twenty lowest voltage levels from a 24-bit DAC compared to approximated JNDs.

In conclusion, we return to the purpose of this article and ask how this hypothetical example supports the value of understanding psychophysics? It illustrates that computational precision, in terms of a single-bit change, is more critical at the threshold of hearing than in the middle ranges. It would explain why a single-bit change would sound different near the threshold compared to a change in the middle of the DAC output range. The example illustrates that modern DAC capabilities still have limitations when evaluated against the impressive psychophysical capabilities of human hearing.

8 Acknowledgment

Preparation of this paper was sponsored by the Office of Naval Research. The opinions herein are those of the authors and do not necessarily represent the opinions of ONR.

Annotated Bibliography

[1] J. C. Baird and E. Noma, *Fundamentals of Scaling and Psychophysics.* New York: John Wiley & Sons, Inc., 1978.

Baird and Noma provide an insightful and understandable description of psychophysics that is unique in showing relationships between different psychophysical approaches that are based upon a common framework throughout.

[2] J. A. Ballas. "Common Factors in the Identification of an Assortment of Brief Everyday Sounds." *Journal of Experimental Psychology* 19:2 (1993), 250–267.

This paper is a series of experiments (five in all) that address "how we identify and perceive everyday sounds" like footsteps, door closings, hammering, etc. The paper also includes data on how often the sounds might occur in everyday environments. The results support the conclusion that acoustic, cognitive, and ecological factors all have to be considered. Additionally, the results provide evidence of many similarities in the perceptual and cognitive processing of environmental sounds and speech.

[3] D. Davis and C. Davis. *Sound System Engineering,* 2nd *Edition.* Indianapolis, IN: Howard W. Sams, 1987.

[4] N. I. Durlach and L. D. Braida. "Intensity Perception I: Preliminary Theory of Intensity Resolution." *Journal of the Acoustical Society of America* 46 (1969), 372–383.

This is the first in an important series of papers that present a theoretical framework, supported by experiments, that explains the detection, scaling and identification of sound intensity. The theory includes both sensory and memory factors, including sensory and memory noise.

[5] J. C. Falmagne. "Psychophysical Measurement and Theory." In *Handbook of Perception and Human Performance, Volume I: Sensory Processes and Perception*, edited by K. R. Boff, L. Kaufman and J. P. Thomas, pp. 1-1–1-66. New York: John Wiley & Sons, 1986.

This chapter, together with the chapter by Scharf and Buus in the same volume, provides a comprehensive treatise on psychophysics.

[6] H. Fouad, J. K. Hahn, and J. A. Ballas. "Perceptually Based Scheduling Algorithms for Real-Time Synthesis of Complex Sonic Environments: Extensible Toolkit for Creating Virtual Sonic Environments." In *Proceedings of the Fourth International Conference on Auditory Display*, edited by E. Mynatt and J. A. Ballas, pp. 77–81. Palo Alto, CA: ICAD, 1997.

Highly complex auditory environments are difficult to synthesize in real-time. In this paper, the authors explain how algorithms can be based on perceptual factors to schedule limited computational resources when the computation must be incomplete in order to meet the real-time constraint.

[7] D. M. Green. *An Introduction to Hearing.* New York: Erlbaum, 1976.

David Green provides an introduction to hearing that includes an analysis of the phenomenal sensitivity of human hearing.

[8] W. M. Hartmann. *Signals, Sound, and Sensation.* New York: Springer-Verlag, 1997.

Hartmann provides one of the few sources that includes a rigorous and comprehensive treatise not only on the sensation/perception of sound but also on the physics and mathematics of sounds as signals.

[9] W. Jesteadt, C. C. Wier, and D. M. Green. "Intensity Discrimination as a Function of Frequency and Sensation Level." *Journal of the Acoustical Society of America* 61 (1977), 169–177.

This is an important original paper on intensity discrimination.

[10] B. Scharf and S. Buus. "Audition I: Stimulus, Physiology, Thresholds." In *Handbook of Perception and Human Performance, Volume I: Sensory Processes and Perception*, edited by K. R. Boff, L. Kaufman, and J. P. Thomas, pp. 14-1–14-71. New York: John Wiley & Sons, 1986.

This chapter, together with the chapter by Falmagne in the same volume, provides a comprehensive treatise on psychophysics.

[11] American National Standards Institute, Standard (ANSI S3.20-1973), "Psychoacoustical Terminology," New York (1973).

[12] American National Standards Institute, Standard (ANSI S3.21-2004), "Methods for Manual Pure-Tone Threshold Audiometry," New York (2004).

[13] G. A. Miller. "The Magical Number Seven, Plus or Minus Two: Some Limits on Our Capacity for Processing Information." *Psychological Review* 63 (1956), 81–97.

This is a classic paper on how human cognitive processing is involved in basic psychophysical processing.

Why the Audiocomputer Is Inevitable

Mark Stahlman

Computing is entering a new and challenging era; our "Crisis of Complexity" is becoming an increasingly pressing problem that must be targeted with innovative solutions. Major causes of this crisis have been architectures designed without an understanding of lessons learned from human physiology. This mismatch between humans and computers is most pronounced in the area of user interface. Since, as humans, we employ a combination of sight and sound to make sense of our world, what is most clearly missing in today's interface designs is an adequate inclusion of audition. Inclusion of features which integrate sound into interface designs as well as their underlying architectures will provide promising opportunities.

1 We Are Auditory Creatures

Humans are principally distinguished (from other higher primates) by having what is known as an auditory integrator—our capacity to communicate through hearing and speaking—despite our frequent inclination to think of ourselves as more biased towards sight.

Whether it was 50,000 or 100,000 years ago (paleontologists continue to refine these dates), it is widely agreed that the last set of biological adaptations that led to the development of our species (*Homo sapiens sapiens*—"man who is wise about being wise") included significant changes to our anatomy and neurology in the closely linked functional areas of speech and hearing.

This combined system—vocal cords, inner ear, related musculature, and the complex of neurological and physiological features that allow us to both speak and hear—appears to develop from a common cluster in the human embryo and, taken together, is often referred to collectively as the auditory integrator.

While recent research has dropped the percentage of genes that we share with chimps (our closest evolutionary cousin) from 98% to 95%, the net is the same... in our zoological class, it is only humans that can speak, hear, and understand "languages" and it is this capacity to integrate (i.e., make intelligible) sounds which most clearly makes us potentially "wise" about the world in which we live.

We hear in the womb (long before we can see), possess no "ear-lids," and continue to sense the world through hearing even as we sleep. Paleoanthropologists agree that our species' fundamental "survival" capacity is intimately associated with our "social bonding" and "task collaboration"—both of which are grounded in the biological adaptations that gave us the capability for speech-hearing-based communications.

While we're on the topic of human development, we must point to the subsequent stage—which is not believed to be "genetic" or the result of biological "adaptations"—through which we developed external storage systems for collecting our knowledge. These later systems clearly rely more on our sense of vision than on our auditory integrator.

While the world created by the alphabet (as well as pictographic and ideographic writing systems) and the cultures of manuscripts and eventually print are not principally auditory media environments, however important these past 2,000 years of visual bias might be, it is not our eyes that make us biologically human; it is our ears.

And, therefore, to match ourselves, computer interfaces need to reflect a balance of both the visual and auditory senses.

2 We Live in a Simultaneous Information Space

Much has been learned about how humanity gradually became biased towards our linear, sequential visual sense, beginning, in some accounts, in the sixth century BCE with the increasing importance of literacy (and specifically the introduction of the complete alphabet by the Greeks) and the displacement of our earlier orality-dominated cultures.

Crucially, it is this same research about these ancient sensory biases which informs us that the dominance of the eye over the ear has been largely set aside in our own times. For better or worse, the eye no longer rules our lives!

Marshall McLuhan's contribution to the study of the environmental character of media is a particularly important guidepost in understanding these transitions in human sensory bias. Human culture endlessly spins webs of inventions that first extend our own biology and then become so powerful, they are overwhelming and scarcely noticed.

Writing reshaped civilization. So did printing. And, most recently, by extending our inventions to operate at the speed of our own nervous systems, we have completely recast our environment with electricity.

From the middle of the nineteenth century, as electricity began to speed up the flow of information—in particular the appearance of a collage of the "news" from around the world on newspaper front pages, made possible by the telegraph, followed by the global reach of radio and then television—we shifted away from our centuries-old accumulated linear, sequential visual bias.

With this shift, we began to experience the strange sensations of being "immersed" in information, surrounded, almost submerged in a cacophonic sea of impressions which has now brought us to the World Wide Web and the feeling of almost drowning in an overload of "information."

Yes, this characteristic of being surrounded by "input"—360 degrees, 24 hours, 7 days a week—is the sensory model of sound, not sight. Our modern information environment is psychologically "auditory," yet we experience it through a variety of "visual" graphic display means! Psychologically, the Internet "speaks" to us, it doesn't "write" to us. No wonder our computing experience is so messed up!

3 Our Sensory Mismatch Buries Us in Complexity

IBM Research has brilliantly and convincingly described the core crisis that computing/networking faces today—we confront a crisis of complexity.

If we do not radically simplify our systems, we will increasingly consume more and more economic resources, "fixing" the exponentially increasing "problems" caused by these ever-more complex computer systems. At some point, we will literally run out of people to make all the fixes/upgrades/repairs demanded by designs that are inherently insecure and incapable of self-diagnosis and self-repair.

IBM Research describes the solution to this crisis as "Autonomic Computing." And, broadly defined, this is a reasonable and hopeful prescription that draws on the biological analogy of adding an autonomic nervous system to the already deployed analog of our central nervous system. Now, what's the prognosis?

Understandably, IBM Sales (or Sun Sales or Microsoft Sales) first attempts to turn this crisis into a more narrowly defined opportunity for add-ons to the existing installed base. New "layers" are spec'ed out and pitched to increasingly overburdened customers. What is not considered, however, in the sales literature of any of the major vendors, is an open consideration of the alternative—scrapping much of the existing installed base of computers and networks in favor of radically simple new architectures.

What is also not considered is an evaluation of how we got into this mess in the first place. Could "standard" digital computer architecture—in some sense—be the problem?

We continue to build more and more complex linear/sequential logic-engines (or what the father of cybernetics, Norbert Wiener, called "arbitrarily complex feedback mechanisms")—exhibiting, in good engineering fashion, our pre-electric *visual* sensory biases—without pausing to consider that we live in a world that cannot be adequately understood (and thus "managed") by piling linear complexity on top of linear complexity. Wiener favored analog computing. Was he "wrong"?

Carver Mead has also had some interesting things to say—albeit largely about vision—regarding the need for VLSI analog circuit design. Is he also "wrong"?

Could our *ancient* bias towards "writing systems" (favoring our linear/sequential visual integrator and disadvantaging our nonlinear/simultaneous auditory integrator) potentially have contributed to pointing us into the apparent dead-end crisis of complexity that we increasingly appear to be rushing towards?

4 New Technology Offers Potential to Resolve Crisis of Complexity

IBM isn't the only one who has been spending R&D dollars on addressing this looming complexity crisis. There is a massive field of computer science research, sometimes called "Human-Centered Computing" (HCC), which allocates billions annually to a wide range of problems that cluster around the periphery of this crisis.

In fact, at the most recent "Olympics of Computer Science," the every-four-year ACM ONE event, the vast majority of exhibited technology could be termed HCC. When ACM ONE event chairman Bob Metcalfe found himself trying to sum up the entire conference and exhibit in one word, to his surprise he simply said, "Human."

Maybe Professor Michael Dertouzos—who spoke eloquently at the most recent ACM ONE—influenced Metcalfe's decision. And, perhaps Dertouzos' most meaningful memorial is the HCC-focused Oxygen Project at MIT that he organized—the foundations for which he details in his recent book, *The Unfinished Revolution.* Moreover (and as shown at MIT as well as dozens of leading research organizations worldwide), the accumulated work of nearly 20 years in computer science—focused on everything from memory architecture to programming languages—can potentially be brought to bear on this crisis.

Everything that we have learned about designing self-repairing/fault-tolerant, artificially "intelligent," secure/robust, and richly data-capable computer architectures takes on new relevance in this context. Fine, but what about audio and the audiocomputer?

5 Audio User Interfaces Might Add 10x More Acuity

It would be disingenuous to suggest that merely migrating user interfaces towards the use of "Audicons" (as described in Roberts and Sikora's article, "Auditory Feedback for Computer Devices" (see *Audio Anecdotes II*)) would solve all (or even most) of our problems.

Indeed, even the full-blown audiocomputer with a new hardware/software architecture that could literally speak to and hear from us—engaging our biological capacity to make sense through "conversation"—will not be enough.

Nonetheless, it is clear that we desperately need a new user interface paradigm among the many elements needed to redirect the computer industry by deploying breakthroughs. It is likely to also become clear that this new user interface must integrate sound in order to permit us to properly use our own inherent biological capacity to sense "meaning" in the world.

Our machines are not only overly complex, but we are also hampered and, in many ways, rendered overly "simple" by current interface limitations—compounding the crisis we now face. We all become, relative to our broader birthright, "dummies" or worse yet, fixated on the minutia of ridiculously complex systems, unable to see the meaningful solutions forest for the trivial technology trees.

With the narrowly focused attention required by the "tunnel-vision" of even the largest graphic display (or cluster of displays), we tend to block out the rest of the world, where most of the important action takes place. Just like the "abstraction" of our designs, we "become what we behold" and abstract ourselves from the larger picture.

How would an interface work that didn't require us to visually fall down Alice's rabbit-hole? How would a fully integrated sound and sight user experience strike us?

We hear and speak in three dimensions. Much is now known about our accuracy of localization in audition and sound reproduction. The sphere of audition is potentially far richer in detail than the narrow cone of visible presentation. What would the overall increase in acuity be for a well-designed interface that employs *both* auditory and visual cues? Might this combination yield enough of an increase in capability—10-fold, for instance—to lead to a basic swing in user acceptance?

QWERTY is, as we all know, a deliberately suboptimal design based on the limitations of nineteenth-century typewriter mechanisms. Nothing has replaced this design since no alternate keyboard layout can overcome the inherent limitations of all keyboards. No keyboard is 10 times better than a QWERTY keyboard.

So, without jumping off the keyboard, we're stuck. A. B. C.

Asking people to become scribes—with any of the various writing tablet designs—doesn't really change things all that much. Writing is still visual—manuscript "culture" as opposed to print "culture"—still linear, and still sequential (despite "drawing" options) and, thus, still fundamentally unlike our daily experience of being "surrounded" by a sphere of simultaneous information. Reading is not hearing writing is not speaking. Only an integrated audio user interface has the potential to correct this problem.

6 Economic Implications of System Architecture Are Enormous

We are what we use (or eat, or behold, or...) and we are often quite unaware of the environment in which we lead our lives.

When Norbert Wiener predicted that robots would replace humans, he was right. In many tasks, they already have. Indeed in the process, to a startling degree, we have become robot-like ourselves—as Wiener also predicted. To the degree that our economy depends on information technology, we are in trouble, since robots aren't yet up to the task of building a richer or more fulfilling human world.

We cannot hope to improve productivity (no, not some oddly measured statistic, but real productivity) or the quality or creativity or even satisfaction in our lives (or the larger economy) by enslaving ourselves to today's inherently visually biased computer architectures.

We need machines that literally encourage us to work smarter, develop our capacity to make crucial judgments, and to become—in a multidimensional sense—more human once again.

Humans make sense of the world with their biologically evolved sensory integrators. In "sense-organ" terms, this means our eyes and our ears. We must use them both as completely as possible.

Our current computer designs have largely continued the centuries-long visual bias handed to us from the Greeks and all those who followed, despite the fact that we no longer experience the world in this linear, sequential fashion.

We are in trouble. We made this trouble for ourselves. Our technological environment must be rebuilt ... again. We will need radically simple new designs and new architectures to overcome the looming crisis of complexity that we are now tumbling towards. This is why the audiocomputer is inevitable.

Annotated Bibliography

[1] Erik Davis. *TECHGNOSIS—Myth, Magic in the Age of Information.* Nevada City: Harmony Books, 1998.

[2] Michael Dertouzos. *The Unfinished Revolution—Human-Centered Computers and What They Can Do for Us.* New York: HarperCollins, 2001.

[3] Merlin Donald. *Origins of the Modern Mind—Three Stages in the Evolution of Culture and Cognition.* Cambridge, MA: Harvard University Press, 1991.

[4] Marshall McLuhan. *The Gutenberg Galaxy—The Making of the Typographic Man.* Toronto: University of Toronto Press, 1962.

[5] Norbert Wiener. *The Human Use of Human Beings.* Boston: Houghton Mifflin, 1950.

Glossary of Audio Terms

Academy Curve: An equalization method associated with the mono, optically-encoded soundtrack in film. The Academy Curve was made an official standard in 1938.

Accidental: A sharp (♯), flat (♭), natural, double sharp (♯♯), or double flat (♭♭), placed in front of a note to either raise or lower the pitch of that note by a specific amount. For example, a sharp placed directly in front of middle C raises the frequency (pitch) of that note by one semitone. Middle C is typically tuned to 261.6 Hz. Raising its pitch by one equally tempered semitone will result in a frequency of 277.2 Hz (C-sharp). A natural cancels the effect of a previously placed accidental in any given measure of music. A double sharp raises the pitch of a note by two semitones (one whole tone), and a double flat lowers the pitch of a note by two semitones (one whole tone).

Acoustic: Pertaining to sound as a physical event, in contrast to *auditory* (pertaining to sound as a psychological event).

Adaptive Transform Acoustic Coding (ATRAC): The digital compressed audio format used in mini discs; operates typically at rates between 64 kbps (ATRAC-3) and 384 kbps (ATRAC-1 and 2).

Additive synthesis: A type of sound synthesis where pure tones are added together to form more complex sounds. Theoretically, we know that additive synthesis may create any sound since the Fourier theorem states that any sound can be constructed from a series of basic sinusoids; however, practically, its use is often limited to the creation of resonant sounds of collision.

Additive white Gaussian noise: A model of noise as a zero-mean Gaussian random process. Used to represent noise in a system from thermal motion of electrons through all electronic circuit elements.

Advanced Audio Coding (AAC): The new digital compressed audio format proposed as part of the MPEG-2; it's an improvement over the MP3 format.

Aeolian mode: The sixth mode derived from the major scale; the same as the natural minor scale. The aeolian mode uses the exact same notes from a major scale, but begins and ends on the sixth note of the major scale (i.e., A up to A with the key signature of C major).

Alias-free: Describes a digital signal which is constructed by summing a set of sine waves, each of which has a frequency which is less than or equal to 1/2 of the sampling rate. See bandlimited.

Aliasing: According to the Nyquist theory, a sine wave can only be represented by a digital sample stream with a sampling rate twice the frequency of the sine wave. In the case where the sampling rate is less than twice the frequency of the wave, the energy from frequencies that are above the Nyquist rate, SR/2, must go somewhere so they appear as phantom tones below the Nyquist rate. This phenomenon is referred to as "aliasing." For frequencies between SR/2 and SR, the frequency of the aliased signal is (Sample Rate – Original Frequency). Thus, a signal with a frequency of 40,000 Hz recorded with a sample rate of 44,100 Hz would sound as an audible tone at 4,100 Hz. This is an important consideration when recording or synthesizing audio because complex signals in the audible range can easily have harmonics that extend far above the Nyquist rate.

Allophone: A variant of a phoneme that is acoustically distinct, but does not constitute a phonemic difference in a language.

Allpass filter: An IIR filter whose gain is unity over its entire frequency range, but whose phase response is variable.

Ambience synthesis: The process of creating a distinct sonic atmosphere through the use of "background" sounds.

Ambient microphone: A microphone placed in a room or hall in such a way as to pick up acoustical properties of the space, especially its reverberant properties. (These properties are sometimes called the "ambience" of an acoustic space.)

Amplitude: The extreme range of pressure levels exhibited by a sound wave, voltage in an electrical signal, or digital value in a digital signal.

Amplitude modulation: See modulation.

Amplitude spectrum: See spectrum.

Analog: **1.** In recording, refers to the process of putting sound on tape resulting from data that are collected by measuring continuous variations in sound pressure level or voltage. (see digital). **2.** In general, refers to any process by which data are represented as measurements along a continuous variable. Analog radios, for example, allow you to tune stations by turning a knob (continuously) that changes the frequency selectivity of the receiver continuously.

Analog synthesizer: A sound-generating device containing circuits that operate over a continuous range of voltages. The components typically include oscillators, filters, amplifiers, envelope generators, etc. The modules produce varying voltages and are also controlled by voltages and can thus be interconnected in complex patterns to create novel sounds. Some well-known brands include Moog, Bucchla, Arp, Serge, and Oberheim.

Analog-to-Digital (A/D) converter: A device that converts samples of a signal to a numeric representation. In some cases, the sampling process is included in the A/D converter.

Articulatory synthesis: A sophisticated form of speech synthesis that forms speech by controlling a mathematically modeled vocal tract in contrast to other systems that build speech from small pieces of sound. Vocal tract parameters include fixed parameters, such as the length of the vocal tract or sinus volume, and dynamically articulated parameters, such as air pressure and jaw, tongue, and lip position. Such a system theoretically should be able to produce very realistic speech, and the vocal model may be tuned to match that of any individual. Unfortunately articulation has many parameters that are not well understood or controlled. The challenges of controlling an articulatory synthesizer are similar to those of controlling a very accurately physically modeled violin synthesizer (an actual violin is challenging to play, but at least there exist musicians who can play a physical violin, no musicians have been trained to modulate the parameters of the violin or articulatory speech synthesizer).

Assimilation: The systematic shifting of the articulation of one speech segment when in the context of another specific segment.

Asymptotically stable system: A control system that, given a stable input, produces output which may fluctuate; however, these fluctuations will eventually die down, settling on a stable value.

Asynchronous granular synthesis: A type of granular synthesis where grains are distributed in time according to one or more stochastic parameters.

Attack time: **1.** The suddenness of a sound's onset. A sound's amplitude envelope is characterized by attack, sustain, and decay. **2.** The time it takes for an audio compressor to reduce its gain when the output signal exceeds the threshold.

Audification: The use of realistic, short-duration sounds to communicate the occurrence of an event. See Auditory icons and sonification.

Auditory branding: Sounds or brief songs (jingles) are often used to enhance the emotional or cultural image associated with a company or product. Successful auditory branding includes the NBC chimes, the AT&T "sparkle tone" and the "you deserve a break today" McDonalds jingle.

Auditory icons: Auditory icons use environmental sounds that have a strong link with the objects or actions represented by the sounds. Examples include the sound of trash being emptied into a trash can, traffic noises, or the sound of a door shutting.

Auditory masking: Effect in which the presence of one sound precludes perception of another.

Auditory Scene Analysis (ASA): Forming separate representations of the individual sounds that are present in a mixture of sounds, given only the sound created by their mixture.

Auditory signature: The distinct formant structure unique to every voice or musical instrument. The combination of auditory signature, transient structure, and dynamic envelope allow individuals to recognize voices and instruments. Instrument sounds cease to be uniquely identifiable if their onsets are removed.

Auditory stream: A set of sounds that are perceived as coming from the activity of a single acoustic source over time.

Augmented fifth: A fifth that encompasses eight semitones (i.e., C up to G-sharp).

Augmented fourth: A fourth that encompasses six semitones (i.e., C up to F-sharp). This interval is diatonic to the major scale between notes 4 and 7 (i.e., in the key of G major, the notes C and F-sharp). This interval is also called the tritone because it encompasses three whole tones (six semitones).

Augmented second: The interval of a second that is one semitone larger than a major second. It encompasses three semitones. An augmented second (C up to D-sharp, for example) occurs between the sixth and seventh notes in the harmonic minor scale. It is one of the intervals that gives the harmonic minor scale such a distinct sound.

Augmented sixth: A sixth that encompasses ten semitones (i.e., C up to A-sharp). This interval is not diatonic to any major scale, but it is an integral part of the augmented sixth chord. This is a complex family of chords used primarily in 19th-century Romantic music in the western European tradition.

Augmented triad: One of the basic triad types (along with major, minor, and diminished). An augmented triad consists of a root, a major third, and an augmented fifth.

Back channel: An alternative means of communication, in the opposite direction of the primary data being communicated.

Backbeat: Traditionally, rhythm devices such as drums are struck on the odd beats so that these beats are known as *downbeats.* The hand or drumstick is pulled back during the even beats and hence these are called *backbeats* and are consequently silent. Some musical genres, such as jazz, accent the backbeat, which would otherwise not be heard. See downbeat.

Balanced modulator: An analog device that combines two signal frequencies and produces only their sum and difference frequencies.

Band-limited: Describes a signal consisting of sine wave partials whose frequencies are all below the Nyquist Limit (SR/2) for a given sampling rate. Band-limiting is desirable because frequencies above the Nyquist Limit can alias back into the audible range and cause undesirable artifacts. See alias-free.

Band-passed: Filtered so that only a certain range of frequencies (the "pass band") is present with substantial amplitude in the output of the filter. Other frequencies are attenuated.

Bandpass waveform: Waveform suitable for Radio Frequency (RF) transmission. A bandpass waveform is frequency translated by a carrier frequency to a frequency much higher than that of the baseband waveform.

Bark scale: Nonlinear scale of frequency scale based on human frequency resolution in which auditory excitation is usually measured. Sounds which are separated by more than about one Bark unit are generally resolvable as separate sounds and do not interact with each other at a sensory level.

Baseband waveform: Waveform suitable for a transmission channel. It is created from the incoming binary (in this case) data commonly by pulse code modulation.

Bass clef: Also called the "F clef." This is the clef that identifies the lower pitches in the grand staff, and is written on the bottom staff of the two staves in the grand staff. The bass clef identifies the pitch F3 (F below middle C).

Beam: A part of music notation. The beam functions as a type of grouping device that shows the beat units in a measure of music. This is especially useful when there are lots of eighth-notes and sixteenth-notes in a measure of music.

Bilinear interpolation: An interpolation that occurs in two dimensions. An example is combining multiple look-up tables to compute a function of two variables. You use the first variable to interpolate between adjacent entries within a table, and then use the second variable to interpolate between the results from two adjacent tables.

Bilinear transform: A nonlinear transformation of a continuous time system to a discrete time system. The output of the frequency response mapping between the two time systems has an arctangent relationship and is very close to linear for frequencies less than half the Nyquist frequency. An example of its use is when a passive or active R-C-L filter is bilinear transformed in order to implement a similar filter on a DSP using discrete time stepped operations.

Bit: An abbreviation of "binary digit." Signals such as sound waves can be represented by strings of numbers. In the decimal system, such numbers (0 to 9) are called "digits." In the binary system, the numbers 0 and 1 are called "bits." In information theory, a "bit" is the amount of information that one must send to a listener (or decoder) so that the latter can tell which of two equally likely alternatives it should choose.

Bit rate: The rate at which bits are transmitted in a communication system.

Bit reversed: A binary number written so that the least significant bit is at the left and most significant at the right. Used in the FFT process.

Bode plot: A method of quickly plotting frequency response by using poles and zeros.

Boundary tone: A marker of certain syntactic boundaries. Examples include the rising intonation at the end of a question or the falling intonation at the end of a sentence.

Bow: A wooden stick strung with horsehair used to play instruments of the viol and violin families. The tension of the hair is varied by means of an adjustable nut attached to one end of the stick.

Brick wall: A term used to describe a filter whose frequency response cuts off very abruptly. A graph of the response resembles a brick wall.

Bridge: In string instruments, a slender wedge-shaped wooden device that holds the strings in place and transmits string vibration to the table for amplification by the body of the instrument.

Brightness: A quality of the timbre of sound in which the sound seems high or sharp. It is correlated with the greater intensities of high frequency components in a sound relative to its low-frequency components. The opposite is often referred to as dullness.

Broadcast streaming: A method of sending a stream of continuous data such as digital audio or video over a computer network, where a server sends out data (broadcasts) without consideration of who may receive it. Broadcast streaming makes very efficient use of bandwidth since no communication is required between the streaming server and clients; however, the lack of a backchannel also makes this technique inflexible in terms of providing flow control or most any other service.

Buzz core opcode: A core opcode in the MPEG-4 Structured Audio standard for creating pulse waveforms with dynamic spectral movement. Also see MPEG-4, structured audio, and pulse waveform.

Chirp: A short windowed sinusoid or bank of sinusoids, where the frequency of the sinusoid(s) changes from one value to another over the course of the window's duration.

Chord: A group of notes played at the same time that have a musical relation to one another and are intended to be experienced as a group. Notes may be played together (a block chord) or melodically unfolded (arpeggiated).

Chorus effect: Produced when a delayed signal is mixed with its original nondelayed version. The delay is modulated randomly or periodically, usually in the 10-40 millisecond range (see modulation). A number of independently delayed and modulated copies of the same signal can be mixed together to "thicken" the chorus effect.

Chromatic: Literally means "colorful." Chromatic typically refers to a note (or notes) that uses an accidental to raise or lower its pitch level in relation to a given key signature. For example, in the key of C major (neither sharps nor flats in the key signature), the note F♯ (F-sharp) is chromatic: It is not a naturally occurring note in the key of C major. It is not diatonic to the key of C major. The term "chromatic" is often used synonymously with the term "accidental." An accidental refers to a specific sharp, flat, natural, double sharp, or double flat that is used in a musical passage. The term "chromatic" typically refers to a larger section of music or to an entire musical composition.

Clef: A notational convention that allows the musician to interpret the grid of a musical staff in terms of the pitch content. For example, in the treble clef, the bottom line is where the pitch E4 (E above Middle C) is placed. In the bass clef, the bottom line is where the pitch G2 is placed (G an octave and a fourth below Middle C). There are many different clefs, but the treble and bass clef are the two most common. The other clefs are moveable C clefs (they determine where on the staff Middle C will be written), and are (from high to low musical range) soprano clef, mezzo-soprano clef, alto clef, tenor clef, and baritone clef.

Clipping: A form of distortion where the normally sinusoidal waveshape is clipped at a maximum amplitude level. Clipping is caused when the dynamic range of the signal exceeds the range of the equipment. Clipping causes both harmonic and intermodulation distortion.

Closed loop system: A control system that uses feedback in the form of a connection from the system's output back to the input(s). This feedback channel is used to adjust the system behavior based on how well the actual output matches the expected output.

Co-articulation (anticipatory/carryover): Temporal overlap of articulatory movements for multiple phones. Anticipatory is influence of a subsequent phone; carryover is influence of a prior phone.

Cochlea: Spiral, snail-shaped organ of the inner ear, in which acoustic waves are converted to electrical impulses.

Codec: A coder and a decoder of sound. The coder converts the sound to a numerical code and the decoder converts the code back into sound. Also, it converts digital audio signals from one form to another and back.

Communications sounds: These are relatively simple sounds derived from traditional electronic tones, used primarily in telecommunications products. Examples include telephone rings, the signal that a telephone line is on hold, and the call waiting tone.

Compact disk (CD): A digital optical recording format created by Sony and Philips in 1979. The initial specification, known as Red Book, specified the storage of digital audio in the form of two channel (stereo), 16 bit, 44.1 kHz, Pulse Code Modulated samples. The CD standards have been extended to include the storage of data and eventually video as well as higher precision digital audio.

The CD rapidly supplanted the existing analog LP-record and cassette-tape formats to become the dominant format for the distribution of prerecorded music because of its comparative durability, low noise floor, high dynamic range, and inexpensive manufacturing.

The CD-ROM, VCD, DVD, Blu-Ray (BD), and HD-DVD standards all derive in some way from the original CD specification. Availability of inexpensive solid state lasers of higher frequencies, with correspondingly smaller feature sizes, has allowed increasingly more data to be stored on the same size disk: a CD using an infra-red laser can store approximately 640 MB, a DVD using a red laser can store approximately 4.7 GB (per layer, with maximum two layers), and a Blu-Ray using a blue laser can store approximately 25 GB (per layer with four-layer (and higher) media being researched).

Comparator: A function that takes two inputs, A and B, and outputs a logical TRUE if A>B or FALSE if A<B.

Complex: A procedure that uses complex numbers (real and imaginary parts) and the associated mathematical rules for operating on them.

Compound time: A type of meter. In compound time, the beat naturally subdivides into three faster rhythmic values. In compound time, the printed note-value equal to one beat will always be a "dotted rhythmic-value." For example, in six-eight time, there are two beats, dotted quarter-notes, and each beat naturally subdivides into three eighth-notes.

Compression: Audio dynamic range compression is the use of an automatic variable gain control system to reduce or compress the dynamic range of an audio signal, i.e., to reduce the difference between the loudest and quietest portions of an audio program. Not to be confused with methods used to compress or reduce the data needed to transmit or store an audio signal (data rate compression).

Compressor: An amplifier whose gain decreases automatically as its input signal level increases. A compressor combines both a fixed gain amplifier for input signals staying below a preset level (threshold) and variable gain amplifier that compresses the input signal automatically when it exceeds the threshold level.

Computational Auditory Scene Analysis (CASA): Carrying out Auditory Scene Analysis by means of a computer program.

Concatenation/stitching: Concatenation is stitching together words and phrases to make sentences and/or a continuous stream of words, phrases and sentences to provide an ongoing commentary for (color), and/or a description of (play by play), and/or reaction to (input response) events as they occur. More simply put, it is producing interactive speech by concatenating specially designed and prepared speech segments.

Consonance: The perceived stability of two or more musical tones sounding together. Consonance has an acoustical definition, and a musical definition. In music, the context of the event in question determines whether that sound is considered a consonance or a dissonance. The syntax of the music, especially in terms of the historical era in which the music was produced, is a large part of how any given sound is perceived.

Continuous spectrum: A spectrum exhibiting nonzero amplitude for one or more broad regions of the continuous frequency spectrum. This is the kind of spectrum that is found for aperiodic sounds, that is, sounds that do not repeat any pattern at all. The "ideal" aperiodic sound is an impulse, that is, a sound consisting of a single instantaneous pressure spike. The impulse is a sound which has equal amplitude at all frequencies. See also line spectrum and harmonic spectrum.

Contrapuntal: A term used to describe the musical texture in a musical composition or musical passage. Contrapuntal music is constructed in such a way as to consist of several melodic lines that occur simultaneously. Any of the fugues by J. S. Bach are examples of artfully crafted contrapuntal compositions.

Control theory: A field of engineering that studies the behavior of dynamic systems over time.

Convolution: A linear method for multiplying the frequency response of two systems in the time domain. The output of this mathematical operation is waveform in the time domain that acts as though the frequency response of one of the input waveforms has been filtered by the frequency response of the second waveform. The convolution operation is independent of which waveform is chosen to be convolved about the other.

Coproduction: Like co-articulation, but the term is intended to emphasize the overlapping, but independent, articulation of speech segments.

Core opcode: A library function for audio synthesis in the structured audio standard.

Crystal oscillator: An electrical circuit that includes a piece of a crystal with piezoelectric properties (often quartz), precisely cut to resonate at a particular frequency. A crystal oscillator circuit is used as a time source for more complex circuits: for instance, a time base for a CD player or microprocessor.

Cue: **1.** A feature of a sensory input that gives evidence pertaining to the interpretation of that input. For example, in vision, the desaturation of the colors of an object is a cue for the distance of the object. **2.** To seek to a location in a linear access medium like a tape.

Cycle of fifths (circle of fifths): A pattern that organizes the major or minor scales into a circle. Each individual scale is a perfect fifth higher or lower than the scales directly adjacent around the circle.

dB Lp: A measure of the loudness of a sound relative to a reference intensity of 10^{-12} watts/m^2. For a measured sound intensity I, DB Lp is calculated as dB Lp$= 10 \log_{10}(I/10^{-12})$.

dB SPL: A measure of the loudness of a sound relative to a reference sound pressure level of 20 μPa. For a measured sound pressure level p, dB SPL is calculated as dB SPL$= 20 \log_{10}(p/20)$. Zero dB SPL is near the threshold for hearing and each dB SPL increment in amplitude is roughly one just noticeable difference in loudness.

dBm: A measure of the level of a signal's power relative to a reference level of 1 milliwatt. Power cannot be measured directly, but must be inferred by measuring a voltage across a resistive load. A standard resistive load of 600 ohms is assumed when inferring power levels for dBm. The voltage level corresponding to a power level of 1 milliwatt across 600 ohms is 0.7746 volts. Given a measured voltage v across 600 ohms, dBm is calculated as dBm $= 20 \log_{10}(v/0.7746)$.

dBv: A measure of the level of a signal's amplitude relative to a reference level of 1 volt. For a measured voltage level v, dBv is calculated as dBv$= 20 \log_{10}(v/1)$.

Decay time: The time it takes for an audio compressor to increase its gain, when the output signal is below the threshold.

Decibel (dB): A unit of measure that expresses the relative levels of two like quantities. Decibels are used to measure sound levels based on acoustic measurements of sound pressure level or sound intensity. The decibel is a logarithmic measure expressed as $\text{dB} = 10\log_{10}(I_2/I_1)$, where I_1 and I_2 are the values being compared. Often I_1 is a reference value like the smallest sound perceivable or a certain voltage. A change of 3 dB corresponds to a ratio of 2x power and 10 dB corresponds to 10x power. A decibel is actually 1/10 Bel which was named after Alexander Graham Bell. Decibels are used because their logarithmic nature allows them to describe vast ranges of value easily and human perception has a natural logarithmic sensitivity (see also dB Lp, dB SPL, dBM, and dBv).

Decimate: **1.** Systematic removal of samples by picking, for example, one out of N consecutive samples. Down-sampling can be used as a synonym. **2.** To divide a single group of samples into a number of smaller groups.

Declination (speech): The tendency for F0 to gradually decline over the course of an utterance.

Delay line: An entity that stores the past values of a signal so they can be later retrieved to reconstruct a delayed version of the signal. Digital implementations of delay lines usually employ a circular buffer into which samples are written.

Delay tap: A signal derived from a delay line with a fixed or variable delay relative to the input of the delay line. When the delay time is not necessarily an integer multiple of the sampling period, some form of band-limiting interpolation is necessary to achieve an alias-free signal.

Detection: The psychoacoustic term that corresponds to a subject's ability to identify the presence of a sound. Sound detection is usually dependent on the frequency and sound-pressure level of the sound to be detected (as described by the Fletcher-Munson curves), as well as the presence of other sounds that might mask the sound's presence.

Diatonic: Any pitch that naturally occurs within a given key. For example, in the key of C major (neither sharps nor flats in the key signature), the pitch G-natural is diatonic. That is, it is a member of the collection of pitches that occur in the key of C major. The pitch G#, is not diatonic to C major. G# is not a member of the collection of pitches that occur in the key of C major.

Diatonic harmony: The manner in which the individual chords that occur in any given major or minor key interact in the context of a piece of music. Diatonic harmony means "conforming to the practice of using notes and chords that conform to the key signature." In other words, diatonic harmony does not use chromatic chords. The study of diatonic harmony is fundamental to the understanding of the way western European music evolved, and is a prerequisite to the study of chromatic harmony.

Digital: Of or pertaining to a process of representing a signal as a series of discrete numerical values, typically created by sampling an analog signal (see synthesis for all digital techniques). To obtain a digital representation of a signal such as a musical waveform, two processes are involved. The first step is to sample the signal by systematic measurement of the signal strength at even intervals (the sampling interval). If this process is carried out on a band-limited signal which contains components up to B Hz, an exact representation is possible if measured at least 2B times per second. The second step is the digitization, which is an approximation of the signal samples to a discrete set of possible amplitudes. The amplitudes are represented by integers, which in turn can be expressed by binary numbers. The digitization process is often called quantization and causes quantization noise. The level of the quantization noise depends on the quantization step size, which is a consequence of the allowed dynamic range of the signal and the number of bits used to represent each sample. The Nyquist theorem and Fourier transform prove, theoretically, that digital representations will be indistinguishable from analog representations providing that the sampling rate is high enough. In practice, cost cutting designs with low-bit sampling, poor antialiasing, and little dithering cause sometimes noticeable and undesirable distortions.

Digital filter: A filter which performs arithmetic operations on digital signals.

Digital-to-Analog (D/A) converter: A device that from a digital signal representation outputs signal samples.

Diminished fifth: A fifth that encompasses six semitones (i.e., C up to G-flat). This interval is diatonic to the major scale between notes 7 and 4 (i.e., in the key of D-flat major, the notes C and G-flat). The diminished fifth is the inversion of the augmented fourth (and vice versa). This interval is also called a tritone because it encompasses three whole tones (six semitones).

Diminished fourth: A fourth that encompasses four semitones (i.e., C up to F-flat). This is not diatonic to any standard major or minor scale.

Diminished seventh: A seventh that encompasses nine semitones (i.e., C up to B-double flat). This interval is used in the diminished seventh chord between the root and seventh, but is not diatonic to any standard major or minor scale.

Diminished seventh chord (diminished-diminished seventh): Also called diminished-diminished seventh chord because it consists of a diminished triad with a diminished seventh added to it. All diminished seventh chords consist of a root, a minor third, a diminished fifth (diminished triad), and a diminished seventh.

Diminished triad: One of the basic triad types (along with major, minor, and augmented). A diminished triad consists of a root, a minor third, and a diminished fifth.

Discrimination: The psychoacoustic term for the ability of a subject to distinguish differences between two sounds that are both above the detectability threshold. These differences may be in any parameter, such as loudness (perceived intensity) or pitch (perceived frequency). The smallest difference detectable, the so-called just noticeable difference (JND), is a core concept that guides the optimal design of sound coding. Generally, the size of the JND is proportional to the size of the stimulus. This relationship is called *Weber's Law* and applies to many but not all areas of perception.

Direct Current (DC): A signal component that remains at a steady voltage, either positive or negative.

Dispersion: Any phenomenon in which the velocity of propagation of a wave is wavelength-dependent.

Dissonance: The perceived instability of two or more musical tones sounding together. Dissonance has an acoustical definition, and a musical definition. In music, the context of the event in question determines whether that sound is considered a consonance or a dissonance. The syntax of the music, especially in terms of the historical era in which the music was produced, plays a large part in how any given sound is perceived.

Dominant seventh chord (major-minor seventh): Also called major-minor seventh chord because this chord consists of a major triad with a minor seventh added to it. All dominant seventh chords consist of a root, a major third, a perfect fifth (major triad), and a minor seventh.

Doppler modulation: Changing the apparent pitch of a sound by moving it away from and/or towards a recording instrument, creating a "Doppler shift" in the wavelength of all the component frequencies. (See modulation.)

Dorian mode: The second mode derived from the major scale. The Dorian mode uses exactly the same notes from a major scale, but begins and ends on the second note of the major scale (i.e., D up to the next octave D with the key signature of C major).

Dot: A part of music notation. A dot on a note simply makes the note length longer by one more of the next shorter rhythmic value. For example, a quarter-note is equal in length to two eighth-notes, but a dotted quarter-note is equal in length to three eighth-notes. Conversely, an eighth-note is equal in length to two sixteenth-notes, but a dotted eighth-note is equal in length to three sixteenth-notes.

Double flat: The accidental that lowers the pitch of a note by a whole tone.

Double sharp: The accidental that raises the pitch of a note by a whole tone.

Downbeat: In the most general sense, downbeat means the beginning, or onset, of any beat in a piece of music. For example, in four-four time, each measure has four beats, therefore, each measure has four downbeats. In a more specific sense, downbeat means the first beat in any measure. It is also used to designate the first beat of a music composition (the downbeat of "Row, Row, Row Your Boat"). See also backbeat.

Duple: Describes the number of beats in a meter. Music in simple-duple time has two beats in each measure, and the beats are simple, in that they naturally subdivide into groups of two faster note values. Music in compound-duple time has two beats in each measure, and the beats are compound in nature, in that they naturally subdivide into groups of three faster note values.

Dynamic range: The range of loudness of sounds, from the softest to the loudest, usually measured in decibels (dB).

Dynamic synchronization: A type of synchronization where the timing relationship between the media being synchronized are periodically examined and adjusted so that they remain in sync, instead of drifting apart over time.

Earcons: Earcons refer to abstract sounds that are musical in origin. The signals may be described as very short snippets of "program music" that are intended to steer the emotional reaction of the listener in support of the desired image.

Edit decision list (EDL): Used in video and film editing, an EDL is a list of the individual clips that form the final sequence. Time codes are used to mark times in the edit list.

Eighth-note: A type of rhythmic note-value in music notation. The eighth-note is the next shorter rhythmic value in relation to the quarter-note. There are two eighth-notes in a single quarter-note.

Electro-acoustic: The use of electric/electronic components (such as an amplifier and a loudspeaker) to produce sounds. Historically, the advent of electrical processing and reproduction of sound provided tremendous benefits over the previously used mechano-acoustic techniques.

Electroglottograph (EGG): A device that measures impedance across the vocal folds during speech using a surface electrode on either side of the larynx. When the vocal folds are in contact with one another, the impedance is relatively low and when the folds are abducted, impedance is high. For this reason, the EGG signal is essentially measuring vocal fold contact area. The EGG signal is also inversely related to air flow: When contact area is low, air flows; when contact area is high, air cannot flow.

Enharmonic: A convention in music notation where two notes with the same frequency (pitch) are spelled differently (i.e., C-sharp and D-flat). The conventions used in music notation to determine which enharmonic spelling is the correct spelling at any given moment are quite complex, and are dependent upon the style of music.

Ensemble timbre: An emergent timbre, arising from the combined sound of an ensemble (group of voices or instruments played together), which is distinct from the timbre of any one instrument or voice.

Entropy: Amount of information carried by a signal; it is a function of the probability distribution for that signal. The information is theoretically infinite for noiseless signals, but is finite if the signal is quantized or has some other noise component.

Entropy coding: Encoding of a signal based on knowledge of the probability distribution for that signal.

Envelope: An imaginary curve (E) that can be fitted to another time-varying curve (T) such that it touches T at its highest (or lowest) points. A temporal envelope of an acoustic wave has two parts: the curve that touches the highest points over time and another that touches the lowest points. It represents the time changes in the amplitude. A spectral envelope is a curve that touches all the points in a spectrum (i.e., points that represent the intensities or amplitudes of all the frequency components). A *smoothed* envelope comes as close as possible to the points it should touch, given the constraint that it should be smooth.

Envelope generator: An algorithm or device for producing a waveform to represent a slowly varying contour of a sound quality such as amplitude or brightness.

Equalization (EQ): The application of gain or attenuation to particular frequency bands of an audio signal. Simple equalization controls are available on most car and home stereos as the bass and treble control, which allows for adding or subtracting energy at fixed points along the frequency spectrum (typically around 200 Hz and 3500 Hz, respectively). Among audio engineers, some believe in an ethic that "no EQ is better" because equalization can lead to audible distortions of the signal in terms of phase shifts.

Equalizer: A device that incorporates a set of filters, each of which can be controlled separately. Its function is to shape the spectrum of the sound. Equalizers generally are of two varieties: multiband and parametric. Multiband equalizers provide a sometimes large set of evenly spaced filters over the 20 Hz to 20 kHz range of human hearing. Multiband equalizers are often called graphic equalizers since the position of the sliders forms a representation of the desired frequency-gain curve. Parametric equalizers allow the user to specify the center frequency that is being affected, as well as the width or "Q" around that center frequency. This control allows a recording engineer to tune the filter very specific applications. See equalization.

Expander: A device that increases the dynamic range of an audio signal. Usually used in conjunction with a compressor to restore the dynamic range removed by the compressor.

FFT Order: Log base 2 of N where N is the number of samples transformed. Also the number of passes through the data arrays required to perform the transform.

Filter: **1.** A mathematical operation or physical device that intentionally changes the frequency content of a signal, usually for the purpose of attenuating or accentuating a range of frequencies. For example, a low pass filter will pass frequencies below a certain cutoff frequency and attenuate those above the cutoff frequency. **2.** A device that alters the amplitude spectrum or phase spectrum of a sound.

Filter bank: A set of filters that are applied simultaneously to the same signal.

Finite Impulse Response (FIR): When referring to a system, this generally indicates a filter that only responds to present (current) and past input signals, and does not employ feedback. In DSP systems, FIR filters are less efficient compared to IIR filters but are easy to design, are unconditionally stable, and can easily be made to have a flat phase response.

First In First Out queue (FIFO): Also known as a Silo. Commonly used to buffer the flow of data between a producer and consumer.

Flap: A speech segment produced by rapidly tapping the tip of the tongue against the alveolar ridge.

Flat: The accidental that lowers the pitch of a given note by one semitone.

Flow control: A way of managing transmission rates between the sender and the receiver where the receiver periodically sends feedback to the sender telling it to either increase or decrease the transmission rate. The simplest forms of flow control limit communication to stop and resume commands.

Focus (speech): The placement of special prominence (including pitch accents, changes in duration, and changes in amplitude) on certain words in a sentence for pragmatic reasons such as to emphasize a particular contrast with a prior utterance.

Formal Language for Audio-Visual Object Representation (FLAVOR): A formal language developed by Columbia University for describing compressed bitstream syntax, especially the bitstreams representing multimedia objects.

Formant Wave-Function synthesis (FOF synthesis): A technique developed by Xavier Rodet and collaborators for the synthesis of sounds that are characterized by the existence of pronounced formants in their spectrum, such as vocal sounds. The technique employs trains of damped or enveloped sinusoids whose envelope characteristics can be modulated to affect the formants of the resulting signal.

Foot: A rhythmic unit in speech consisting of a stressed syllable and any immediately following unstressed syllables (definition for English).

Formant: **1.** A peak (region of enhanced amplitude) in the spectrum of a sound. The intensities and arrangement of formants, and their change over time, alters the timbre of the sound and helps the listener to distinguish between different musical instruments or different speech sounds. **2.** A spectral prominence resulting from a resonance in the vocal tract. The average spacing of formants is largely due to the length of the vocal tract and the exact frequencies at which formants appear are determined by the shape of the vocal tract. Formants are normally referred to as F1, F2, F3, etc., meaning the first, second, third, and so forth formants from lowest to highest frequency.

Formant synthesis: The rules-based speech-synthesis technique that presently is the dominant form of speech synthesis used in commercial devices. Formant synthesis uses rules to dynamically vary over time parameters, such as fundamental frequency, amplitude, and voicing, to form speech. Formant synthesizers emphasize intelligibility over naturalness and can be understood by trained listeners at very high rates of words per minute (such as text readers for the blind). In contrast to concatenative or articulatory synthesizers, formant synthesizers do not require large databases of speech or computationally expensive vocal models. Consequently, formant synthesis can be used in applications with low-power processors and small memory footprints such as in PDAs, automotive electronics, toys, or other embedded applications.

Formant transition: Change in frequency of a formant typically associated with the change in articulation from one phonetic segment to the next.

Four-four time (simple-quadruple meter): There are four beats in each measure, and the quarter-note is equal to one beat.

Fourier Transform: Forward: Conversion of a sample set from the time domain into a spectrum (the frequency domain). Inverse: Conversion of a spectrum (frequency domain) into a sample set in the time domain.

Frame: The number of digital audio samples presented at one time. One for a mono signal, two for a stereo signal, four for quad, etc.

Frequency component: That part of a complex wave having a particular frequency, amplitude, and phase. If the wave is periodic, each frequency component will be a harmonic.

Frequency modulation: See modulation.

Frequency Modulation (FM) synthesis: A technique for generating sound that involves adding the output of one sine wave generator known as the "modulator" to the frequency control input of another sine wave generator known as the "carrier." Traditionally, this was accomplished using a voltage-controlled oscillator, but may now be accomplished purely digitally. Harmonically rich sounds can be generated inexpensively by controlling the depth of modulation and the frequency ratios of the carrier and modulator. Multiple oscillators, typically 2 to 6, can be combined in patterns referred to as "algorithms." This technique was patented by John Chowning of Stanford University and licensed to Yamaha for use in their popular DX-7 line of synthesizers. See modulation.

Frequency response: **1.** A complex valued function of frequency which indicates the modification performed by a filter on a sinusoid of a given frequency. The frequency response can be split in a magnitude response (the magnitude of the frequency response), which is responsible for amplification or attenuation of the different frequencies, and a phase response, which is responsible for relative delays of different frequency components. **2.** The frequency response of the highest quality audio systems vary less than 1 dB over the range of audio frequencies from 20 Hz to 20kHz.

Frication: The broadband turbulent noise source we use in spoken sounds like /s/ and /f/.

Friction: Force that appears, for example, whenever one surface rubs against another.

Fugue: A specific type of contrapuntal composition.

Fundamental frequency (F0): The fundamental frequency is 1.0/T0, that is, the inverse of the period. Normally, we express F0 in units of cycles per second or Hz. This can be slightly confusing since we often express T0 in units of ms. You must remember to multiply T0 by 1000.0 if it is expressed in ms to arrive at F0 expressed in Hz. For complex sounds, F0 will normally be the frequency of the first, or lowest, frequency harmonic. See harmonics.

Fusion (perceptual): Hearing a set of concurrent sounds—which might otherwise be heard as separate sounds—as a single sound.

Gate: **1.** An electronic circuit that either does or does not allow an input signal to appear at the output, depending on the state of another signal that controls the gate. **2.** An amplifier whose gain decreases automatically to zero (at a preset rate of decay) as soon as its input signal level drops below a certain threshold value that has been set in advance.

Gated reverberation: Reverberation passed through a gate that attenuates it as soon as the reverberation level drops to a threshold that is set so that it will occur shortly after the onset of the reverberation. This produces a dramatic ambient effect, used most often on drums and percussion to increase their explosive quality and loudness.

Gibbs phenomenon: The ringing and overshoot that can occur when constructing a waveform by adding together harmonics and abruptly stopping the harmonic series after a finite number of terms. The ringing can be reduced by gradually tapering off the harmonics being used. It also refers to the ringing that can occur when using a brick-wall lowpass filter that effectively chops off high frequency partials in the same manner.

Grand staff: The combined staves of the treble and bass clef. The grand staff is the most commonly used full-range musical grid, and is the clef used for piano music (as well as concert harp, marimba, and others).

Granular synthesis: A synthesis technique involving mixing very short sounds called grains to form a layered result. Granular synthesis can vary the grains used, the pattern of grain excitation, and the volume and pitch of the individual grains to create sounds that are difficult to achieve using other techniques, specifically sounds of nature: waterfalls, wind, and shifting sands. See pitch synchronous granular synthesis.

Group modulation: A variation of gain, time delay, frequency, or phase that is applied equally to a number of independent sound streams.

Half-diminished seventh chord (diminished-minor seventh and/or minor seven flat-five): Also called a diminished-minor seventh and/or a minor seven flat-five chord. This chord consists of a diminished triad with a minor seventh added to it (thus, the diminished-minor designation). It is also possible to conceive of this chord as a minor seven chord with a lowered fifth (flat five). All half-diminished seventh chords consist of a root, a minor third, a diminished fifth (diminished triad), and a minor seventh.

Half-note: A type of rhythmic note value in music notation. The half-note is the next longer rhythmic value in relation to the quarter-note. There are two quarter-notes in a single half-note.

Harmonic: **1.** A frequency component of a periodic waveform having a frequency of I/P where P is the period and I is any positive integer. **2.** A line (or near-line) in the spectrum of a periodic (or near-periodic) signal that can occur at any integer multiple of the fundamental frequency. In a harmonic spectrum, the harmonics are spaced F0-Hz apart.

Harmonic consonance: A sound comprised of at least two musical tones that produces a consonant (pleasant) effect in the context of a piece of music.

Harmonic dissonance: A sound comprised of at least two musical tones that produces a dissonant (tense or unpleasant) effect in the context of a piece of music. The V7 chord, in traditional Western classical music, is perceived as a dissonance that produces harmonic tension. This tension is resolved when the chord changes to the I chord (in a major key). This movement from dissonance to consonance is called a cadence.

Harmonic distortion: Distortion of an audio signal caused by a nonlinear process that produces unwanted harmonics of the original waveform. Usually expressed as a percentage of power, high-quality audio equipment will have a small fraction of a percent harmonic distortion.

Harmonic minor scale: A form of the minor scale. The harmonic minor scale has one chromatically altered note from the natural minor scale: The seventh note is raised in pitch by one semitone. This alteration creates an augmented second between the sixth and seventh notes of the scale. This augmented second gives the harmonic minor scale its characteristic sound. The scale is historically derived from the combination of the tonic subdominant, and dominant chords (i, iv, and V) used in musical compositions written in minor keys during the Common Practice era (1600–1900) in western European music history.

Harmonic relation: The relation between frequencies when they belong to the same harmonic series. Good harmonic relations are produced when the frequencies (or fundamental frequencies) of two simultaneous sounds form a simple ratio to one another (e.g., 1:1, 2:1, 3:2, 4:3 ...). These ratios are those that relate the component frequencies of a harmonic series.

Harmonic series: A summation of sine waves, f, $2f$, $3f$, $4f$, $\ldots$, whose frequencies are integer multiples of a base frequency, f, called the fundamental of the set of harmonics. The waveform produced by a harmonic series yields a strong pitch sensation.

Harmonic spectrum: Similar to a line spectrum except that sounds giving rise to harmonic spectra are not purely periodic, but only approximately so. Such sounds produce a harmonic spectrum in which the lines have some discernible width. As sounds deviate increasingly from true periodicity, their spectra deviate increasingly from line spectra to approach a continuous spectrum. For example, any sound that has finite duration is not strictly periodic. Many natural sounds, like the human voice, are quasi-periodic in that the sound deviates in a variety of ways from one period to the next. See also line spectrum and continuous spectrum.

Harmonics: Most sound can be analyzed into a number of frequency components. These components are called harmonics when their frequencies are all multiples of the same frequency (which is called the fundamental frequency of the set of harmonics.

Harmonizer: A digital signal processing device that generates copies of the original signal transposed in pitch by a specified musical interval(s). It does it by writing and reading audio data at different clock rates and compensating for any resulting changes in signal duration.

Head-Related Transfer Function (HRTF): A mathematical model of the highly directional spectral filtering (experienced) by sounds before reaching the eardrums. This filtering is caused by the sounds' interaction with the torso, head, and pinnae (outer ears). The brain interprets the spectral signature of a signal to help determine the location of the sound's source in three-dimensional space. HRTFs are similar in structure but ultimately distinctly based on the shape and size of an individual's features. An HRTF may be applied to a raw sound to emulate the filtering that the sound would have experienced if it were actually physically encountered. The result when processed for the right and left ears and applied directly to each eardrum via headphones will contain the three-dimensional cues. Unlike stereo processing, HRTF processed sounds contain elevation cues and can actually make users believe sounds are coming from behind them.

Helmholtz motion: Characteristic motion of a bowed string whose name derives from the physicist who discovered it. In it, the bow sticks to the string for the longest part of the period, slipping only once every cycle. It is the motion that every player tries to achieve.

Hertz (Hz): Frequency expressed in cycles per second.

House-sync: A distributed master time code signal to which all devices in a video or film production facility to are synchronized.

Imperfect consonance: Two tones that encompass one of the "imperfect" consonant intervals: major or minor thirds, and major or minor sixths.

Impressionistic transcription: Identifies all perceptible speech features.

Impulse Response: The output of a system, usually a filter, in response to an impulse at the input. An impulse is an infinitesimally brief input pulse. The impulse response is a mathematical representation of the system in the time domain and is directly related to the frequency and phase response. The Fourier transform converts between the time domain and the frequency domain, i.e., between the impulse response and the amplitude/phase response of a system.

Infinite Impulse Response (IIR): **1.** When referring to a system, this generally indicates a filter that responds to both present (current) and past input signals, as well as past output signals. An IIR system employs feedback and has an impulse response that is, in theory, infinite in duration. In DSP systems, IIR filters are more efficient compared to FIR filters, but are more difficult to design and can be unstable. **2.** A signal process that changes the frequency response by implementing poles and zero using a feedback loop.

Integration: The tendency of sounds containing certain properties to be perceived to be indistinct.

Intensity: The power per unit area at a distance from a sound source.

Intermodulation Distortion (IMD): Distortion of an audio signal that contains two or more tones caused by a nonlinear process that produces the unwanted sum and difference frequencies of the original tones. Because the new tones are not harmonically related to the original tones, intermodulation distortion is very noticeable and objectionable. Usually expressed as a percentage of power, high-quality audio equipment will have a small fraction of 1% intermodulation distortion.

Interonset time: The time between the onsets of adjacent events in an ordered event series.

Interval: The distance in pitch between two notes. Intervals are categorized by size and quality. The size is a number which represents the number of generic note letter-names between the two notes (C up to G is a fifth: count C, D, E, F, G=5). This is often called the diatonic size of an interval. The quality represents the relative amount of consonance and dissonance in an interval, which we determine as the number of semitones encompassed by the given interval (C up to G encompasses 7 semitones which equals a perfect fifth).

Intonation: The pattern of pitch changes in speech characteristic to individual languages or dialects. So-called *Intonation Languages* use pitch changes to convey meaning (i.e., English speakers raise the pitch at the end of a sentence to indicate a question). Intonation is one element of prosody.

Inversion: Literally "flipping something upside down." To invert an interval, take the bottom note, transpose it up one octave, which makes it the top note of a new interval. One can also invert an interval by transposing the top note down one octave, which will make it the bottom note of a new interval.

Ionian mode: The first mode, same as the major scale.

Isochrony: **1.** Events taking the same time. **2.** The notion that the intervals between stressed syllables in a stress-timed language should be equal.

Jitter buffer: A buffer that is used to compensate for variations in the transmission rate, when the average transmission rate is equal to the average consumption rate of the data at the receiver. The buffer temporarily stores data that is sent too fast, which is consumed when the transmission rate slows down again. Similarly data stored in the buffer may be consumed even when new input data is temporarily delayed.

Just noticeable difference (JND): The smallest change that a subject can differentiate. Any change smaller than the JND is indistinguishable from the original. Knowledge about the JND of various domains allows algorithms like lossy compression to distort a signal in ways that are undetectable.

Key signature: The pattern of sharps or flats written at the beginning of a musical composition, and at the beginning of every line of music. The key signature is a notational shorthand that communicates to the individual musicians the key of the music.

Lagrange interpolation: Fitting of polynomials to make the resulting polynomial function exact at the data points. If N data points are given, an $N-1$ degree polynomial can be applied.

Laplace domain (S domain): Continuous time domain.

Laplace transform: Method of transforming a continuous time function to the Laplace domain.

Larynx: The cartilaginous structure above the trachea containing the vocal cords. It is within the larynx that much of the sound for speech is generated.

Leading tone: The note that is a major seventh above the tonic note in any given key. This note derives its name from the practice of melodically moving the leading tone to the tonic at an authentic cadence (V-I in a major key or V-I in a minor key).

Leakage: An artifact of Fourier transform-based spectral analysis caused by transforming nonperiodic waveforms or waveforms having a nonintegral number of cycles in the analysis record. When present, strong frequency components in the analysis spread out and obscure weaker components even if far away in frequency. See window.

Leger line: A short horizontal line that extends the musical staff above or below the standard five lines. Leger lines are used to accurately distinguish the pitches that are either too high or too low to fit within the musical staff regardless of the clef being used.

Leslie loudspeaker: A loudspeaker system employing a rotating horn-type transducer at the top and a rotating low-frequency transducer at the bottom of a wooden enclosure. Its characteristic time-varying polar pattern due to the rotation produces spatial and spectral modulation able, for example, to enrich the sound of a Hammond organ.

Lexical stress: The pattern of syllabic prominence that is specifically identified with a word. It is primarily a lexical stress difference that distinguishes the verb conVICT from the noun CONvict (upper case representing the stressed syllable).

Limiter: An application of dynamic range compression characterized by high threshold, high compression ratio, and fast attack time. The limiter is used to prevent brief audio transients from exceeding an upper amplitude limit.

Line spectrum: The kind of spectrum that is found for sounds that are purely periodic, that is, for sounds that repeat the same pattern infinitely. Each line in a line spectrum is a harmonic of the fundamental period of the waveform and represents a sinusoid at a particular frequency and amplitude. Line spectra are the ideal case of harmonic spectra. See also harmonic spectrum.

Locrian mode: The seventh mode derived from the major scale. The locrian mode uses the exact same notes from a major scale, but begins and ends on the seventh note of the major scale (i.e., D up to D with the key signature of C major).

Lossless compression: A compression technique in which the original data can be recovered exactly.

Lossy compression: A compression technique in which the original data can only be approximately recovered.

Loudness: The perceptual correlate of amplitude. Equal steps in loudness are roughly equal to logarithmic steps in amplitude.

Loudspeaker panning: A spatialization technique whereby the level of sound emanating from a set of loudspeakers is manipulated to give the listener the impression the sound is emanating from a particular point or region in space.

Low-pass filter: A filter that passes low frequencies and attenuates high frequencies.

Lydian mode: The fourth mode derived from the major scale. The lydian mode uses the exact same notes from a major scale, but begins and ends on the fourth note of the major scale (i.e., F up to F with the key signature of C major).

Major scale: The scale that is comprised of this specific interval pattern above a tonic note: whole tone, whole tone, semitone, whole tone, whole tone, whole tone, semitone. Constructing an ascending collection of pitches based on this interval pattern will result in the creation of the major scale. The major scales can be easily organized into a memorable pattern called the "circle of fifths" (or "cycle of fifths"). Each major scale has a unique key signature, which is the pattern of sharps or flats contained in that specific scale.

Major second: The interval that is equal in sound to a whole tone. A major second is the interval of a second (adjacent letter named notes) that encompass two semitones (i.e., C and D). It is also the diatonic interval between the tonic and second notes of any major scale.

Major seventh: A seventh that encompasses eleven semitones (i.e., C up to B-natural). This interval is diatonic between the tonic and seventh notes of a major scale.

Major seventh chord (major-major seventh): Also called major-major seventh chord because this chord consists of a major triad with a major seventh added to it. All major seventh chords consist of a root, a major third, a perfect fifth (major triad), and a major seventh.

Major sixth: A sixth that encompasses nine semitones (i.e., C up to A-natural). This interval is diatonic between the tonic and sixth notes in a major scale.

Major third: A third that encompasses four semitones (i.e., C up to E-natural). It is also the diatonic interval between the tonic and third notes of a major scale.

Major triad: One of the basic triad types (along with minor, diminished, and augmented). A major triad consists of a root, a major third, and a perfect fifth.

Manner of articulation: The classification of speech segments on the basis of the type of articulation needed to produce the segment such as stop, fricative, glide, etc.

Marginally stable system: A control system that, given a stable input, produces output which fluctuates but does not get better or worse over time.

Masking: The ability of an interfering sound (the masker) to make a listener unable to detect the presence of a target sound (the masked sound).

Measure: A notational convention consisting of one instance of the metric pattern in a given music composition. The printed measure is identified by the placement of a vertical bar-line printed through the five lines of the musical staff at the end of the metric pattern. For example, in two-four time, there are two beats in every measure, and the quarter-note is the rhythmic value equal to one beat. Each measure will have two quarter-notes (or their rhythmic equivalent, such as four eighth-notes) before the bar-line is printed.

Mechano-acoustic: The use of mechanical components to produce sounds. A bell is a simple example of a mechano-acoustic device. Sound reproducing devices such as the Victrola expose many of the limitations of these techniques.

Mel scale: A logarithmic scale of frequency based on human pitch perception. Equal intervals in Mel units correspond to equal pitch intervals.

Melodic minor scale: A form of the minor scale. The melodic minor scale uses two chromatically altered notes, only in the ascending version, from the natural minor scale. In the melodic minor scale, the sixth and seventh notes are raised by one semitone in the ascending version of the scale, and are returned to their original pitch level in the descending version of the scale.

Metadata: Data that describes other data. For example, a common mp3 file contains data, the compressed digital representation of the music, and metadata such as the artist, genre, and album name.

Meter: An organized hierarchical system of beats into regularly occurring patterns. These patterns are called measures. The first beat contains the most gravitational weight, and is therefore the most important beat in the measure. It is the psychoacoustic perception of the first beat that makes the pattern recognizable to the listener.

Meter signature: A notational convention consisting of two numbers, one printed directly on top of the other, that communicates to the musician the type of meter for a given music composition. Synonymous with time signature.

Metronome: An electronic or mechanical device that outputs a regular "click" sound at selectable speeds. A metronome is commonly used as a learning tool during practice sessions when a musician is learning to play a piece of music at a specific tempo. Metronome markings are also commonly used in music notation to indicate the tempo at which a specific composition should be performed.

Middle C: The C that is approximately in the middle of the piano keyboard. Middle C is written one leger line below the staff in the treble clef, and one leger line above the staff in the bass clef.

Minor scale: Also called the natural minor scale. The scale that is comprised of this specific interval pattern above a tonic note: whole tone, semitone, whole tone, whole tone, semitone, whole tone, whole tone. The minor scales can be easily organized into a memorable pattern called the circle of fifths (or cycle of fifths). Each minor scale has a unique key signature, which is the pattern of sharps or flats contained in that specific scale.

Minor second: The interval equal in sound to a semitone. Minor seconds are distinct in their spelling because they always encompass adjacent note names (i.e., C and D-flat, as opposed to C and C-sharp). Therefore, all minor seconds are intervals of a second (adjacent letter named notes), that encompass only one semitone.

Minor seventh: A seventh that encompasses ten semitones (i.e., C up to B-flat). This interval is diatonic between the tonic and seventh notes of the natural minor scale.

Minor seventh chord (minor-minor seventh): Also called minor-minor seventh because this chord consists of a minor triad with a minor seventh added to it. All minor seventh chords consist of a root, a minor third, a perfect fifth (minor triad), and a minor seventh.

Minor sixth: A sixth that encompasses eight semitones (i.e., C up to A-flat). This interval is diatonic between the tonic and sixth notes in the natural minor scale.

Minor third: A third that encompasses three semitones (i.e., C up to E-flat). It is also the diatonic interval between the tonic and third notes of a minor scale.

Minor triad: One of the basic triad types (along with major, diminished, and augmented). A minor triad consists of a root, a minor third, and a perfect fifth.

Mistuning: Altering the pitch of a sound (e.g., that of a musical instrument) so that it is not related to other sounds by a good harmonic relation.

Mixing console (audio mixer, soundboard): An electronic device often used in recording studios or live performances that allows a sound engineer known as a mixer to dynamically set the relative volume, pan, and other audio effects, for often a large number of audio tracks. The resulting *mix* will combine formerly independent tracks with a final mix creating a single left and right track for stereo recordings, or four to six channels for a surround sound recording. Pan controls are used to control how much energy from a source track will be placed in any given output track. The commonly seen, and sometimes quite physically large, consoles with rows and rows of knobs and sliders are slowly being displaced by much more compact and less expensive computer-controlled devices.

Mixolydian mode: The fifth mode derived from the major scale. The mixolydian mode uses the exact same notes from a major scale, but begins and ends on the fifth note of the major scale (i.e., G up to G with the key signature of C major).

Modality: In perception, the particular sense used in perceiving something. (e.g., the visual modality, the auditory modality).

Modal synthesis: A synthesis technique that uses a bank of resonators to realistically model the resonances of actual objects. The resulting model may be excited by signals that emulate striking, scraping, or otherwise manipulating the actual object. While not as accurate as a true physical model, modal synthesis is highly efficient.

Mode: One of the forms of scale typically derived from the major scale. By building a scale using the exact same pitches from a major scale (called the parent scale in this context), but starting and ending on a different note, one is constructing a modal scale. Since there are seven different pitches in every major scale, there are seven distinct modes that can be derived from the major scale.

Modes: The family of scales derived from the major scale which is thought of as the "parent" scale. These modes are Ionian (same as the major scale), Dorian (second mode), Phrygian (third mode), Lydian (fourth mode), Mixolydian (fifth mode), Aeolian (sixth mode and the same as the natural minor scale), and Locrian (seventh mode).

Modulated Lapped Transform (MLT): Similar to Fourier and cosine transforms, with the exception that the MLT functions extend beyond block boundaries, overlapping orthogonally with the functions from adjacent blocks. Also known as the MDCT (modified discrete cosine transform), the MLT is used in most digital compression formats, including MP3, AAC, ATRAC, etc.

Modulation: The change, over time, of some property P of a sound, often in a periodic (repetitive) way. If the modulation is periodic, it can be viewed as a wave that is "modulating" (changing) property P. If P is amplitude, the process is called amplitude modulation (AM) and when P is frequency, it is called frequency modulation (FM). See also side-bands.

Motion Picture Experts Group (MPEG): The ISO/IEC working group that determines standards for coding digital audio and video.

MP3: File format for the MPEG-1 Layer III audio compression system. It provides good-quality stereo audio encoding at bit rates of 128 kbps and above.

MPEG-4: The latest set of standards for audio and video compression issued by the MPEG committee.

Multirate systems: Systems where more than one sampling frequency is involved. A digital interpolator where the input and output sampling frequencies are different is a typical example.

Multitrack recording: A sound recording technique that allows multiple sound sources to be simultaneously recorded onto distinct *tracks* in a synchronized manner. These tracks may be recorded simultaneously, perhaps by micing each musician's instrument, or independently, perhaps even at different times and locations. Additionally, any given track can be rerecorded without affecting the other tracks, essentially providing the ability for a musician to rework their contribution. Originally, multitrack recording was achieved using analog tape with compound recording heads to create multiple independent parallel tracks on the linear tape, but now it is commonly achieved digitally using standard computer hard disks.

Multitrack techniques were innovated by guitarist and inventor Les Paul in the 1940s. Multitrack recording revolutionized how many forms of music were recorded and allowed formerly impossible scenarios. For the first time a single musician could accompany themselves and essentially play all the instruments on a recording if desired, or even to accompany a musician they have never met. More commonly, multitrack recording is used to *lay down* each musician's contribution to a recording separately in a controlled environment where the musician may listen to the recording as they themselves are recording their own track (percussion and rhythm tracks are recorded before the lead and vocal tracks). This methodology allows tremendous freedom to change the character of the music in the final mix, where tracks can even be eliminated or perhaps added at the last moment.

Murmur: The low frequency and low amplitude energy found during the closure interval of a consonant.

Natural: The accidental that cancels the effect of a previously placed sharp, flat, double sharp, or double flat, in a measure of music.

Natural Minor Scale: see minor scale.

Network Time Protocol (NTP): The standard method of synchronizing clocks on computers connected via the Internet. The clever technique uses multiple trusted time sources to deduce Internet packet time delay between this system and the reference time servers and then uses this information to both determine the actual time and to correct for inaccuracies in the local machine's time source.

Nine-eight time (Compound-triple meter): There are three beats in each measure, and the dotted quarter-note is equal to one beat.

Node (FFT): A graphical representation of the fundamental unit of computation in the fast Fourier transform.

Noise-to-Masking Ratio (NMR): A measure of the noise level of an audio signal with respect to the masking threshold; an NMR of 0 dB means that the noise is barely audible. High-fidelity digital audio systems should have NMRs of several dBs negative.

Nonlinear editor (NLE): A modern film or video editing system that allows random real-time access of frames in a video sequence, thus allowing the creation and immediate playback of arbitrarily complicated edits. Nonlinear editors are also nondestructive, allowing editors to change or make multiple versions of an edited sequence as they choose. Traditionally, editing was accomplished by physically cutting and splicing bits of film together to form the edited sequence (linear editing).

Nyquist frequency: One-half the sampling rate.

Nyquist rate: This is equivalent to the necessary sampling frequency for obtaining an aliasing-free representation of a band-limited signal. If the signal is band-limited to B Hz, the Nyquist rate (or frequency) is equal to 2B. For digitally sampled representations, the Nyquist rate is one-half the sampling rate. Any energy of frequency higher than the Nyquist frequency will alias down into the audio range and cause undesirable artifacts.

Octave: **1.** The interval between two notes of the same name whose frequencies exhibit a 2:1 ratio (i.e., A4 at 440 Hz and A5 at 880 Hz). The interval between these two specific notes is an octave. **2.** A popular signal processing library.

Open loop system: A control system where there is no connection from the system's output back to the input(s). Open loop systems are not able to adapt to unexpected variances in the system and consequentially will drift over time.

Oscillator: An algorithm or device that generates a periodic waveform signal, usually a sine wave. See voltage-controlled oscillator.

Overflow: An undesirable situation involving the loss of data. Overflow will eventually occur if data is added to a buffer faster than it is consumed. While this situation is the reason buffers are used and may safely be maintained for short periods of time, during which the buffer fills, at some point flow control must intervene by throttling the input or the buffer will finally become full. Once full, any new data is lost or, alternately, displaces unconsumed data in the buffer. A larger buffer may alleviate the situation only if the average rate of production exceeds the average rate of consumption and the variance may be contained by the large buffer.

Partial: Fourier theory tells us that any sound can be constructed by adding together a sufficient number of sine waves of the appropriate frequency and amplitude. Each sine wave is a "partial." If the ratio of the frequencies of two partials is a whole number (2, 3, 4,...), then the higher one is said to be a "harmonic" of the lower one. Some sounds, like pipe organs, have partials that are mostly harmonically related. Percussive sounds, like bells, are often rich in enharmonic (not harmonically related) partials.

Pascal: A unit of air pressure measurement, named after the physicist and mathematician Blaise Pascal, that is used to establish an absolute reference for comparing loudness or intensity of sound waves. The standard reference of 0 dB SPL corresponds to 20 uPA or 20 micro Pascals. One thousand Pascals or 1 kPa = 0.145 PSI = 7.52 mm Hg.

Perceptual Quality Audio Measure (PQAM): An audio quality metric that includes measurements such as NMR and others. It is an important metric for digital audio systems, for which traditional measurements such as SNR are not meaningful.

Perfect consonance: A consonance that is comprised of one of the "perfect" intervals: unison, octave, perfect fifth, or perfect fourth. This is a mathematical definition. In practice through most of the Common Practice era (1600–1900), perfect fourths were treated as a dissonance when the lowest sounding tone of the interval was found in the bass part of the musical ensemble. The implications of this are beyond the scope of this book, but are worth mentioning nonetheless.

Perfect fifth: A fifth that encompasses seven semitones (i.e., C up to G). This interval is diatonic between the tonic and fifth notes of a major scale.

Perfect fourth: A fourth that encompasses five semitones (i.e., C up to F). This is the diatonic interval between the tonic and fourth notes in a major scale.

Period: For a repetitive waveform, the time between repetitions.

Period (T0): The duration of a single complete cycle of a periodic waveform. We sometimes refer to the period of a signal as T0.

Periodic: A waveform that continually repeats its shape in time.

Phase: The time relation between two sinusoidal waveforms having the same frequency or the relation between one sinusoidal waveform and a fixed reference.

Phase-Locked Loop (PLL): An electrical circuit that keeps an input signal's phase aligned with the phase of a reference signal. The PLL is often used in a communications device to synchronize its clock to the clock of an incoming signal.

Phaser: A function that corresponds to the phase angle of a rotating vector mapped into the range -1.0 to $+1.0$. It can be used as the phase input to a band-limited oscillator and looks like a "sawtooth wave."

Phonation (voicing): The periodic impulsive sound source that is characteristic of all vowels and many consonants.

Phonemic transcription: Identifies just sounds that are phonemic in a language.

Phonetic feature: Minimal characteristics of segments that distinguish one speech segment from another (e.g., voicing, stricture).

Phonetic transcription: Identifies allophones as well as phonemes.

Phrase final lengthening: The tendency for the final syllable of phrases to be substantially longer in duration that the same syllable would be in a phrase medial position. We use the drawing out of syllables at the end of phrases (and to some extent, smaller units as well) to signal the presence of a boundary.

Phrygian mode: The third mode derived from the major scale. The Phrygian mode uses exactly the same notes as a major scale, but begins and ends on the third note of the major scale (i.e., E up to E with the key signature of C major.

Physical modeling: A synthesis technique that uses mathematical models to simulate the vibrations of the physical source of sound. This technique produces very accurate and realistic results for the simple objects that we understand how to model, such as circular membranes, strings, cylinders, bars, and tubular bells. Unfortunately, we don't yet understand the physics required to directly model non-trivially shaped objects, and instead we use techniques such as *finite element analysis* (FEA) to break a complicated object into a large number of simple objects that we can model. These techniques work very well but quickly become computationally prohibitive, especially if we would like to synthesize the results in real time. While FEA may be appropriate for modeling a bridge design, it is likely unnecessary for synthesizing the sound that such a structure would make with wind blowing over it to be used in a movie or video game.

Piezoelectric effect: The characteristic of certain materials (especially crystals) to convert mechanical stress to electrical voltage, and vice versa.

Pipeline: An implementation of the Silo or FIFO first in first out) data structure where data may be inserted at arbitrary locations in the buffer to control the time in the future when the data will be delivered.

Pitch: **1.** A perceptual quality—running from "low" to "high"—that is a function of the repetition rate (or frequency) of a sound wave (inversely proportional to the sound's wavelength). Higher repetition rates are heard as higher in pitch. For example, as one moves to the right on a piano keyboard, the notes produced by the keys are considered to be higher and higher in pitch. Humans can hear a wider range of frequencies than that to which they can attach a strong sense of pitch, however, with the range of strong pitch roughly spanning the range of the keyboard, from approximately 40 Hz to 3500 Hz. **2.** In humans, the ability to vocally reproduce a stable tone at the same frequency that a recently heard tone occurred is considered one of the criteria in determining one's sense of pitch. **3.** Pitch also means the specific pitch of a given note. For example, the note middle C, is also the pitch middle C. The pitch that is 440 Hz is the "A" above middle C on the piano. **4.** (Speech) The perceptual correlate of frequency. Normally, the pitch of a complex sound is a function of its F0. Equal steps in pitch are roughly equal to logarithmic steps in frequency.

Pitch accent: A prominence-lending peak or trough in the intonation contour of an utterance. Pitch accents mark words for special emphasis and guide listeners in interpreting the meaning of utterances.

Pitch class: One of the 12 distinct names of pitches regardless of octave and of enharmonic. For example, the letter name C is a pitch class regardless of which octave any given C occurs. Consequently, there are seven letter-named pitch classes that correspond to the musical alphabet (letters A through G). Also, the notes C-sharp and D-flat belong to the same pitch class because they are enharmonic.

Pitch period: The waveform associated with a single closing and opening cycle of the vocal folds. Each pitch period contains information about both the sound source generated in the larynx and about the structure of the vocal tract about the larynx.

Pitch shifting: The process of changing the apparent pitch of a signal without noticeably altering its temporal evolution. The musical analogue of pitch shifting is transposition. Algorithms for pitch shifting are related to those used for time stretching.

Pitch smearing: An audio effect that results in the smearing of frequency components across the spectrum of a signal.

Pitch synchronous granular synthesis: A technique for synthesizing periodic tones with one or more formant regions developed by Aldo Piccialli and Giovanni De Poli. Grains are generated at a rate related to the fundamental frequency of the tone and are overlapped and added to create smooth spectral transitions. The content of the grains is generated by filtering a pulse train according to parameters acquired from analysis of an existing musical signal.

Pitch Synchronous Overlap Add (PSOLA): A method for operating on speech in the time domain that allows timescale modification and pitch modification.

Place of articulation: The location of primary constriction needed in the production of a speech segment.

Pole: **1.** Signal processing terminology used to describe the characteristic of attenuating frequencies. **2.** An element of a linear system that causes the frequency response to increase in magnitude. For instance, if we were to describe the frequency response of a system with $h(\omega) = 1/(1 - \omega)$, the point at $\omega = 1$ would represent a pole because the graph would clearly show the frequency response approaching infinity as ω approached 1.

Polyphonic: Referring to music in which two or more concurrent parts are meant to be heard individually (at least sometimes), and no part is simply an accompaniment of another.

Polyrhythm: A rhythmic structure that simultaneously combines two or more independent rhythms. While polyrhythm is a feature usually associated with western music, it is commonly found in other traditions, especially music of African origin. See rhythm.

Power: The amount of energy per unit time being emitted by a sound source. Power is usually measured in Watts. A power level of one Watt is equal to one Joule of energy per second.

Preroll: Traditionally, the amount of time a tape deck must be started early (and the corresponding retarded tape position needed) so that the deck can overcome mechanical inertia and be up to speed (with the tape at the correct location) to make an edit at the appropriate time. Digital systems might avoid inertia but can never eliminate latency. Consequently preroll also refers to the latency on digital systems.

Prosody: Patterns of stress (amplitude change), intonation (pitch change), phoneme duration, and other characteristics of human speech. Prosody is an important, and not completely understood, component of speech that is unique to each language, dialect, gender, and even individual. Lack of sophisticated prosody modeling limits a speech synthesis algorithm's ability to sound completely human, or for these systems to convincingly mimic women, children, or speakers of specific dialects.

Psychophysicist: A scientist who attempts to establish the relationships between physical variables, such as the amplitude of an acoustic pressure wave, and psychological variables, such as the loudness of the perceived sound.

Pull model: A description of how data flow is induced in a system. In the pull model, the consumer of the data dictates how much and how often the data is produced.

Pulse wave: An idealized oscillator waveshape that can be drawn with a series of straight lines whose intersections make right angles (add sketch of a pulse, if possible). See oscillator.

Punching-in: A sound editing technique where a very brief portion of a recording is replaced by a portion of another take. The edit may be as short as an off-key vocal or even a wrong note. Using this technique, even mediocre musicians can create, apparently, virtuoso recordings.

Push model: The opposite of a pull model, where the producer dictates how much and how often the data is produced.

Quantization: Approximation of an arbitrary real value by the nearest entry in a finite table of values. It is a key step in audio data compression.

Quantization error: Errors that emanate from the limited precision of digitally represented numbers during mathematical operations.

Quarter-note: A type of rhythmic note-value in music notation. In the majority of popular music, the quarter-note is the written value that is equal to one beat.

Real-time: **1.** An area of engineering that involves designing systems that must meet certain time constraints. Real-time systems are classified into two main types: hard real-time, where the result of computation is useless if the deadline is not met (e.g., airbag control system in an automobile), and soft real-time, where occasionally missed deadlines are tolerated (e.g., maintaining frame rate in video playback—a dropped frame once in a while can be tolerated). **2.** A description of a process intended to play its results immediately as it proceeds. This requires that the computation needed to synthesize the results is able to occur in less time than the result takes to play.

Record: A group of consecutive samples representing a short segment of sound.

Release burst: The "explosion" of air at the release of a stop consonant. The burst is a brief period of frication which may be followed by a period of aspiration.

Resampling: Also known as sample rate conversion, resampling involves changing the number of samples in a digital signal without unduly distorting the signal it represents. For instance, resampling the 44,100-sample-per-second digital audio from a CD to the 48,000 samples per second required for DAT (digital audio tape).

Resonance: Oscillations that are self-reinforced by the dynamics of a system, causing an increase in response.

Resonant frequency: A system's natural frequency of vibration, related to the fundamental frequency. It refers to the frequency at which a vibrating body generates the most power or, alternately, the frequency at which a body absorbs the most energy.

Reverberant: Having high amplitude and a slow decay of reverberation.

Reverberation (reverb): **1.** The persistence of a sound after its source has stopped, caused by multiple reflections of the sound reflecting off surfaces within an enclosed space. This term usually refers to the later reflections, in which individual copies of the sound (echoes) cannot be heard because the sound is a mixture of so many repeated reflections from a variety of surfaces. **2.** The total description of all reflections, echoes, and spectral qualities of sound in an enclosed space. **3.** The application of delays and echoes by use of a signal-processing device to achieve the simulation of particular acoustic spaces.

Rhythm: A strong, recognizable pattern of sound or motion. Also known as beat. Western musical tradition provides a system for describing many beat structures.

Ring buffer: An efficient implementation of the FIFO queue. Also known as a cyclic buffer.

Root Mean Square (RMS): Square root of the mean of the squares. Found by squaring a function, calculating the mean, then taking the square root. Also known as the effective value, the RMS value is important because it represents the *average* power of a waveform and also closely represents the perceived loudness of a waveform. Note the RMS value of a current, voltage or pressure is proportional to the *average* power. The term RMS power, while widely used, is strictly speaking, *not* correct.

Roundoff error: Computational error resulting from the limited number of bits (digits) used in the computation.

Rubato: A style of playing employed by soloists in which they deviate slightly from the note durations that are shown in the musical score, sometimes leading and sometimes lagging behind the other musicians.

S domain: Laplace domain for continuous time systems.

Sample: The amplitude value of a signal measured at an instant of time (see frame).

Sample accurate: Presenting a digital signal at the closest audio frame position to the intended time. This is the finest granularity of timing available when presenting a digital signal. For professional 48 kHz audio, this is approximately ± 21 μSeconds. Also implies that the system will not drop audio samples causing quality and timing issues.

Sample rate conversion: See resampling.

Sampling: The process of systematic measuring analog (time continuous) signals at regular intervals. If a signal is sampled at the Nyquist rate, the representation is theoretically exact.

Sampling frequency: The number of samples per time unit employed is sampling. If the time unit is seconds, the sampling frequency is measured in Hz.

Sawtooth wave: A repeating waveform commonly used in audio synthesis that resembles the edge of a saw. It has a straight section that rises or falls punctuated by a sharp edge. It can be constructed by adding even and odd harmonics of a fundamental frequency.

Scale factor: An assumed multiplier applied to one or more numerical values.

Score: A generic term for any musical composition that is written in standard musical notation. Lots of popular music is not written in music notation, and therefore has no score, in the traditional sense of the word.

Search for Extra-Terrestrial Intelligence (SETI): Relies on gigantic Fourier transforms of radio signals received from space to detect periodicities that may indicate an intelligent origin.

Segmental: Having to do with individual speech sounds or phonemes. Syllables can be broken down into a sequence of segments. For instance, the syllable (and word) *sat* consists of three segments, "s," "a," and "t."

Segregation: The tendency of sounds containing certain cues to be perceived to be distinct.

Semitone: The smallest interval in the western equally tempered scale. A semitone is the difference in pitch between any two adjacent keys on a piano keyboard, regardless of color (black or white). A semitone is often called a "half-step" in music slang. Physically, moving the pitch of a note upward by a semitone is equivalent to multiplying its frequency by about 1.06 (i.e., the twelfth root of two).

Series summation: A method of describing a function as the sum of many component functions.

Seventh chord: A four-note chord consisting of a triad with an added seventh. All seventh chords consist of a root, third, fifth, and seventh. There are five basic types of seventh chords: major seven chord, minor seven chord, dominant seven chord, half-diminished seven chord, and diminished seven chord.

Sharp: The accidental that raises the pitch of a given note by one semitone.

Side-bands: When a periodic modulation is applied to either the frequency or amplitude of a wave, it creates side-bands (other frequencies that were not present in the unmodulated sound). The frequencies of these added frequencies are related to the frequency of the wave that is modulated (the "carrier") and to the frequency of the wave that is modulating the carrier (the "modulator").

Signal-to-Noise Ratio (SNR): Usually measured in decibels (dB). High-quality sound reproduction will feature an SNR better than 60 dB which is a power ratio of 1×10^{-6}.

Silent movie: A motion picture film that doesn't have a synchronized sound track. The earliest films were silent movies and were often accompanied by live music played by musicians in the theater. Silent movies quickly gave way to talkies (movies with a sound track including effects and dialogue) after their introduction in the 1920s.

Simple time: A type of meter. In simple time, the beat naturally subdivides into two faster rhythmic values.

Sinusoidal: A waveform having the shape of a sine wave. A sine wave is heard as a pure tone.

Six-eight time (Compound-duple meter): There are two beats in each measure, and the dotted quarter-note is equal to one beat.

Sixteenth-note: A type of rhythmic note-value in music notation. There are two sixteenth-notes in a single eighth-note, and there are four sixteenth-notes in a single quarter-note.

Sonification: The mapping of data to sound in order to acoustically display information, such as trends (the acoustic analog to visualization). For example, pulse rate is conveyed aurally with a hospital-monitoring device.

Sound classifier: A device that can automatically identify sounds based on characteristics such as their amplitude envelope, spectrum, fundamental frequencies, duration, and other parameters. A military application might be to detect the presence and type of aircraft at a distance. Often these systems analyze signals for a large number of parameters then *learn* the parameter signatures characteristic to specific sounds.

Sound-on-disk: An audio storage/reproduction technique using a phonograph record or similar device to store the audio. This technique requires a separate mechanism to synchronize the sound and the image tracks. The Vitaphone is an example of a motion picture system that employs a sound-on-disk device.

Sound-on-film: A audio storage/reproduction technique where the sound track is physically inscribed on the same film as the image track. With the sound and images next to each other on the same substrate, there is no way for the two tracks to lose synchronization during playback. In such a system, synchronization is accomplished in the post production process.

Sound track: Technically, it refers to the optical audio track on motion picture film stock (in contrast to the picture track). The term also commonly refers to the collection of music found in a film.

Spatialization: Creating illusionary or virtual sound sources that are perceived to have a direction and distance relative to a listener.

Spectrogram: A two-dimensional visual representation of the intensity of frequency components of a sound or series of sounds. It has time as its x-axis and frequency as its y-axis. It depicts the intensity of the acoustic energy at each point of frequency and time by the darkness (and sometimes the color) of the spot that represents it.

Spectrum: A description of a sound, giving some measure (m) of each of its frequency components. Usually presented as a graph with frequency as the x-axis and the measure m as the y-axis. The measure can be amplitude ("amplitude spectrum"), power ("power spectrum"), phase ("phase spectrum"), etc.

Speech detector: A device used to detect the presence of speech, as opposed to noise or other sounds. Speech detectors are used in applications such as conserving network bandwidth in VoIP (by only sending packets that contain speech, conserving battery life in a handheld unit by only activating the power-hungry transmitter to send actual speech) or in echo cancellation schemes to disable transmission of sound by the party not actively speaking (the actual echo cancellation algorithm is then only needed when both parties are speaking simultaneously). Speech detectors have to be used with care to avoid clipping the beginning or ends of utterances.

Speech synthesis: Any technology for synthetically creating an intelligible but not necessarily human sounding voice. While the earliest techniques involved analog methods, some electronic, some pneumatic, most modern systems are digital and either completely synthesize speech waveforms or piece together prerecorded components. See also text to speech.

Square wave: A pulse waveform whose high and low sections are constant values of equal length (add sketch of a square, if possible). An ideal square wave contains the fundamental component and only odd harmonics. See pulse wave.

Staff: The grid upon which musical notation resides. The staff contains five horizontal lines with four spaces between them. Musical pitches of specific rhythmic duration are placed on the staff to represent the sound of the music. Staff lines are always counted up from the bottom. The first line is always the bottom line.

Start synchronization: A type of synchronization that ensures that all the media are started together at precisely the same moment in time.

Steady-state sounds: Sounds that stay constant, over time, in all their properties.

Stereophonic (stereo) sound: The overwhelmingly popular two-channel format for the recording, distribution, and playback of musical recordings. Stereo recordings may be reproduced using a pair of widely spaced loudspeakers, a pair of closely spaced, near field monitors, or via headphones. Although stereo sound may be recorded using a pair of microphones, it is more often the result of multitrack recordings panned and *mixed down* to two channels. The best stereo recording and reproduction produce a three-dimensional sound stage mimicking the experience of attending the live performance. Stereophonic recordings superseded earlier *monophonic* recordings by the 1960s, and various *surround sound* technologies with five and more channels have recently displaced stereo playback in homes at least for film and video reproduction.

Stiction: A term used to describe interactions that are characterized by periods of sliding and sticking. Typically, the interaction will be in a state of high friction, until a force threshold is exceeded, and then the system will shift into a low-friction sliding state for a period of time before returning to the initial high-friction state. Stiction may be found in many real-world interactions such as an automobile disk brake (squeal) or wiping a wet finger around the rim of a crystal goblet (hum). Stiction is also found in the bow-string interface of a bowed musical instrument, where it is responsible for imparting energy to the strings. In this case, it is the rosin that initially causes high friction, where the bow will deflect the string instead of slipping along it. Once the energy level exceeds a critical threshold, the string will begin to slip. This slipping causes the rosin to melt, which yields a low-friction interface. As the bow passes with low friction over the string, the rosin once again hardens, yielding a cycle of sticking and sliding that adds pulses of energy to the string.

Stochastic: A description of signals or sets of values that possess random characteristics defined by (usually) nonuniform probability distributions. In generative contexts, a *stochastic parameter* is defined in terms of the statistical distribution of its possible values rather than its actual value.

Structured audio: A part of the MPEG-4 standard, for coding sound as an algorithm. The compressed version of the audio consists of a computer program that, when executed, generates audio output. See MPEG.

Subdivision: The act of dividing the beat, or pulse, into faster regular rhythmic divisions. This is a human response to rhythmic stimuli and a skill all trained musicians master.

Subtractive synthesis: A sound synthesis method, which works by dynamically filtering a static, harmonically rich waveform.

Suprasegmental: Characteristics of speech such as intonation and timing that are defined over syllable and larger sized units.

Syllable coda: The final consonants of a syllable.

Syllable nucleus: The vocalic portion of a syllable.

Syllable onset: The initial consonants of a syllable.

Syllable rhyme: The nucleus plus coda of a syllable.

Synchronization: To cause to occur with exact coincidence in time or rate. In digital media, this has to do with starting with and then maintaining the correct relationship in time between streams of media.

Systematic transcription: Identifies all acoustic differences known to be systematic in a language.

Talkie: A movie including synchronized sound and images. Always a goal of the movie industry, commercially viable technology to produce, distribute, and present talking films wasn't created until the 1920s.

Telephony: The act and technology for communicating voice over distance. Once limited to conventional analog telephones and the corresponding POTS (plain old telephone service) technology, telephony is now digital and significantly integrated with digital computers. See Voice over IP (VoIP).

Tempo: The rate at which the beats progress in a piece of music. Humans respond to tempo in relation to one's heart rate. The perception of "fast" and "slow" passages in music depends upon the tempo of the music in relation to the heart rate of the listener.

Text to speech (TTS): A system that renders text to synthetic speech. Text to speech is closely related to but distinct from speech synthesis. Among other things, text to speech systems need to be able to determine the correct, sometimes context-specific, pronunciation of words or names and to be able to provide the correct, language-specific articulation such as raising pitch at the end of a question.

Three-four time (Simple-triple meter): There are three beats in each measure, and the quarter-note is equal to one beat.

Tie: A part of music notation. A tie is a curved line that connects different rhythmic values of the same pitch together into a longer sustained note or sound.

Timbral: Of or related to timbre. For example, "timbral variation" refers to variations in timbre.

Timbre: That quality of sound that distinguishes two instruments (or voices) sounding at the same pitch and loudness. Also known as "tonal color." Timbre encompasses differences in attack, steady state, and decay of a musical tone. It is what makes a trumpet sound identifiably different from a clarinet, for example, when both are playing the same tone. Sounds are said to be different in timbre when their perceived qualities are different, even though their pitches, locations, and loudnesses are the same.

Time base: An independent time coordinate system.

Time code: A sequence of numerical codes generated by a film and video editing system to keep track of time. Time codes are often used for synchronization or to describe edits.

Time freezing: An audio effect that creates the illusion that the passage of time in an audio signal has halted. Since audio signals only exist in time, time freezing essentially involves the generation of a signal with a constant or quasi-constant spectrum that reflects the spectrum of the input signal at the time it was frozen. This effect can be implemented in a number of ways including looping, granulation, and additive synthesis.

Time signal: The description of a sound in the time domain as fluctuations in some physical property like pressure over time. Often, because the pressure fluctuations have been transduced by a microphone or other measurement instrument, we have converted pressure fluctuations to voltage fluctuations over time.

Time signature: A notational convention consisting of two numbers, one printed directly on top of the other, that communicates to the musician the type of meter for a given music composition. Synonymous with meter signature.

Time smearing: An audio effect that smears the content of an audio signal forwards and/or backwards in time. Reverberation can be thought of as a type of time smearing, although the latter term is more general. Depending on the application, this effect can be the result of artifacts in certain types of processing (such as some types of overlap add resynthesis,) or as an intended outcome as is the case with reverberation or granular time smearing.

Time stretching: The process of altering the perceived passage of time in an audio signal without the intention of modifying its spectral characteristics, such as changing its pitch for example. Implementing generalized time stretching is difficult to achieve without introducing audible artifacts. However, in some musical contexts, artifacts may be acceptable, or even useful, as they add additional spectral interest when stretching ratios are large.

Time varying filter: A filter where the components/coefficients are time-dependent. This means that the output signal from a given stimulus will generate different outputs depending on the onset in time of the filtering.

Tonic: The most important note in any given major or minor key. The pitch that gives the key its name (i.e., the note C in the key of C major). The first note of a major or minor scale (i.e., the note E in the E minor scale).

Top-down: Perception, memory, attention, and other mental activities can be influenced by the prior knowledge of the class of signals that the person may encounter and also by the cues provided by the signal itself. The former are called "top-down" influences because they are assumed to come from higher parts of the brain, whereas the latter are called "bottom-up" influences because they are assumed to originate at lower levels of the nervous system (the sense organs and the early processes that operate on sense data).

Torsional waves: Waves in which the displacement of the medium is a twist in a plane perpendicular to the direction of propagation of the wave. For example, when a bow is drawn across a violin string, the string twists and a torsional wave travels down the string.

Track: In audio recording, a specific instrument or group of instruments is often recorded together on a "track" and this track is later mixed with others. See multitrack recording.

Transducer: A device that changes a signal from one physical form to another. For example, a microphone changes the signal from a pressure wave in the air to an electrical voltage whose values change over time in exactly the same pattern as the pressure wave in the air does. Because of the one-to-one correspondence, the original signal can be recovered from the transduced signal.

Transduction: The activity of a transducer.

Transfer function: An equation describing the system given by output/input.

Transients: Rapid changes in a signal (e.g., at the onset of sounds).

Transpose: To move a note (or notes) to a different pitch level. If a melody starts on the note C, and one wanted to transpose the melody up a perfect fifth, the new starting note would be the G above the original C. By continuing this process (moving each note up a perfect fifth), one can transpose a given melody up a perfect fifth. It is possible to transpose pitch information by any interval up or down.

Transverse waves: Waves in which the displacement of the medium is perpendicular to the direction of propagation of the wave. For example, when a bow is drawn across a violin string, the string moves in a direction perpendicular to the excitation and a transversal wave travels down the string.

Treble clef: Also called the "G clef." This is the clef that identifies the higher pitches in the grand staff, and is written on the top staff of the two staves in the grand staff. The treble clef identifies the placement on the staff of the pitch G4 (G above middle C).

Triad: A specific type of three-note chord. All triads consist of a root, a third, and a fifth. The root of the chord is the note that gives the chord its name (i.e., the note C in a C major triad). Triads come in four basic types: major, minor, diminished, and augmented.

Triangle wave: A repeating waveform commonly used in audio synthesis that has a rising straight section followed by a falling straight section. It can be constructed by adding odd harmonics of a fundamental frequency in the proper proportion.

Triple: Describes the number of beats in a meter. Music in simple-triple time has three beats in each measure, and the beats are simple, in that they naturally subdivide into groups of two faster note-values. Music in compound-triple time has three beats in each measure, and the beats are compound in nature, in that they naturally subdivide into groups of three faster note-values.

Two-four time (Simple-duple meter): There are two beats in each measure, and the quarter-note is equal to one beat.

Underflow: An undesirable situation where a buffer runs dry because data is being, on average, consumed faster than it can be produced, resulting in the consumer having to stall as it waits for the producer.

Uniform sampling: The process of sampling at regular intervals, usually called the sampling interval. CD recordings use uniform sampling with 44100 samples per second, which indicates that the sampling interval is equal to $1/44100$ s = 22.67 microseconds.

Unison: Two notes with the same frequency are in unison. This can be an aural event, as when a musician tunes his/her instrument to a given pitch, and can be a visual event, when two notes of the same pitch-class are written on the staff (two middle C quarter-notes, for example).

Unstable system: A control system that, given a stable input, produces output which fluctuates over time; these fluctuations get worse over time.

Upbeat: In the most general sense, upbeat means the portion of a beat that occurs after the downbeat. Typically, upbeat refers to the second half of an individual beat. For example, in four-four time, there are four quarter-notes. Each quarter-note can be subdivided into two eighth-notes.

Virtual acoustic environment: A sound field created by spatializing a set of sounds. See spatialization.

Voice concatenation: Also known as voice stitching, voice concatenation is a form of voice synthesis that combines small utterances to form natural sounding speech. The speech elements could be as small as phrases, words, or even individual phonemes. (Theoretically, recordings of the 40 phoneme sounds found in English may be concatenated to form any statement; however, there are many practical complications that would make such a system unpractical.) Voice concatenation can create a wide variety of speech that matches the vocal characteristics of an actual individual using a relatively small collection of recorded sound and is often combined with rules-based dynamic parameters found in formant synthesis.

Voice Onset Time (VOT): The time from the release burst of a stop consonant to the onset of voicing for a subsequent voiced segment.

Voice over IP (VoIP): A general term that describes any telephone protocol that uses the Internet protocols to transmit voice conversations. Commercial software such as Skype has popularized the use of VoIP for individuals as an alternative to conventional telephone service. The Asterisk open source project remarkably allows inexpensive personal computers to act as a PBX (private branch exchange), enabling even small businesses or individuals to have advanced telephone services once limited to large businesses, such as the ability to connect multiple extensions, call between extensions, provide voice mail, support phone menus, have a central operator, use trunk lines to connect to the public telephone network, use the internet for long distance calls or phone calls to other offices (toll bypass), and more.

Voltage-Controlled Oscillator (VCO): An electronic component that generates a sine wave whose frequency can be varied via the input control voltage.

W function: A complex function of a real angle, $i/N : W(i) = \cos(2 * \pi * i/N)$, $\sin(2*\pi*i/N)$. It is the fundamental multiplier used in the fast Fourier transform and represents a pair of "probe waves" 90 degrees apart.

Waveform: Sounds are pressure waves in the air. The sequence of instantaneous pressures that passes a fixed point in the air or other medium, over time, can be plotted as a wave. The shape of this wave is called the waveform. Sounds may also be encoded as time-varying voltages, currents, or approximated by a series of numerical sampled values.

Wavetable: This term most accurately describes an area of memory containing a single cycle of a sampled or synthesized periodic signal that is usually used in oscillator synthesis. In a common corruption, wavetable is used synonymously with "stored sample" to describe any sequence of audio samples stored in computer memory for use in sample-based synthesis techniques.

Wavetable synthesis: A technique for generating repetitive waveforms of an arbitrary shape. A simple phase accumulator is used to index into an array (table) that contains the shape of the desired waveform. The output is usually generated by interpolating between adjacent values in the table. The term "wave table synthesis" is also sometimes used incorrectly to refer to sample playback systems which play a digital recording of a sound.

Whole-note: A type of rhythmic note-value in music notation. There are two half-notes in a single whole-note. There are subsequently four quarter-notes in a single whole-note.

Whole tone: The interval that encompasses two semitones (keyboard steps). It is often called a "whole step" in music slang. Physically, moving the pitch of a note upward by a whole tone is equivalent to multiplying its frequency by approximately 1.12.

Window: A special kind of amplitude envelope or weighting curve given a signal before Fourier transformation in an effort to reduce spectral leakage. See leakage.

Windows Media Audio (WMA) compression: The digital audio component of Microsoft's Windows Media product; it can represent high-fidelity stereo signals at about the same bit rates as AAC.

Z domain: Discrete time domain.

Zero: An element of a linear system that causes the frequency response to decrease in magnitude. For instance, if we were to describe the frequency response of a system with $h(\omega) = (1 - \omega)$, the point at $\omega = 1$ would represent a zero because the graph would clearly show the frequency response approaching zero as ω approached 1.

Contributor Biographies

Richard Bailey is a software developer and architect specializing in computer and human interaction at Microsoft. Most recently, Richard developed the audio and rumble system and authoring tools for *Forza Motorsport*, a simulation racing game on the Xbox. Currently Richard is developing authoring tools to be used for creating applications for Windows Vista.

James A. Ballas received his PhD with a dissertation on the sensory and cognitive factors in the classification of sounds. His research in auditory perception has focused on understanding the processes involved in identification of everyday sounds and characterizing the information in non-speech sound. He is currently leading a team at NRL that is developing advanced audio systems for virtual reality and augmented reality. He is past president of the International Community for Auditory Display (ICAD) and was co-chair of the technical program in 1997.

Ronen Barzel received his undergraduate and master's from Brown University, then completed his PhD at Caltech in computer graphics, researching physically based modeling techniques. He has worked at Pixar on production of the first *Toy Story* movie (among other things, he built the Slinky Dog model) and in R&D of modeling and lighting software. He is the editor in chief of the *journal of graphics tools*.

Ross Bencina is an internationally-recognized composer, performer, and software developer who works at the leading edge of electro-acoustic music practice. In collaboration with Phil Burk and a team of open source developers, Ross designed the PortAudio cross platform audio API. He is the creator of AudioMulch, a widely-used software environment for the manipulation of sound in real time.

Albert Bregman is emeritus professor of psychology at McGill University in Montreal, Canada. He received a BA and MA from the University of Toronto and a PhD in psychology from Yale, and he spent three years at Harvard as an instructor and a researcher at the Center for Cognitive Studies. He introduced the teaching and research of cognitive psychology at McGill and taught a generation of students who have gone on to have distinguished careers of their own. He developed a computer-based laboratory for working with auditory signals and testing human subjects. Bregman has been called the "father of auditory scene analysis" (ASA). He has published more than 50 articles on ASA, which describe the cues for and the perceptual results of ASA and its role in the perception of speech, music, and other sounds. His 1990 book, *Auditory Scene Analysis: The Perceptual Organization of Sound*, is considered a classic treatise in modern hearing science.

Derek Brock is an expert in human-computer interaction. He earned his MS in Computer Graphics and Multimedia Systems from the George Washington University. Derek is presently with the U.S. Naval Research Laboratory's Center for Applied Research in Artificial Intelligence, where his research includes the application of sound and models of human language use to the design of standard and novel user interfaces for computational systems.

Bob Brozman's life is defined by an all-consuming passion for music. In addition to being an accomplished slide, fingerstyle, and percussive guitarist with an extensive touring schedule, Bob is also an adjunct professor at Macquarie University in Sydney, Australia. He is a respected ethnomusicologist and has been featured on NPR.

Evan Buehler is a noted Seattle Jazz vibraphone musician and sound designer for Sierra Entertainment. His game credits include *SWAT 3: Urban Justice*.

Tim Bunnell received his PhD in experimental psychology from Pennsylvania State University in 1983. He worked as a research scientist in the Center for Audiology and Speech Sciences at Gallaudet University and later served as program director for Speech Processing Research at the Alfred I. duPont Hospital for Children, where he currently heads the Speech Research Laboratory and the Bioinformatics Core Facility. He is also a member of the research faculty in several departments of the University of Delaware. Tim's primary research interests are speech perception, speech synthesis, and speech recognition. With his colleagues at both the hospital and university, he is actively involved in projects to develop personalized synthetic speech for users of augmentative communication devices, application of speech recognition techniques to speech training for young children, and basic research into the phonetics and phonology of prosody.

Hesham Fouad has been involved in various aspects of audio for the past 15 years. After receiving a doctorate in computer science in 1997, he founded VRSonic, Inc., a company focused on developing new techniques for creating compelling virtual auditory environments.

Bo Gehring is a self-taught inventor and serial entrepreneur. He is a three-dimensional graphics pioneer, his Los Angeles studio having created some of the earliest examples of computer animation used in film and advertising. He is also an early developer and proponent of spatial audio, where he developed early patents and worked with many applications including helping the US Air Force develop three-dimensional audio cues to improve fighter cockpit displays. Bo presently has returned to an early love where he is applying his technical background to fine art sculpture.

Ken Greenebaum is a software engineer who has developed digital media technology over the past 20 years for companies that include Silicon Graphics, Microsoft, and now Apple. Ken's research interests include the creation of reliable, sample-accurate, low-latency media engines; language systems to describe time varying behaviors; and human perception motivated optimization. Ken is an adjunct member of the DigiPen Institute of Technology faculty where he develops and teaches the interactive audio for gaming curriculum.

Frank Haferkorn has a degree in physics from the Technical University of Munich where his thesis topic was spatial audio. Frank continued at the university as an electro-acoustics lecturer until he left to pursue a software engineering career in industry. When Frank isn't pursuing his interests in acoustics and physics, he is dancing or making music.

Jay Kadis attended California State University Hayward, where he received Bachelor's and Master's degrees in biological science. He worked for many years as research assistant for the Stanford University School of Medicine, doing electronics and computer programming in support of the Neurology Research Lab's epilepsy research program. In 1988, he joined Stanford's Center for Computer Research in Music and Acoustics (CCRMA) as audio engineer and sound recording lecturer. He has worked with many electro-acoustic music composers including John Chowning. Jay is also a performing guitarist and songwriter and has recorded dozens of CDs for rock, blues, and classical artists in the San Francisco bay area. His research interests include the physiology of hearing and audio electronics.

Mark Kolber has been working as an electronic circuit design engineer for more than 20 years. He has designed circuitry for processing audio signals and other AGC circuits for broadcast, CATV, and commercial avionics equipment. Mr. Kolber is currently an engineering manager in the CATV Head-end group of Motorola's Digital Networks Systems group.

Daniel Lee lives in Sydney, Australia. He holds a bachelor of engineering (electrical) degree from the University of New South Wales, where his thesis focused on dynamic range compression in conjunction with multirate signal processing to develop a multiband compressor. Although he works in the telecommunications industry, his interest in audio stems from his involvement as part of the production team at Hillsong Church—a vibrant contemporary church in Sydney.

Eric Lee is a PhD candidate at RWTH Aachen University in Germany, where he conducts research on time-based interactive multimedia systems. Eric holds a bachelor's degree in Computer Engineering from the University of British Columbia and a master's degree in electrical engineering from Stanford University. Interspersed with his studies, Eric has worked in industry, including Sony and Apple Computer, developing image and audio processing software.

Daniel J. Levitin holds the Bell Chair in the Psychology of Electronic Communication and the FCAR Strategic Professor Chair in Psychology at McGill University in Montreal. He has worked as a record producer, recording engineer, and consultant for all the major record labels, and his custom-designed guitar amplifiers produced the guitar sounds on albums by Joe Satriani, Blue Öyster Cult, and Chris Isaak. He currently conducts research in psychoacoustics and music cognition and has published more than 30 scientific articles and more than 300 commercial articles on popular music.

Ian Merritt is an old hand in the telecommunications field. He most recently has been developing telephony services at Microsoft.

Dinesh K. Pai is a professor of computer science at Rutgers University and previously was a professor at the University of British Columbia. He received his PhD from Cornell. His current research interests are in multisensory computation. This includes multisensory simulation (integrating graphics, haptics, and auditory displays) and multisensory modeling (based on measurement of shape, motion, reflectance, sounds, and contact forces). His other interests include robotics and human-computer interaction. He developed the UBC Active Measurement Facility (ACME), a robotic facility for acquiring comprehensive models of three-dimensional objects, including models of sound, appearance, contact texture, and deformation. He is currently developing the Rutgers Haptic, Auditory, and Visual Environment (the HAVEN).

Susan E. Rogers is a PhD candidate in the Department of Psychology and a fellow at the Center for Interdisciplinary Research in Music Media and Technology at McGill University, Montréal, Canada. In a career spanning over twenty years, she produced, engineered, or mixed albums for Prince, David Byrne, Barenaked Ladies, Tricky, Michael Penn, Rusted Root, and Crosby, Stills and Nash.

Stefania Serafin holds a degree in computer science from the University of Venice, Italy. She has studied violin and music theory at the Conservatorio di Musica B. Marcello of Venice. She later moved to Paris where she worked in the Analysis-Synthesis team at IRCAM. There she obtained her DEA degree in acoustics, signal processing, and computer science, applied to music at Ircam on the Analysis-Synthesis team, and also served as visiting researcher at CCRMA working with Julius Smith. Stefania received a PhD from Stanford in computer-based music theory and Acoustics and is currently an assistant professor in Medialogy at Aalborg University in Copenhagen, where she teaches and performs research on sound models and sound design for interactive media and multimodal interfaces.

Mark Stahlman is an analyst, entrepreneur, and investor involved with next generation computing platforms. His focus on technology-driven economic cycles led him to become one of the investment bankers who brought America Online public and an architect of New York's "Silicon Alley." He is currently Managing Director, Technology Strategist, and Senior Equity Analyst at Caris and Company.

Craig Utterback is a composer/sound designer who has created and produced music, sound effects, voice content, and integration schemes for more than 30 computer games as well as numerous music projects and products for other markets. He is currently director of the Office of Audio Creation, Rehabilitation, and Corrections at the TCS Memorial Sound Abuse Clinic and Mental Health Spa (for Oui Gnu Development) in Kent, Washington. Craig plays, builds, and restores electric guitars, basses, and audio tube amps.

Kees van den Doel received a PhD in theoretical physics from the University of California at Santa Cruz. After a postdoc at the University of Tel-Aviv, he pursued his interest in music and studied music composition at the University of British Columbia. He obtained a second PhD in computer science from the University of British Columbia. He worked in industry for some years and is currently a research associate at UBC. He is interested in reality-based audio modeling for simulated immersive environments.

Wieslaw Woszczyk is the founder of the graduate program in sound recording at McGill University and of the Centre of Interdisciplinary Research in Music, Media, and Technology, which he currently directs. He currently holds the James McGill Professor Research Chair in Sound Recording. He has served as visiting professor at the Bang and Olufsen A/S, Research and Development Department, in Denmark, and was the first foreign scientist invited to join the R&D department. He has been the recipient of a Board of Governors award from the AES, a Hoso Bunka Foundation award, and the AES Fellowship Award. As a recording producer and/or engineer, he contributed to more than 50 compact discs and LP records (with such artists as Philip Glass, Brian Eno, and Harry Belafonte). Wieslaw designs Acoustic Pressure Equalizers (APE) and microphone attachments manufactured by several microphone companies.

Debra Yarrington received a master's degree from the University of Delaware in computer science. She is a member of the Speech Research Lab at Alfred I. duPont Hospital for Children and the University of Delaware Applied Science and Engineering Lab, where she is currently pursuing her PhD.

Index